1815

THE RETURN OF NAPOLEON

1815
THE RETURN
OF NAPOLEON

PAUL BRITTEN AUSTIN

Greenhill Books, London
Stackpole Books, Pennsylvania

TO JOHNNY
My childhood's first playmate
and still my best critic

1815: The Return of Napoleon
first published 2002 by Greenhill Books, Lionel Leventhal Limited, Park House,
1 Russell Gardens, London NW11 9NN
and
Stackpole Books, 5067 Ritter Road, Mechanicsburg, PA 17055, USA

British Library Cataloguing in Publication Data
Britten Austin, Paul
1815: the return of Napoleon
1. Napoleon, I, Emperor of the French, 1769–1821
2. Napoleonic Wars, 1800–1815 – Sources
I. Title II. Eighteen hundred and fifteen
940.2'7'092

ISBN 1-85367-476-1

Library of Congress Cataloging-in-Publication Data available

Edited by Ian Heath, typeset by DP Photosetting
Printed and bound in Great Britain by Creative Print and Design (Wales),
Ebbw Vale

CONTENTS

LIST OF ILLUSTRATIONS

LIST OF MAPS

'*Ma foi*, I'm a man. I wanted people to see I still wasn't dead.'
– Napoleon to Gourgaud, at St Helena

'It's almost always on the past one bases one's conduct and one's hopes.'
– M. Mignet, *Histoire de la Révolution Française*

'Our judgment of the course of political events depends on our conception of the men who were engaged in them. As soon as we see these individual men in a new light we have to alter our ideas of the events.'
– Ernst Cassirer, *An Essay on Man*

GERMAN

STATES

AUSTRIA

Paris

F R A N C E

SWITZERLAND

Geneva

Lyons

Grenoble

Venice

KINGDOM

OF

SARDINIA

PARMA

MODENA

PAPAL STATES

Genoa

Nice

TUSCANY

Antibes

Marseille

Cannes

Toulon

ELBA

Rome

SPAIN

CORSICA

Barcelona

Mediterranean Sea

SARDINIA

0   50   100   150   200

Miles

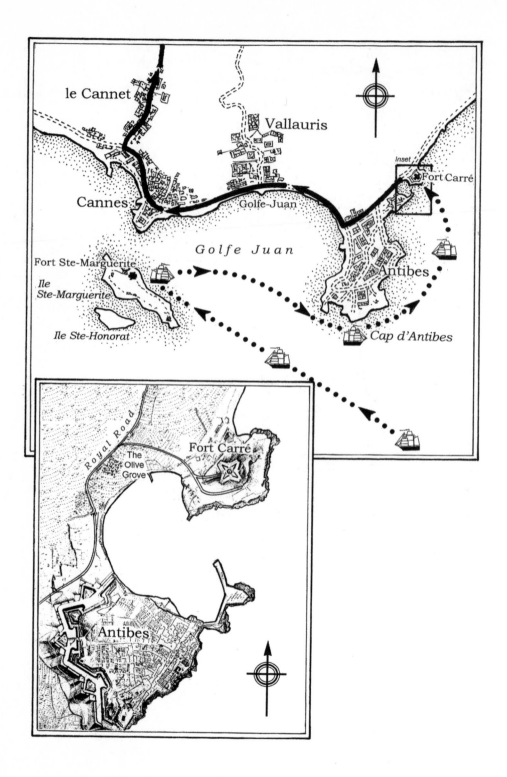

Tournus

Mâcon
Pont de Veyla
Thoissey
Belleville
Roanne
Villefranche
Trévoux
Neuville
LYON

Bourg

GENEVA

Switzerland

R. Rhône

Vienne

Bourgoin

Chambéry

Voiron

Tullins

St.Marcellin

GRENOBLE

Vizille
Laffrey
la Mure

St Jean
de Maurienne

Kingdom of

Sardinia

Valence

R. Rhône

Corps

St.Bonnet le Pont

Gap

Briançon

F r a n c e

le Poet

Sisteron

Orange

Carpentras

AVIGNON

Malijai

Barrême

Digne

Senez
Castellane
Séranon
Escragnolles
St.Vallier

NICE

Grasse
CANNES

Antibes

Draguignan

MARSEILLE

TOULON

St.Tropez

M e d i t e r r a n e a n

S e a

0   10   20   30   40   50
Miles

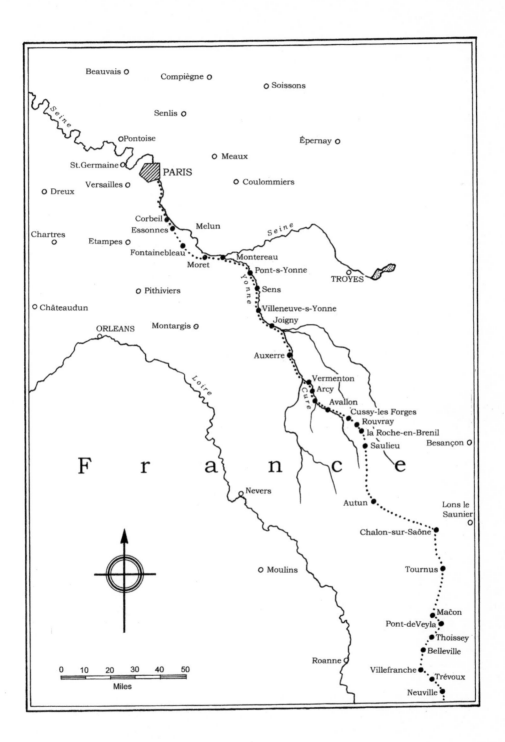

Beauvais ○

Compiègne ○

Soissons ○

Senlis ○

○ Pontoise

Épernay ○

St.Germaine ○

○ Meaux

PARIS

Versailles ○

Coulommiers ○

○ Dreux

Corbeil

Melun

Seine

Chartres ○

Essonnes

Etampes ○

Fontainebleau

Montereau

Moret

Pont-s-Yonne

TROYES

Sens

Yonne

○ Pithiviers

Villeneuve-s-Yonne

○ Châteaudun

Joigny

ORLEANS ○

Montargis ○

Auxerre

Vermenton

Arcy

Cure

Avallon

Loire

Cussy-les-Forges

Rouvray

la Roche-en-Brenil

Saulieu

Besançon ○

F   r   a   n   c   e

Nevers ○

Autun

Lons le
Saunier ○

Chalon-sur-Saône

Moulins ○

Tournus

Maĉon

Pont-deVeyla

Thoissey

Belleville

Villefranche

Trévoux

Roanne ○

Neuville

0   10   20   30   40   50

Miles

PREFACE

This book is a kind of sequel to my 1812 trilogy. English-language accounts of The Hundred Days naturally emphasise British experiences, or else (in proper historical fashion) hover over both sides (or indeed, in this case, several) all at once. But this is the story of 1815 as seen wholly from the French points of view – for there were at least two, above all among military men.

Napoleon's unheralded return from Elba, which split France diagonally in two and startled an admiring but also terrified Europe, would lead to a catastrophe every bit as great as that of 1940. Once again Frenchmen were faced with the implacable hostility of all Europe's 'legitimate' sovereigns and aristocracy determined to have done with the detestable Bonaparte once and for all, with revolutionary ideas and French militarism. And France would have to pay the price of his astounding comeback.

Once again I've tried to describe events as far as possible in the participants' own words.[1] More particularly, I was curious to see how things fared with some of my survivors from Russia. With perky little Coignet, for instance? With slippery handsome Flahaut, 'the best dancer in France'? With impeccably honest but unamiable Davout? With that annoying knowall Pion des Loches and his comrades of the ex-Guard artillery, such as Lubin Griois, he whose hair had turned white in the Russian snows? The patient reader of my 1812 trilogy will come across many an old acquaintance in what might be called the Grand Army's terminal circumstances; but will also make many new ones. Once again I've italicised their names at their first appearance in the text, and have marked them with an asterisk where they also appear in the Russian trilogy.

Here, in a different way from what was the case in 1812, the question of veracity and source values arises. To a much greater degree than in 1812, many of my 1815 'cameramen' wrote not merely to record vivid memories, but also to justify ex post facto their choice of sides in an anguished ideological situation. Yet their pages, even so, contain so many vivid and obviously authentic glimpses of what actually happened as to yield us as close a close-up as we're ever likely to get. History, after all, reposes ultimately on contemporary documents and on its actors' memories. Whether such memory traces are fresh and recent or unconsciously manipulated with the passage of time, in either case they can be equally enthralling.

For all kinds and conditions of Frenchmen, but notably the veterans of the Republican and Napoleonic armies, the Hundred Days weren't just a great military catastrophe, but a great socio-political trauma. At risk of their careers, even in some cases of their lives, they had to decide overnight where their sympathies lay and which side their bread was likely to be buttered on.[2] And then, three months later, decide again. Most famous and tragic of the victims, of course, would be the hero of the Great Retreat, Ney, the 'Bravest of the Brave'. Headstrong, passionately patriotic, but no friend of Napoleon and wavering between the parties, his fate overwhelms him – first in the *Golden Apple* inn at Lons le Saulnier; then at Quatre Bras; then on the 'grim plain of Waterloo'; and at last under a wall (near what today is the Montparnasse Métro station) before a firing squad. Nor, of course, should we forget the thousands who perished during the disastrous campaign. Or even Napoleon himself, 'that genius, angel or demon who was dominating us all!', as Sergeant-Major Larreguy de Civrieux puts it. More sharply here than in the Russian tragedy, I think, that charismatic personage comes into focus: an enigmatic middle-aged genius, who after succeeding so brilliantly with his 'crazy' but (as it transpires upon analysis) unavoidable enterprise, becomes less and less sure of himself and succumbs to what seems to have been a half-expected fate. This time Napoleon himself, who'd spend the rest of his life rewriting history and creating the legend of his own martyrdom, is one of my 'cameramen'.

Thanks to the singular French gift for pen portraiture 1815 provides us with a gallery of very different individuals. From the foxy but in some ways, if his memoirs are to be trusted (which of course they aren't), oddly naive Fouché – who'll manage to swing the whole thing his own way at the crisis, only to be himself ousted by the even foxier Louis XVIII – to the women who were so passionately in love with these gilded heroes. All played their parts in the disaster. Who, in imagination, isn't the secret hero of his own fate?

Farsta, Sweden, 2002

16

Chapter 1

'A CRAZY ENTERPRISE'

I f there'd been a sentry on one of the sharply jutting bastions of the Gabelle Fort, just across the harbour from Antibes, at dawn on 1 March 1815, he'd have noticed on the horizon a small flotilla. Mostly lateen-sailed, its largest vessel is a twenty-six-gun brig of war, the *Inconstant*. And if his officer had steadied his telescope on his shoulder, he'd have seen something even more startling: the Elban ensign, crimson-and-white with imperial bees, being hauled down from its gaff and the tricolour, symbol of republican and imperial France, being broken instead. For the last eleven months – months when Europe, for the first time in twelve years, has been at peace – it's been strictly banned.

But the other day twenty-three-year-old artillery captain Gazon had stripped the Gabelle Fort (also known as Le Fort Carré) of its guns. So there's no sentry and no officer. It's deserted.

'Like most young men at that time,' Gazon prefers
> 'the pleasures of society to the tobacco and liqueurs of cafés. The foreign colony and garrison officers were living on the best of terms with the townspeople. Our drawing rooms were truly places where people could mingle agreeably and where perfect union reigned. We did a lot of dancing.'

Unlike some 12,000 other *demisoldes*[1] he's content with his existence. And Brigadier-General Coursin, too, the Antibes military governor, is fond of making 'pleasure trips into the countryside'. Only today he has invited young Gazon to join his other guests on a trip out to the Lerin Islands, opposite Cannes, where Paris has just ordered him to establish a company of veterans in the St Marguerite fort, similarly dismantled. Unfortunately – or perhaps fortunately, for what will follow will be his 'life's most memorable experience' – Gazon has had to decline. He's already promised the day to his good friend Lieutenant Léandre Sardou at the village of Cannet, just inland from Cannes, and early this spring morning has set out, after borrowing his father's mare and faithfully promising his mother to be back by nightfall. Taking boat with his picnic party, Corsin has entrusted Antibes to his second-in-command, the Corsican colonel *Cuneo d'Ornano*, of the 87th Line.

All day yesterday a heavy sea was running – or at least so it had seemed to *Guillaume Peyrusse*[*].[2] A 'young southerner, full of spirit, vivacity and frank-

17

ness, always cheerful, always obliging, and strongly attached to his duties', Peyrusse is Napoleon's treasurer, who, if anyone asks him why he'd followed him to Elba, laughingly replies: 'I didn't. I followed my cashbox.'

But just now he's in no laughing mood. All yesterday he'd sat crumpled up on the *Inconstant*'s deck, with his back to the mainmast. Given an imperial kick in the ribs and told to 'join the other pen-pushers' down in the cabin, he'd pleaded a headache and begged to be excused:

'Pooh pooh,' Napoleon had said. 'Seine water will cure all that.'

And when Peyrusse with 'an incredulous shrug of a shoulder' had made so bold as to doubt it, the Emperor had told him they'll be in Paris on 20 March in time to celebrate his son's fourth birthday – that son who just now is a prisoner in Vienna. Down in the cabin, meanwhile, all who can wield a quill are busy making a hundred copies of two proclamations. 'I should have taken a portable printing press,' Napoleon will later say to Gourgaud on St Helena, printed proclamations making so much greater impact. But the imperial printing press has been deemed too cumbersome to bring along. The first of his proclamations is to France. The second to the army:

> *'Soldiers! We were not defeated. Two men from our ranks betrayed our laurels, their country, their prince, their benefactor! Tear down those colours* [the Bourbon fleurs-de-lis] *proscribed by the nation and which for twenty-five years have served to rally all France's enemies! Show the tricolour cockade! You wore it during our great days. Come and range yourselves under the standards of your chief. . .'*

— the two 'traitors' being Marshal Marmont, his oldest friend, who had led his corps over to the Russians after surrendering Paris (admittedly in consultation with Napoleon's own brother Joseph); and Marshal Augereau, who, a republican at heart, had welcomed an end to his master's tyrannical régime and released his troops from their allegiance to him. To the always admiring First Valet *Louis Marchand*, watching his master dictate these stirring – if not strictly truthful – proclamations it seems

> 'his whole soul stood painted on his face. When speaking of the fatherland, of France's sufferings, it was electrified. Genius was on the tripos. *Deus ecce Deus.* I've seen the Emperor on various occasions, but never more handsome.'

The other proclamation, addressed to the French nation and 'dictated with the same rapidity', flings *Talleyrand*'s newfangled label 'legitimacy', under which he'd brought back the Bourbons, in his enemies' faces:

> 'Raised by your choice to the throne, all that's been done without you is illegitimate. For twenty-five years France has had new interests, new institutions, a new glory, that can only be guaranteed by a national government and a dynasty born in these new circumstances. . .'

namely his own.

Among the quills busily copying out these stirring effusions is doubtless that of the middle-aged *André Pons de l'Hérault*. A staunch Jacobin who'd been with the young Bonaparte at the siege of Toulon but afterwards objected to his Empire as 'putting force in the place of law', for years he has been managing the Rio iron mine on Elba, a job he'd owed to Napoleon's dissident brother Lucien. When the exiled Emperor had first landed on the island, Pons had been utterly fascinated by

'this extraordinary man I'd so often blamed and at the same time admired. My heart was fit to burst, my spirits were dejected, my mind distracted, a general trembling took from me the free exercise of my faculties, and I felt I was going to faint.'

But several times since then he's been dismayed by Napoleon's dictatorial ways, not least by his lack of common honesty[3] and consideration for others. Despite at least one head-on dispute, however, Napoleon has learnt to appreciate Pons, and since it had been Pons who'd scraped together his little flotilla it had been to him before anyone else he'd confided his plan to return to France. If he has brought him along it's because he's a personal friend of Marshal Masséna, in command of the 8th military division at Toulon, whose unpredictable reactions can make or break the whole 'crazy project'.

For that's what the forty-one-year-old General Antoine Drouot*,[4] the troops' immediate commander – he too suffering the agonies of seasickness, on a mattress in Napoleon's cabin – thinks it is. Who has ever heard of anyone conquering a large country, the largest in Europe, with a mere 800 men?[5] And Drouot has 'done everything humanly possible to dissuade the Emperor from it'.[6] Dubbed by Napoleon 'the Sage of the Grand Army' on account of his bookish habits, Drouot creates an impression of great probity in all but his former subordinate *Pion des Loches*. And for Pons, who hadn't hesitated to stand up to Napoleon,[7] he's

'the equal of Plutarch's heroes, the perfection of the moral man. He'd followed the Emperor [to Elba] on condition he didn't pay him any salary – the only one of Napoleon's companions to make this reservation. Inside him were two men: the private man, who was too good; the public man, who was too severe.'

Neither quality, alas, staves off seasickness. To Peyrusse, too, a man who, although torn between ambition and fondness for his creature comforts, has fulfilled his ambition of becoming Napoleon's treasurer, the whole enterprise seems utterly risky. So much so that before leaving Porto-Ferrajo and the 'agreeable relationships' he'd formed there, he'd 'in greatest secrecy' laid up his own little stock of 'flours, wine, potatoes and salt beef'.

'How much does 100,000 francs weigh?' Napoleon had asked him musingly. Then: 'How much a trunkful of books?'

And in fact it's books that at first glance seem to fill the two wooden crates Peyrusse is in charge of – filled in reality with little sacks, each holding two million francs in gold.

So packed with troops are the *Inconstant*'s decks there's hardly even standing room for her sixty to eighty civilian passengers. Less than a year ago at Fontainebleau, after Napoleon's abdication and attempted suicide, these Grenadiers, Chasseurs and gunners of the Old Guard, its *crème de la crème de la crème*, hand-picked by him, had marched south to join him on Elba.[8] The rest, '100 Polish lancers[9] and 200 Corsican infantrymen of small stature and poorly equipped,' are either on the *Saint Esprit*, a cargo ship, or else 'on the Emperor's xebec, the speronade *Caroline*, two vessels from Rio, and a little felucca belonging to an Elban businessman'.[10] Though the guardsmen are the soul of discipline, the Corsican volunteers certainly aren't – Drouot hadn't been at all happy to see a Corsican battalion set up in the first place, their Commandant Guasco being 'the worst officer on Corsica, whose only merit was to bear the name of one of the noble Corsican families.' He's sure they'll only be a nuisance.

Among the brig's many non-military passengers are, of course, Napoleon's two valets. Never has the old saying that no man is a hero to his valet been less true than of the twenty-four-year-old Louis Marchand, a pleasant-mannered young man, in his spare time even something of an artist, who'd been promoted at Fontainebleau after his predecessor Constant Wairy* had absconded, taking with him with 100,000 francs.[11] Admittedly the usually judicious Pons finds Marchand 'very conceited, occasionally playing the confidant'; but from these minor charges his subsequent devotion on St Helena must absolve him. His assistant is the twenty-seven-year-old *Louis-Etienne Saint-Denis*. Originally having been taken on to assist the Armenian mameluke Roustam* (who'd also quit at Fontainebleau), he's become known as 'Ali' since he wears the same oriental costume. Shut up in the besieged fortress of Metz, he'd rejoined his master on Elba at the earliest opportunity. Notable for his immaculate handwriting, Ali has a quite remarkable memory for detail. Both valets are veterans of the Russian and Leipzig disasters[12] and worship the ground – or at this moment the deck – beneath their master's feet. Exigent Napoleon may be;[13] but also whenever possible considerate toward both his valets. And it never occurs to either not to accept their master at his own valuation.

Besides the folding iron campaign bed, standard-issue for a French general, with its green curtains and a 'bedcover of embroidered linen, very beautiful work', that can be put together in 'five minutes', Marchand has in his charge three objects of great value: (1) the gold travelling case (*la nécessaire*); (2) the privy purse – a casket containing 80,000 gold francs; and

(3), not least valuable, a diamond necklace worth 500,000 francs. It had been entrusted to him at the very last moment by Napoleon's sister Pauline, who'd begged him 'with tears in her eyes never to abandon the Emperor and to take good care of him'; mere valet though he is, she'd even allowed him to kiss her hand. And when Marchand, dazzled by her beauty,[14] had countered her heart-broken *adieu* by respectfully saying it'll more likely turn out to be an *au revoir*, had replied sadly: 'That's not how I see it' – 'A secret presentment,' he'd thought, that 'seemed to tell her she'd never see him again.'

Otherwise the valets' duties are to wait on His Majesty day and night and, just now, brush his 'one grenadier and one chasseur uniform' and 'a few shirts' – all the clothing he has brought with him.[15]

There have been anxious moments. Yesterday evening Peyrusse had 'shared everybody's joy' when a line-of-battle ship outward bound for Sardinia from Leghorn – a single broadside from half her sixty-four guns could have blown them all out of the water – had sailed unsuspectingly past. Nor had one of the two French frigates forever tacking to and fro between Corsica and Elba, to prevent Napoleon's escape from his absurd little kingdom, suspected anything. And another brig, the *Zephyr*, had made so threateningly for them that all the troops had been told to lie down on deck and prepare to board her until she'd come within hailing distance of the *Inconstant* (the rest of the convoy had scattered for the crossing) and her master, recognising her, had merely asked through his loud-hailer where they were bound.

'For Genoa!'

'And how's The Man?'

'Marvellous!'

It had been at dawn the Italian coast had been sighted, then the French. Whereon Napoleon had told Marchand to replace the Elban cockade in his hat with a tricolour one and to pass it up to him through the hatch as he appeared on deck. It had also been at that moment the crimson-and-white Elban flag had been struck, and to the troops' 'delirious' enthusiasm the tricolour run up instead. 'The other vessels had rallied to us. They were told through the loud-hailer to hoist it.' Marchand had handed up the famous hat

'through the hatchway. It was the affair of an instant. The Emperor put it on. Such was the enthusiasm at the sight of this cockade, of the little hat with the colours of Austerlitz gleaming on it, that the Emperor, though he tried to speak, couldn't make a word heard. Indeed it'd be difficult to depict the joy, the enthusiasm, the tender feelings that manifested themselves on the brig.'

Ali too, presumably below deck, hears Pons de l'Hérault reading out the

proclamation; and to Marchand, under the open hatch, it seems as if
 'the vivats, the hand clappings, the stamping feet made such a noise as
  if all the brig's batteries were firing at once. It was delirium. Knowing
  the Guard had exhausted its rations, he ordered his *maître d'hôtel* to
  bring up the provisions laid in for his own household and had them
  shared out among the grenadiers.'
Why is the flotilla leaving Antibes' spacious harbour and rocky promontory
to starboard and heading for the Lerin Islands instead? How much does
Napoleon know about the state of affairs at Antibes?[16] Is he intending to
disembark on the long sandy beach at Cannes? Even if he knows the ancient
Sainte Marguerite fort's guns, which normally could prevent it, have also
been dismantled, it isn't easy to interpret the flotilla's movements, which
must surely by now have given the alarm in Antibes? However this may be, at
9:00 am – doubtless to General Coursin's and his picnic guests' amazement,
not to say dismay – the *Inconstant*, the tricolour flying from her gaff as it also
is from all the other boats, comes under the island's lea and lowers her
longboat.
    Down into it climb an advance party of twenty-three Chasseurs and
Grenadiers, commanded by Captain Lamouret, the Guard's senior captain.
'A strictly military man but highly esteemed' (Pons), his orders are to go on
ahead, 'visit the coast, make verbal contact, and sound out the terrain', and,
if possible, 'seize the citadel at Antibes'. Afterwards Napoleon, who never
admits to making mistakes, will make Lamouret responsible for misunderstanding his orders. Is he already doing so? Ali sees how
  'instead of making for the goal indicated, he orders his men to row for
  Antibes. Napoleon, astonished at such a manoeuvre against his will
  and order, has a gun fired to recall him: "Where are you off to,
  Captain?"'
By now General Coursin, faced with this 'unprecedented situation to which
history offers no parallels', must be worried indeed and wishing he was at his
post in Antibes and hoping that Cuneo d'Ornano has his wits about him.
    Wading ashore on the short stony beach of the Le Canu promontory, not
far from Cannes,[17] Lamouret's party find the coast road lies only a few
hundred yards away. Turning right, they've begun to march for Antibes
when they run into no less a personage than the commander of the Cannes
National Guard. In company with his wife and a borrowed donkey, 'Monsieur D——'[18] is on his way home after buying some olive groves. The flotilla
has already been pointed out to him by a local naval official who, 'following
the news that had been spread', had supposed it to be bringing invalids
home from Elba. Last January a party of such invalids had come home. This
news
  'hadn't prevented Monsieur D—— from attending to his purchases

and loading his olives on the donkey. It's in the midst of these domesticities he finds himself, his wife and the donkey arrested. Astonished by such unexpected treatment, he complains loudly and demands sharply to be set at liberty.'

Lamouret assures him it won't be for long. He must just wait for his two parties of soldiers to leave, one for Cannes[19] the other for Antibes. And he tells him confidentially that his men have 'brought back the Emperor of France, where his return is so strongly desired, above all,' he adds, turning to Mme D——, 'by the ladies.' 'At this word she almost fainted.'[20] And a few minutes later Lamouret sets the couple at liberty, but 'not the donkey, which this troop kept for its own use.'

Meanwhile the flotilla, still presumably under Coursin's anxious gaze, has again weighed anchor. Putting about in the lazy onshore breeze – it must be coming from the south-west for it to do so – it's tacking back eastwards along the coast toward Antibes. If Napoleon, doubtless assured to that effect by spies, has chosen to land there, it's certainly because he's assuming its garrison will come over to him, thus, from the outset, more than doubling his force. From his arsenal he can obtain what Ornano knows to be 'a considerable amount of field artillery and its magazines with all kinds of resources, weapons and food'. As well, perhaps, as a base to fall back on in case of a setback.

Now it's 3:00 pm and out in the roads opposite the deserted Gabelle Fort, well out of range of the Antibes guns across the harbour, the *Inconstant*, for a second time, lets go her anchor, and again lowers her longboat. Summoning General Cambronne, the commander of the so-called 'Elba battalion' (the Grenadiers and Chasseurs), Napoleon orders him

'to take some forty men to form the advance guard on the Fréjus road, in the direction of Cannes. We heard his last words: "General, I entrust you with my finest campaign. You won't have to fire a single shot. You'll only find friends."'

Optimism, theatre, calculation? All three, but also a needful caution. Cambronne's military career, Pons concedes (he speaks well of almost all these officers), 'was illustrious for many traits of devotion, but the violence of his character was sometimes terrifying'.[21] More specifically, Cambronne is to tell everyone he meets that 'the Empress and Murat*, King of Naples, are entering France simultaneously with the main body of troops via Toulon.'

All of which is completely untrue.

Cambronne's men approach the shore and from the brig's deck Peyrusse sees how

'muskets held high above their heads and without waiting for the landing to become easier, they were jumping into the water and wading ashore near the Gabelle Fort,' whose ramparts they find 'unoccupied'. Immediately patrols are sent out to control the approaches, notably

'a detachment to bar the main road, to intercept all communication and survey all passages. Others were to beat the countryside and occupy the village of Valauris. When all this was done Captain Adjutant-Major *Laborde* reported back on board the brig and also told the Emperor that the commandant at Antibes was a Corsican colonel by name Cuneo d'Ornano. At which Napoleon summoned Baron Galazzeani, his former prefect on Corsica, and asked him whether he knew Ornano. "Yes, Sire." "Very well, then! Take someone with you you can rely on. Go to Antibes and tell Colonel Cuneo to hand over the town to me together with its garrison, and I'll reward him for the service he does me today."'

Galazzeani takes with him 'the army's postmaster Pulicani.' Peyrusse, that bad sailor, makes 'the greatest haste to get myself put ashore.' Summoning a certain Captain Bertrand, Napoleon tells him to get into plain clothes, thrusts a packet of the proclamations into his hands, and orders him to enter Antibes, where he's to obtain three blank passports, and then go on to Toulon to make contact with Masséna. 'The Emperor was the last to leave the brig. At 5:00 pm the flotilla's guns announced his disembarkation. All the troops had landed.'

Today, if any, is an imperial *journée*, and as such ripe for rhetoric. As Napoleon steps ashore,[22] Marchand hears him declare histrionically:

'Soil of France! Fifteen years ago I decorated you with the name of Country of the Great Nation. I salute you anew, and in the same circumstances. One of your children, the most glorious to bear this beautiful title, comes again to deliver you from anarchy. Nothing for me! Everything for France.'

Rhetoric? Certainly. But in this initial phase, with only 800 men, two 4-pounder guns and only two horses, words are crucial.

What does Europe's most admired, most hated and most feared man look like on this afternoon of charming spring weather? Aged forty-six years, seven months and fifteen days, according to the notions of the time he's already almost old. And indeed his appearance is

'that of a man rather older than he was. Remarkably strong, well-built, about five feet seven inches high,[23] his limbs particularly well-formed, with a fine ancle [*sic*] and very small foot, his hands were also very small, and had the plumpness of a woman's rather than the robustness of a man's. His eyes light grey; and when he smiled, the expression on his face was highly pleasing. When under the influence of disappointment, however, it assumed a dark gloomy cast. His hair, though a little thin on the top and front, had not a grey hair amongst

24

it. His complexion was a very uncommon one, being of a light sallow colour',[24]

or rather, just now, all observers will note, strikingly bronzed – whether from the Mediterranean sun or some other possibly more sinister reason.[25] Though corpulent, he isn't squat. Rather it's his bull neck, his large head and generally stocky but well-proportioned appearance that, together with his habit of surrounding himself with notably tall and handsome men, creates an impression of compact smallness:

'The depth of his head, the shape of his handsome forehead, the well-set eyes, his well-modelled lips turned down at the mouth's corners – his piercing glance, veiled rather than gentle, his smile, rather disparaging than gay and more mocking than caressing,'[26]

all this, together with his boundless – but now, in middle age, somewhat more intermittent – physical and mental energy, a photographic memory and a computer-like appetite for facts and people, together with his steel will, his unprecedented fame and a devastating instant charm – all this gives him a charismatic ascendancy over everyone, whether friend or enemy. His allusion, as he steps ashore, to his return from Egypt sixteen years ago, when France, instead of arresting him for deserting his army, had acclaimed him as its saviour, certainly isn't haphazard. If then, why not now?[27] Yet perhaps the strangest thing of all is that this extraordinary Corsican man, who for so long had seemed to symbolise France itself, can't even speak correct French[28] and mispronounces many words.

Having 'furtively introduced himself into Antibes', Staff Captain Bertrand, before requesting the three passports, 'wants to circulate among the troops and inhabitants the hand-written proclamations the Emperor had himself thrust into his hands.'

A serious mistake.

Instantly everything begins to go wrong. Very wrong indeed.

For here in the deep Catholic south Bonaparte, though himself a southerner, is anything but popular. Indeed detested. At Orgon, en route for Elba less than a year ago, it had only been thanks to his seven-foot Swiss bodyguard-cum-coachman Noverraz's courage and presence of mind that he'd escaped lynching, seen himself burnt in effigy, and only escaped by disguising himself in an Austrian uniform and pretending to be his own outrider. Now word must certainly have got around that something serious is afoot. Proclamations? By Bonaparte? So far from letting themselves be suborned,

'two individuals, NCOs of the 87th Line, arrested Captain Bertrand and took him to Colonel d'Auger, their CO, who took his papers off him. Not wanting to let go a prisoner carrying so important a secret, he sent to the town commandant, asking him to come, since he had to inform him of a matter of the greatest importance, which could stand no delay.'

And Ornano, who obviously (even allowing for the fact that it's he himself who's telling us all these details) is an officer of quite another stamp than his inept relative who'd died in Russia,[29] comes immediately. Upon d'Auger handing him the hand-written proclamations,

'the arrested officer confessed frankly to the two commanders that Napoleon himself was present in person out in the roads, at the head of his grenadiers. He exhorted them to recognise their Emperor and be the first Frenchmen to raise his standards on French soil and share his new fortunes.'

Neither have the least intention of doing so:

'There was absolutely no other answer to give this emissary than to secure his person; seize his papers; and as far as possible hide from the inhabitants the danger menacing them and take needful precautions to avert it.'

One battalion of d'Auger's regiment is drilling with 'wooden bullets and flints on the marine glacis'. Ornano orders him to assemble it and prepare for all eventualities. He's just about to go back to his head-quarters when

'he's approached by an NCO who'd been sent from the watch-house of the Royal Gate to notify him that some grenadiers from Elba were asking to be allowed in. It was Captain Lamouret's detachment. Instead of waiting on the high ground overlooking Antibes, as the Emperor had ordered him to, he, off his own bat and on his own responsibility, and hoping to seize the town and suborn the garrison with shouts of *Vive l'Empereur!* had advanced toward it.'

Now things become even more dramatic. So far only Ornano has had time to grasp the peril.[30] And on his own he goes straight to the Royal Gate to explore the situation:

'There wasn't a moment to lose. To his great surprise he finds that this detachment of twenty-one grenadiers and chasseurs, commanded by two officers, is partly on the glacis and [partly] between the barrier and the protruding drawbridge. What to do in so critical a situation? The posts in the demilune and the main fortifications were too feeble to put up the least resistance to the well-known impetuosity of Napo-leon's men. So swiftly had all these events succeeded one another, no one inside the town knew what was afoot outside it.'

Ornano, keeping a very cool head,

'decides to parley with the officer commanding the detachment, thus

26

hoping to gain the time needed for the execution of the orders he'd given to d'Auger and the town gatekeeper.'

Which in effect means, first, drawing up the 87th in line just inside the Royal Gate and, 'second, raising the advanced drawbridge and closing its gates as soon as the Elban unit should have advanced to within the works.' Above all he judges it

'wise not to precipitate an attack on a handful of brave and desperate men, so as not to spill French blood and compromise, perhaps uselessly, both his own existence and that of the fortress. He was alone amidst some imperial grenadiers who, if they'd suspected he knew the Emperor had landed, could have tossed him into the moat and forced their way in. Having presented themselves as the advance guard of a battalion that had left Porto Ferrajo which was requesting billets for the night, they couldn't adopt a hostile attitude if they, ostensibly as friends, were to penetrate into the town and, glass in hand, suborn the garrison.'

Ornano isn't a Corsican for nothing; and opposes

'ruse to ruse. They're not to be allowed in until a special sign tells him his orders are ready to be carried out. Then he lets them into the demilune; and the sound of the gates closing and the clanking of the chains of the drawbridge behind them makes them realise, but too late, the trap they've fallen into. They pass through under the vaultings of the fortifications and between hedges of men whose faces express fidelity. There is no shout of *Vive l'Empereur* raised, so great is these warriors' surprise and mortification at having failed.'

Turning to Lamouret, Ornano says: 'Captain, make your men lay down their weapons.'

'Colonel,' replies Lamouret, 'don't submit grenadiers of the Imperial Guard to such an affront. They'll refuse, and I can no longer answer for them.'

Instead Lamouret proposes Ornano shall let them proceed under arms to any place he designates, where they'll hand them over. It's a distinction, evidently, with a difference; and Ornano accepts,

'to preserve so many brave military men for France who otherwise, on both sides, would have seen their last day at Antibes, and whose blood would neither have held up Napoleon nor usefully served the cause of Louis.'

He orders his adjutant to take 'these unhappy grenadiers to a room in the curtain quarter, receive their weapons, place them under lock and key in the next room, and to place squads of guards at the entrances of all the streets, as much to prevent them from communicating with the garrison as to shelter them from the popular fury. 'As soon as you've done this you'll tell the officers, from me, to go with you to the town hall,' where he'll meet them as soon as he has taken all due measures to secure the town. Ornano's idea is to separate the men from their officers. But though the muskets and swords are duly handed over, everything's still within an ace of going wrong. The adjutant's on his way with Lamouret and his lieutenant to the town hall, when 'a wretched policeman intervenes in something that's none of his business', and tries to put them in prison.

'We're betrayed!' shout Lamouret and his lieutenant, turning and running back to their men. 'They're putting us in prison! Grenadiers, to arms!'

The men of the Imperial Guard break down the door of the room where their muskets are stacked and prepare to defend themselves. But Ornano, told about what's happened, hurries to the spot and gets the two officers to see reason, 'as much by threats as by frankly explaining the whole business.' And the weapons are locked in again. After which he takes Lamouret and his lieutenant to the town hall, where he tells them he's known all along that it's Napoleon who's landed, and that he intends to hold Antibes for the King. With these words he places them both under arrest, with a sentry at the door.

But arrests are a game two can play at. 'At the moment when he was jumping into a boat to go out to Sainte Marguerite with a despatch to Coursin to tell him what's going on, an orderly is arrested by some grenadiers of the Guard.' Their captain, Combe by name, ironically receipts his missive as 'addressed to General Drouot', who of course passes it on to Napoleon,

'who, reading it, could convince himself that fidelity reigned at Antibes and that one Corsican knew how to keep his honour intact when faced with a crowned compatriot.'

Ornano also sends out two vessels to reconnoitre the coast, 'one to the west of the island, the other to the east,' and confides despatches to a coastguard gunner, by name Blaise Elina, who, 'eluding the troops from Elba guarding the roads, deposits them at the post office at Luc for urgent transmission to the War Ministry and General Abbé', the department's other subdivisional general.

Already, at around 4:00 pm, Peyrusse has landed his boxes of book-covered gold. Going over to 'a bivouac established in a copse between the sea and the main road,' he hears Napoleon

'recommending care be taken to pay meticulously for everything anyone took and to respect the properties passed over. The baggage had been landed. Some mules were bought in the neighbourhood to carry the treasure.'

The early spring afternoon is 'mild and beautiful' as young Captain Gazon, having 'passed a day filled with good memories and reciprocal marks of friendship', suddenly remembers his promise to his mother to be home before nightfall.

'The evening was wonderful, the air calm, the sea tranquil. From afar off the sky, reflecting the dusk's last rays, had begun to exude that undulating haze that announces our spring evenings.'

At 5:00 pm he's jogging on along the winding sandy Royal Road from Cannes to Antibes on his father's mare, when he sees an acquaintance, an employee of the Bridges and Highways Department, who's 'superintending some repairs' to it. And reins in his horse to chat. But . . . why's his friend so taciturn, so unwilling to talk? (Doubtless he has seen Lamouret's party, recognised the imperial uniforms, and thinks prudence the better part of valour.) Puzzled, but all the while charmed into 'a veritable ecstasy' by the lovely view out over the bay, Gazon rides on, Antibes and the sea to his right, the hills to his left. Rounding the rise in the road which overlooks the town he also comes 'within view of the Gabelle battery'. And notices 'some soldiers on its parapet.' Now what can they be doing there? Isn't the fort 'well out of bounds to the Antibes garrison?' Hasn't he himself only recently dismantled its guns? So what's going on? Passing the town's drawbridge, he even makes out 'their bearskins, their red facings. I recognised gunners of the Imperial Guard. I thought I must be dreaming.' Reining in the mare at the gate of the fort,[31] he asks some of them who they are. Well, yes, they reply evasively,

'they'd gone to Elba with the Emperor; but been stricken by the local sickness and given leave to return to France. "We've just been taking a little stroll while waiting for our comrades. You can see them over there, disembarking from the brig."'

Indeed, a lot of small boats are coming and going between the *Inconstant*, where she rides at anchor 'opposite the Gabelle hamlet', and the rocky beach. Some of the flotilla's smaller vessels have even been run ashore and are discharging soldiers. Surely the whole thing must be an hallucination?

Riding on slowly, his thoughts filled with 'the great captain whose eagles, after victory upon victory, we'd carried into all the capitals of Europe', he has left the fort a hundred yards behind him when a customs official comes galloping toward him, reins in his horse, and supposes 'he too must be on his way to see him.'

'Him? Who?'

'*Parbleu!* Napoleon, the Emperor! He's not stand-offish, I can tell you. Anyone can approach him.'

And away goes the customs man at a gallop – evidently for Cannes – with the imperial proclamation.

'A thunderbolt wouldn't have stunned me as did these few words. In a flash I grasped the gravity of the situation. On the one hand the Bourbons, whom France was growing daily more disaffected with, but who were supported by all the powers of Europe. On the other the common people and the army, who hadn't forgotten how high he'd raised France among all the nations.'

Napoleon's return, he realises, can only mean a civil war, coupled in all likelihood with and aggravated by a new and even more frightful invasion. 'My brain assailed and troubled by sad forebodings, I stood rooted to the spot.' Well, Emperor or no Emperor, no one has a right to prevent him making good his promise to his mother. So on he jogs, passing a sentry – then an outpost – then a *grand'garde*.[32] All let him pass without comment. Last of all,

'opposite the point where they'd landed, some groups of officers were walking about on the road. As I'd retained my moustaches these gentlemen, taking it for granted I was an army man, honoured me with a salute; to which I, without slowing down and impatient to leave them behind me, replied.'

He's just about to spur his mare to a gallop when, a few yards from the point where the road branches off down to the shore, he sees,

'a young *sous-lieutenant* of voltigeurs (I recognised it from his yellow collar) coming toward me, saying: "No one's allowed to pass." "By whose orders?" "The Marshal's." "Which marshal's?" "Marshal Bertrand."'

Count Henri-Gratien Bertrand, dubbed by Napoleon 'Europe's best engineer', is the expedition's most senior officer. Ever since Duroc* had been killed by a roundshot in 1813 the forty-two-year-old Bertrand has been Napoleon's Marshal of the Palace, or Grand Marshal. 'In every sense of the word a decent, conventionally minded [*bien pensant*] man,' Pons de l'Hérault has seen that

'the events that shattered the imperial throne had also shattered Bertrand's soul. Ceaselessly preyed on by the upsetting memories of that vast catastrophe, he was no longer a friend to hard work, but to repose. His heart was completely with his family. His wife and children took up all his thoughts. From all I saw, Napoleon's and Bertrand's natures weren't in harmony, and the bonding of their union, more apparent than real, was more a matter of habit than of feeling.'

Gazon demands to be taken to him, but the lieutenant says he doesn't know where he is: 'He can be here any moment.' But an order's an order. 'I sat my horse.' And here, 'brought by curiosity', are some peasants, among them an Antibes locksmith who tells the young artillery captain that one of 'these gentlemen' – *viz* the officers – has just been asking after him. And now here's another, a former comrade at the Saint-Etienne arms factory.

Hastening up to Drouot, he's just told him a Captain Gazon's here. And here's yet another friend, Engineer Captain Larabit,[33] 'my hall corporal at Polytechnic School'.

'Gazon?' says Drouot, and rather naturally assumes he must be a relative of one of the district's two sub-divisional generals, General Gazon. Gazon dismounts, and they take his father's mare – saying it makes the expedition's fourth horse. 'I asked them whether they weren't worried about bringing down terrible misfortunes on France.' No, says Drouot, coming forward and seeing from his moustaches that he's an artillery officer: 'The whole of France has been longing for the Emperor and has called him back. And on 20 March he'll enter Paris.'

That's right, Larabit confirms eagerly, and begs his former comrade-in-arms to join them. But 'standing on my oath of fidelity to Louis XVIII' Gazon refuses 'point-blank'. Taking him aside, Drouot asks him about the state of affairs behind those ramparts in full view only half a mile away. What about the Antibes garrison? 'Notably he asked me whether I thought the 106th Line[34] was really devoted to the King.' And – above all – what can have happened to Lamouret and his detachment? Gazon has no idea. But when asked to carry some of Napoleon's proclamations 'to General Gazon at Grasse' he again refuses, saying he 'must be in Antibes this evening.'

'So you aren't coming with us?'

'*Mon général*, I'm bound by an oath, and mustn't.'

There's no answer to this – hadn't Napoleon, after his abdication, ordered the army to swear allegiance to Louis XVIII? Oh, but come now, just a moment, says Larabit, upset. Surely he isn't going to leave without even meeting the Emperor? Leaving Gazon for a moment, he goes and fetches Drouot, who comes back. Larabit takes him by the hand: 'Come along, I've spoken to the Emperor about you. He wants to see you.'

And there 'walking in one of the strips of ground between the vines set at right angles to the road between the hamlet and the highroad',[35] Gazon finds Napoleon

'wearing his little hat, a grey riding coat, a black cravat that hid his collar, in the uniform of the Grenadiers of the Imperial Guard. The two first strips of open ground to his right and left were empty. In each of the neighbouring ones a rank of grenadiers stood posted. At each moment the Emperor was receiving communications from his high functionaries, who also came to take his orders.'

Though he's standing in 'a group of five or six persons', Gazon's eyes are 'so fixed on him' and he's 'so moved to find myself in his presence,' that he can't identify them. Drouot, persisting in his error of mistaken identity, presents him as the nephew of General Gazon, 'of whom I've spoken to you.'

'The Emperor took a step toward me and said: "Well! And Drouot's given you my proclamations? You're leaving for Grasse?"'

Captain Gazon says he knows nothing about *General* Gazon (to whom he's no relative at all) at Grasse. What's certain is that he must be back in Antibes before nightfall, when he has faithfully promised his mother to be back with his father's mare.

'But you won't get in, they've closed the gates.'

'Sire, I'm a local man, and for me they'll open up.'

Napoleon walks over to the group of his officers; comes back; and, almost as if he hadn't heard what Gazon's just said, asks again:

'Well, and you're leaving for Grasse?'

Gazon repeats his refusal. But Napoleon never wastes time on futile argument,[36] least of all when he knows his interlocutor's in the right. Well then, Gazon will at least sell them his horse? And when told the animal isn't his to sell,

'he again walked away from me. And a few minutes later a gentleman
in a sky-blue coat with silver lace on it came and said: "You may retire.
His Majesty will call for you if he needs you."'

Who's the wearer of this sky-blue uniform, denoting an *officier d'ordonnance*? An Elban perhaps, by name Perès, from Longone? If so he's already 'fearing the consequences of the enterprise' and planning to desert. Or perhaps he's a young Elban aristocrat called Vantini, another of the ADCs? Gazon, at all events, can't identify him. Passing out through the line of sentries, he again falls in with Larabit, who's deeply shocked at his refusal to do the Emperor's bidding:

'It'll be your undoing. Come on, now! Go to Grasse.'

And when Gazon still refuses, but asks him, as a friend, to recover his father's mare for him, Larabit says:

'Don't you worry on that score. We don't want to do violence to anyone.'

By now dusk is beginning to fall. Larabit goes with him to the road junction. In 'the big olive grove under which the general was giving orders and supervising the copies of the proclamation that were being made by the light of [candles placed] on drums for tables' he asks Drouot to return the mare.

'So, Monsieur Gazon,' Drouot too urges, 'you're quite sure you don't want to join us?'

'*Mon général*, I've sworn fidelity to another sovereign. But if the Emperor again ascends the throne I'll serve him as I used to.' Words that will speak for thousands during the weeks to come. But at least, Drouot persists, he'll take the Emperor's *Proclamation to the French People* to Antibes? But no, he won't do that either – to publicise such acts isn't the business of 'simple private individuals'. Only when Drouot insists does Gazon agree to take it – on condition that he hand it straight to Ornano.

'Adieu, Monsieur Gazon,' says Drouot, handing him a copy. And adds dryly: 'I hope I'll soon have the pleasure of seeing you again at some less problematic moment.'

Gazon puts his father's mare 'to such a gallop as she'd never made before'.

Not every passer-by is getting off so lightly. 'Having oriented ourselves,' Peyrusse goes on,

> 'we looked for the main Antibes road. It wasn't far from where we'd landed. We'd seized all means of transport that presented themselves.
> I was on the road with Squadron-Leader Jerzmanowski, four grenadiers, and as many Poles.'

Jerzmanowski is the Poles' CO, and in Pons de l'Hérault's judicious eyes 'a very superior man'. Just then Peyrusse sees 'a heavy coach' lumbering towards him along the road:

> 'We decided it should be for me. It came closer. Our little troop barred the road. Hiding my coat's gold lace under my greatcoat I stayed a little in the rear. The coachman, stupefied, tried to resist. The travellers, surprised by this hubbub, stuck their heads out of the windows, and seeing before them some Poles, some quite handsome grenadiers and the tricolour cockade, seemed turned to stone. I went up to the coach and showed my coat.'

One of its occupants, he sees, is a sub-inspector of reviews who's on his way to Antibes with his wife – 'she could hardly get over her terror. They thought they had to do with Algerians'. Pointing to the bivouac in the olive grove, the treasurer tells them it's the Emperor who's come back, and promises to return their coach to them at Cannes:

> 'They gave in. Having got over their emotions, they were obliged to take out their belongings and wait for the first vehicle to come along to take them on into Antibes. The carriage was brought into our camp. My trunks were placed in it.'

Another 'well-dressed individual, arrested in a vineyard, who said he was a Corsican and a retired captain', is brought to 'the Emperor who, taking him by the collar, hands him to his generals and superior officers, saying: "Gentlemen, here's the first recruit we've made in France. Place him in the entourage with his rank of captain."

> 'But this officer, head of a numerous family, unwilling to exchange the unsure for the sure, managed to escape and soon afterwards returned to Antibes, where he reported all he'd seen and heard to the commandant.'

Among the 'astonished individuals' who've been watching the troops come ashore Marchand also sees some peasants who 'when they realised it was the

Emperor, and that he was thinking of marching on Paris, expressed their amazement at his having so few troops with him.'

The Guard, the Grand Marshal sees, is boiling 'to go and free their comrades arrested in Antibes. This spread a lot of melancholy among us.' A wagoner too, who has crossed France recently, is interrogated by him, and replies

> 'with heavy common-sense "Ah monsieur, we're very annoyed to see you. It's true you've friends, but I was just beginning to feel calm and who knows what'll come of all this?" This reply put more blackness into our hearts.'

What the philosophically gloomy Drouot is feeling – he who'd 'done everything humanly possible' to dissuade Napoleon from trying to make a comeback – is anyone's guess.

Meanwhile the Antibes town council is all at sixes and sevens. Reprimanding Ornano 'for his lack of prudence' in letting Lamouret and his party inside the walls, they order him at all costs to disarm them. Which of course he's already done. By now it's between 7:00 and 8:00 pm, and Napoleon, waiting in the olive grove for news of his grenadiers and chasseurs, must be realising something's gone seriously wrong. Ali has seen him

> 'walking hither and thither, waiting for his dinner, stopping at his men's bivouacs, conversing with them or else directing his footsteps to the road bordering the meadow to the north, where he talked to passers by, who were rather rare, and questioned them. Dinner over, he again began walking about, talking with either the Grand Marshal or General Drouot, or some other person in his entourage.'

What's become of Captain Bertrand, of Baron Galazzeani, of postmaster Pulicani?

> 'Amazed at all this warlike activity outside the town's closed gates and drawbridge, an infinity of peasants and craftsmen coming back from their work in the countryside were blocking the approaches to the barriers and demanding to be allowed to come home.'

But the municipality is 'too apprehensive of an enterprising and audacious enemy, to lower the drawbridges'; and it's amidst this protesting crowd that Galazzeani and Pulicani are trying to get in. Finding all the gates closed and all approaches guarded and realising Antibes, both garrison and inhabitants, are compactly hostile, they 'slip along the glacis toward the Rosni bastion, to try and get in through the Marine Gate', but are prevented from doing so 'by the sea and the mud at the base of the walls. Not risking showing themselves in Antibes in so muddy a state,' they return to the olive grove, where they find Napoleon surrounded by his grenadiers, who've protected him 'with an overcoat against a fresh damp breeze soughing in the bran-ches. He was asleep on a chair set up for him near the main road, his elbows on the table. Someone had brought his campaign armchair and lit a big fire for him. His Majesty, wrapped up in the cloak he'd worn at Marengo,[37] had sat down in front of it and fallen asleep, his feet stretched out on another chair. His horse was brought ashore.'

He's been resting like this 'for nearly two hours' when 'on his awakening, two soldiers of the Antibes garrison who'd climbed down the ramparts to join him' are presented. And it's from these two men, doubtless very much excited and out of breath, he finally hears what's happened to Lamouret and his men. At that moment (as Ornano will hear afterwards) he's

'chatting with a lady and her husband who'd come to present their compliments, when Galazzeani, back from Antibes, comes up and reports the failure of his mission. "*Bon*," the Emperor said after a moment's silence. "*Bon*." And without being disconcerted took a pinch of snuff and went on talking with the lady.'

But of course it's anything but *bon*. His enterprise has, it seems, opened with a serious error of judgement and a supererogatory manoeuvre. If instead of sailing blithely toward Cannes and thus giving the alarm to Ornano, he'd promptly landed on the Gabelle promontory, surely his 600 veterans would have been able to rush the town gates? Suborn the garrison? Antibes itself, perhaps, is of no great importance. But what does its resistance portend for the future? 'The army will obey me,' he'd said when he'd wanted to march on Paris last year. And Ney and Macdonald had replied: 'The army will obey its generals.' And so it had. Peyrusse sees how 'His Majesty's mood darkens' as he sends for another captain, Casabianca by name, and orders him, too, to go to Antibes and get him back his grenadiers and chasseurs. At the same time, as if to visibly stress there's no turning back, he orders the *Inconstant* and the chartered cargo ship *Étoile* to sail back to Elba to fetch his mother and his sister Pauline and their households.[38] Peyrusse settles the vessels' masters' bills totalling 11,304 francs, and is thereto ordered to advance every man a fortnight's pay. 'Everyone dined as best he could. The troops didn't sleep. They were preparing their weapons.' Though Peyrusse, by his own admission, is no warrior, he finds it necessary to place his 'mind and spirit at the level of all possible outcomes' and like everyone else awaits the order to leave. Marchand sees that the Guard, after its ever more tedious existence on Elba[39] is 'overjoyed' to be back in France. 'It didn't sleep at all.'

Meanwhile, Captain Gazon's worrying about his mother – who by this time is certainly worrying about him. He too has found 'both the outside barrier and the demilune gate shut'. Luckily, in the excited buzz behind it, he makes out the voice of 'Lafon the gatekeeper, whom I knew very well', and shouts up to him that he has an extremely urgent mission to d'Ornano. Is it Captain Gazon? Yes. Alone? Yes. Lafon lets him in. Galloping through the streets on the mare, he sees candles burning at every window. Falls into his mother's arms. Where's his father? At the town hall, with the National Guard, which is under arms all the clock round. The town council too is in permanent session 'for fear of the town being assaulted.'

At first not even his father believes his story. Surely it can't be the Emperor? Not Bonaparte himself? Not really? Surely it's some impostor? How can he be sure, the councillors ask him? Has he ever seen him before? Where? When?[40] The questions hail down. Waving aside Gazon's stipulation that he would show Napoleon's proclamation to Ornano, in person, Mayor Tourre insists on seeing it. Well, it's true! Bonaparte's back! Stepping forward, Colonel Chantron, in command of the fortress artillery, tells Gazon to help his colleagues mount the rampart guns. 'Captain,' he says, 'I requisition you. From this moment you're on active service.'

> 'I thanked the colonel, but observed to him that in view of the fact that the Emperor had to be in Paris on 20 March he certainly wouldn't hang about in front of Antibes.'

Gazon finds that, under Ornano's and the mayor's joint supervision – the municipality electrifying the population by its example – 'already, within a few hours, pieces had been placed in battery at the threatened points. Infantrymen, gunners, National Guards, rivalled each other's zeal,' and Ornano is being perfectly seconded by his officers. It's in the midst of all these urgent arrangements that Casabianca turns up. Brought before Ornano, he

> 'orders him in the Emperor's name to accompany him at once with his staff and the municipality. The only answer he got was to be arrested, taken to the guardhouse at the Royal Gate and, after again being interrogated as to Napoleon's mission and plans, to prison.'

Likewise the Guard's medical officer Maramoud, 'captured on the glacis while apparently either examining the fortifications or trying to get in by stealth'. He gets the same treatment. And when,

> 'in the middle of the night, an officer sent to parley presents himself at the outpost gate with a packet addressed to the commandant Ornano, the duty officer relieves him of it in a [lowered] basket. Opening it, Ornano finds inside it hints, orders, promises, rewards, officers' commissions, etc. But, always incorruptible, he sends it back to the flag of truce, with the inscription: "Returned to H.E. Marshal Masséna, Prince of Essling, governor of the 8th military division, at Toulon".'

And when a fourth emissary, Adjutant-Major Laborde, approaches, a sentry of the 87th shouts at him: 'Go back, sir. Or I'll fire at you.' Which Laborde does, hastily. Finally, allotting War Commissioner Vauthier one of the very few available horses, Napoleon sends him 'to make sure of the real state of affairs' and if possible get Lamouret's men released, calling after him as Vauthier rides off:

'Above all don't get yourself trapped in the same way!'[41]

'M. Vauthier being mounted, he was soon back and reported that the town gates were indeed closed'.

Not until 11:00 pm does Napoleon finally accept defeat.

His attempt on Antibes has failed. But Gazon's assessment of what he'll do now is perfectly correct. Though 'some people around me' (now it's Napoleon himself who's reminiscing)

'murmured at my not marching on Antibes to make them give me back my twenty-five men – a few shells, they said, would suffice – I calculated it'd take me two hours to get to Antibes[42] and two to return, and at least three or four in front of its walls, which would be half a day lost. If I succeeded, it would be a trifle. If I failed, as was probable, this first setback would give my enemies confidence and time to get organised.'

What use are two 4-pounders to reduce a Vauban fortress? All the Imperial Guard can do is stand outside the walls and shout to the men of the 87th to come over to them. But Ornano obviously has his men well in hand. A mortifying setback it certainly is. Does he, as he stands there in the olive grove, glance up at Gabelle Fort and his thoughts go to the few days after Robespierre's fall when he'd been incarcerated in it, like his friend Augustin Robespierre in danger of the guillotine, only being released thanks to his appeal to Representative Albitte?[43]

During the crossing Napoleon has told his officers he's counting on:

'the astonishment of the locals, the state of public opinion, the resentment against the Allies, my soldiers' love for me; in a word, all the Napoleonic [sic] elements still germinating in our beautiful France. No historical precedent is making me attempt this bold enterprise.'

And when Colonel Malet had asked him what he thought his chances were, he'd said he was

'counting on the stupor produced by such a great novelty, and on people's minds being unable to reflect and being swept away when suddenly stricken by a bold and unexpected enterprise. I'll be there before anything's been organised against me.'

But what if the whole 'crazy enterprise' is turning out to be a fiasco? Marchand too sees that 'this scuffle' has put him 'in a bad humour'. Can it herald others, perhaps fatal? The valet also hears

'some officers expressing it as their opinion that to avoid the bad effect that could result from this fortified town's resistance we should go to Antibes and try to seize it. The Emperor replied that Antibes counted for nothing in the conquest he had in mind. The way to remedy the effect would be to march faster than the news'

– just like when he'd come back from Russia.

'Several soldiers and officers wanted to go to Antibes to free their comrades. But on reflecting I decided to march promptly for Grenoble, and told them: "Even if more than half of your men were prisoners in Antibes I shouldn't change my plan."'[44]

At 10:00 pm, as if to concretely stress the impossibility of a retreat, both the *Inconstant* and the *Étoile* set sail. And at 1:00 am

'at moonrise, knowing how important it was to march fast, I got going. No one, not even Bertrand, knew which road I meant to take.'[45]

'This first march,' Peyrusse goes on, 'was made in silence. We were embarked on a most perilous enterprise. The Emperor rode at our head.' So far, indeed, only Bertrand and Drouot have horses, and are riding beside him. 'Everyone else was on foot.' As for the 4-pounders, their ammunition wagons, and some carts containing 1,500 spare muskets,[46] they're having to be dragged along by hand. A few late travellers, encountered in the moonlight on the winding sandy road, are induced to part with their horses or donkeys; but though the mayor of La Colle accepts three copies of the proclamations, 'one for his own village', he refuses to part with any mounts. So the Polish lancers are having to carry their heavy saddles on their shoulders.

Cannes is a large fishing village clustered around a hilltop monastery an hour's march to the west. Ever since 5:00 pm yesterday it's been occupied by Cambronne's advance guard,[47] with orders to 'intercept communications and obtain bread rations for 3,000 men and the same amount of meat, to be distributed at midnight precisely.' At first the Cannes mayor hadn't realised it's Bonaparte himself who's come back, and has had time to send off a corporal of gendarmes to notify his colleague at Fréjus, further along the coast, that 'some troops from Elba had landed'. Now Pons de l'Hérault and two Elbans, sent on ahead to join up with Cambronne and find out what's going on there, come back to the column to report that Cannes is in fact complying with Cambronne's demands. Marchand hears Pons 'telling of the inhabitants' amazement at seeing the grenadiers,' to whom, when they'd first got there, Cannes had seemed deserted. After flushing out the mayor and making 'various requisitions, notably twelve four-horse carriages' and ordering 'all bread and wine that can be procured' – 3,600 rations – 'to be brought to the road and an embargo placed on all post-horses,' Cambronne had stationed his men at the France Gate with 'orders to let people in, but no one out.' Only a local gendarme had managed to give his grenadiers the slip and made for Grasse with his startling message to its town council. Now Cambronne too, 'passing to and fro several times,' has joined the column. He has something to report.

While he'd been issuing orders to the mayor, 'a more important personage' had been announced – 'the Duke of Valentinois, on his way to Monaco'. Prince Honoré's tiny feudal principality, confiscated during the Revolution like so many others of its kind, has been restored to him under the Treaty of Paris.[48]

> 'Arriving with an escort of gendarmes outside Cannes, this duke had run into a general officer [Cambronne] who, alone and hat in hand, had invited him to get out of his carriage and told him he had something most important to tell him. The carriage hadn't halted. Whereupon Cambronne showed the duke his tricolour cockade, which he'd been concealing, and said: "You see we're not of the same party. I heard you'd arrived. I've sent to headquarters to know how I'm to act toward you. Meanwhile you're my prisoner..." The duke said that as a French officer he only knew of one party in France – the King's. And that he didn't understand a word of this brusque declaration. At this moment he was surrounded by the platoon of the advance guard, composed of Chasseurs, which unmasked itself. Its officers, and Cambronne himself, seemed most impatient and agitated. The inhabitants of Cannes were sombre, gloomy.'[49]

Having taken Prince Honoré to the local inn and placed him under lock and key, Cambronne had resumed his parleying with the mayor. But though that dignitary had had to furnish the rations, he'd refused to go out along the Antibes road in the moonlight

> 'to compliment Buonaparte. Asked what he thought of the Emperor's return, he'd remained profoundly silent. And when pressed to explain himself, replied: "As I see it, I've sworn allegiance to the King, and I'm not going to betray him." "But you'd also sworn allegiance to the Emperor." "That's true, and I stood by my oath until he abdicated. Now all I see in him is a man who wants to be France's downfall. I repeat: my oath to the King is sacred. You can do what you like with me."'

Napoleon (the mayor will report tomorrow) gets to Cannes

> 'when it was nearly 2:00 am and set up his bivouac on the sands outside the town, near Notre-Dame, where he had a big fire lit that was surrounded by his troops and a lot of locals.'

To Peyrusse, Cannes seems to be deserted

> 'at the rumour of a horde of corsairs having landed. Here and there

windows were half-opened, lights appeared, and some cries of *Vive l'Empereur* were heard.'

Were they? Local legend will tell of a loaded gun pointed at the Usurper and a terrified neighbour who knocks it up and tells the would-be assassin it'll unleash a massacre. And the would-be assassin riposting: 'What does Cannes matter, if Europe is saved?'

Neither does the mayor mince his words. Going up to Napoleon, he tells him:

'We've just begun to be happy and tranquil. And here you come upsetting everything.'

'I can't say how much these words troubled and hurt me,' Napoleon will confess afterwards.

As for Prince Honoré, 'a trifle ill-used by Cambronne', Ali sees he's brought from the inn to the big fire that's been made up 'on the right-hand side of the road near the sand dunes', where Napoleon welcomes him 'as someone he knew. One of the many aristocrats who'd rallied to the Empire, he'd been ADC to Murat and chamberlain to Josephine. Standing there 'hat in hand' in the chilly night, he's 'at first embarrassed'; but when Napoleon urges him to retail the gossip of the Paris salons, makes no bones about the dangers facing the expedition. 'He told me he was doubtful my enterprise would succeed, seeing how few people I had with me'; though once beyond Provence he thinks he'll 'find everyone ready to follow him'. Also arrested, between Antibes and Cannes, has been his outrider, 'epaulettes and all'. 'A former member of the Empress' stables in Paris', he's telling how 'his handsome livery has been an object of disfavour and insults' but is assuring everyone they'll 'have all the populace on their side.' Now, formed in a 'wide circle' around Napoleon and the prince, the officers, unavailingly trying to eavesdrop, hear the latter 'firmly demanding to be allowed to go on to Monaco'. And they come to the conclusion that he's

'retailing drawing room opinion; the other, his outrider, the mind of the common people. In our imaginations the details he gave made up for the mortification caused by our failure at Antibes.'

What in fact are they talking about? 'I avoided questioning him on political matters,' Napoleon will afterwards relate:[50]

'There were witnesses at the bivouac. He was being observed, and I didn't want to expose myself to hearing any detail that might make a bad impression on the bystanders [already sufficiently upset by the Antibes setback]. So the conversation went in a bantering tone. It was about the ladies of my former court at the Tuileries, about whom I gaily informed myself.'

But Peyrusse does hear him ask the prince:

'Are you coming with us?'

But for Prince Honoré, too, discretion is the better part of valour: 'Sire, I'm going home.'

'So am I,' says Napoleon. 'You won't be staying at Monaco. You'll come back to Paris. It's the only place to live in.'

'From the Emperor's gaiety' as he sets off inland along the Grasse road Marchand assumes that he's 'satisfied with the details he'd obtained about Paris, and with public attitudes in France.'

'At one hour after midnight [Cannes' mayor goes on] the rations had been very nearly complete. I'd been asked to provide several drivers, carts and horses. All were furnished and the whole troop marched off toward Grasse; and at 5:30 am Cannes had the happiness of seeing itself completely delivered. For a few moments the inhabitants, who'd been too scared even to go to bed, had been astonished at this apparition, and were very content it had left. When it was known the Emperor was gone, a troop of the most ardent of his Cannes enemies rushed off in pursuit, sure that the populace along the way would rise en masse. Since nothing of the kind happened, we very soon saw them come back again.'

Marchand notices how much his master, 'almost in a state of levity', is enjoying the chatter of a local guide whom he 'goads on with his own funny remarks.' Admittedly the mayor of the first village, Napoleon will recall afterwards, 'refused to come out and speak with us.' Once again Cambronne, his Poles gaped at by early-rising peasants along the roadside, has gone on ahead.

The mayor of Grasse, chief town of the Var district, is as staunch a royalist as his Cannes colleague. Assembling the town council, M. de Gourdon has sought the advice of General Gazon de Perrières, the man Bertrand had been so keen to contact. Instead, Gazon has instantly sent off the alarm to Paris – but been so jittery he's dated it 28 February in lieu of 1 March. Meanwhile a party of young royalist hotheads have gathered and are urging the town council to sound the tocsin in all the villages and arm the population. This is all very well, says Gazon, but how many muskets can the town muster? Only thirty, it seems, and of them only five in a state to be fired – even if they had cartridges, which they haven't. Gazon counsels prudence: 'Don't they realise a thousand of Buonaparte's veterans are enough to disperse several thousand National Guards?' Anyway, who knows – maybe Bonaparte won't pass through Grasse anyway. Maybe he'll take the Aix road, and it'll be none of our business to bar his way.

Deaf to these reasonings, a party of the young royalists sets off down the Cannes road, where a messenger sent from Grasse to Cannes has already run into Cambronne's advance guard. Suspecting him for a spy, Cambronne takes him by the arm:

'My friend, you seem exhausted. No need to go so far. I'll tell you anything you want to know.'

The royalists have bivouacked for the night, when 'at 4:00 am a gendarme who seemed to be on his way from Cannes on some mission, came and told them "Fall back on the town. We're going to sound the tocsin."' They do so, only to be told by the councillors that their zeal is 'stifling us'.

Two hours later Cambronne arrives in Grasse, where he sees 'lots of old heads and white ones', and demands 4,000 rations. 'In the name of whose sovereign are you demanding them?' asks Mayor Gourdon. And when told it's the Emperor Napoleon, objects: 'We have our own sovereign and love him.'

'*Monsieur le maire,*' Cambronne replies in his rough way, 'I'm not here to discuss politics with you, but to insist on getting some rations, seeing as how my column will be here at any moment.'

'Nothing would have been easier than to kill me, alone as I was amidst the population. It wasn't enough just to say "I love the King". He should have shown it.'[51]

But what can M de Gourdon do, with five unfireable muskets? Cambronne goes back to Napoleon, who's 'advancing only slowly' along a road the Bridges and Highways Department has allowed to deteriorate so that the twelve commandeered four-horse vehicles that are now carrying the baggage are finding the going heavy. Napoleon halts at the Grasse youngsters' abandoned bivouac. Near a village called Mouan he has heard its church bells ringing and 'thought it was the tocsin[52] but been relieved to hear from a passing carter that it was tolling for a funeral.' 'I had my lively apprehensions', he'll confess afterwards. Is he having momentary doubts about the success of his enterprise? 'No one, not even Bertrand, knew which road I was going to take. Only as I reached the fork in the Avignon and Grasse roads did I give the order "to the right," through Grasse.'[53]

Now it's midday. And there, in front of them, on the lowermost slopes of the Maritime Alps, stands Grasse. Centre of the French perfume industry, in which many of its 12,000 inhabitants are engaged, its interests are firmly anchored in the upper and middle classes.

Napoleon's two valets always take turn and turn about; and today it's Marchand who's on duty:

'We halted until the whole battalion had joined. Then we marched through this town. Everything was silent. The inhabitants were out of doors. The town was totally royalist. Its municipal authorities had been

changed. The shops were shut. The Emperor wanted to have lunch
and it had been prepared for him,'

by a M. Camette, proprietor of the Hôtel du Dauphin, 27 Place des Aires.
But struck by the 'profound silence' of a citizenry aghast at the sudden
reappearance of this man they'd thought had vanished for good from the
political scene, he prefers to go on and 'breakfast on the high ground
dominating the town.' But Ali's party, bringing up the rear – the headquarters group had overtaken them half an hour after they'd left Cannes –
are hungry:

'Like most members of the Household I was on foot. The Emperor
had gone on far ahead of us. We heard he'd left to go further. Before
resuming our way my companions and I wanted to restore our ener-
gies by having something to eat. We entered an inn and had ourselves
served enough to make up a small meal. Heartily determined not to
fall behind, we swallowed what was given us as quickly as ever possible.'

By now the townsfolk are in the streets, and to Ali it seems they're

'neither hostile nor aggressive [farouche]. In a small square where we
halted a moment there was a fountain, and on it a phrase praising the
Bourbons, followed by the indispensable Vive le Roi!'

At the same time they're astonished to see

'our two cannon and the Emperor's carriage. We got going again.
Leaving the town, we had to climb up a steep mountainside. Arrived at
a plateau, we saw on our right a circle made up of quite a lot of people,
townsfolk and peasants, women and children, with the Emperor and
his staff in their midst.'

Neither M. de Gourdon nor General Gazon have waited for him. Jumping
on his horse and accompanied by his ADC, a Captain Fabreguettes – does
Napoleon (as legend will relate) gaze after the two mounted figures in their
officers' greatcoats? – the general has made off up into the hills to Peyrière,
where he owns a country house with a view out over the rocky windings of
the Castellane–Digne–Grenoble road. 'I'd no wish at all to rest in Grasse,'
Napoleon goes on, slightly modifying the facts – actually it's been his
intention to print off an edition of his proclamations here, 'but the printer
had fled and the two fusiliers placed at his door didn't encourage him to
come back – so I just halted on some rising ground beyond it, and let my
troops eat there.'

Grenoble, beyond the Maritime Alps, lies 200 miles away. Success depends
on

'swiftly seizing Grenoble, where there was a numerous garrison, an
arsenal, cannon; in a word, all sorts of assets, and in assuring myself of
the troops. And above all in not wasting time.'

Back in 1802 he'd given orders for the Grasse–Digne road to be developed as a post-road, viable in winter. 'In his pocket' he has Cassini's map, which shows it as such, though the work has never been done. Setback. Unless his original scheme – as Ornano assumes, priding himself on having scotched it – has been to march, reinforced by the Antibes garrison, its field artillery and its other supplies, on Lyons via Aix, Napoleon has evidently been assuming that his decree had been implemented and that the mountain road is already viable for wheeled traffic.[54] Otherwise why the dozen four-horse vehicles commandeered at Cannes?

But now two guides offer their services. With the snows still melting, they assure him, the road is nothing more than a crude mountain track, traversed by torrents and crumbling at points into precipitous abysses. Speed is more important than artillery. He must reach Sisteron, on the broad Durance river, before Masséna can send troops to command and block the passage. This is why he has ordered the two 4-pounders – brought more for effect than for use since the least armed conflict must end in disaster – to be left behind. He 'entrusts them' together with his own carriage 'to the Grasse municipality.'

In its own eyes the bourgeoisie, sole rightful beneficiary of the Revolution, is *la nation*. For years it had supported his régime. It was his genius that had fended off the forces of feudal reaction, first and foremost, secured the rights of proprietors of nationalised property, bought up for an inflated song during the Revolution. So far so good. He'd been a Roman-style dictator, appointed in a crisis. But then his personal ambitions had taken over; and the price of a substitute for a conscript had risen sharply, in the end to more than most middle-class families could afford. Dismay had replaced enthusiasm; and already on the banks of the Niemen[55] the loyal but plain-spoken Caulaincourt* had warned him that the new war against Russia wasn't regarded in France as a 'national one'. Though still haunted by a fear that the returning emigrés may force them to disgorge, and already becoming disenchanted with the Bourbons, the bourgeoisie has been adjusting itself – money speaking louder than words, loyalties or ideologies – to the new situation. So Grasse's prosperous bourgeoisie, living off its famous perfumes, is one thing. Its employees – *le peuple*, the working classes he'd 'tamed by putting them into uniform' and of whom he's as distrustful as any *aristo* – quite another. Yet it's mainly peasants and factory workers who've turned out en masse to greet him.

Is this going to be the seismic crack in his whole enterprise?

When the troops appeared and the Emperor's name was announced, Marchand goes on, telling perhaps for once a mingled truth,

'the common people came out in crowds. The shops reopened. The authorities presented themselves. Supplies were abundant, and were

44

instantly paid for. Soon the whole population followed him out there. Some horses and mules were brought, and some Poles and members of the entourage were provided with mounts.'

'Some terrorists,' Napoleon will relate afterwards, 'offered to revolutionise Grasse. I told them not to stir, even to leave wearers of white cockades in peace, and said that not for fifty millions was I going to be stopped.'

Two posies of violets presented to him are symbolic. One is from a workman in one of the perfume factories, the other from a country labourer. 'The violet,' writes the ultra-reactionary *F-A-V. de Frénilly*, a Breton gentleman of overweening pretensions, for whom Napoleon is 'the detestable Buonaparte' and even the liberally inclined Louis XVIII a 'royal Jacobin',

'had long been his friends' password. While waiting for the natural flower to blossom, people had been wearing artificial ones in their belts and cross-belts and putting violets in perfumes. All of which meant "I'm conspiring".'

Not that there's been any conspiracy. Nor has anyone expected him back. Albeit dictated, as we shall see, by extremely cogent reasons, the decision had been his and his alone.

'One inhabitant [Marchand goes on] made himself spokesman and said to the Grand Marshal: "General, His Majesty has punished us enough by not doing us the honour of breakfasting in our town. If he only knew how badly we've been treated by the emigrés since they've come back, our silence wouldn't lend itself to such nasty interpretation, and His Majesty would see we're worthy of being counted among his faithful subjects."'

The gruff and taciturn Bertrand, for whom 'the Emperor isn't a man like other men, one to whom no ordinary standards can be applied',[56] replies sententiously:

'It's the only way you can serve him properly.'

Since Napoleon tolerates neither beards nor moustaches at his headquarters, the officers, 'hanging up their pocket mirrors on a wall opposite a sheepfold', are taking a much-needed shave while His Majesty chews a chicken sent up from the Hôtel du Dauphin.[57] Lunch over, Marchand sees him 'turn to the women and cheer them up by telling them funny stories.' But though Ali, as he draws abreast, sees him 'chatting one by one with most of those around him and despite all his efforts to put himself out,' it seems to him 'all those people remained more or less cold. We didn't stop there. The best thing we could do was to get on ahead and arrive as early as possible at the overnight halt.'

Cold? To his fellow-valet the enthusiasm seems to be gradually growing. A blind ex-officer, brought by his wife, asks to be allowed to kiss his hand. And is embraced. But where's *officier d'ordonnance* Perès from Longone? He has 'hidden himself, so as to go home at the first opportunity'.[58] So far only four persons – 'a retired veteran, now a tanner, the two deserters from the Antibes garrison and a gendarme' – have actually joined the Elbans. The loss of the two 4-pounders, Bertrand notices, 'affects' Napoleon, the one-time lieutenant of artillery. Likewise the 1,500 useless muskets and his travelling carriage – another gift from Pauline. All must be left behind. Since the requisitioned vehicles, too, are to be sent back to Cannes, Peyrusse, leaving the books in his wooden cases, extracts his gold millions and loads them on muleback. This done, and the two-hour halt at an end, the drums beat the fall-in:

'The whole assembled population made the air resound with cries of *Vive l'Empereur!* And for the second time the shouts of the common people accompanied His Majesty along his way.'

The mountain track winds upwards;[59] and by and by the expedition, its tail brought up by the Corsicans, disappears round a bend in the road.

This time no one pursues it.[60]

Antibes, so efficiently fortified by the great Vauban, is as difficult to get out of as into. Toward midnight on 3/4 March

'a nocturnal alert momentarily troubles the tranquillity of its inhabi-tants. The four officers and the health officer [Maramoud] impri-soned in the same house, with a sentry at the door, all five together break out of their lodging, overthrowing the sentry, who however fires the alarm shot.'

Ornano, afraid it's some surprise 'combined by the officers and their gre-nadiers or some party outside', rushes up onto the ramparts. One of the fugitives, having knotted two sheets, is captured in an embrasure of the seaward bastion. And at the foot of the rampart outside the Marine Gate a patrol finds Captain Casabianca, his back broken, lying in agony. But his three other companions have returned lamely to their lodging.

Much later, on 11 April, Masséna will order General Coursin without delay and by the promptest means to send to Toulon

'the twenty muskets, twenty bayonets, twenty-one sabres, twenty car-tridge boxes and accessories, twenty-one sabre belts, one drum-case, one drummer's collar and drumsticks, taken at the time when the grenadiers of the Imperial Guard landed at Antibes.'

By then there'll be a desperate need of all military equipment.

CHAPTER 2

A FURIOUS ARMY

W hen Louis XVIII, a sufferer from gout and elephantiasis, had waddled ashore at Calais last year, escorted by the British navy and subsidised by a £100,000 British government loan, he'd been given an ecstatic welcome. In the utterly confused situation at Napoleon's fall he'd been brought back by Talleyrand, not so much out of wisdom aforethought but as the only discernible 'principle',[1] who'd prevailed on the all-powerful Tsar Alexander to accept the Bourbons, however little he liked them. Anything else, Talleyrand had stressed, would have been an intrigue. And at least to a large part of the French nation, Marshal Oudinot's young wife the *Duchess of Reggio**[2] assures us,

> 'the Bourbons truly presented themselves as a pledge of peace. It was under that head they were accepted by most people who, without knowing them, welcomed them as the olive branch.'

Like many other well-off people, the former Mlle. de Coucy has shed imperialist sentiments in favour of her 'childhood's royalist impressions'.

Not that she or anybody else had known much about Louis, who'd always styled himself the eighteenth of that name, or about his handsome brother, the mealy-mouthed fanatically Catholic ex-roué, the Count of Artois: a man who frankly acknowledges he has no ideas in his head 'except those he was born with'. Colonel *Montesquiou de Fezensac*'s*[3] officers, prisoners of war in faraway Hungary, had never even heard of

> 'these princes who, so far from having been called back by the country's wishes, had marched behind foreign bayonets, triumphed at our reverses, grieved over our successes, and had had no other wish than for France to be defeated.'

To someone who'd told him the King was back, one young officer had replied, surprised, 'How odd! I thought the King perished in the Revolution!'

Which of course he had, twenty-two years ago, without his younger brother, the new Louis XVIII, lifting a finger to save him from the scaffold.

Even five days after Napoleon's abdication Davout's men, bottled up in Hamburg and still fighting on, hadn't yet heard of it. So that when, at dawn on 9 May 1814, they'd seen

> 'the enemy line decked out in white flags, the marshal ordered us to fire on them. After a quarter of an hour they'd been knocked down by our gunfire. New flags quickly appeared, out of range of our round-shot.'

To *Paul Thiébault*, a lieutenant-general just now of Orléanist sympathies,[4] this had 'seemed rather significant.' He'd 'heard some rumour, but dared envisage anything except the Bourbons' return.' Could those white flags have borne fleurs-de-lis? 'It even made us wonder whether it had been altogether wise to have knocked down the first ones.' When Davout next day summoned his officers and told them Napoleon had abdicated 'both for himself and his family'[5] it had been to Thiébault's ready pen – he's the author of several books on military matters – that the task had fallen of writing a letter of submission to the new government, though another officer with an even glibber tongue had been sent off to deliver it to the Tuileries. 'The Revolution,' its first historian *J.M. de M. de Norvins* assures us, 'had annihilated the very memory of what it had destroyed.'

King Louis had entered Paris seated beside his sad-eyed niece, the *Duchess of Angoulême*, Marie-Antoinette's daughter and sole survivor of the former royal family. The moods and attitudes of crowds, even their very composition, lie very much in the eye of the beholder; and the event had seemed different to different onlookers. 'The procession,' the royalist diarist *Mme. de Boigne* had seen,

> 'was escorted by the Imperial Guard. Its aspect was imposing, but it froze us. It marched quickly, silent and gloomy. With a single glance it checked our outbursts of affection. The shouts of *Vive le Roi!* died on our lips as it strode past. The silence became immense, and nothing could be heard but the monotonous tramp of its quick pace striking into our very hearts.'

Even the royalist writer Châteaubriand had noticed how the veterans had 'pulled their bearskins down over their eyes and presented arms with a gesture of fury'. As for the populace, the republican *A-C. Thibaudeau*, who'd been Napoleon's prefect in Marseilles, scrutinising 'the slowly moving cortège from several points to judge the effect it was making as it went by,' had thought that the 'immense mass of people who were out was cold, sad, silent. Only at moments did it emerge from its calmness to laugh at the costumes of these ghosts.'[6]

Such acclamations as had met them he'd been sure were 'provoked', and the occasional vivats had come from

> 'upstairs windows occupied by upper-class ladies. The marshals and generals escorting the King cavorted shamefully under the crushing weight of their swift conversion. Grim and threatening, the Imperial Guard, some of whose detachments closed the procession, seemed to be present at the burial of our national glory rather than at the Bourbons' triumph. The common people knew it and applauded them. The Bourbons had opened the road to Paris over French corpses. Had anyone ever seen such a shameful spectacle?'

The cross of the Legion of Honour proudly dangling on his chest, and despite a leg still stiff from a serious ankle wound, Lieutenant *J.J. Henckens**, that peasant from Brabant who's made of himself a highly professional soldier and for whom the military life is a sacred calling and who 'had only one country, France,' had managed to mount his horse and ridden at the head of his troop of the 6th Chasseurs. 'Cold and submissive, like the Imperial Guard,' they'd followed in the procession's wake:

> 'The houses were packed to the roofs, there was no great enthusiasm. Shouts of "Long Live the King" alternated with "Long Live the Prussians! Long live the Cossacks!" to make us realise people had had enough of the Empire. We accompanied the King as far as the Tuileries.'

To the young Estonian baron *Boris von Üxkull*,[7] a Russian cuirassier lieutenant in civvies who'd been watching from the pedestal of Henri IV's equestrian statue by the Pont Royal,[8] the Parisians had seemed singularly 'light-headed and characterless. They turn to the wind like a weathercock. They need constant change.' As for the city itself, it had seemed

> 'like an immense fair. From its gates to Notre Dame it was teeming with people in various costumes, of all ages, making as much noise as they could. The women were wearing white hats and dresses embroidered with lilies. The carriages and riders and our army were all in gala costume. It was really beautiful and curious to see. With my own eyes, I've seen the same populace which had clamoured at and condemned its kings at the time of the Convention, applaud the arrival of the illustrious exile! The people of Paris had to be seen that morning! The enthusiasm was general, though perhaps artificial or paid for by the legitimist party.'

With his entourage, Louis XVIII – like another famous liberator 130 years later – had gone straight to Notre Dame – where only a generation ago a naked actress impersonating Liberty had danced a fandango on the high altar to the strains of the Marseillaise, and, scarcely a decade later, Napoleon had crowned himself Emperor to the strains of Méhul's coronation anthem, *Ave Napoleone immortalis!*, and, though himself a complete sceptic, had attended a thanksgiving mass. Meanwhile the Old Guard had had to run at the double to form up outside the Tuileries; and when it was all over had found itself without even billets for the night.

Out at Malmaison, meanwhile, an embittered ex-empress had written to a friend who'd promised to describe it all, but hadn't, that she didn't want to know any more about a topic

> 'that can only remind me painfully of the past. It saw the same transports of joy, the same professions of love, for a hero no one speaks of

except to malign him and whom, after making him into an idol, they
want to see as a tyrant.'

But on the whole, insists young Major *Théodore de Rumigny*,

'and despite everything that may have been said or written, it's obvious
the whole population of Paris, with few exceptions, was happy about
Louis XVIII's return, and saw in it a guarantee of tranquillity for the
future.'

But to her faithless correspondent Josephine had added a PS:

'You are too young to have seen how far the changeability of the
French mind can go. I've convinced myself our compatriots can't be
moderates – they always have to go to some extreme. See how the
enthusiasm for one man lasted for twenty years! They'll be avenged for
such constancy.'

And indeed a mere eleven months in office have sufficed for the new régime
to make itself detested. Notable among its innumerable mistakes has been to
alienate the army. 'They'd committed one blunder after another,' the
'honest republican' Colonel *J-N-A. Noël*[*9] – in command of the 2nd Horse
Artillery Regiment at Valence, not far from Lyons – is thinking; and goes on,
speaking perhaps for a broad segment of middle-of-the-road opinion:

'First, they should have tried to conciliate the army. They'd done
everything they could to alienate it. For the tricolour cockade, so dear
to the soldiers, they'd substituted the white one. And, as if to have
fought against our regiments was a superior entitlement to command
them, they'd given the army too many superior officers who'd only
served as émigrés.'

Of course the army had had to be cut down to a peacetime footing.[10] Louis
XVIII's government had inherited a national debt of 759,175,000 francs and
in the last years of war, though comprising only 2.85% of the population,[11]
the army had been consuming over half the national budget. Why did he
flout Marshal Ney's advice to rename 'the Imperial Guard the Royal Guard,
and your throne will last for ever' but insist – it was, his acting Secretary of
State baron *E.A. de Vitrolles* tells us, 'the only decision he had insisted on' – on
creating his own ruinously expensive 20,000-strong *Maison du Roi?* 'We must
have splendour, outward show', he'd declared. 'This, without giving the
King a single soldier, swelled our military establishment with an enormous
and costly staff and 5,000 cavalry officers.'

Otherwise Louis, so unwieldy he can't get out of his armchair unaided, is
almost pathologically loth to make decisions of any kind.

These household troops consist almost exclusively of aristocrats, all having
officer rank. Many are returned émigrés. Most inappropriately – since
Britain, France's triumphant enemy, also dresses her army in red – they're

dressed up in a spectacular scarlet-and-gold uniform, for which a single plume costs fifty francs.

'Improvised in a week, 700 men from the best families in France had been accepted, dressed, equipped and mounted, all at their own expense, and given a little drilling. The handsome Duke of Mouchy, on the fat side, a bit stupid, a bit bright, avowed enemy of a thousand things and a thousand persons, little loved and less esteemed, had aspired to command it. But Count Charles de Damas had been preferred.'

Even so, commissions had only been found for 500 of the 6,500 émigrés, all aristocrats, who'd applied.

Almost worse, Noël goes on, 'they were so lavish with the Legion of Honour, hitherto so honoured, they seemed to want to cheapen it.' A Napoleonic institution, membership is 'by no means an insignificant distinction', conferring as it does a minimum pension of 200 francs and the right for even the lowest-ranked legionary to have every sentry present arms to him as he passes. That it's being 'vilified', even 'sold', to all and sundry, disgusts all truly military men, not only its proud wearers such as Lieutenant Henckens, who has served with the 6th Chasseurs ever since the Consulate. 'These were so many insults the army keenly resented.'

As for the tricolour, it too is a matter which 'though little understood' by the Bourbons 'is only apparently a frivolous one', Napoleon's treacherous one-time Police Minister, *Joseph Fouché*, Duke of Otranto, has warned them. 'The colour of the flag will decide the colour of the reign.'

The army's necessary reduction from half a million war-hardened (if in many cases very young) veterans to a peacetime footing of 200,000 – helped, admittedly, by the desertion of some 180,000 conscripts – had come to it as a severe trauma. Of the 206 infantry regiments there are now, at the turn of February/March 1815, only 107. Of 99 cavalry regiments, only 61. The 340 artillery companies have been reduced to 184. And so on. At first, to make this possible, all recent conscripts, whether they'd wanted to or not, had been sent home on indefinite leave and without pay. All symbols of Bonaparte's 'military tyranny' are ordered to be destroyed. Though by no means all the handsome new flags and eagles issued one per regiment in February 1812 had been to Russia or Spain, the colonels had been ordered to hand them in for burning and melting down. What this wholesale destruction of the '*sacrés coucous*' ('sacred bloody cuckoos') can have meant to such veterans as the many times wounded Captain *François* – he who at peril of his life had limped back to pick up the 30th Line's eagle from the snow as the regiment had panicked into Krasnoïe[12] – may be imagined. Nor have all these glorious totems been destroyed. The 41st

Line's colonel had even admitted to the mayor of Limoges he had its eagle in his trunk.

For economic reasons, but also as a deliberate attempt to shatter the Line units' esprit-de-corps, the regiments' numbering has been shuffled. When Sous-Lieutenant *Honoré de Beulay** had come home to Le Mans last year after captivity in Russia[13] he'd found his beloved military family, the 36th Line, renumbered as the 35th.

> 'The 112th Cohort, amalgamated with it, had flung into its bosom a whole gang of noisy, troublesome, quarrelsome southerners, ambitious braggarts. This had completely transformed the morale of my old 36th. Anything that didn't speak with a Gascon accent[14] wasn't deemed worthy to be alive. The NCO cadres, as well as the commissioned ones, were packed full. At the bottom, as at the top, the dry, lively, over-temperamental lads from the South, having elbowed their way forward and taken the least positions by assault, weren't going to let themselves be dislodged.'

Only after spending many weeks kicking his heels at Le Mans had this seasoned young officer, who'd gone to such infinite trouble to be sent to the Grand Army in Russia and above all has a horror of pen-pushing, been graciously 'permitted to kill time' in the quartermaster's office. Can this really be his whole future?

The 36th is by no means exceptional. In May 1814 eighteen-year-old Sergeant-Major *Larreguy de Civrieux*, a veteran from Spain,[15] had witnessed 'the touching spectacle of this great family, the proud 116th, so long dispersed over Europe's battlefields, reunited on the banks of the Isère', near Lyons. But when the regiment had realised that its various battalions were going to be dispersed among other regiments without even getting their arrears of pay, it had mutinied:

> 'Efforts were made to bring us to more moderate sentiments. But the regiment declared it wouldn't budge until its pay was settled. The men implored the officers, who secretly sympathised with us, to stay in their lodgings. The mutiny was organised with new leaders. The regiment took up arms, threatened to see justice done to it.'

And in the end the authorities had had to yield. After which each battalion had 'tamely marched with its officers to its new destination' – in Larreguy's case (dramatically, as things will turn out) to the eastern fortress town of Besançon, headquarters of the 6th Military District, whose military governor was old General Lecourbe (who, because of his pigtail and 'pigeon wings' hairstyle, had been taken 'for a voltigeur from the days of Louis XIV'). Together with 'the débris of I don't know how many other regiments', Larreguy's battalion had been incorporated in the former 99th Line, now renumbered as the 77th; whose fate has been a far from a happy one. One old officer who by mistake shouted *Vive l'Empereur!* on parade instead of *Vive le Roi!* had been sent home on half-pay:

'My NCOs and I were put in the glasshouse for four days. A general fatigue was inflicted on our grenadiers. Ah, how the Bourbons seemed in that moment the very consecration of our defeat! We imagined them and their friends as all being fitted out as if for another century – shoes with big buckles, a steel-hilted sword, a trumpet-shaped pigtail, powdered hair in pigeon wings!'

Lodged in dreary dilapidated barracks that had hardly been used while the imperial armies had been living at the expense of occupied countries, 'we were piled up on top of each other in huge poorly whitewashed halls, slept two to a bed, all in an atmosphere that made us regret our old bivouacs'. Almost worst of all, they can envisage no more battles. Thus no more swift promotions either:

'The 77th's discipline was of unexampled severity. The least flaw in one's turnout or faintest sign of disrespect for the hierarchies was rigorously punished. When under arms one had to be a marble block, a mechanical automaton. A movement of the eyeball sent us to the guardroom. At each moment the drum, with its different beats, sum-moned sergeants-major, sergeants, quartermasters. If, at the last stroke of the drumstick, you weren't on the spot, fully turned out, you were shoved in clink. A second offence plunged us into the dungeons of the citadel's casemate.'

Napoleon's army, in a word, is to be remodelled on Frederick the Great's. Small wonder if in June last year the 77th had 'offered shouts and insults to the royal emblems,' so that when the King's commissioner, a M. de Cham-paigne, had realised that instead of disappearing examples were multi-plying, he'd written angrily to Paris: 'Savage punishments are the only remedy.'

Nevertheless the new 77th had been singled out for an exquisite honour: a visit by no lesser a personage than 'Monsieur', the heir to the throne. At Besançon His Royal Highness the Count d'Artois positively sprinkles the 77th with the Order of the Lily, which Larreguy's comrades have to pin to their jackets like 'one more button' – and on which they set no value at all. After which His Royal Highness,[16] having signally failed to win their affec-tions, goes on down to Lyons, the second city in France, where he does no better. 'Even if they meant well when in front of the men', Colonel Noël goes on, 'the princes had the misfortune not to know how to speak the language that would have gone to their hearts.' Artois had been no less liberal with the Cross of St Louis when reviewing the Grenoble garrison: 'a promotion [*sic*]', writes Lieutenant-Colonel *Guiraud* (a man who, having suffered a severe skull fracture while working on the Kremlin fortifications, likes to keep his hat on in all circumstances), 'that included myself'. On Guiraud, too, whose refusal to doff his hat even in front of the Emperor at the Tuileries had earned him a severe rebuke from Caulaincourt*, Artois had made a bad impression:

'I was pained to see him give a cold accolade to everyone who'd made a career during the Revolution, but shake hands warmly with officers of the *Ancien Régime* or who'd come from the Vendean armies, types like Cadoudal,[17] who was at my side.'

Urged on by his younger brother, an impassioned royalist who'd none-theless penned a poem in praise of Mme. de Staël*, Guiraud had applied for a position in the Royal Guard but – can the hat have had anything to do with it? – been turned down. As with so many other experienced senior officers who're being laid off, he can count himself lucky to have the post he has. For half-pay officers, *les demisoldes*, are hardly better off than the rank and file. And France is full of them.

As Major *Victor Dupuy**[18] has found out – he who three years ago had galloped sword-waving into Vilna and five months later almost been tram-pled to death in the crush outside its town gate[19] – no one who doesn't belong to the feudal aristocracy can be sure of his own fate. His 7th Hussars having just recently in the last days of February been the last of the hussar regiments to be 'recomposed', Dupuy had been thoroughly in the dumps:

'For three posts as squadron-leader we found eleven candidates. Each was trying to assert his rights. My own hopes dwindled when I heard Lieutenant-General Count de Pully, charged with reorganising the unit, say that to get a place you had to be of good birth, have a private fortune, and some little seniority.'

Dupuy, alas, has none of these qualifications. But just when he'd given up all hope, his luck had turned. The senior colonel had sent for him and told him: 'Hurry up and fit yourself out, you're staying with us.' Given the third and fourth squadrons – the other two have gone to his comrade Roch, who'd been wounded in the throat at Smolensk ('the third squadron-leader, an ex-émigré, I believe, had no definite command') – they've had to get busy training recent recruits,

'which meant a lot of work. The colonel got the happy idea of giving each squadron horses of the same colour. The 1st got the blacks, the 2nd the bays, the 3rd the chestnuts, the 4th the greys. The effect was handsome, and fine for garrison duty. But to maintain these distinc-tions on campaign would have been hard, not to say impossible.'

Being renamed 'the Duke of Orléans' Hussars' is of course quite a distinc-tion, since *Philip, Duke of Orléans*, the King's cousin, is the whole army's colonel-general. But when Dupuy, who in 1813 had been wounded and captured at Altembourg with three lance-thrusts in his body, had donned his full uniform and gone for an audience at the Palais Royal, all he'd seen in its salons had been 'a host of generals or superior officers, most of whom didn't seem to me to be in the habit of wearing a uniform'. Though Orléans receives him graciously and sends him to *Marcelline Marbot**, the regiment's new colonel, Dupuy feels utterly out of place among these pseudo-soldiers:

'Seeing nothing but unfamiliar faces perched on these bulky epaulettes, and not knowing the proper or polite way of waiting until dismissed by the prince and moved perhaps – I admit it – by what was left of the Emperor's leaven, I left, clattering my spurs on the parquet floor, doubtless to the indignation of the noble courtiers I left behind me.'

Not that Dupuy or his comrades have anything against the Duke of Orléans personally:

'His fine conduct in the army during our first [revolutionary] campaigns, his behaviour during the emigration, his constant refusals to fight in the ranks of our enemies, all made him an object of our veneration.'

As for Dupuy's new colonel, though fond of grossly inflating his own exploits, Marbot is the very type of the *beau sabreur* of the Empire. And only the day before yesterday (1 March) on reporting for duty at Valenciennes, Dupuy has found that his new chief's 'open and frank countenance and military bearing and demeanour' immediately inspired his 'attachment and confidence'.

As for the arrogance and sumptuous scarlet-and-gold-lace uniforms of the blue-blooded *Maison du Roi*, one can imagine what such men as Marbot and Dupuy think of them. Few have ever smelt powder, or only in their faraway youth in Condé's émigré army, so ignominiously routed by the Republic. When the Oudinots had received Orléans' thirty-year-old son the Duke of Berry with all due pomp and ceremony at their château – half-burnt down by the invaders – at Bar-le-Duc, out of sheer commiseration they'd even encouraged

'some of the district's poor old gentlemen to put on something resembling a uniform. There they stood at the main entrance, a drawn sword on their shoulder, as they said, to guard their prince. Those rusty old blades! Those superannuated uniforms! Those antique faces intermingled with the 100 grenadiers of the Old Guard and with the marshal's brilliant ADCs and the Duke of Berry's no less elegant ones and a large number of officers from nearby garrisons!'

Admittedly Berry had shown great presence of mind during a mock naval battle on the lake, when Oudinot's son Victor* had fallen overboard and Oudinot's ADC Jacqueminot* had jumped in to save him. Berry had reached him an oar and fished him out. But the fireworks display which should have climaxed that fine autumn evening had been a fiasco. When a match had been put to the two great fireworks mounted on a nearby hill, only the one showing the cross of the Legion of Honour had lit up. Of the other, showing the Cross of Saint Louis, 'only a few fragments. We waited in vain.' Tactfully, the matter hadn't been looked into. But when some such 'voltigeurs of Louis XIV' – as people are mockingly calling them – had turned up at Tortoni's Bonapartist restaurant in Paris in their 'super-annuated uniforms, with heads powdered white', even the waiters had burst out laughing, and Oudinot had had to reprimand son-in-law Jacqueminot for joining in in the general hilarity.

Even the Oudinots' young duchess, ardent royalist though she's become – she'd only had to take one look at Louis XVIII to be sure he possesses every royal virtue – can hardly condone Berry's egregious dinnertime habit of throwing eggs (hopefully hard-boiled ones) at his ADCs' resplendent uni-forms. Nor has he ever seen a shot fired in anger. Yet he regards the army as his domain. Among other absurd military pretensions – in ridiculous imi-tation of 'The Other One' – he even sports a green chasseur uniform and ... pinches people's ears! Heir presumptive to the greatest throne in Europe, his manners wouldn't grace any régime. Attending a reception at the Tui-leries, Thiébault had been on his way to the King's reception in the Blue Drawing Room when he'd heard

'someone coming up behind me with big strides. It was the Duke of Berry. I stand aside to let him pass. A few steps ahead of me, bent almost double, the aged Marquis de Letourneur, captain of Artois' guards, receives a sharp kick in his backside. Surprised and furious, and putting his hand – not to his sword hilt – but to the stricken part, the marquis turns round, fury on his face. And finds himself in the presence of His Royal Highness, who was roaring with laughter. Instantly the courtier's expression changed. Putting his hands toge-ther as if to say grace and bowing to the ground, he exclaimed with a happy smile: "No one is so amiable as Monseigneur."'

Berry's tours of inspection have been, if possible, even more counter-pro-ductive than his father's. True, when he'd visited the northern frontier fortress of Mézières, Colonel *Lubin Griois** hadn't had anything to complain of personally. Not even reacting to the sight of Napoleon's effigy on the Iron Cross of the Kingdom of Italy dangling on Griois' chest, the prince had admired his horse, invited him to dinner, and listened eagerly to his tales of his campaigns. Yet even Griois had thought Berry's

'brusque tone of voice and harsh manners indicated a rough and impetuous character, unsoftened by education. Either out of tact-lessness, or because he didn't trouble himself to please, he didn't give us a very favourable idea of the Bourbons. Reviewing the troops, he said he thought the cuirassiers' manoeuvres inferior to those of the English cavalry – a backhanded compliment which when it became known rightly wounded the cuirassiers' self-esteem.'

The grenadiers at Oudinot's party had been fetched from nearby Metz, where the ex-Grenadiers of the Guard, mortifyingly, are stationed. For a few months they and the Foot Chasseurs, the most admired élite force in Europe, had kicked their heels at Fontainebleau, scene of their idol's pathetic leave-taking.[20] These battle-hardened men who've so long been under Napoleon's spell, lived solely in and for his magnetic field and felt his personal charm. For them he'd been 'the demigod of battles, that idol of France's glory, the first captain in the world.' Now they are still feeling like masterless dogs, 'workmen out of work'. Chevalier, for instance, a Chasseur à Cheval of the Imperial Guard who, when he'd been making up a fire for him during the Great Retreat, and had been in such a hurry to adjust his dress when he'd come up to him, but been forgivingly told 'we aren't at the Tuileries now' – he and his comrades feel they've 'lost their entire future', and when marching do so 'sad, silent and resigned, like young ladies.' Berry had come and inspected them, fancying he could win over 'the old moustaches' by drinking with them. From the looks on their weather-tanned faces afterwards Oudinot had been pretty sure he hadn't. After which, pay cut by a third, reduced to Line status and relabelled *Le Corps Royal de Grenadiers et Chasseurs de France*, each infantry unit had been reduced to four battalions of six companies apiece and been marched off to do garrison duty in the northern frontier fortresses – Grenadiers at Metz and the Chasseurs at Nancy – 'as if,' writes Sergeant *Hippolyte de Mauduit* of the 1st battalion 2nd Grenadiers, indignantly,

'they needed to go there as apprentices to their craft. For a great number it was an affront, and for all a keen disappointment – a miserable piece of economising that a few months later would cost France two billions!!!'[21]

At one moment, says General *Brun de Villeret*, friend and assistant to Marshal Soult at the War Ministry,

'the idea occurred to Berry, who in the Guard only saw its beauty, to make it come to Paris to manoeuvre in the Champ de Mars. The minister hesitated. But since the prince insisted, he felt he'd have to give the order. I told him it would be to organise a permanent conspiracy in the capital's barracks, and showed him certain reports which showed the Guard to be in a hardly describable state of exasperation. He took them, showed them to the King. No more question of summoning it to Paris.'

A prime example of such exasperation is the 2nd Grenadiers' one-time drill sergeant Captain *Jean-Roch Coignet**, during Napoleon's last campaigns Imperial Headquarters' baggage-master. Not being one of the 607 guardsmen who'd been selected by Generals Petit and Cambronne to go to Elba, now, in this cold rainy spring of 1815, he's one of the innumerable half-pay captains who've been 'sent to plant cabbages in our own departments on sixty-three francs a month'. In his case that had meant going to his native town of Auxerre, two days march south of Paris. After seventeen years of intensely active service – Coignet claims he'd been in every major campaign from Marengo onwards – he has been trying to take legal action against certain locals who've taken advantage of his long absence to strip him of his property; and is being exposed to humiliations from lawyers and local bigwigs who don't know a sword from a goose quill. Particularly aggravating to little Coignet is to have to attend Sunday mass in the cathedral, strictly ruled over by its vicar-general Abbé Viart. Non-attendance can cost him what's left of his pay.[22]

> 'They withheld 2½ per cent in advance, and then, very gently, dealt us the knockout blow: retained our 120 francs a year as members of the Legion of Honour, in such fashion that our half-pay was reduced to a third.'

Usually a *demisolde* Line captain is only getting seventy-four francs a month, a lieutenant forty-four, and a *sous-lieutenant* forty-one – just enough to buy bread. So considering that an ordinary labourer can often earn two francs a day, it's not surprising if many feel they're 'starving'. And some perhaps really are:

> 'Recourse was had to the purses of comrades who possessed a little personal capital. When no more was to be had from that source, then silver watches, epaulettes, old uniforms, weapons went to the junk merchant. All some half-pay officers had to wear was their long regulation greatcoat – minus its copper buttons – their tall boots and a pair of trousers. When any of them wanted to go out, then the others, even poorer and crowded four or five together in a miserable attic, would hand over the sole hat and overcoat in their group's possession.'[23]

The ranks of these unemployed – and all too often unemployable – men who've only known the killer's trade have been further swollen by the 400,000 returning prisoners-of-war, 70,000 of them from Britain alone. 'All indigent' and begging on the streets, they're costing the state 420,000 francs; and in the eyes of the émigré general Langeron*, who'd served with the Russians in 1812–14, are 'a real pest.'

Lavish with promises, the Bourbons neither are nor ever have been noted for keeping them. For instance, promises of places in the Red and Black

Companies of the *Maison du Roi*, the Royal Guard. This has led to a host of disappointments. It had, for instance, dashed the hopes of so sincere a royalist as Colonel *A-A-R. Saint-Chamans**, recently returned from captivity at St Petersburg. In January he'd been given the command of a new élite 1st Chasseur Regiment which was to have formed part of the Royal Guard, with all that this would have meant in higher pay, residence in Paris, the right to take his pick of the finest horses, etc, etc. But then, suddenly, no reasons given, he'd been told that, so far from being able to enjoy the delights of the capital for all futurity, he was to march the regiment off to Béthune, a dreary little garrison town in Picardy, best known for its bottomless muds. Whereupon forty of his veteran troopers had instantly deserted. Admittedly, the hastily granted compensation of being allowed to call themselves 'a King's regiment' and dangle aiguilettes from their left shoulders had seemingly had some small effect – desertions had fallen off. But it hasn't prevented officers and men alike from feeling intensely embittered:

'Every day these old soldiers were hearing how their military juniors, whom they'd left behind in their former regiments, were being promoted to the élite companies or decorated with the Legion of Honour, or else honourably discharged. When we set out for Béthune on 24 January 1815 their discontent no longer knew any bounds, and on the eve of our departure they'd been uttering the most terrifying opinions.'

As police spies who'd 'spent part of the day with some of these military men' – universal spying on everything and everyone being not the least of the Empire's legacies – confirm:

'Above all the officers and NCOs regard their having to leave Paris as an affront to them as a royal regiment. The police agents have also heard from some of them that the Cuirassiers who left for Blois on the 20th had shouted *Vive l'Empereur!* en route. One of them had declared that, in losing Napoleon, French military men had lost everything.'

Despite all Saint-Chamans' attempts to bring them to a more reasonable state of mind at Béthune, 'since soldiers prefer grumbling to reasoning', his men have since then been becoming even more resentful.

The Napoleonic army, though its choice officer ranks had been increasingly filled with young aristocrats who'd rallied to the imperial régime, is a 'national' one— *ie* the first in history to represent a whole nation. Yet this is far from meaning it's universally popular. Certainly not in the country towns. And least of all in the fanatically Catholic south, where every Protestant is a suspected Bonapartist. In ultra-royalist Marseilles the horrors of the Revolution are far from forgotten[24] – last year Thibaudeau had had to do a moonlight flit from an enraged populace. There the army is positively hated. In the eyes of a certain *Mme. J-J. Pellizzone,* seated at her window overlooking the main square and writing everything down in her diary, it consists of 'cossacks. Bonaparte is universally detested'. After suffering from the French and British blockades, the principal Marseilles merchants – 'ruined, discontented, exasperated', Thibaudeau had seen – have 'no feeling for patriotic solicitudes'.

And certainly the almost inconceivable arrogance of army officers on leave during the Empire hasn't mended matters. Any officer coming into Tortoni's could, as of right, snatch your newspaper from under your nose. For twenty years a military uniform had been the outward and visible sign of an ethos, and therefore a self-assurance, denied to the mere *pékin* (civilian). It had entitled its wearer to take the centre of the pavement (insofar, that is, as there is one[25]). And to look askance at one had been to risk one's life. True, the hard-worked bureaucrat also wore one.[26] But in the eyes of the high-bosomed ladies in their slim Greek-style dresses neither he nor the wealthy son of some contractor, sitting on a fat contract for manufacturing or supplying endless quantities of tasselled bearskins for grenadier companies or bootees for the Imperial Guard, or beplumed and crested brass helmets for the dragoons, lancers and cuirassiers, or Hungarian-style pélisses for hussars, not to mention muskets, bayonets, swords, sabres ad infinitum, etc – neither the one nor the other individual, in his mere English-style civilian *redingote* (riding coat), could hope to rival such glorious apparel.

Duelling, which goes with the honour of the uniform, is still very much in fashion. Especially, writes surgeon *L-D. Véron,* between real army men and the

> 'young officers who made up the King's military Household, whom one tried to wound to the heart by making incessant comparisons, and who didn't tolerate the least disdain. This led to daily duels and a whole little population of duellists. Men fought in the morning; in the evening under the street lamps. I attended to more than one sword-thrust, carried out more than one amputation. A duellist came into the Café-Français on the boulevard at the corner of the Rue Lafitte, threw a scornful glance on everyone present, and declared: "I find no one here this morning worthy of my least sword-thrust." A gentleman in glasses replied: "Monsieur, you're mistaken! Give me your card!" On it stood written Count ——. The spectacled gentleman gave him his. He was the Marquis de ——.[27] With utter aplomb the latter, a royalist of course, gives the waiter 2,000 francs, telling him to step round the corner to the undertakers and order, for tomorrow afternoon, a first-class funeral, suitable for a marquis, for the count. They soon made it up between them.'

Henckens, too, is witnessing other duels, 'often over silly little trifles', between officers on half-pay and those who've been kept on in the regiments. A *demisolde* can be as dangerous as a starving bull-dog turned out into the street.

The extreme south is by no means alone in detesting the military. To Colonel Lubin Griois of the Guard Horse Artillery even the Parisians, always frivolous, always sceptical, seem utterly unpatriotic. A year ago, dropping with fatigue from the Emperor's forced marches to save Paris, if possible, from the invading Russians and Prussians – marches the like of which he and his comrade Colonel Hulot 'had never seen' – Griois had been disgusted with its National Guard. With the exception of a few brave fellows who'd fought the Russians among the windmills of Montmartre,

> 'they'd evinced such martial prowess before things had got dangerous and had seemed ready for anything. But in the moment of peril had prudently stayed inside the town walls. Twelve or fifteen hours could have been gained and given the Emperor time to arrive.'

And in the end they'd been only too happy to surrender – yes, even fallen in love with their conquerors! For the ultra-royalist *Frénilly* the fall of Paris hadn't been

> 'a conquest, but a deliverance. Never had the city worn such a festivous air. Young Russian officers saluted the ladies saying "Here we are, *mesdames*, the barbarians from the north."'

A certain Colonel Count Tschoubert of the Russian Guards, billeted in Frénilly's house on the Rue du Faubourg St Honoré 'only a few hundred yards from the Elysée Palace where Tsar Alexander had installed himself', had turned out to be

> 'the politest man I'd ever met. Refusing all further hospitality and squeezing himself into the third-floor rooms, he'd only needed one stable for his horses and a few bales of hay for his Guard Cossacks, superb men hewn out like Hercules but gentle as children, and the darlings of my servants.'

Admittedly, Tschoubert had taken the liberty of mildly contrasting his men's behaviour with that of French soldiers who in 1812 had 'crucified his steward on his front door, herded all the women into the church and raped them'. To such ultra-reactionaries as Frénilly even the victorious sovereigns' formal entrance into Paris had seemed idyllic: 'The Revolution, the Terror, the Directory, twenty-five years of tortures, had seemed to vanish in the sunbeam of a new hope.' Hopes which, from Frénilly's and many another returned émigré's point of view, had been immediately dashed by Louis XVIII's fatal addiction to liberal principles. Since then, in his eyes, everything has gone to the devil. Alas, he grumbles, by espousing English-style liberalism Louis XVIII has forgotten that

> 'the real enemy hasn't been Buonaparte, but the spirit of revolution,

Jacobinism, without which he'd never have reigned; without which he
wouldn't have conquered Vienna, Berlin, or Moscow; the Jacobinism
which only a long and firm absolutism had so far been able to keep
chained up until religion and education should have time to neutralise
its terrible germs. The Allies thought they'd liberated Europe from
Buonaparte's tyranny. All they'd done was to set free the tiger he'd
kept muzzled.'

Here, of course, Griois and his comrades couldn't disagree more:

'But what above all made me indignant and what I could hardly believe
was the welcome the Parisians had given to the Allies and the base
adulations they'd been so despicably cowardly as to shower on them.
Never in my life shall I forget reading the *Journal de Débats* which
complacently reported a solemn performance at the Opera at which
the sovereigns had *deigned* to be present. An actor called Laïs had sung
"Long live Alexander/Long live this king of kings!/Long live William
[of Prussia]/And his valiant warriors!" to enthusiastic applause!'

Griois, over whose head since returning from Russia 'twenty years had
passed, whitened my hairs and changed my tastes', would even have

'preferred a civil war with the horrors it brings in its wake to the shame
of submitting to the foreign yoke and the cowardly abandonment of
the man we'd been serving for fifteen years.'

Frénilly's reactionary sentiments certainly aren't confined to Paris. After
resisting an impulse to follow Napoleon to Elba, Griois, whose sole terror, he
tells us, is of being laughed at (how awful it would have been if his application had been turned down!), had been sent with the Guard Artillery, Old
and Young, foot and horse, to the 'rather pretty little town of Vendôme with
its charming surroundings', well away from the centre of events. On Sundays, like Coignet at Auxerre, he and his colleagues Colonel Boulart* and
Major Pion des Loches had had to listen to sermons comparing the royal
family's virtues with 'the crimes of the tyrant'. The always superior, always
sarcastic, and now wholeheartedly royalist *Pion des Loches*, coming out
afterwards, had heard his colleagues 'criticising the curé in the most scandalous manner, almost out loud.'

After a tolerably agreeable stay at Vendôme, the proudest gunners in
Europe had been ordered to leave for La Fère, the great northern artillery
base, there to be disbanded or merged into other units. But before leaving
Griois had had to get the obligatory certificate of good behaviour from the
mayor. That worthy, probably to curry favour with the new authorities
('afterwards he became a member of the Chamber of Deputies'), had added
the supererogatory observation to Griois' certificate that, during its stay at
Vendôme, the regiment's morale had 'perhaps improved'. Two words too
much! What a rumpus! For then there'd been the devil to pay. Accom-

panied by two other officers, Griois, 'without losing a moment, my certificate in my hand', had gone to the town hall, burst into the room where the municipal council was in session, and told the mayor

'in no uncertain terms, what I thought of his insolence and perfidy, and insisted he immediately specify the facts that made him think ill of our morale; or else do the regiment frank and open justice, without any kind of reservations. I was in a towering rage. My expressions showed it, so did my gestures. I tore up the certificate and flung it in his face. Terrified, without replying, he wrote me out another, a magnificent certificate that lacked nothing.'

Scenes like this, or worse, have been going on all over France. In Picardy, for instance, a party of prisoners-of-war returning from British hulks had attacked and killed thirty royalist volunteers. Everyone is suspicious of everyone else. In January at La Fère, Pion des Loches, by now second-in-command of the 2nd Artillery Regiment stationed there, has seen half its effectives moved to the École Militaire in Paris, under 'one of the chief malcontents', a Major Bobilier, a protégé of General Maison*,[28] and appointed commander of all the 1st Military Division's artillery. For his chief-of staff Maison has chosen – to Pion's intense suspicion –

'Colonel *Gourgaud**, one of the Emperor's former *officiers d'ordonnance* [actually his *premier officier d'ordonnance*, ie chief staff officer], who was already showing himself at the Tuileries with the cross of the Legion of Honour with Bonaparte's effigy on it;'

– instead, that is, of the new royalist version engraved with the head of Henri IV. As might be expected in so wholly military a town as La Fère, Pion des Loches, who'd 'never liked Bonaparte, but feared for the results that must follow from his fall', and who in the absence of the colonel is effectively in command, sees the population is 'Bonapartist at heart'. Finding the other officers' womenfolk not to his taste – and probably also realising his own unpopularity with them – Pion and his wife are mostly consorting with the ex-émigré mayor. But once a fortnight they give

'a dinner for sixteen of his officers to know their state of mind and principles. I let them talk on, in such a way as to know whether I could count on them in the event of a revolt.'

It's all very worrying. The young lieutenants from the Saint-Cyr school, 'malcontents, ignoramuses or bunglers of the worst sort', hardly even know their infantry drill. On the other hand such lieutenants as have risen from the ranks and the NCOs are 'models of docility and good conduct.' As for the captains, it seems to Pion all they want is

'peace and repose. They talked loudly about the Emperor and his follies. "We're only being kept on," they said, "because they've no one else to replace us with. But, you see! Little by little we'll be ousted by émigrés and noblemen's sons. Even the luckiest among us won't rise higher than captain. What hope of promotion is there under a king who can't even get on a horse and will never go to war? Under the Emperor we at least could count on being captain after three or four years' service.'"

One day when it's been announced that Berry's going to come and inspect them, the humourless Pion assembles his officers in the mathematics hall and particularly recommends they study their drill – and is staggered to hear them burst out laughing:

'Ah yes it's true, he's a terrific tactician, this Duke of Berry!'

'Gentlemen,' ripostes Pion after a moment, 'if I thought you'd said that knowingly, I'd put you in solitary confinement until the Minister of War cashiered you and dismissed you from the regiment!' Fortunately the NCOs and their gunners are

'wise and disciplined. Short of civil war breaking out, the regiment, despite the superior officers' and lieutenants' discontent, was ready to stay within the bounds of its duty.'

There's the insurrectionary talk of Colonel Lallemand, also formerly of the Imperial Guard artillery and now supposed to be trying to sort out its tangled accounts. 'To anyone who'd listen to him' Lallemand, whose brother is in command at nearby Laon, is saying 'the King and princes are daily committing new errors, and that their reign won't last long.' One day Pion hears two of his captains, Marin and Servois, talking in the same vein in the public square. The latter, 'an absconded priest who was afraid the police were on his tracks and was as strong in mathematics as he was weak in politics, had been indoctrinated by the malcontents in the Guard artillery' – men, one supposes, like Griois and Boulart. Marin, for his part, despite lucrative Spanish pillagings and ample rewards from Napoleon, is utterly dissatisfied with his 'mediocre' pension (2,007 francs). Servois is telling him to be patient. Very soon there'll inevitably be another revolution. And when a furious Pion intervenes, Servois says quite simply that if Napoleon should come back

'"the entire army will range itself under his flags. The Royal Bodyguards are a pack of cowardly nitwits. And if he, Servois, had 600 men as determined as himself, he'd go and overthrow the King and the royal family tomorrow." I put a stop to him by grabbing his arm, striking him on the shoulder, and countering forcefully: "Six hundred idiots like you would find sixty men like me barring their way, who'd put an end to them. Because sixty honest men like me are worth 60,000 brigands like you. Remember what I've just said. I don't doubt you're a man to dabble in any conspiracy against the throne. But if you do, you'll have me to reckon with."

Such are Pion's sentiments. Soon to be severely tested.

Many of the regiments are literally in rags. Only one million francs of the four million allocated to their maintenance have actually been disbursed. In more than twenty regiments the men lack boots or shoes. At Cambrai, a day's ride from Béthune and La Fère, the troopers of the once so prestigious Chasseurs à Cheval of the Imperial Guard, redubbed Chasseurs de France, lack even shirts. The Duke of Orléans will soon be seeing they've 'received neither clothing nor equipment since the Restoration.' Few if any heavy cavalry not of the Royal Guard have cuirasses – the Prussians had taken them last year as war indemnities. Likewise large numbers of cannon. As for the Line infantry, for two years now the men of the 14th Light have been wearing light canvas trousers summer and winter in lieu of their blue serge ones. And the Ministry of War owes the 27th Line some 30,000 francs just to clothe its returned prisoners.[29]

These and many similar measures, or lack of them, have turned the army into a wasps' nest of resentments. The higher the rank – up to a point – the fiercer they are. Pion des Loches can't believe the top brass's precipitate adhesion to the restored régime can have been whole-hearted:

'As to the army as a whole, and particularly the crowd of marshals and generals the Empire had overwhelmed with favours, I couldn't convince myself their rallying to the Bourbons had been sincere. They'd lost immense grants of land and money, yet they'd sworn fidelity to the King. Their conversion had been too general to be sincere.'

Napoleon's devoted Postmaster-General, Count *A-M.C. de Lavalette*, now prudently retired into private life, has been noticing too how

'the most discontented among the generals were the youngest and most ambitious. Checked abruptly in mid-career, thrust back into the crowd, they'd been finding dignities and high fortune slip out of their grasp just when they'd only one more step to take to get their hands on them. Accustomed to a superb style of life, their big salaries cut, they were deeply resentful of not being able to maintain their brilliant position in the army and in society. I shan't say patriotism and devotion to the Emperor didn't also count for much. But taken together all this added up to an intolerable situation.'

As for the marshals, their generous endowments (*dotations*), too, have vanished with their conquests. Ney, for instance, is demanding compensation for his vanished estates in Italy and Poland. But when the question had been raised in the Chambers it had been found that 'all the money in Europe wouldn't suffice to fill such an abyss.' No longer really popular with the army, the marshals' social status is nevertheless immense, and unassailable.

Receiving them in a body at Compiègne on his way from Calais to Paris, Louis XVIII, among whose gifts is a flair for saying the right thing at the right moment, even if he doesn't mean a word of it, had told them: 'You've always been good Frenchmen'. And called them 'the chief props of his throne.' Berthier, who'd promised to come back to Fontainebleau but never had, is a Captain-General of the Royal Guard. Marmont likewise.

Though by far the least popular of the marshals, the steely loyalty of *Louis Davout**, Prince of Eckmühl, bald, bespectacled, has never been in question, either as military administrator or as field commander. But despite all his applications (via Macdonald, Oudinot and others) he alone hasn't been received at the Bourbon court, or allowed to justify his stubborn defence of Hamburg and those roundshot that had 'knocked down the white flags' outside it. Nor is he liked. Far from being a charming personality, he's above all feared for his rigid principles and fierce discipline.[30] The Iron Marshal's intense, if impersonal, devotion to Napoleon, the military genius, the conqueror, is notorious. But in the end even he had written a letter of submission, if only to secure the social status of his dearly loved wife and daughter. But though his friend Oudinot has repeatedly tried to get him reinstated at court as one 'totally devoted to the profession of arms, who has always been a loyal soldier', all such attempts have failed. He's the odd man out.

More problematic is the case of Marshal Ney. 'Nature,' writes his young ADC *Octave Levavasseur*, to whom he's been a second father since his own had died,

> 'had given Ney an iron body, a soul of fire. His build was athletic. He had a big face, a flat nose.[31] His physiognomy was reminiscent of the Nordic type. His voice resonant. He only had to give an order for you to feel brave. Ney's genius only awakened in face of the enemy and at the great voice of the guns. No matter how brave you were or wished to appear, if this man was near you in the midst of a fight you had to confess him your master. Even under grapeshot his laughter and pleasantries seemed to defy the death all around him. His recognised superiority made everyone obey his orders.'[32]

Alone among the marshals, perhaps, since his heroic performance during the Great Retreat,[33] he's still really popular with this seething resentful army. An army that's at least sure of one thing: that it's never been defeated, only 'betrayed'.[34]

CHAPTER 3

A CHAPTER OF ERRORS

Is there then no relic of the imperial court in Paris, no Bonapartist faction? Certainly. And it revolves on the one hand around Napoleon's Secretary of State, *Hugues Bernard Maret*, Duke of Bassano*. On the other, around Josephine's[1] daughter *Hortense*, for a brief unhappy while Queen of Holland. It's out at her château of Saint-Leu, surreptitiously watched by the police, that a brilliant group of young Bonapartist officers like to foregather. Notable among them is her much-loved but chronically faithless lover, the thirty-year-old lady-killer *Charles de Flahaut*. Also the twenty-nine-year-old Colonel Charles de Labédoyère. Flahaut may be 'the best dancer in France' and also possess a fine voice, which he deploys singing duets with Hortense. But he's the sort of charmer who, unfaithful as a dog, can always convince himself he's in love with a woman – indeed several at the same time – and has no difficulty, of course, in convincing her too. Labédoyère, on the other hand, is the soul of chivalry,

'a very good lad, a distinguished young man, who conducts himself with every sense of delicacy, has a charming cast of mind, a very nice face and figure and something noble about his physiognomy that must come from his heart and gives a rather good idea of it.'

During the last campaigns he'd behaved 'with such quite exceptional valour' that his superior had wanted to promote him general. At the same time he's a Bonapartist of unusual stamp. His attachment to the Emperor dates from his abdication, and is largely motivated by disgust at the wholesale defections at Fontainebleau. And more especially with the way the marshals, themselves so wealthy, have accepted France's humiliation. 'The marshals, having the swiftness of their defection on their conscience, feared nothing so much as the Emperor's return. Devotion was in inverse ratio to rank.' Disgusted also at the cheapening of the Legion of Honour, Labédoyère and Flahaut are even refusing to wear it except when visiting Hortense, who insists they shall.

Having earlier stayed with Mme. de Staël at Coppet, Labédoyère has imbibed many of her liberal ideas. And last year he'd married into an old royalist family, the Chastelluxes, who're at a loss to understand his devotion to the detestable Bonaparte. It's to cure him of it that his brother-in-law, an officer of the *Maison du Roi*, has just secured for him the colonelcy of the 7th Line, currently stationed at Chambéry, near Grenoble, where it's been sent together with the 11th Line in case France has to help the Austrians to oust Murat from the throne of Naples. Not that Labédoyère's choice of the 7th

67

rather than any other regiment has had anything to do with that scheme, but simply because its 1st and 2nd battalions contain so many men from his former 112th. Only with misgivings had the Minister of War, General Dupont[2] – who'd seemed to know more than Labédoyère's brother-in-law about his political sympathies – agreed to the appointment. But Chastellux had stood surety for his loyalty, admonishing him that though

> 'some people have been so imprudent as to show opposition to the Minister's wishes, your position at present is quite simple and in order. Above all bear in mind it isn't Monsieur de Flahaut who's your brother-in-law.'

Only a few days ago, after lingering an unconscionably long time with his wife and new-born son in Paris, has Labédoyère wrenched himself away from them and left for the South, staying en route with another in-law, Count Damas, governor of Lyons.

Among the innumerable Napoleonic officers in Paris, either on half-pay or still employed, is the sensitive and intelligent Captain *Planat de la Faye**. After bringing back his 'dear general' Lariboisière's corpse from Berlin in spirits of wine, Planat, finding his 'bellicose' instincts temporarily sated by the Russian disaster, had found a job in the War Ministry, under General Évain, head of the artillery section,

> 'a great worker, but taciturn and surly, whose great capacities were as much appreciated by the ministers of the Restoration as they had been by those of the Empire.'

But on the eve of the 1813 campaign Drouot had sought Planat out and insisted he be his ADC; so he'd had plenty of opportunities of admiring Drouot's brilliance as commander of the Guard Artillery and to admire Napoleon's as field commander of his dwindling armies. Badly wounded in both legs in 1814 at Château-Thierry, he'd been lovingly nursed by Lariboisière's grief-stricken widow. Grieved to the heart to see her, like her surviving son Honoré*, exposed to the arrogance of not only the Austrian officers billeted in her big house in the Faubourg Saint Germain, but also of her triumphant Vendean and Chouan[3] relatives, he'd offered to accompany Drouot to Elba as soon as he could again stand on his legs. But Drouot's letters from there – not all had reached their destination[4] – have advised him to stay in Paris. Just now he's sharing an entresol flat on the Quai Voltaire, just across the Seine from the Tuileries, with his friend and fellow staff captain Résigny.

During the winter they've been associating with other Bonapartists, of whom Flahaut is one and the emotional *Gaspard Gourgaud**, Napoleon's *premier officier d'ordonnance*, another. Hot-tempered, always touchy and obsessively ambitious, the thirty-one-year-old Gourgaud is never tired of pointing out that he'd had 'access to the Emperor at all hours'. A man at his best on a battlefield, exercising a sure eye for positioning the artillery, or else making technological calculations, he's also obsessed with getting married. At the Berezina he'd saved the life of senator Roederer's son with half an eye to marrying the daughter. But it's all come to nothing. 'In 1814 I was colonel, and yet I wasn't happy'. He's one of those people who obviously aren't destined to be. But Gourgaud's mother, wife of a Versailles violinist before the Revolution, had been the Duke of Berry's wet nurse; which makes them foster-brothers. And Berry, doubtless in a vain hope that something of the imperial charisma will rub off onto his own preposterous person, has made him his ADC. Very probably it's from his violinist father that Gourgaud has inherited his fiery unbalanced temperament. At first he'd meant to follow his idol to Elba, but had changed his mind, gone to say good-bye to his mother in Paris, and stayed. 'I'd like to send M. Gourgaud to Elba to know what Bonaparte's up to,' Louis XVIII has told Soult in confidence. But nothing's come of that either. No more has the government honoured Napoleon's last-minute dotation to his fiery *premier officier d'ordonnance*. All Berry has done is to grant his wet nurse, Gourgaud's mother, a very small pension. Worst of all, having had to fit himself out with horses and a sky-blue and silver uniform for the Russian campaign, Gourgaud, like many another officer who'd lost everything in the snows, is still heavily in debt.

Nor must the youngest generation be forgotten – youngsters like Carnot's and Montalivet's sons, both at the prestigious Collège Henri IV – up to yesterday the Collège Napoléon. Brought up, like all their contemporaries, to tap of drum, they've imbibed the mystique of Empire, its rousing events and amazing victories, with their mother's milk. So to them Restoration France seems a very tawdry, humdrum, uninspiring affair. Just now *M-C.B. de Montalivet*, whose father had been Napoleon's devoted, indeed obsessively meticulous, Intendant-General of the Crown, is a fourteen-year-old schoolboy:

'In 1814 the drawing room of the Hôtel Lambert, which in those days belonged to my family, was being visited assiduously by the former servants of the Empire. Each day off school presented me with a spectacle of nostalgia for the past, of an ardent desire for revenge on the foreigner, and hopes for the future, all summed up in the name of Napoleon. I recall how my brothers and I, ignoring our parents' very natural counsels to be prudent, covered walls with inscriptions calling for an imperial restoration, but without actually pronouncing that great name. Children and ex-soldiers thought they'd done enough to disguise themselves when they wrote up "Long live the Man!"[5] all over the place.'

One of young Montalivet's classmates is the son of 'the great Carnot', the military engineer who together with a colleague had organised victory for the armies of the Republic. Afterwards Carnot, objecting to Napoleon making himself Emperor, had retired from public life, only volunteering again for service in 1813, when France had once more been threatened by invasion. Accepted by Napoleon, then very short of capable officers, he'd brilliantly defended Antwerp. To royalists he's anathema – hadn't he been a member of the Committee of Public Safety of odious memory, signed all its commitments of arrested persons to Fouquier-Tinville's fatal tribunal? Even so, Carnot had presented himself at court:

'When the name of Carnot was pronounced Louis XVIII pretended to avert his glance and fixed it obliquely on an angle of the ceiling, stammering out a few unintelligible words accompanied by a cold nod. Carnot passed in front of him and left.'

But he'd published an open letter to the King pointing out the mistakes he was committing and referring to Bonaparte as a '*parvenu*' – a letter Louis XVIII had taken in good part, saying: 'The author certainly hasn't spared us, but the work is that of an honest man and a good citizen.'

Yet only last January, when the decapitated remains of Louis XVI, Marie Antoinette and Madame Elizabeth were taken out in solemn procession to Saint-Denis to be decently reinterred amidst all the other jumbled relics of France's kings and queens, Carnot, joined by a handful of officers, had had to barricade his modest home against the rumour of a new St Bartholemew's Eve to massacre Bonapartists. True, nothing had come of it. But as it had passed through the working-class suburbs the royal procession had been booed; and afterwards a policeman had heard the good-natured Oudinot, as he emerged from the ancient church after listening to the Bishop of Tours' hellfire sermon against all regicides, past, present and to come, quip to his ADCs: 'All we've got to do now is cut each other's throats, to show how sorry we are!'

Looking out of their classroom window, the boys can just see the tip of the column in the Place Vendôme, its platform vacant since last year when the Emperor's statue had been toppled by royalists. When, oh when, is something really *real* going to happen again? Will it ever?

Yet if the police are really searching for a conspiracy, it's not out at Saint-Leu they'll find one; but at the town house of Napoleon's former Secretary of State and Foreign Minister, Maret, Duke of Bassano. Here, for some time now, a group of generals have been plotting a military coup to oust the ever less popular Bourbon régime. At Lille, on the northern frontier, the kindly if not very efficient general *Drouet d'Erlon* shall raise the 10,000 men of Marshal Mortier's 16th military division, march them on Paris, joined en route by the hot-headed Lefebvre-Desnouëttes and his crack cavalry regiment, the former Chasseurs à Cheval of the Imperial Guard, who'll have ridden from their base at Béthune, and by the two Lallemand brothers. The younger of these is to suborn the garrison of the La Fère artillery base and add it and its guns to the rising. Joined then by the Paris garrison, they'll brush aside the 'antechamber soldiers' of the *Maison du Roi*, seize the Tuileries, depose fat King Louis, and either 'force' the Duke of Orléans to ascend the throne; or else, should he refuse – and as others prefer (but no one's quite clear which) – set up a regency of the Empress Marie-Louise in the name of her three-year-old son, as Napoleon II, virtual prisoners though they both are of the Austrian court.

At the conspirators' discussions, Thibaudeau, who has a watching brief on behalf of his fellow republicans, assures us 'no one doubted that the populace would support the movement.' But there's one fly in the conspiratorial ointment. Mortier's in cahoots with the Bourbons. So what's to be done? Everyone seems to be consulting and confiding in everyone else. Only the police – hopefully – are in the dark.

Also 'more or less permanently installed'[6] at Maret's house, Thibaudeau finds the ex-Postmaster-General Lavalette. Throughout the Empire he'd been responsible not merely for the post-relay system which slowly but reliably linked the new centralised France with its capital, but, more surreptitiously, for the Black Chamber, where letters deemed interesting to the State were opened, read and invisibly resealed before being forwarded to their unsuspecting addressees.[7] Lavalette comes from quite a humble family. His tall, graceful, if somewhat neurotic wife is (as the sequel will show) a woman capable of heroic actions.[8] The ex-Postmaster-General himself has wisely withdrawn into private life, and is therefore not being molested by the police. In *Laure d'Abrantès'* sharply observant eyes – but his profile portrait belies it – he's a funny-looking little man with a pot belly and a potato nose. Yet no one has ever doubted his personal integrity. And Napoleon had set great store by it:

'Entirely devoted to Napoleon, discreet, concentrated, he wore the air
of someone deep in a conspiracy; spoke little, listened, observed, only
gave himself away by deep sighs and strong handshakes.'

'Less discreet,' his wife, whose beauty had been marred by smallpox – an affliction, says Junot's widow, that 'had thrown her into a lifelong despondency,' a veritable neurosis which had 'done more to sadden Lavalette's life than the effects of the smallpox' – 'is openly recruiting adherents' to the conspiracy. Most of all Lavalette is deeply worried how this plot, should it be discovered, may affect the Emperor's fate. 'Judge what effect,' he begs the conspirators, 'such a correspondence would produce on the Allies! I'm sure they'd send the Emperor to the ends of the earth, perhaps even kill him!' Besides, what do they know of any plans His Majesty himself may have,

> 'and which yours perhaps can counteract or destroy? Has his head grown weaker? Has he no friends in Italy? Can't he be well-informed about what's going on here? It seems to me you're taking a considerable freedom in disposing of the Emperor. Isn't it going a bit far to let him be only part of an enterprise on which he hasn't been consulted in advance, to dispose of his destiny without his consent?'

Bothered by Lavalette's objections, the older of the Lallemand brothers tells him to 'go and tell Bassano all this.' For his part he's afraid that if they don't act soon, then one fine morning Napoleon, 'despite the brave men around him', will be abducted and 'sent to the ends of the earth'. And all will be hopelessly lost. Lavalette, troubled, goes to Maret. Yes, says Maret, only the other day – admittedly before the plot's details had been finalised – he has sent off a secret agent, a young man named *Fleury de Chaboulon*, to Elba. When Lavalette doesn't remember the name, he reminds him that last year Fleury had been sub-prefect at Reims, where he'd shown such resoluteness against the Russians that Ney had presented him to Napoleon as 'the intrepid prefect'. Papers being utterly dangerous things to have about one's person, he, Maret, had made the ardent young Bonapartist learn by heart 'a secret only known to him and Napoleon' as a password. Fleury, for his part, had been impressed by Maret's

> 'candid air. He converses agreeably, is equally polite to everyone. His dignity is sometimes affected but never offensive. Naturally inclined to hold men in esteem, he obliges them gracefully, perseveres in helping them.'[9]

'What shall I say if he asks whether you think the time's ripe for him to return?' Fleury had asked.

'I can't take it upon myself,' Maret had replied, 'to give such grave advice. Expound the situation to the Emperor. He, in his wisdom, will decide what he must do.'

Whereafter Fleury had left for Italy...

But riskiest of all, so it seems to Lavalette, is to have involved Fouché in the plot. Isn't the fabulously wealthy Duke of Otranto notoriously on no one's side but his own? And therefore the most dangerous of personages to make cognisant of one's affairs? The sudden appearance of what Laure d'Abrantès calls Fouché's 'mean foxy face' in the young Duchess of Reggio's hotel room at Tours last year, when he'd been hurrying back from Italy, had produced a startling impression:

> 'I saw him enter. What an astounding face! Hair, eyebrows, complexion, eyes, all seemed to me to be exactly the same pale shade of colour.'

Fouché's strange glance had 'strayed restlessly round the room.' To Laure d'Abrantès he 'seems to have stolen a skeleton's head'. And *Paul Barras*, the one-time head of the Directory who'd been ousted by his protégé Bonaparte, has found his very handshake has something frightening about it:

> 'The dryness of the bony paw made it feel like an iron nail or a bit of wood one was holding. He had two or three fingers contracted, and this made it seem to anyone he honoured with this handclasp that his own contained a foreign body.'

Apart from his love for his ugly children (his no less ugly wife Bonne-Jeanne had died in 1812) Fouché has only one passion. Power. Power at any price. The one-time terrorist, who'd mown down royalist prisoners at Lyons with grapeshot and posted up the words 'Death is an eternal sleep' over the entrances to graveyards, knows infinitely more about what's afoot in France than its government does.[10] Nor has anyone a more sensitive nose for a régime's imminent demise, or is more willing to assist in it than Fouché. Sometimes he's having long chats with Thibaudeau, his fellow-regicide,[11] whose principles are as firm as his own are non-existent. And on one thing they're agreed. The present state of affairs can't last much longer.[12] So what's France to do instead? Some monarch, however nominal, there must be – now, in 1815, no one, not even Thibaudeau, is envisaging a republic. And they certainly don't expect to see the terrifying Man on Elba reappear – no more than the royal favourite Count Blacas does. For him Bonaparte's 'nothing more than a corpse without influence buried in a little corner of the earth cut off by an arm of the sea'. In Fouché's fierce little 'fiery' eyes – why do they remind his friend the Countess de Vaudémont of 'soapsuds'? – Napoleon Bonaparte is 'finished' (*'un personnage usé'*). Hasn't he, Fouché, only recently sent him a friendly word of good advice to flee to America before he's assassinated or deported to some even remoter place – St Helena, for instance? And then sent a copy to Chancellor Dambray, thus buttering his toast on both sides? (Fouché's successor at the Police Ministry, *A-J-M-R. Savary*, Duke of Rovigo, is even sure he's planning to have the Emperor assassinated himself – and then book the crime to the Bourbons!)

Having taken over the leadership of the generals' conspiracy, Fouché, just now, in these first days of March, is waiting for a suitable moment either to unleash it – or alternatively, at the least sign of it failing, to denounce it to the government, whose fault it'll have been, for not heeding his wise advice. Should it on the other hand succeed, then he's toying with the idea of a regency under Marie-Louise, with himself, of course, as head of government. And oddly enough Maret's sure that 'this time', at least, Fouché won't betray them.

Heads or tails, Fouché wins.[13]

73

Napoleon has had every reason to leave his puny kingdom. Only thanks to the Tsar, who'd chivalrously relied on his enemy's word 'as a sovereign and a soldier' that he'll never leave it, had he been given Elba 'as a place of retirement'. But Metternich, Austria's more sceptical and all-puissant chancellor, has all along been sure the island lies much too close to France.

'You see,' he'd said, 'he'll be back in a year.'

Ever since the opening of the Vienna Congress powerful voices have been urging his deportation to 'the islands of the ocean – St Lucia, for instance', where one British newspaper is thinking the vile climate 'would soon purge this world of our friend Bonaparte'. Or how about the Azores? – Foreign Minister Castlereagh approves of the Azores. Or – why not? – St Helena. Hadn't Pitt, at the time of the royalist conspiracies against his life, deemed that isolated rock in the South Atlantic a suitable place of exile, should they ever lay hands on him? And hadn't Wellington, on his way back from India in 1805,[14] concurred? Last October Talleyrand, in one of his letters to Louis XVIII, had written:

> 'People are showing their intention of sending Bonaparte away from Elba. Some are proposing to transfer him to St Lucia or St Helena, others to one of the Azores. Everywhere people have been mooting this project.'

More and more worried about Bourbon ineptitude and the growing tensions in France, the sovereigns and the Prussian, Swedish and Spanish plenipotentiaries in Vienna have been seeing it as 'a powder barrel liable to explode any moment.' What, for instance, if Murat, anxious for his 'illegitimate' throne in Naples, should attack the Austrians in the north and – with or without Napoleon's participation – try to unite Italy? Then surely both birds can be felled with one stone?

All of which, of course, has come to Napoleon's ears.

A court, however small, costs money to keep up. So does a guard. All he'd brought with him last year was 3,980,915 francs of his private Civil List savings[15] – all the rest had been spent on defending France in 1813–14. And already half those millions had gone. As for the two million the Treaty had guaranteed him from the French budget, they've not been paid, nor has he ever expected they would be.[16] And to his sharp, ever-calculating mind it had swiftly become obvious that his nest-egg wasn't going to last for ever. As early as October the British Commissioner Sir Ian Campbell had noticed that his ward was worried about money. The Elban climate may be 'delicious',[17] but its tiny confines are too small for his restless energy. And its actual income, including the yield from the Rio mines, 'an inexhaustible highish mountain that's nothing but a mass of iron,' amounts to only 606,309 francs, a mere nothing against Napoleon's expenses of 2,432,886 francs, whereof 1,446,309 francs was needed for military and naval outlay.

And despite Pons de l'Hérault's admirable management of the mines and a sizeable but hardly repayable loan from Genoa, it seems from Peyrusse's accounts that Napoleon's economy would soon have been on the rocks,[18] and that he'd above all have had to get rid of his guard.

On at least one occasion it had been put on an alert and trained to aim fireballs at any enemy – Algerian pirates, for instance – trying to burst into the harbour, 'which can accommodate even the largest warships.'

The idea of having him assassinated may be abhorrent to Louis XVIII. But it certainly isn't to Artois, who has earlier mounted any number of such attempts. When Soult had replaced the inefficient, long-imprisoned Dupont at the War Ministry, his assistant and lifelong friend Brun de Villeret had found correspondence from the Governor of Corsica, Brulart,[19] lying on his desk, telling the Tuileries that the proposed victim was too well-guarded. Then there's the Spanish government which, not having signed the Treaty of Paris, still regards itself to be at war with him, and has been nurturing plans to send a squadron to bombard Porto-Ferrajo; hence the fireball practise. Lastly, there's the Bey of Algiers who – doubtless in connivance with Paris – has issued an order to his corsairs to

'seize shipping navigating under the Elban flag, likewise the person of that island's sovereign, should an opportunity arise to seize him.'

One morning when staying at Marciana, valet Marchand had heard a rumour that Brulard

'had sent an emissary to Algiers to carry off the Emperor during one of the excursions he made when he'd left Porto-Ferrajo and was returning by sea. From his bedroom window he saw some small vessels he thought were Barbary pirates. Asking me to get his telescope, he placed it on my shoulder and soon saw he hadn't been mistaken.'

Sent for from Porto-Ferrajo, the *Inconstant* had anchored off Longone; and Jerzmanowski had been ordered to put on board 'an officer, a sergeant, four corporals and twenty-four chasseurs, taking care to select those who didn't suffer from seasickness.' Also an equivalent party from the Corsicans.

'The embarkation over, the brig immediately put to sea. For a long while the Emperor's eyes followed it, but saw the vessels disappear, and that evening the brig came back into the port.'

The idea of making an eventual comeback had been in Napoleon's mind even when he'd left Fontainebleau. But not until December perhaps did he actually begin to devise one. Garrulous about his ideas in general, Napoleon is always silent as the grave about his actual plans. First and foremost he must wait for the Vienna Congress to dissolve itself and the sovereigns to go back to their capitals. In February he'd sent his trusted Corsican secret service agent Franciso Cipriani[20] to Vienna, to report back as soon as the Congress' dissolution was imminent. But then, just after nightfall on 12 February (or perhaps the 13th), Fleury de Chaboulon – after 'at risk of his life' having braved brigands in the Ligurian Alps and eluded the French government spies, thick as mussels along the coast – had landed at Porto-Ferrajo 'disguised as a common sailor'.[21] Reporting immediately to Bertrand, he'd been summoned by his idol 'walking in his garden'; and after giving the secret password – those 'facts known only to Maret and the Emperor himself' – Napoleon had made him sit down beside him and 'recount in greatest detail' everything that had passed between him and Bassano:

> 'I reported that interview word for word. I listed all the errors and excesses of the royal government. Incapable when moved of listening to any account without interrupting and commenting on it at every instant,'

Napoleon had launched out against the said faults (at such grandiloquent length, indeed, that one suspects Fleury of embellishing them[22]): 'Pacing to and fro and seemingly violently agitated' he inveighs against Brulard and his emissaries:

> 'Each day I uncover new ambushes, new plots. They've sent one of Georges'[23] hit-men, a wretch whom even the English newspapers have indicated to Europe is a bloodthirsty assassin. But let him take care! If he misses me, I shan't miss him. I'll send my grenadiers to flush him out and I'll have him shot to serve as an example to the others.'

To his questions about the army Fleury replies that it regards itself as having been betrayed, but never defeated. In a word, Fleury and Napoleon mirror each other's sentiments. "The race of the Bourbons is no longer in a state to govern," Napoleon declares – 'he seemed rather to be talking to himself than to be addressing someone else.' – "Their government is good for priests, nobles, old countessses of former days. To the present generation it's worthless." But what else is France thinking about?

"Will you restore the Republic?" he asks.

'Republic, Sire? No one gives it a thought. A regency perhaps.'

Told about the generals' plot and Fouché's plans for either putting the Duke of Orléans on the throne or setting up a regency in the name of Marie-Louise, Napoleon's 'vehement and surprised' comment is:

"What for? Am I dead?"

Fleury: 'Sire, in your absence...'

Napoleon: 'My absence has nothing to do with it. If the nation recalled me I'd be in France in two days. Do you think I'd do well to return?'

> 'In saying these words the Emperor averted his eyes, and it was easy for me to notice that he attached more importance to this question than he wanted to seem to, and was waiting anxiously for an answer.'

After a few moments Fleury, ordered to reply, says:

'Like Maret, I'm convinced that the common people and the army would receive you as a liberator.'

Napoleon, 'uneasy and agitated': "So M. de Bassano thinks I should come back?"

After a second interview next day, when he'd been struck by the shabbiness of the drawing room furniture ('the dyes of the shot silk were half worn out and discoloured. The carpet was threadbare and had been repaired in several places. A few poorly upholstered armchairs completed the furniture'), Napoleon – of whom Fleury had thought 'it was easy to see he'd been through a violent agitation, his manner betrayed a calm belied by his eyes' – had declared:

"My intention has been no longer to mix myself up in politics. What you've said has changed my resolution.[24] It is I who am the cause of France's misfortunes, it's I who must repair them."

Pons totally discounts Fleury's claim to have brought fresh news from France – 'after all he'd been four weeks en route and Napoleon knew more than he did.' But some effect his visit certainly has. Sent back to France via Naples, with more commissions than he can possibly carry out in short measure – one of them being to send in a report, via a private intermediary on Elba and in the form of a commercial traveller's list of business connections, listing the names of the commanding officers at places along the road to Paris – Fleury, not realising he's been sent on a wild goose chase and obviously filled to bursting with a sense of his own importance (hasn't his visit changed the course of history?) had departed for Naples, where he was to pick up a passport.[25]

Without waiting for Cipriani to get back from Vienna, Napoleon had immediately got busy. Never one to give advance notice of his movements, he'd kept silent about his last gamble until the very last moment. 'For several days,' Marchand had noticed, 'the Emperor had been silent and reflective,' and Drouot and Bertrand were being summoned

'much more often than usual, likewise Cambronne. The map of France lay constantly spread out in the office, with pins stuck into it. Profiting from the return of the fine season, he decided on several building projects to resume or carry out. Leaving his serious thoughts in the office, outside it he affected to be very gay, laughed with the princess [Pauline], visited his mother, dined with her; went to see his Guard and ordered it to begin work on a garden around its barracks. With the engineers he drew up projects for improving the town – in a word did everything to disguise the project he had in mind.'

Two or three days before Fleury had landed, his mother's chamberlain Colonna d'Istria, who has also been Murat's representative in Vienna, had returned from Naples with news – premature, as it'll turn out – that the

Congress is in fact closing, and that the Tsar has already gone back to Russia. 'He didn't even think he need wait for it to be confirmed from Vienna. He decided to leave, and prepared to do so.'[26]

Now Marchand sees the 'big map of France unfolded on the drawing room floor', the Emperor 'on his knees tracing the route he proposed to follow', which only Drouot and Bertrand are allowed to know about.[27] Ali the second valet, the seven-foot Swiss valet-cum-bodyguard Noverraz, and Vantini, have all been sent to the island's various harbours to find out how many vessels are in port: 'Several were chartered and were to sail on a given day, and during the night of 25–26 February put into Porto-Ferrajo.' Peyrusse too – not to mention Mariotti's spy – has suspected something's afoot. But only the previous evening at bedtime does Napoleon actually tell Marchand he's going back to France, and "to prepare for this journey, taking only a few effects." Without thinking too much about what he's been told, the First Valet spends part of the night hours putting his master's effects in order, and

> 'drawing up a list of what was to be left behind, to give to Madame [*Mère*]. I took care to take with me, as I'd been urged to, a tricolour cockade to hand to him at the moment when he asked me for it. All these measures were to be carried out unperceived by the servants on duty, and I was to tell anyone who asked me that the Emperor was going to spend a few days at [his summer house of] San Martino.'

Speculation is rife as to the convoy's destination. Some people even think it's bound for America – hasn't His Majesty provisioned the *Inconstant* for a three-month voyage? But so far is anyone from envisaging a return to France that Marchand is believed. Even next morning, as Ali's holding up the shaving mirror and Dr Foureau[28] comes in, when Napoleon says "have you packed your trunk? we're leaving for France," Foureau just throws Marchand a sceptical smile,

> 'thinking it was a mystification the Emperor was fabricating for his doctor. Great was their astonishment, both of them, when the Emperor having dressed and gone out into his garden, I told them nothing was truer. By midday it'd be known all over the town.'

If they don't want to be taken by surprise, Marchand respectfully adds, "they'd better hurry up and get their things packed."

That Sunday morning Napoleon comes into his room where his valet is drawing up his list of effects and gives him a watch with a gold chain and a key, saying:

"Take this watch with you. I give it to you. It dates from when I was Consul."

At that moment, to everyone's dismay, the British frigate HMS *Partridge* is sighted. Has Campbell suspected something? Everyone's in a state of intense anxiety. No, apparently not. Her captain comes ashore and, as usual, presents his compliments to Bertrand. By 10:00 am, while Napoleon is already hearing Mass – an hour earlier than normal – the *Partridge* has left again. And after mass, at his usual Sunday morning reception, Napoleon announces his departure.

Seeing the 194-ton merchant ship *Saint Esprit* come sailing into the harbour, Napoleon, who has realised he's short of transports, orders Jerzmanowski to take twenty of his Poles and their harness, board her, and toss the cargo of Turkish grain into the dock – Peyrusse is ordered to pay for it:

'Captain Cardini became extremely agitated to see himself boarded in this way. Each case, each barrel thrown into the water excited his jeremiads.'

But, realising he's going to be paid for them, he

'resigned himself to deliver up his ship to His Majesty's troops. After giving his orders to his first mate, he took me down into his cabin. I went through all his accounts as best I could. I found them rife with double entries. From Genoa he was bound for Naples. His bills of lading didn't seem to me to be sincere. His pretensions were excessive. Not all the Poles yet being on board, I lost no time in verifying and buying up, as cheaply as possible, the sustenance offered us.'

But for Napoleon, looking out over the port from his terrace, all this is going too slowly.

'He gets into his sloop, comes on board the *Saint Esprit* and finds my hands full of papers. When I inform him of how much her master is asking for, His Majesty throws all my papers in the air, calling me a *papperassier*. And orders me to give the master whatever he wants. I put up with this moment of bad temper and paid out 25,000 francs,'

as against only 5,795 francs for all the other chartered vessels. Napoleon and his treasurer go ashore again:

'The town was all topsy-turvy. The inhabitants were sad. The same affliction reigned in the palace. His Majesty had assigned me my place on the *Inconstant*. All my trunks went aboard. The fall-in was being beaten. The troops came flying out of their barracks. Soon the roads were being ploughed by boats. The populace filled the port, making the air ring with its prolonged shouts of *Vive l'Empereur!*'

At 7:00 pm, in bright moonlight, Napoleon leaves the palace and rides down to the quayside in a little carriage, followed on foot by Bertrand, Drouot and the entourage. His sloop passes closely by each of the six other vessels, where the troops are piled up 'pell-mell'. At 8:00 pm one of the *Inconstant*'s guns fires the signal to depart:

'At once the ships were covered with sails. The evening was superb. The wind seemed favourable. On the ramparts the inhabitants saluted the Emperor with a thousand vivats.'

Anticlimax.

> 'Hardly had we doubled the St André Cape than the wind dropped,
> the sea became calm.'

Not a breath of a breeze to waft the convoy on its way. But what's sauce for the goose is also sauce for the gander. Only a few sea miles away, across the bay at Leghorn, Campbell, tipped off that something's afoot and determined to get to Porto-Ferrrajo and prevent a disaster, has boarded HMS *Partridge*. Only at dawn does the breeze freshen, wafting Napoleon's flotilla northwards – and the *Partridge* to Elba, only to drop again to a dead calm when she is a few miles offshore. Not seeing the *Inconstant*'s masts in the port, an agitated and becalmed Campbell has himself rowed into Porto-Ferrajo, where a British tourist tells him what's happened. When he furiously insists that Fanny Bertrand shall tell him the convoy's destination, *Madame la Grande Maréchale*, like the other ladies, has to remind him he's speaking to a lady.

Ordered to scatter, the Elban flotilla eludes both of the French frigates tacking to and fro between Elba and Corsica to prevent just this eventuality.[29] And with the surprising candour which at moments can be as typical of him as his reticences, a delighted Napoleon assembles his officers on the *Inconstant*'s deck, and tells them:

> 'To have stayed would have been more dangerous than to have left.'

CHAPTER 4

THROUGH THE MOUNTAINS

Ａnd now he's sitting on a circular stone bench round a plane tree in the village of Saint-Vallier-de-Thiey. It's the first halt after Grasse. The column has climbed twelve kilometres to 730 metres above sea level. Fast though it's marching, the news has travelled faster and

'disturbed the locals and thrown them into terror. Above all they were afraid there'd be a razzia after their mules, and to be on the safe side they'd shut them up in the village's remotest sheep-pens.'

The mayor has fled – even the smallest village has one. Instead his deputy, a M. Chautard, appears. Can he provide some mules? Chautard, who speaks with a broad country accent[1] has prepared his reply:

"Sire, all the mules are in Champagne."

'At which the Emperor, adopting his interlocutor's tone and without laughing, said: "Bugger it! But that's a very long way away!" Chautard, reassured by his familiar tone, replied: "I beg your pardon, *mon Empereur*, they're out in the country [*à la campagne*]."'

But forthcoming, even so – at a price.[2] And soon the villagers, having first 'prudently shut themselves up in their houses', are 'timidly forming a circle' around him. But when the local innkeeper offers His ex-Majesty some refreshments on a tray, he turns his back on him. Only after Bertrand has ordered the innkeeper: "Fill the glass and drink!" does Napoleon quench his thirst – always this fear of poisoning! And upon the appearance of a local magistrate who says he has a son in Paris, Bertrand 'without any motive one could see', but presumably fearing a spy, again intervenes: "Sire! It's getting very hot!"

'The Emperor immediately got up and gave the signal to leave for Escragnolles. We took the Castellane road among rocks, boulders and precipices, where we seemed to hang in the air. Night made our march perilous.'

Ali, himself unused to such physical exertions, sees how it's 'virtually only the advance guard' that's

'marching in some order. The body of the little army, scattered along the route, formed a lot of more or less feeble little platoons. Many soldiers were making it on their own. It seemed that, being at home [*chez soi*] we had nothing to fear. Though in Provence, the ill-intentioned had had no time to take any measures.'

It's the first two days he's going to find heaviest going:

'At each moment mountain peaks had to be climbed, or rather narrow

81

defiles to be passed through. Now snow was preventing us from quickening our pace as much as we'd have liked to, now mud. We of the Household had all of us left all our effects at Porto-Ferrajo, only brought with us what was indispensably needed for the journey.'

Peyrusse's gold is too heavy for his mules, which by and by refuse to go on: 'Little by little their escort, tiring of such sloth, left my convoy behind. I was dead beat. While the muleteers were giving them some oats I dismounted and went a little to one side, holding my mule's bridle in my hand. Sleep overwhelmed me. The cold woke me up. The convoy had left! My mule, no longer feeling himself restrained, had followed on after it.'

In the pitch darkness he presses his repeater watch – and finds he has 'slept for two hours! I can't describe the worry, the anxiety, the disquiet that fell on me as I woke up to realise I was alone in a gorge.' But his very imprudence and terror lend him wings. Following a path that

'seemed freshly churned up, I'd hardly gone one league [four kilometres] when a little straw lying by the roadside led me to two of my boxes of gold. The mule that had been carrying them had got stuck. And since he hadn't been able to go on, they'd had to unload him. I made haste to hide them under a pile of stones and marked it with a stake. After an hour, redoubling my pace, I reached the village of Escragnolles, where my convoy had halted, but at once went back to look for my money. Having reloaded it, I went back to Escragnolles.'

But the halt's only a brief one – three hours, he says. Then that tiny hamlet too is left behind. Now the column, in pitch darkness, is staggering on 'through snow and ice', much of the time in single file along the sharply winding mountain track, with sheer cliffs on one side and bottomless gorges on the other: 'Our little column,' Adjutant-Major *Laborde* estimates, 'took up as much space as 20,000 men would have done on a proper road.' To have to lead a horse by its bridle in the dark along a path broken by melting streams and crossed by icy gullies is dangerous enough, but those of the Polish lancers who haven't got one are almost in a worse case than their comrades who have (either requisitioned at Cannes or taken from the abandoned guns at Grasse). 'Embarrassed by their heavy waxed oilskin trousers, spurs, big sabres and lances, they were still having to carry their saddles and bridles on their shoulders.' To the 300 Corsicans bringing up the rear there's perhaps nothing extraordinary about such terrain. Corsica, too, is all mountains. But after eleven months in barracks and despite an intense last-moment three-day fit of gardening work[3] the Guard's *grognards* can hardly be in such good physical trim as in the days when they'd marched all over Europe. How about the man with the big drum, for instance – for the bandsmen are here?[4] Or the Chinese chimes player, his unwieldy

82

instrument strapped to his pack? Are there no twisted ankles? No broken bones? No stragglers to fall into the hands of Prefect Bouthillier's gendarmes? Not as far as Ali will recall: 'no one was left behind.' Isn't Maria, an Elban girl who, opting to follow her lover, a man who's served for thirty years and become his company's *vivandière*, finding it harder and harder to keep up as its *serre-fil* ('last man')?[5] Or is she simply being dragged on, her arms around her lover's and his *copain*'s shoulders, like so many a novice before? And how are things with a certain Captain Loubers? A fanatic for the Emperor, how is it with his nervous disposition?[6] The column scrambles on as fast as anyone can on foot. Or ever has. Or will.

For it's a race against time, if ever there was one. What dispositions has Masséna taken at Toulon?[7] Has he already perhaps despatched a superior force, with artillery, to cut them off at Digne? Or, more probably, at Sisteron? Two days march away, it's there the only bridge crosses the broad swift-flowing Durance river.

But here at least are some more mules. Their owners, from the mountain village of Caille, are bringing corn to the Grasse market. They won't get there. Cambronne's weary men make them offload their sacks, replace them with packs, and force them to turn back. Napoleon himself, pushing on 'through snow and ice, sometimes on horseback, sometimes on foot', is in no better case than anyone else. Perhaps worse. Has his portly physique been debilitated by daily ninety-minute hot saltwater baths on Elba?[8] Apparently not. And his will is the strongest in Europe. Soon he and those of his Headquarters group who've no units to command are far ahead of the rest of the battalion, not to mention the Corsicans, bringing up the rear. Walking with a stick and leaning on the arm of Captain Raoul, his *premier officier d'ordonnance,*

> 'the stick he held in his hand didn't save him from slipping and falling. His Majesty got up again cheerfully. "Never mind," said a grenadier at his side, "today John the Sword[9] mustn't twist anything.[10] First he must be *Jean de Paris*."'

Now, as perhaps never before, success depends on speed.

At long last, at about 8:00 pm, this second night's bivouac is reached. Overhung by a sheer wall of high cliffs at the opening of a wide plain, more than a thousand metres above sea level, lies the village of Séranon. In a mere twenty hours the column has covered almost fifty kilometres,[11] forty kilometres of it amidst melting snows, threatened at every moment by avalanches and rockfalls along an impossibly difficult mountain track.

Here at Séranon the honours are done by the curé, 'a very polite handsome man. The amiable and modest Abbé Chiris,' who has his servant spread an ample repast in front of his parsonage at the village's end. But all his illustrious guest eats of it, once again, is 'two boiled eggs, presented to him on a silver platter'. Eggs at least are safe. Meanwhile the conversation turns to one of the abbé's relatives, a certain General François,[12] the first man to sing the *Marseillaise* in Marseilles, who, like 8,915 others, had left his bones in Egypt. But his mother's still alive, and Napoleon says he'd like to see her. But all she does is 'deplore her son's death'. Turning to Marchand for the privy purse, he puts a roll of twenty-five gold napoleons (500 francs) into her outstretched hand. And Abbé Chiris gets a similar gift – just how much he'll never disclose – for the parish poor.

'What you need,' says Napoleon 'is a mitre.[13] It'd suit you much better than your shovel hat!'

But where's the mayor? It's the same M. de Gourdon who'd taken to his heels at Grasse! At first he'd assumed that though the 'tiger had escaped from its cage' it would get no further. But since it has, he has thought it prudent to send word to the steward of his country house, a Sieur Blaise Rebuffon, to make suitable arrangements here at Séranon. 'Everything had been prepared to receive him.' On the other hand neither the folding bed nor the gold *nécessaire* have arrived. And both Marchand and the Elban chamberlain Vantini are worried, since they're sure it's going to take the battalion 'several hours' to catch up:

> 'The cold was intense. The Emperor was very tired, his boots were soaked through, and he had great difficulty in getting them off. He stretched himself out between two chairs in front of a big fire.'

The First Valet's just beginning to be very worried indeed when Ali and Noverraz turn up: 'We instantly assembled the Emperor's bed, and he slept for three hours.' So does the battalion when it debouches into 'Séranon's pleasant plain', and seizes poor Blaise's precious stock of firewood to light huge campfires in the village square. Not so the wretched muleteers from Caille. Terrified they'll again have to provide transport tomorrow, they and their mules slip quietly away into the night.[14]

For Napoleon three hours' sleep are always enough. At dawn, Marchand goes on,

> 'he got dressed and had the kindness to say to me: "You must be tired. You'll take one of my horses until we find some we can buy." After which I heard him say to the generals: "The battalion must be worn out! Come on, courage! The main thing is to get past Sisteron. Masséna can have no idea how fast I'm moving, and his orders will reflect his uncertainty."'

But supposing Masséna's quicker on the uptake than Napoleon supposes? Supposing he has already sent troops to blow up the bridge? From Toulon to Sisteron is only 135 kilometres along the main highway.

The mules having given them the slip, Marchand mounts one of

Napoleon's own horses (he evidently now has several). But poor Sieur Blaise is treated less complaisantly. 'Deploring the disappearance of his woodpile', now a heap of smouldering ashes in the village square, he's worried for his wife, who's just gone into labour. But though 'far from sharing the enthusiasm of two veterans who'd joined at Saint-Vallier', he's pressed into service, even so, to guide the advance guard as far as Castellane. Still badly needing horses, the column, as it climbs over the Lèsques Pass, encounters a peasant who's riding one. Napoleon asks him how much he wants for it.

"A thousand francs."

"My friend, the price is too high for my purse."

In the meanwhile Blaise has managed to slip away and got back to his wife at Séranon in time for her delivery. He'll 'always remember the infant's date of birth'. It's 3 March. The third day.

Castellane, spectacularly situated underneath an immense 185-metre high boulder-like crag that each moment seems ready to fall on it, is the administrative centre of the Department of the High Alps. Its sub-prefect Francoul has recently been dismissed – presumably on account of his political sympathies. But hasn't yet been replaced. And it's in his house Napoleon stays 'for three hours, lunching on victuals brought from the inn', washed down by wines from Francoul's cellar. The mayor, a M. Saint-Martin, is also prevailed upon 'to issue three blank passports and forbidden to notify the prefect until after three days.' Napoleon also summons the gendarmerie, which *Fabry*[15] concludes 'was struck dumb with amazement' and has left town.

One of the passports is for Pons de l'Hérault. Peyrusse advances him 1,900 francs for his journey. He's to take the direct route through the mountains to Marseilles. When he gets there he's to tell his friend Masséna the Emperor's back, and take particular care to add that he has the support of the Austrian government and the British navy.[16] Perhaps that'll be enough to make the marshal hold his hand for a few hours? Another passport is made out for the Guard's chief surgeon, the well-liked Dr Eméry. A man, Pons thinks,

'of distinguished talent, a man of science and the sword, generous-
minded, devoted, religiously caring for the wounded, one of the finest
examples of that eminently illustrious body.'

On Elba Eméry's been in secret contact with a certain well-to-do glovemaker and ardent Bonapartist of Grenoble, his native town, by name Jean Dumoulins. Smuggled through the French customs in his glove consignments, Dumoulins' letters have been full of useful and encouraging information on the state of public opinion, at least as perceived by himself. Now Eméry, described in his passport as being 'on leave from Elba', is to 'push on as far as he can', announce the Emperor's return to Bonapartist circles, and, in general, smooth His Majesty's path. Like Pons de l'Hérault, he's to

'announce the landing and the Empress's arrival with a considerable force. They're to announce that this simultaneous arrival had been combined with and favoured by the Emperor of Austria.'

The third emissary is one of Lavalette's former coachmen.

Already, even before the column's arrival in Castellane, its authorities have sent on an official messenger to Barrême, the next village, to announce to its mayor that the 'ex-emperor Bonaparte' will shortly be arriving with his troops. At about 3:00 pm the news has reached Barrême and the tocsin is being rung, assembling the peasantry from the surrounding hamlets. Two hours later, just as night is falling, Cambronne's arrival with the advance guard startles the Barrême villagers. And at once he gets busy arranging Napoleon's lodgings and dinner. Requisitioning the village's largest house, the home of its magistrate, a M. Tartanson,[17] he goes into its kitchen:

"What have you got for dinner?"

"It's Friday," says a startled Mme. Tartanson, "so we only have lentil soup, an omelette and some cod." The lentil soup is only for some employees who're out in the fields.

"Let me taste it!" says Cambronne, picks up a spoon and finds it excellent. And orders the sentry he places in the kitchen doorway not to take his eyes off the pots and pans. The meal is to be eked out by 'a haunch of kid and a few other dishes, fetched from the inn, where they were cooked under the eyes of two sentries.' Also summoned, the mayor, a M. Béraud, is ordered to find 500 rations of bread and as much again of wine and other provisions. Likewise mules. All of which, Cambronne assures him, will be paid for.

By and by 'preceded by fifty mounted lancers, and accompanied by Drouot, Bertrand and Pons de l'Hérault', the 'ex-emperor, saluting to right and left, comes riding in on his white horse.'[18] Salutations the villagers at first don't respond to. Dismounting with difficulty – it's extremely cold – outside the Tartansons' house, he goes upstairs to a first-floor room where a rousing fire has been lit and a bed made up. There follows a cross-examination, Napoleon's usual way of addressing individuals he doesn't know:[19]

"Are you the house's proprietor?"

"Yes, Sire."

"What's your name?"

"Tartanson."

"And this young man?"

"He's my son."

"What's he do?"

"He's receiver of taxes."

Upon the younger Tartanson's wife, embarrassed by his greeting, saying

clumsily "Monsieur, I have the honour to salute you," Cambronne takes her
by the arm and reproaches her: "Madame, it's the Emperor."[20]

> 'While Buonaparte installed himself in the apartment set aside for
> him, the rest of the house filled up with a crowd of officers, and the
> ground floor rooms were encumbered with baggage,'

though the Headquarters' own will only arrive 'during the course of the
night.' Summoning Mayor Béraud again, he questions him at length about
the road from Barrême to Sisteron, where he proposes to stop tomorrow
night – 'but was told it was impossible [to get so far in that time] on foot.'
Impossible isn't a word he likes to hear.[21] With Mayor Béraud he studies
several maps of Provence and compares them with Cassini's:

> 'He requisitioned 200 two-horse vehicles, taking pains to point out the
> villages that were to supply them and choosing by preference those on
> the road to be followed by his troops, so that they couldn't refuse the
> requisition.'

Then, selecting a deep armchair, he drops into it and summons the fifty-six-
year-old magistrate and his son, who find him with his feet up on another
chair. He has taken off his grey overcoat and is still wearing his blue uniform.
In a majestic blend of fact and fiction he tells them:

"There have been several landings at various points in Provence simultaneously with mine. My cavalry and artillery are taking the main road. We'll
be joining up later on. The whole army's on my side and the Bourbons won't
be able to hold on. But they needn't worry for their fate!"

"The troops may be for you," Tartanson makes so bold as to put in, "but
not the populace, at least not in this part of the country."

> 'Buonaparte let this observation pass; and seemingly unconcerned,
> turned the conversation to vaguer matters, in the middle of which he
> interposed these remarkable words:[22] "The day after tomorrow in the
> evening the Bourbons will hear I'm back. The Empress, too, is on her
> way to Paris, where we'll arrive simultaneously. On 20 March I'll sleep
> at the Tuileries."'

Then, turning to the younger Tartanson: "So you'll be coming along with
us, eh? You'll be one of ours, isn't that so? I shan't forget you. I'll make your
fortune. I'll give you a high rank."

The young man, responding perhaps to a nudge from his father, replies
that he's an only son and has a wife and child to consider: "I'll be more use
to my country by staying here at Barrême." Is he timid, or a royalist,[23] or just
cagey? Napoleon insists, and is only distracted when his interlocutor's little
boy is brought into the room. What's his name? Alphonse. How old? Four.

"The age of the King of Rome!" he says; and "his eyes filled with tears."[24]

Mayor Béraud is dismissed, with a promise to run a post-road (Fabry says
'a military road') through Barrême. But once again neither is Bertrand – no

more than with Captain Gazon at Antibes – taking no for an answer. Taking young Tartanson aside he renews

'the same propositions in the liveliest way: "I'll make you a squadron-leader on the spot. After we've left Lyons behind you'll have an even higher rank, and when we get to Paris I'll make it my personal responsibility to see you're promoted.'

But Tartanson jr isn't only stubborn. He's also resourceful. The village's two gendarmes having been posted at the front door, as he goes out he privily urges one of them to despatch a messenger to announce 'the Emperor's return', prudently scribbling the prefix 'ex-' in front of 'emperor'.

'After the mayor, the gendarmerie was summoned. There was only a corporal and one gendarme. He called for the curé, Abbé Galland. But that clergyman didn't present himself. During these interviews the little town was filling up with troops who were received in an amazed and stupefied silence.'

But now dinner's served up here in this upstairs room, Napoleon, Bertrand and Drouot dining at the same table and rounding off their meal with fruits and the Tartansons' oldest wines.

'Buonaparte drank some coffee which he'd brought with him ready-made in a bottle and which was served to him in some of the household's cups, his own not yet having arrived. While the family's supper was being consumed by him and his companions at table, his very numerous entourage laid their hands on all the household's provisions, in a few instants devouring the fruit of several years' economies. After supper all the beds and mattresses were commandeered and spread out in every room in the house, even on the stairs. Buonaparte had an iron bed which was put up in five minutes. The house supplied only the sheets and mattresses. He went to bed and was guarded by two mamelukes [*sic*, presumably Noverraz and Ali] placed as sentries at each door of his room. The stairs were littered with officers lying on mattresses or straw.'

Meanwhile the villagers, plucking up courage, have begun to mingle with the troops. Other 'peasants, informed of the Emperor's march, were coming down in torrents from the mountain. From their way of expressing themselves', Marchand and the others can 'see how much they feared the restoration of church tithes and feudal rights.'

By now it's snowing again, and the night outside is both bitterly cold and pitch dark – or would be, if every window didn't have a candle in it – whether placed there spontaneously or 'forced to by the troops' will depend on one's point of view. Those troops not 'posted at the village's various entrances and on the main square' have lodged themselves with the inhabitants. Anyway, Peyrusse, who has paid for mules 'for persons in the entourage', hears fireworks being let off, and 'dancing and singing'. At the Tartansons' house some officers

> 'instead of turning in were passing the night writing and despatching emissaries. Several had already been sent off at the moment Buonaparte had arrived. He could be heard asking Bertrand: "Has that man left?" "Which one, Sire?" "The one in correspondence with Grenoble [*ie* Eméry]?" "Yes, Sire." "And the ones from the north?" "They've left too."'

Now it's 3:00 am and Napoleon, 'who hasn't slept a wink', asks Marchand for a cup of coffee. At 5:00 am, having finished his breakfast ('a few cubes of broth from his travelling case' served – as the Tartansons notice – from, among other objects, 'a magnificent silver-gilt service') he declares he's ready to leave – but doesn't. Instead he spends another half-hour in the big armchair,

> 'his legs stretched out on a chair, and in the posture of a man wearing a cuirass, impeded in his movements and stiff as an iron bar, bareheaded, in his blue uniform and riding boots with spurs.'

Chatting again with his hosts, he tells them of his plans; asks about the department's needs; promises improvements to certain inheritance laws; interrogates them about taxes. Are they having any difficulty in getting them in? And what are those layabouts, the returned émigrés, up to? And how about the sales of church property, nationalised during the Revolution, "there must be those of the Senez diocese, did they go at a fair price?" Well, more or less, yes. Remembering a certain Squadron-Leader de Moriez who'd owned a property in the neighbourhood, he enquires about him:

"He's dead isn't he?"

"Yes."

Who's the prefect at Digne? – Duval.

"Oh, Duval," Bertrand exclaims, "he's a fine fellow!"

Another hour passes. 'All these questions were jumbled up with others in which the interrogator didn't shine by reason of consequentiality.'[25] His hosts notice that he 'never uttered the words *the King*. Said always *the Bourbons*. Nor did either he or his men used the word *royalists*.'

By now some 200 peasants from the neighbouring villages are filling the village street, and at 6:00 am some of their mayors, too, are admitted. One of them has forgotten in his haste to unpin the Order of St Louis from his tailcoat.

"What kind of dicky birds are they?" exclaims Cambronne scornfully, referring to the lilies. Rips off the medal and kicks the mayor's backside. Sending for the bill, he's told by their hosts that "not being innkeepers they haven't made one up." So he gives the Tartansons five gold twenty-franc pieces 'to distribute among the servants'.

It's still pitch dark when the torches are lit in the square; and at 7:00 am Napoleon, evidently very thoroughly dressed indeed against the cold mountain by Marchand, appears in the doorway. As 'two or three equerries' hoist him onto his horse he seems to some bystanders 'like a man whose clothes are too stiff [*engoncé*] for him' and to others 'like an iron bar'. Can it be he's wearing armour under his uniform, they wonder?[26] Gallantly saluting the ladies, he shakes hands with Tartanson father and son; and leaves. Going back into their kitchen, his hosts find a handsome colander engraved with a crowned *N* that's been left behind by mistake and which they'll hand down as a family heirloom. 'For guides Buonaparte took the Barrême gendarmerie, which consisted of a corporal and two [*sic*] gendarmes.'

'The first two days,' Ali will always remember,
> 'were the most burdensome. We left before daybreak, and it was always very late before we got to the night's halt. At every town, walled village or hamlet we passed through we bought up all the horses in a state to carry a man, and it was in that way we found mounts for the Poles, for many officers and all the Household staff.'

From Barrême, which 'it took all day for the troops to pass through', Treasurer Peyrusse goes on, 'we took the Digne road.' Digne is a spa – only a couple of years ago Pauline had visited its warm baths, at a natural temperature of 42°C. It lies eighty-nine kilometres distant, through mountains all the way. This time the baggage is laden on the peasants' mules:
> 'The cold was sharp. A thin layer of ice made our march painful and perilous. We warmed ourselves by charcoal-burners' fires we came across in the mountains.'

Halting at Bédéjun, a tiny mountain hamlet, the Headquarters warms itself
> 'at a big fire made up in the middle of a field. And there, a quarter of a chicken in his hand and a bit of bread under his arm, he [Napoleon] most philosophically broke his fast.'

Again, at Chaudon or La Clappe, two other small hamlets, he seats himself on a stone, to have a second breakfast of two hard-boiled eggs. Not that the stone is comfortable, for he comments:
> "Gentlemen, we're ill-seated."

Since when the stone has been called *Le Mal-assis*.

Once again the bystanders are 'stupefied. Such a spectacle had never presented itself to their eyes. They contemplated His Majesty with gaping mouths.' While eating his two eggs he has a long conversation on religious topics with the local priest, young Abbé Laurent. And upon the innkeeper demanding an exorbitant sum for the eggs, quips:
> "Eggs must be rare hereabouts."

To which the quick-witted innkeeper responds: "Not eggs, but emperors."

And everyone has a good laugh. When they've left, Abbé Laurent goes straight home and writes down their conversation.[27]

The painful march over the mountains continues, 'the Emperor walking on foot.' Two persons of consequence at Barrême coming in the opposite direction – one of them is the local priest – are obliged to yield up their horses, turn back, and follow the expedition as far as Digne 'to get paid for them'.

Of all the expedition's members Peyrusse is sure he's 'the unhappiest, on account of the great responsibility weighing on me.' Once again his mules aren't able to keep up. At about 10:00 pm he's just congratulating himself on the prospect of soon reaching the main Aix–Grenoble road and getting some wheeled transport to carry the balance of his two million gold francs, when

'coming down the mountainside that leads to the baths at Digne – the track is narrow – one of my mules loses his foothold, slithers, falls, and tumbles over a precipice. The night being so dark, we can't climb down after him. Still being far from the bath house, I decide to leave a sentry there to keep an eye on things and go on to Digne.'

Is it this mule Ali, too, sees plunge to its death 'in one of the narrowest and worst precipices'? Doubtless there are others which suffer the same fate. Peyrusse enters presumably by the same exceedingly narrow Rue Mère-de-Dieu (Mother of God Street) – no broader than that a man only has to stretch out both arms to touch both its walls at once – that Napoleon has just done. Seeing him and his staff come riding along it, some of the ladies at their narrow elongated windows with red and blue shutters so typical of this part of France, had called out, asking which was the Emperor. And he'd called up to one of them: "Madame, it is I!" And gone to the *Petit Paris* inn.

No sooner has the headquarters party entered the public square than they hear what's been going on here. Only a week ago, by sheer force of personality, the local commander, Colonel Loverdo, a veteran from Spain, has had to quell a mutiny of his men. And now, though it hadn't been connected with Napoleon's as yet unheralded return, in view of the impossibility of defending Castellane he has thought prudence the better part of wisdom and withdrawn them. News of the landing had in fact reached Prefect Duval

'at 3:00 pm on 3 March. The despatch from his colleague in the Var had told him Buonaparte had 1,600 men with him and told him of his own dispositions to hold him up. M. Duval, having receipted the despatch, had put it in his pocket. That evening he'd given a social reception, at which he appeared looking more radiant than usual. The fateful despatch didn't prevent him from joining in the evening's diversions and prolonging his game of billiards until 11:00 pm or midnight.'

Meanwhile Eméry and (Fabry goes on) 'several others' had arrived, and 'at 4:00 am the express from Barrême had spread the news that Buonaparte would be entering Digne during the course of the day. It was only then that the Prefect had informed M. de Loverdo, commanding the military district of the Lower Alps, of the despatch from the Var prefect and of that of the Barrême corporal he'd just received. M. de Loverdo went at once to the barracks where was the depôt of 150 men,'

(or, to be more exact, 132). Received there with shouts of *Vive l'Empereur!*, Loverdo had informed Duval, 'adding that he couldn't count on a single one of his soldiers,' he had exhorted him to instantly call out the National Guard. 'At 6:00 am the engineer of the Bridges and Highways Department came and offered his services, either to cut bridges or break the roads. But the Prefect thanked him and told him to go and look to his womenfolk (his wife and mother-in-law).'

Obviously Duval's Bonapartist reputation isn't undeserved. But by now the news has unleashed the

'zeal of a crowd of good citizens who came running to the town hall, demanding weapons so as to bar the road to Buonaparte and wait for him at the narrow point by the Baths: an inexpugnable position, where a handful of men could hold up a whole army.'

But the mayor says he must refer the matter to the prefect who, 'far from seconding these citizens' generous ardour, forbade the mayor to arm them and made him responsible for everything that might ensue if he violated his ban.' All probably in tune with the town's notables, who've panicked and begged them 'not to commit any hostility against Bonaparte and so avoid the town suffering utter disaster.'

It had been at that moment Eméry had turned up.

'Arrested at first, he'd soon afterwards been released at the request of one of his compatriots [from Grenoble] who took on himself the responsibility for doing so, received him in his home, gave him his own horse to continue on his way, and a certificate in lieu of a passport.'

A Lieutenant Julien, 'formerly an officer in his Guard', had been sent out to report on Napoleon's advance,

'but in the meanwhile one of the latter's orderlies had entered Digne, demanding 5,000 rations, thus swelling his body of troops to terrify the citizens. Toward 11:00 am the lieutenant of gendarmerie came back with the news that Buonaparte was arriving.'

Whereon Duval, with an escort of only four gendarmes, withdraws to his country house at Champtercer, 'together with his secretary-general and some other officials.[28] M. de Loverdo had already left earlier and made off with his unit, which at least didn't swell Buonaparte's. Buonaparte entered Digne to the sound of his drum; but was met with silence and consternation. The shops were closed, the citizens had withdrawn into their houses. Only a few children were in the town square. In the grim silence Bertrand threw them some coins and said "the Emperor's here. Shout *Vive l'Empereur!*" And in fact these children did take up the cry, whilst others at the windows shouted *Vive le Roi!* Such, exactly, was Buonaparte's entrance into Digne.'[29]

On the other hand it seems the children also know some anti-Bourbon ditties, for Napoleon will remember how they 'raised our spirits a little.' Who, then, are really his partisans at Digne? Certainly not the fashionable folk who're taking its health-giving spa waters, a couple of miles up the road. As Napoleon himself will admit: 'At Digne they showed no more joy at seeing me [than at Grasse]. Everywhere people were surprised to see us go by.' Is he beginning to despair of his extraordinary enterprise? In front of Bertrand he exclaims:

'Can it be we've been fooling ourselves? Aren't the troops on our side?'

'He dismounted at the *Petit Paris* inn,' Fabry goes on, 'where he stayed a few hours. He summoned five individuals, one after the other.' One is the wife of a local hero, the thirty-six-year-old Colonel A. Desmichels, who'd served in Italy in '96 and is famous for having captured 600 Austrians with only thirty of his 31st Chasseurs back in 1805. Unfortunately he isn't at home; but his wife is, and she too is quite sure the further His Majesty advances the readier he'll find the population to rise in his favour. Nor does Desmichels' nephew need any urging – unlike Gazon, unlike the younger Tartanson – to join the column, where he replaces the pusillanimous *officier d'ordonnance* Perès.

But all this while Peyrusse is worrying about his missing mule-load of gold coin:

'After depositing all my funds with the Grand Marshal, I had [my men] take lanterns and provisions, and we retraced our steps. Reaching the foot of the precipice with difficulty [we found] the mule all torn to pieces, but still breathing. One of my cases, containing 200,000 francs, had burst open.'

Hard though it is to lay his hands on the rolls of gold coins in the dark, in the end he finds them under freshly fallen snow. Or at least most of them. Perhaps if he goes on searching he'll find more. But at first blush of dawn he is reached by a message from Bertrand, with orders to relinquish further searching and rejoin headquarters. Not all the money's been found.

'Such rolls as had escaped our searchings must have fallen into the stream, swollen by the night's snowfall. I drew up my account. I found a deficit of 37,000 francs [the exact net loss he books is 37,520]. I went back to Digne, got hold of a carriage, handsomely paid off my muleteers, and settled the mayor's account for the supplies he'd provided.'

A sum of 1,124 francs. The inhabitants, meanwhile, have 'promptly torn down' the prefect's royalist proclamation. And the local printer finds he has other work to do. Written proclamations, Napoleon knows, aren't going to make at all the same impact as the printed word – 'I should have brought a printing press with me', he'll reflect afterwards, 'the peasants said they didn't believe hand-written proclamations.' Though how even a portable printing press could have been humped across the mountains is hard to say. Anyway, the Dauphiné province, which lies ahead of them, is no less strongly Bonapartist than Provence was anti-Bonapartist. And the imperial proclamations, properly printed, can be counted on to 'spread like lightning'.[30]

From this little spa on the fringe of the mountains, where the plains start, Napoleon also writes to his blonde young Empress in Vienna. Hasn't he long ago realised something's amiss? He hasn't heard a word from her since last August. But on this point, as on his hopes the Emperor of Austria will stand by him as his son-in-law, he seems to be stubbornly deluding himself. '*Ma bonne Louise,*' he writes, as always to her, in his own illegible scrawl:

'I've written to you many times. I'm sending you a man to tell you that everything's going very well. I'm adored and master of everything. All I lack is you, my good Louise, and my son. – *Nap.*'

Pons doesn't say exactly when or who this messenger is who's 'sent on a mission to her'. Can he be a certain 'distinguished officer' by name Hurault de Sorbée, whose wife, too, is with Marie-Louise? And does Marchand slip into the emissary's hand a greeting to his mother, who's nurse to Napoleon's boy? If so, he omits to tell us.

'Master of everything' is a trifle precipitate. So far no *troops* have joined. And this, as everyone realises, is the crux of the matter. Far from welcoming his old friend Pons de l'Hérault, news has just come in that Masséna has put him in prison,[31] as he also has Captain Lamouret and his grenadiers. By now Masséna (says his friend Thibaudeau) is 'very ill. He had no love for the Emperor, but he was attached to the Revolution and to France's greatness and glory.'

No doubt. But meanwhile, as Napoleon doubtless suspects, he's sitting on the fence in ultra-royalist Marseilles, where public opinion is loudly demanding action.[32]

In the other direction Drouot sends off two letters, one to Loverdo, the

other to the unit's battalion commander, inviting them to join "the brave fellows of the Imperial Guard."

There's no reply.

Though the atmosphere is still icy and Napoleon is 'always sensitive and susceptible to colds'[33] at last they're out of the mountains. From now they'll be following a broad flat plain until they join the valley of the Durance. Towards 3:30 pm, still seeming

'as rigid as an iron bar – everyone noticed it and was sure he was wearing a breastplate – Buonaparte, with the help of three or four servants, remounts his horse. A beggar who was there came to kiss his hand. From that liberal hand he received five francs and though ordered to shut up began shouting *Vive l'Empereur! Down with Napoleon!* several times over. Buonaparte crossed the public promenade, where there was a large number of persons. He addressed salutations to right and left, to which no one responded except with a gloomy silence.'

And here – at last – is another recruit. A former grenadier of the Imperial Guard.

'Jerzmanowski, informing him of the enterprise he was engaged in, tried to persuade him into the service. The soldier being told it was the Emperor who was advancing, laughed heartily, and said: "Good! I'll have something to tell them at home tonight."'

But convinced in the end, if only with some difficulty, that it's true, says: 'My mother lives three leagues from here. I must take leave of her. But I'll be with you tonight.' And sure enough in the evening, 'some time after arriving at his quarters', Jerzmanowski is

'accosted by his recruit, who tapped him on the shoulder and wouldn't be satisfied until promised the Emperor should be instantly informed that Melon the grenadier had kept his word and was with his former master.'[34]

It is at Digne that Ali notices someone has at last provided the column with an eagle:

'We hadn't any eagle when we'd landed.[35] It was only on the second or third day we acquired one. It was of gilded wood. One can only suppose it had come from some bedpost or some curtain rod. It had been put on the end of a stick. And with some bits of cloth of the three colours, nailed on, someone had made a flag.'

From Digne to Grenoble is 215 kilometres. Between them lies the important town of Gap. But before Gap comes Sisteron, where

'Masséna, if he wanted to oppose us, could open a passage for troops from Marseilles. Cambronne, with an advance guard of forty

grenadiers [according to Marchand 100] was ordered to seize its
bridge and fortress.'

While the column had been scrambling through the mountains there'd
been little order in its ranks. But now, after Digne, where the road joins the
Grenoble highway, its march order has been re-established.[36] First come the
three companies of the Chasseurs of the Old Guard, commanded by
Colonel Mallet, with the few Sailors of the Guard and the Polish Lancers,
progressively mounted. Then come the three companies of the Grenadiers,
under Captain Loubers, a highly strung character.[37] Then the gunless
gunners, the thirty or so officers without units, Napoleon himself and his
staff, and Peyrusse and the treasure, now being properly transported on
wheels. The 300 Corsican volunteers under Commandant Guasco bring up
the rear.

> 'We marched with greatest rapidity. The advance guard eight leagues
> [thirty-two kilometres] ahead, then the army [sic], then the rearguard
> two leagues behind with the treasure. The gendarmes we met with sold
> us their horses to mount our 100 [sic] lancers.'[38]

Cambronne goes on ahead. This evening of 4 March the advance guard
doesn't halt. But the rest of the column does, twenty kilometres from Digne,
at the château of Malijai.[39] For four more hours Cambronne pushes on
along the left (east) bank of the Durance, aiming for Sisteron, with its
soaring citadel perched on an immense cliff and the stone bridge it commands. What if Loverdo has already occupied the one and blown up the
other? A few volleys of grape or roundshot and all's over...

In the small hours Cambronne rounds the last bend in the road. The
bridge is intact! Loverdo has done neither. Lacking any barrels of gunpowder to blow it up or cannon to defend it, and sure anyway his 132 ex-
mutineers of the 87th can't be made to fight the veterans of the Old Guard,
he's busy evacuating the town,[40] where Eméry, after sending his friend
Valès' horse back to Digne, has already prepared lodgings. At midnight the
sub-prefect, forewarned, has gathered the commander of the local National
Guard and the mayor, the Marquis de Gombert ('the only one along our
route who'd tried to raise the commune's inhabitants, depicting Napoleon's
soldiers as brigands and incendiaries'), at the town hall. The two officials are
just expressing surprise at his orders to put the municipal funds in a place of
safety and at his insistence that 'all resistance will be futile', when, at 1:00 am,
Cambronne suddenly enters, and demands 5,000 rations for the column.
When the mayor demurs, he orders him to

> 'go out and meet the Emperor on the bridge, adding when he sees
> them hesitate, that they've nothing to discuss because if they're don't
> go willingly he'll take them there by force. The mayor, confounded by
> Cambronne's suddenly appearing armed only with his sword, changed

Napoleon in 1815. Many eyewitnesses noticed what a lot of weight he'd put on and his peculiar bronzed complexion. It wasn't the green uniform jacket with its order of the Legion of Honour, however, that electrified his supporters, but the grey overcoat and the little hat. Louis Marchand, his faithful First Valet, says none of his portraits were good likenesses, and that Napoleon himself was indifferent to them. (Courtesy of the Anne S. K. Brown Military Collection)

The harbour at Porto-Ferrajo could accommodate big warships. Under threat of a rumoured raid by the Spanish navy Napoleon had ordered his gunners to train at firing red-hot shot from the forts. When he left his little convoy was mostly made up of small lateen-rigged vessels of the type shown.

'Napoleon coming ashore in Golfe Juan, 1 March 1815', an early 19th-century engraving. In the evening of 20 March Napoleon was swept back into the Tuileries by several hundred disgruntled half-pay officers. (Courtesy of the Anne S. K. Brown Military Collection)

A rather accurate representation of the landing at Antibes, around 5 pm 1 March 1815. The two square-rigged vessels in the background are the 26-gun brig Inconstant and the cargo ship Saint Esprit. The latter had come sailing into Porto-Ferajo harbour just as the convoy was about to leave and been commandeered 'rather roughly' to join it. Napoleon himself, as always, is shown as a good deal less corpulent than all eyewitnesses agree he actually was. The staff officers with him are presumably meant to be Bertrand ('the best engineer officer in Europe') and perhaps Drouot, who'd been opposed to the 'crazy enterprise' of trying to reconquer France with some 6-800 men. The abandoned Fort Carré, whose guns Captain Gazon had just recently dismantled, is out of frame on the left.

The spot where he landed at the foot of the deserted Gabelle Fort, today part of the Antibes yacht harbour. The event is re-enacted annually on 1 March by the local authorities, who however like to represent him as wearing his famous green (chasseur) jacket. In fact, as Marchand the 1st Valet tells us, he was wearing the blue (grenadier) jacket he wore on Sundays – it had been on a Sunday he'd left Elba. (Courtesy of Granada Television)

A contemporary propaganda print of the Antibes landing. While the Fort Carré is shown correctly in the background, most details are imaginary. Napoleon didn't mount his horse till late that evening and thanks to Colonel Cuneo d'Ornano's prompt action in locking up the Antibes garrison, there were no troops on the spot to welcome him.

"An act of bounty by the Emperor" contemporary Bonapartist print. In contrast to Louis XVIII, Napoleon certainly had the common touch, or knew how to feign it. Certainly he was a superb actor in his rôle. Nor did all the women faint with terror when they heard he was back, as the royalist writer Fabry likes to make out. (Courtesy of the Anne S. K. Brown Military Collection)

Napoleon's first bivouac in France, in an olive grove between the Fort Carré and the fortifications of Antibes, whose commander and citizens stubbornly refused to open the city gates. The olive grove, according to Captain Gazon, was located more or less on the site of the present Antibes railway station. "At 1 am, moonrise, we got going" – for Cannes. (Courtesy of the Anne S. K. Brown Military Collection)

Napoleon's march through the Var, a contemporary coloured print by Friedrich Campe. Again, it is reasonably accurate, except that he was surrounded by a largish group of officers without units to command, and looked by no means so pathetic or thin as in the picture. The scene supposedly shows his column as it penetrated the mountains of the Lower Alps, along a track which, in early spring, still didn't permit the passage of wheeled traffic, making him leave his 4-pounder cannon and his carriage at Grasse. All the baggage, including the 2 million francs in gold watched over by treasurer Peyrusse, had been laden onto mules. The civilian speaking to Napoleon might be Pons de l'Hérault, whom he'd send to Toulon to chat up his friend Marshal Masséna military governor of Provence.

The house at Barrême, where he and his staff overnighted on 3 March and 'his officers encumbered the stairs'. Cambronne, commanding the advance guard, had commandeered it as the village's finest. Tasting the lentil soup the Tartanson family was preparing for its peasants, he found it 'excellent'. The house was afterwards cut in half to widen the road, and is today very dilapidated. (Courtesy of Granada Television)

The Rue Mére-de-Dieu at Digne, down which Napoleon entered the town, politely greeting ladies at their windows on either side. It's so narrow one can touch the walls on either side.

The crisis outside the village of Laffrey, when Napoleon's column first encountered a royal regiment. 'It was the most emotional moment of the encounter. The Emperor appeared to us amidst his rays of glory, untarnished in the men's eyes by any setback. More than ever, Napoleon was the idol of the army, the man of the people. All these feelings exalted minds, set hearts violently beating', writes the future Marshal Randon, then only a lieutenant, who vainly tried to get their commander Major Delessart (both omitted from the picture) to fire on him, or else retreat back to Grenoble. Napoleon went forward and said in a voice hoarse probably not very resounding on account of a bad cold, 'Here I am. Soldiers of the 5th Line, recognise me. If there's a soldier among you who wants to kill his Emperor - unbuttoning his grey overcoat - he can do so.'

Young Colonel Charles de Labédoyère, "a very good lad, a distinguished young man, who conducts himself with every sense of delicacy, has a charming cast of mind, a very nice face and figure and something noble about his physiognomy that must come from his heart." Though married into a royalist family, he was the first to take his regiment, the 7th Line, over to Napoleon outside Grenoble. After Waterloo he, like Ney, would die by firing squad.

The artillery general Antoine Drouot, a self-educated son a baker. Nicknamed by Napoleon the Sage of the Grand Army on account of his bookish habits and gloomy disposition, he'd followed the fallen emperor to Elba on one condition: that he received no pay. He'd ever afterwards reproach himself for having lost valuable hours on the morning of Waterloo by advising a delay until the ground had dried out to enable the guns to manoeuvre. Generally respected (except by his one-time subordinate Pion des Loches, who calls him 'a military Tartuffe') he would be acquitted of treason and die blind. (Courtesy of the Anne S. K. Brown Military Collection)

Cambronne, in command of the Elba Battalion of the Old Guard, was noted for his rough bad tempered ways. When Napoleon had asked him what he'd thought of his plan to make a comeback in France, Cambronne had replied that "it wasn't his business to have opinions on his Emperor's decisions." He would command the advance guard.

Colonel Saint-Chamans, of the renumbered 1st Chasseurs, was favoured by Berry, but though he tried to remain loyal to the King he was obliged to escort Napoleon into Paris in the evening of 20 March, the day he'd predicted he'd arrive.

Marshal Macdonald, who together with Ney and Lefébvre had forced Napoleon to abdicate at Fontainbleau last year, would fail to get his troops to resist him at Lyons.

The Duke of Berry, Louis XVIII's nephew and heir apparent to the Bourbon throne, was an ebullient character who imagined himself a military man and even imitated The Usurper's uniform and idiosyncrasies. But at dinner he'd bombard his ADC's splendid uniforms with (hopefully hard-boiled) eggs. (Courtesy of the Anne S. K. Brown Military Collection)

Baron E. d'A. de Vitrolles, the only livewire in the King's cabinet. After vainly trying to get the almost pathologically imperturbable Louis XVIII to raise the royalist West against the Usurper, he was given permission at the last moment to go and do so.

Joseph Fouché, Napoleon's one-time police minister. Laure d'Abrantés writes of his "mean foxy face. What an astounding face!" Oudinot's young duchess agrees: "Hair, eyebrows, complexion, eyes, all seemed to me to be exactly the same pale shade of colour." When Napoleon heard of his astuteness in evading arrest, he'd declare laughingly "he's the smartest of us all." And so he'd prove to be. "I'd like the Emperor to win the first two battles," he'd tell his friend Thibaudeau with uncanny prescience, "but lose the third."

Grenoble, evening of 7 March: 'No sooner had the Emperor had supper, than, to the sound of fanfares, the inhabitants came to deposit the debris of the Beanie Gate under the balcony of the Town Hall. Since they hadn't been able to offer the Emperor the keys of his good town of Grenoble, they said, they were bringing the gates instead. The town was spontaneously lit up.' (Courtesy of the Anne S. K. Brown Military Collection)

PROCLAMATION

DE S. E. LE MARÉCHAL NEY,

PRINCE DE LA MOSKUA.

—————————————————

A Lons-le-Saunier le 13 Mars 1815

OFFICIERS, SOUS-OFFICIERS ET SOLDATS!

La cause des Bourbons est à jamais perdue! La dynastie légitime que la Nation Française a adoptée va remonter sur le trône : c'est à L'EMPEREUR NAPOLÉON, notre Souverain, qu'il appartient seul de régner sur notre beau pays! Que la noblesse des Bourbons prenne le parti de s'expatrier encore, ou qu'elle consente à vivre au milieu de nous, que nous importe! la cause sacrée de la liberté et de notre indépendance ne souffrira plus de leur funeste influence. Ils ont voulu avilir notre gloire militaire, mais ils se sont trompés : cette gloire est le fruit de trop nobles travaux pour que nous puissions jamais en perdre le souvenir. Soldats! les temps ne sont plus où l'on gouvernait les peuples en étouffant tous leurs droits ; la Liberté triomphe enfin, et NAPOLÉON, notre auguste Empereur, va l'affermir à jamais. Que désormais cette cause si belle soit la nôtre et celle de tous les Français! Que tous les Braves que j'ai l'honneur de commander se pénètrent de cette grande vérité!

Soldats! je vous ai souvent menés à la victoire, maintenant je veux vous conduire à cette phalange immortelle que L'EMPEREUR NAPOLÉON conduit à Paris, et qui y sera sous peu de jours. Là, nos espérances et notre bonheur seront à jamais réalisés.

VIVE L'EMPEREUR!

Le Maréchal de l'Empire

Signé, Prince de LA MOSKUA.

Ney's printed proclamation, declaring that "the Bourbon cause is lost for ever" was greeted with delirious cheering. Its authorship is uncertain. Napoleon would deny having sent it to Ney, but from its style it seems almost certainly to have been dictated by him. "Ney only got what he deserved," he'd declare when he heard he'd been shot. "He should have gone back to Paris. It'd have been nobler. It wasn't Ney's business to dispose of crowns."

Ex-Queen Hortense, by Gérard. Royalists regarded her, unjustly, as at the heart of a conspiracy to bring back 'the Man of Elba'. Delighted to see him back, she would be scathingly reprimanded for accepting the title of Countess of St-Leu from Louis XVIII and trying to get wardship of her two sons from the neurotically jealous Louis Bonaparte.

Louis XVIII suffered from elephantiasis and gout. Though impressively regal, he maddened Baron de Vitrolles, his acting Secretary of State, by never taking decisions or, apparently, having any policy. Though he swore to 'die on the throne' on 16 March, three days later he fled to Belgium, followed dismally through the rain of Holy Week by his Maison du Roi (Household Troops).

"They could have spared me these emotions," Louis XVIII complained to his entourage as he fled from the Tuileries on 19 March, at midnight for fear of the Paris mob. "We didn't need daylight to illuminate this shameful flight," comments Vitrolles. (Courtesy of the Anne S. K. Brown Military Collection)

Napoleon's triumphal return, 9 p.m. 20 March. Captain Routier, one of the half-pay officers who welcomed him: 'Suddenly some very simple carriages present themselves at the waterside gate and announce the Emperor. It's beyond me to describe that moment. The grill opens, the carriages enter. We all rush to surround them.' Ali, the 2nd Valet: 'It was impossible even to move it on as far as to the pavement. Seeing he could get no further, the Emperor got out amidst the immense crowd pressing around him.' (Courtesy of the Anne S. K. Brown Military Collection)

his tune; seemed only afraid of not getting paid. Coldly, Cambronne tossed him his purse. Said: "Pay yourself!"'

When Napoleon, after passing the village of Salignac, rounds the last bend in the road and looks ahead through his spyglass, he's so relieved to see the bridge intact that he exclaims joyfully:

"*Messieurs*, we're in Paris!"

Reaching it, he dismounts and is met by the two officials:

'Placing himself between them, he entered the town chatting with them. Casting a glance at the mayor's fleur-de-lis, he asked him what it was. "It's the decoration of the lilies." And when the mayor tells him he'd been given it when he'd offered the town's homage to the King, advises him: "Take that thing off while my troops are here, they might insult you."'[41]

Asking for an inn, he's taken to the *Bras d'Or*, where he dismisses the two officials,

'telling them to come back in an hour's time and to fetch all the town's half-pay officers. There were a dozen of them. They were informed by the town's trumpeter to go to the Emperor.'

Some, it seems, do. Others not:

'However, he found five individuals devoted to his cause who joined his entourage: *viz* Barrière, a retired officer; Avisse, an old military man in charge of tobacco sales; the fortress' military engineer and his son; and a young man, formerly a drummer.'

The locals 'can't help noticing that Buonaparte's soldiers,' presumably above all the Corsicans,

'worn out and exhausted, were dragging themselves along in his wake, isolated and in no order. Everywhere they were saying Buonaparte had told them that he was only coming back by arrangement with the chief Powers, and certainly not to fight. If they'd run into the least resistance discouragement would have seized on them and then only a single shot would have sufficed to make them lay down their arms.'

Napoleon asks M. Bignon, the sub-prefect, what people are saying about his reappearing on the scene. Everyone, says Bignon, is chiefly surprised, a feeling absorbing all others.

"But will they be pleased to see me back on the throne?"

"I think so, if they weren't afraid of seeing conscription and all the other scourges return with you."

"I know there've been any amount of stupidities committed. I've come to repair everything. My people are going to be happy."

"But you'll certainly run into obstacles before getting to Paris."

"I've got troops at Gap and Corps. The Grenoble garrison's waiting for me. I've 10,000 men at Lyons. Not a drop of blood will be shed. It's all been arranged with the foreign powers.''

After dining at the *Bras d'Or* he's followed by an entranced populace who've provided even more food than they've been asked for, the Vauthier brothers – the column's two commissaries – indenting to Peyrusse for cash to pay for everything. The mayor's bill comes to 1,295 francs. 'One man came up closer than the others to Buonaparte, who, hearing he was a tipstaff of the court, said: "I'll make you a judge".' The populace offers the battalion 'a tricolour flag, made by a workman in less than an hour'. Leaving town by the narrow bridge

'over the Buech (a little rivulet that throws itself into the Durance at the foot of the citadel) Buonaparte was under extreme pressure and seemed afraid. He held out his hand to the son of a baker who was close to him, and overwhelmed him with amiabilities. Once out of his trouble, he mounted his horse and went on along the road to Gap',

and dismounts at Le Poêt, the first village. At that moment the local curé, 'who's been waiting for his little children in the church and has already three times rung the bell for them', comes out to see what's become of them. Sees first the soldiers. Then the Great Man himself, standing there in the middle of the road, between the church and the mayor's house. Sitting down on the stone ledge along the church's east end, he calls the curé over and tries to talk with him. 'But so stricken was the good curé by the sight of this ghost [*revenant*] from Elba he couldn't give any clear reply to his questions and he had to terminate the conversation.'

The populace's reception of him at Sisteron and Loverdo's failure to blow up the all-important bridge have been encouraging. Yet the crucial confrontation is approaching, and for once Fabry may well be right when he assumes Napoleon's

'not without worries. He knew he was marching on the chief town of a department at whose head was a prefect, M. Harmand [d'Abancon[42]], faithful and devoted. He hesitated as to whether he should march on toward Gap or take off to the left and throw himself into the department of the Drôme, whose prefect didn't give him such apprehensions. Both from the mayor and the curé he enquired most carefully whether there weren't any roads from Le Poêt to Valence.'

Valence is the 2nd Horse Artillery's base, where he'd once served as a newly fledged second-lieutenant. Such a deviation, however, even if feasible, presents dangers hardly less than those at Gap, and would mean leaving in his rear a fortress and a much larger – and potentially friendly – force at Grenoble. Weighing one risk against the other as he sits there with his back to the church wall, he decides to pursue his original plan, the more so as there's no short cut to Valence through the mountains. Not much further on, the column runs into a gendarme bringing a proclamation by the Gap prefect. 'Very strongly against him, it treated him as an adventurer'. Prefect Harmand's proclamation orders all mayors to sound the tocsin, arm the populace and gather them at certain indicated points: 'The gendarme, as one may imagine, was arrested and the proclamation's distribution suspended in this direction.' A bit further on they meet a defrocked priest by name Abbé Sechier. 'Buonaparte welcomed him as a most valuable agent and appointed him sub-prefect at Gap'. He only has a couple more miles to go when more encouraging news comes in. Eméry, who'd 'got there last night, been arrested and then released (as at Digne), has gone on to Grenoble.' Even so he needs all his celebrated sangfroid to conceal his anxiety, most of all perhaps from Bertrand and the even more jittery Drouot, who've never believed in the expedition anyway.

The next halt is at the village of Vitrolles. Its inn, like everything else, is the property of the local châtelain.

'Buonaparte was given a chair from the coach house with a cushion doubtless borrowed from a carter's bed. He promised some veterans from Egypt a pension of 100 crowns. Finally, coming out for a moment and holding in his hand a map of the country, he examines the surroundings, and turning toward the château says: "that must be the château of the celebrated Baron de Vitrolles we hear so much about!"'

CHAPTER 5

A THUNDERCLAP

The thirty-one-year-old *Eugène d'Arnauld de Vitrolles*, the only live wire in Louis XVIII's otherwise inept cabinet, has just come out from Sunday mass, and is sitting by the fireside in his apartment in the Tuileries, interviewing a visiting general 'on some personal matter'. For months now he has been 'trying to bring some order and system into the high direction of affairs'. At that moment

> 'we were startled out of our sleep, as it were, by a thunderclap. An usher announced M. Ciappe, fat Chappe,[1] director of the Telegraph, who wanted to speak to me at once. All out of breath and beside himself, he was clutching a sealed telegraphic despatch, addressed, as was customary, to myself.'

Does he know what's in it? No, replies Ciappe, such knowledge is restricted to the 'translator'. But from Ciappe's flustered manner Vitrolles sees he's lying. Why otherwise bring it himself, 'something that never occurred'? Can something have happened to the Duke or Duchess of Angoulême at Bordeaux, where they're celebrating the first anniversary of their landing? – 'We already knew they'd had reason to be discontented with the Poitiers garrison.' Well, Vitrolles will have to take the ominous despatch to the King.

To the most energetic of monarchs has succeeded the most slothful. Delighted to have resumed what he insists on calling his 'twenty-year reign', Louis is certainly not fond of the work involved in administering it. When one of Napoleon's hard-working aides, *Jacques-Claude Beugnot*,[2] had first brought him documents to sign and had 'attached to each report the documents supporting it' so as to be able to find them in a hurry, together with

> 'a table summarising each, its number, the nature of the business, its degree of urgency, and a list of observations, and asked him to glance down it and tell me which to start with',

Louis had observed dryly:

> 'That's very nice, monsieur. But as I'll always have all the time you ask me for, you may abandon your ways of working with Bonaparte. I don't care for them at all. Begin at the beginning.'[3]

At the next session the King had taken three-quarters of an hours to sign a score of documents with his maddeningly slow handwriting. But even that's too long. And when the Finance Minister, Abbé Louis, heard of it he'd laughed aloud:

"What! Didn't you realise the very first day you're boring him to death? What's the use of all these reports? You might as well present them to a saint in his niche. *I* don't bore him. It's he who bores me."

'All he saw in me,' Beugnot concludes, 'was a robust workman who'd served his apprenticeship under a nasty master.'

Above all Louis XVIII is averse to making decisions. Sometimes, when faced with one, his forefinger plays with his pendulous Bourbon nether lip. Vitrolles hands him the despatch:

> 'Clumsily, with his gouty[4] hands, he broke the seal. And then, doing his best to get hold of it inside its envelope, held it out to me to extract. I turned away slowly to throw that bit of paper into the fire; then, placing myself again at the table in front of the King, I waited . . . and waited . . . while he read its contents two or three times. There he sat, his eyes fastened on the paper, much longer than was necessary to read it. Then threw it onto the table.'

Does Vitrolles know what it's about?

"No, Sire, I've no idea."

In an 'apparently unchanged tone of voice' Louis says:

'What it is, it's Bonaparte, who's landed on the coast of Provence.'

Vitrolles picks up the despatch. Dated 3 March, he sees it's been forwarded from Masséna in Marseilles via Lyons – 'the telegraph in those days went no further.[5] I was more upset than the King was. And said so, with some vivacity.'

But all Louis the Imperturbable observes 'with the same calmness' is:

"This despatch must be passed on to the Minister of War. He'll see what's to be done."

Vitrolles takes a short cut through the 'château' (as it's now being called – 'palace' smacks too much of Napoleon's ever-mobile headquarters), jumps into his carriage, and orders his coachman to drive over to the left bank to the Rue de l'Université, where Soult has his magnificent residence (packed with pillaged works of art from nearly every country in Europe).

> 'It was rather a fine day. A numerous crowd was coming out of the Tuileries gardens, and the Pont Royal bridge[6] was crowded. My carriage was mounting its ramp rather more slowly than I'd have wished, when, near the parapet to my left, I caught sight of Marshal Soult, on foot, followed by one of his staff, carrying his briefcase. He was on his way to the preparatory meeting held every Sunday by the departmental heads in M. de Blacas' apartment.'

Blacas, the royal favourite, is a singularly solemn and self-important gentleman whom Vitrolles can't help teasing. Though only Master of the Royal Wardrobe he regards himself as superior to any mere minister of state. A singularly inept personage completely out of touch with the times, he spends his spare time, so Fleury de Chaboulon will find on going through his papers, 'exhuming' the files of individuals eminent or prominent since the Revolution and writing minutes and memoranda, just in case they'll have to be indicted. Another of Blacas' pastimes is inventing reactionary laws. It's been hard work. Not because anything is lacking from the files, but because Blacas finds writing difficult:

> 'Hatred of the Revolution emanated from every line. By their laborious corrections they showed how little imagination or facility he had. Often he made three or four drafts before giving his ideas any consistency or coherence. His familiar style was dry and inflated. He took extreme care to vary the formulations.'

But he too has round-the-clock access to the royal ear, and is a major nuisance to Vitrolles in all conceivable matters.

Marshal Soult – 'the best manoeuvrer in Europe' – is a big strong man in the prime of life. A dry, charmless personality lacking basic education, but an immensely hard worker, ever since January he and his friend and chief aide Brun de Villeret have been struggling to reorganise the army, a task utterly complicated by the conflicting claims of Bonapartists and émigrés.[7] Once an ardent republican, then a no less ardent imperialist, Soult's just now a no less ardent royalist,[8] and is busy raising subscriptions to erect a column in memory of the 'whites' – but not of course the 'blues' – who'd died at the inept landing in Quiberon Bay twenty years ago.

Vitrolles halts his carriage. Waving away the footmen who've opened its door, he beckons to Soult to come over:

> 'From my seat in the carriage, in the midst of the crowds of passers-by all round us, I held out the open despatch to the marshal, who stood at the door. The impression it made on him was just what it should be: above all surprise. Even incredulity.'

While Soult seems to be casting about in his mind for a reason to doubt its truth, Vitrolles passes on the King's order to take whatever measures he sees fit. Yes, says Soult. But first he must himself see the King. Vitrolles turns his carriage around on the bridge's crowded slope. Drives back to the Tuileries.

Louis XVIII may be the soul of lethargy. But he can also be surprisingly shrewd. And when Soult says it'll be a 'mere matter for the gendarmerie' to deal with Bonaparte, he tells him, on the contrary, that the outcome will "depend on the behaviour of the first regiment Bonaparte encounters." With many regiments already on the march southwards to liaise with the Austrians against Murat in Italy, Soult says, it shouldn't take very long to concentrate all available forces at Grenoble. Meanwhile, they decide to keep the landing a secret for as long as possible.

Which isn't very long – not on a fine Sunday morning in Paris.

119

Only a stone's throw from the Tuileries, on the other side of the (still building) Rue de Rivoli, the Palais Royal – residence of the Orléans branch of the royal family – is

'a vast picturesque animated noisy bazaar, offering all the most shameful passions of an advanced civilisation. Almost unenclosed and devastated [since the Revolution] most of its businesses were open day and night, where tomorrow's buzz and inebriation will be the same as yesterday's.'[9]

It's the heart and soul (if it has one) of the city. About midday,[10] the twenty-six-year-old staff-major *Théodore de Rumigny*,[11] ADC to General Gérard, is passing through this 'beehive of all the vices',

'when a man I didn't know inclined his head toward my ear and said in a low voice: "The Emperor has landed!" I stared at the man. He walked away, leaving me stupefied.'

The secret has taken less than an hour to be blown abroad! Rumigny bears the régime a grudge for not confirming his last-minute promotion to lieutenant-colonel at Fontainebleau last year. Gérard being an Orléanist, he's doubtless on his way to the Duke of Orléans' newly restored apartments. Going straight to Gérard he hears him confirm:

"It's true. But nothing more is known."

At the Tuileries, Vitrolles, pretty sure the secret's not being kept, decides to contact Artois, whose agent he is in the Council.[12] Going to the Marsan Pavilion, headquarters of the Ultras, he's so taken up with his own agitation he doesn't even notice that

'none of all the officers who ordinarily filled the big *salon de service* were there. I was just going to open the door to Monsieur's office, when an usher who'd followed me, astonished by my absence of mind, told me Monsieur wasn't at home, but at vespers. "Vespers, vespers!" I said aloud to myself, and began pacing the great hall. "How can anyone be at vespers in such circumstances? James II of England lost his kingdom for a mass. Are this lot going to lose theirs for a vespers?"'

But at last here comes Artois, 'followed by his gilded flock'. At first he tries to dissimulate by talking about the Angoulêmes at Bordeaux. But then, inviting Vitrolles into his office, says offhand: 'Oh, by the way, and the news of this landing, what do you say about it?'

'To me this "by the way" seemed rather singular. I got him to envisage all the danger threatening us and the need to face this storm with calm and dignity.'

But where's Bonaparte making for? Italy, to join up with Murat? If not, then there's not a moment to lose. Salvation, Vitrolles urges,

'"lies entirely in the first shot fired at the enemy. And for it to be fired, a prince must be there. And it's you, Monseigneur, who can best secure us the army's fidelity and revive what there is of zeal and love for the royal cause in the population." During this allocution, which I abbreviate, I was walking to and fro at Monsieur's side along the whole length of his office, without his answering me a single word.'

They stride backwards and forwards, Artois' pace becoming ever swifter, 'so much so that in the end we were almost running. My voice was certainly becoming a trifle impatient.'

"Very well," he says at last, without halting. "I think you're right and that I'll have to grease my boots."

"No, Monseigneur," Vitrolles replies, "you'll have to leave without greasing them."

He must go at once to his brother the King, formally declare his fidelity to him, and get his orders. What's more, the Duke of Orléans, the second most important personage in the kingdom, must go too, to show his solidarity with the family's senior branch. The other princes don't trust him further than they can see him. Hadn't his father triggered off the Revolution, voted for the death of Louis XVI, and called himself *Citizen Philippe-Egalité?* And isn't a large part of the army devoted to him? A marshal must also go – *Macdonald**, for instance. Or Ney. Hadn't they, with Lefèbvre, forced Bonaparte to abdicate? Certainly *they* don't want him back.

'I went back to the King at 5:00 pm and again at 8:00 pm. He didn't seem to be the least bit worried; it was Louis XVIII's passive courage. He listened and made no difficulties about agreeing to what was proposed. Angoulême would take command in the south, assembling the troops on the right bank of the Rhône. In the Franche-Comté the Duke of Berry, of brilliant valour,[13] enterprising, ardent, though sometimes lacking moderation in his ardour and intoxicating himself with his own fire, would more than anyone else be able to enthuse the regiments by his graciousness and chivalrous eloquence, and could take command of the garrisons of Lorraine and Alsace, to be assembled there. Thus supported to right and left, Artois, with such troops as were on the spot and quickly reinforced by those already set in motion to form a camp of 24,000 men at Chambéry, would march against the enemy.'

So at least Vitrolles supposes. Does he think the Chambers should be recalled? No:

'I knew how dangerous it is in principle to summon political bodies to deliberate at a moment when the royal authority is threatened. Assemblies, in such circumstances, are pitiless and try to extend their own rights and privileges rather than public liberties. Not that we weren't sure that not a single voice would be raised in favour of the exile from Elba.'

For once the King heeds Vitrolles' advice. And at 11:00 pm this Sunday evening, Orléans is

'still in the drawing room at the Palais Royal when M. de Blacas was announced. He was in my antechamber. Though he didn't wish to come in, he was asking to speak to me. I went out at once, and he said with a mysterious air and in a low voice: "The King wishes to speak to Monseigneur immediately, at once." – "I'll go and put on my uniform and present myself to the King." – "No need, " he said. "The King's asking for you as you are, and with your permission I'll take you there in my carriage." "What!" I said. "In civvies at the Tuileries! All Paris will be talking about it. What's so urgent?"'

That, Blacas replies, is something the King will tell him: "But I can tell you in advance. *Buonaparte's in France.*"

Telling his wife he'll be back in half an hour, Orléans leaves. Since 2:00 pm, Blacas says as they cross the Rue de Rivoli, there've been five despatches by the Lyons telegraph. And Bonaparte's only got a thousand or perhaps 1,400 men with him.

"Makes no odds," Orléans says. "The danger's immense."

"That's not how the King sees it, and you'll find him very calm."

"Just as well," Orléans replies. "But do try and save him from entertaining illusions."

It's the very last thing Blacas is likely to do.

"I can see this news is making a great impression on you."

"Oh! Very great," Orléans replies.

By now they're at the Tuileries. As they pass through the guard room the bodyguards 'lying on matresses on the ground, opened their eyes with amazement to see me going through it at this hour, and in civvies.' Orléans immediately realises Louis is suffering from 'a light attack of gout, which nonetheless was enough to prevent him from walking and getting out of his armchair.'

"Well, Monsieur, Buonaparte's in France."

"Yes, Sire. And it makes me very angry."

"Ah! I'd just as soon he wasn't. But since he is, we must hope this'll be a crisis that'll rid us of him."

"I hope so, Sire, but I'm afraid that once the troops contact him it'll snowball. We must be sure of only sending against him troops we can be sure will fire at him. For if there's any hesitation among the first, it'll get serious."

But Louis is certain generals Marchand, at Grenoble, and Mouton-Duvernet at Valence, will put a stop to him before he can reach Gap. Orléans is by no means so sure, least of all of the 2nd Horse Artillery at Valence, Colonel Noël's regiment, 'one-third of which consists of débris from the Imperial Guard, which won't do anything against Buonaparte and will probably join him.'[14] Louis says he hopes not, and Orléans says he admires his sangfroid. But when Louis tells him he's sending Artois to Lyons and wants him to go with him as his subordinate, Orléans jibs. Is it really so prudent to send princes against Bonaparte, but no troops? Wouldn't it be better if he assembled his forces between Lyons and Paris and made sure of their attitudes?

"'Not at all,'' the King interrupted me very dryly. "You'll be much more use with my brother, who'll give you a division or an army corps, well, something or other, as he thinks fit.'"

Surely it's not a good idea, Orléans persists, to send off all the princes of the blood – Angoulême to Nîmes, Berry to Franche-Comté, Artois to Lyons, and not keep one of them with him? For his part he'll be happy to stay. No no, says Louis obstinately, he doesn't need him. He can grease his boots and leave for Lyons, "if not exactly this evening, then tomorrow."

However, Orléans manages to convince Artois, who's just leaving, that the troops down in the south are ill-disposed toward the régime.

"Very well, then,'' says Artois. "If the troops won't go to the attack, I'll collect the National Guards. After all, I'm their colonel-in-chief. I was very well received at Grenoble, even with a lot of enthusiasm."

"That may very well be so. But have no illusions! Buonaparte with a thousand men of the Old Guard isn't going to be halted by 10,000 National Guards.'' To call them out will, anyway, be inadvisable. "Take care it doesn't give rise to jealousy in the Line units."

Orléans goes back to his palace, and there passes 'a very sad and agitated night.'

And now it's Monday morning, 6 March. Towards 9:00 am Lavalette is

'crossing the Tuileries gardens when, on the steps of the gate out to the Rue de Rivoli, I spotted M. Paul Lagarde, formerly commissioner-general of police in Italy. As we passed each other I raised my hand in salutation and went on my way under the trees to reach the waterside terrace.[15] I heard someone coming up close behind me, and was just going to turn round when these words were pronounced in a low voice: "Make no gesture, show no surprise, don't halt! The Emperor landed at Cannes on 1 March. Artois left last night to fight him.'"

Lavalette is staggered:

'I can't describe the confusion these words threw me into. I was half-choked by emotion. I walked on like a drunken man, saying over and over to myself: "Is it possible? Isn't it a dream, or the cruellest of jokes?'"

Nearing the terrace, he catches sight of Caulaincourt, formerly Master of the Horse.

'We came together. And I, word for word and in the same tone of voice, gave him the news I'd just received. But he, with his irascible character and too accustomed to seeing things from the dark side, said: "What extravagance! What! Disembark without any troops? He'll be captured, he won't get two leagues into France. He's lost. But it's impossible! However," he added, "it's true Artois left in a hurry last night."

Caulaincourt's 'bad temper and forebodings' upset Lavalette:

'They made me feel ill. I parted from him to yield myself up to all the inebriation of my own feelings. But at first I didn't find anyone in my own home to share them with. My wife was terrified by the news and deduced sad forebodings from them. I hastened to the Countess of Saint-Leu's place.'

'Weighed down by sad thoughts' about the court's decision to give her husband wardship of her children, Hortense has this morning been on her way home from a ride in the Bois de Bologne when Lord Kinnaird, one of the many English aristocrats in Paris and a notable art connoisseur, had come riding up to her carriage:

"Has Your Majesty heard the big news? The Emperor Napoleon has landed at Cannes."

'I turned stiff with amazement. He told me he'd just come from the Duke of Orléans, who was ready to go to Lyons. That Artois was already on his way there. And that the greatest emotional commotion prevailed at court.'

Her first thoughts are for her boys. Does Kinnaird think she need worry on their account? No, "but of course it's always possible the Bourbons might want to take them as hostages."

Poor Hortense, she who's so sensitive that Napoleon had once 'feared for her sanity', who loves the arts and hates politics – in which, she assures us, she never gets involved. She's panic-stricken. And Kinnaird himself seems so anxious regarding what a popular rising in Napoleon's favour may mean in the way of danger to foreigners in Paris that she offers him refuge in her house on the Rue Cerutti – 'after all he was an Englishman. For my part I knew I'd nothing to fear from the populace'.

She drives home, where Lavalette finds her 'bursting into tears of joy and emotion. After the first reaction, we began to consider the immense distance between Cannes and Paris. "How will the generals in command of the troops along this route act? The authorities? The troops? What will be the effect of Artois getting there?" It seemed to us nothing could resist the Emperor, and that once he'd got to Lyons all further obstacles would be impossible.'

Hortense sends her two boys with Mlle. *Cochelet*, their governess, out to Saint-Leu.

But the Council has overruled Vitrolles on one point. Assembled this same morning, it has decided that the Chambers, prorogued until May, shall be immediately reconvoked.

As for Orléans, though far from keen on the prospect of having to go and fight the invincible Bonaparte, he has assembled his six ADCs, and at 11:00 am reports back to the Tuileries, where he – though by no means sure of Artois' military prowess – declares himself ready to leave for Lyons. If Vitrolles can't stand Abbé Montesquiou, the prime minister, and loathes Blacas, he likes Orléans not the least bit more:

'At the moment when the doors were thrown open to admit him, he detained me by his deep bowings, so profound no one could return their like. "But, M. de Vitrolles," he said in a voice of deep emotion, "tell me, I beg you ... are we going to leave *alone* ... with Monsieur?"'

Vitrolles 'isn't in the habit of counterfeiting' his facial expressions, but evidently they betray his astonishment:

"But no, Monseigneur the Marshal Macdonald should be on his way at this moment to take command under Monsieur's orders."

'At these words, the Duke of Orléans grasped my hand and squeezed it. "Ah!" he exclaimed. "You give me back my life." He went into the office, leaving me stupefied. "There's one," I said to myself, "who hasn't much confidence in himself, and I don't know how much we should have in him."'

Orléans – his memoirs don't even mention the officious Vitrolles – goes in to the King, who asks at once:

"Well, and your boots are greased?"

"Always," comes the reply, "when it's a question of serving Your Majesty." Told to depart as soon as ever he can, Orléans reiterates his doubts. To send him to Lyons is both useless and injudicious. 'My observations on the King's need to keep one of the princes by his side had no greater success, Berry's departure for Besançon having already first been put off, then countermanded.'

At 11:00 pm he and his ADCs leave for Lyons.

This evening more carriages are drawing up in the Rue Cerutti as more guests than normal are turning up at Hortense's usual weekly reception:

'I pretended not to know anything. Everyone followed my example. And not one word was said about what had happened. Yet next day a rumour spread all over Paris that my salon had rung with congratulations, and that songs had been sung in the Emperor's honour.

Even the name of the songs' author was known, a M. Etienne, a gentleman I'd never seen in my life'.

At first it seems to Hortense that Parisians are taking the extraordinary news as light-headedly as they take everything else, almost as a joke. Just as they'd taken their city's occupation by the Russians, Prussians, British and Austrians last year.

It's an age of multiple infidelities and desperate love affairs. The Swiss writer *Benjamin Constant*, the most lucid of the age, has at last made up his mind to escape from the silken clutches of Juliette Récamier, by general acknowledgement France's most beautiful woman whose return to Paris last autumn had been regarded as marking the resumption of the capital's normal life. Hardly was she back than she'd had a letter from Naples. Her friend Caroline Bonaparte, Murat's queen, begged her to find them 'a pen' that could defend their shaky throne in Vienna, where its continued occupancy by Napoleon's brother-in-law, though legitimately a perquisite of the Bourbons, is felt to be a last foul blotch on the map of Europe. Juliette had bethought herself of Benjamin Constant. He'd come to Juliette's house in the Rue Basse-du-Rempart (the one from whose first-floor window Mme. de Boigne had witnessed Louis XVIII's return last year). Had seen. And been conquered, like so many others. Lucien Bonaparte and, latterly, the Duke of Wellington among them.

Constant scribbles in his private diary:

'6 [March]: Arrangements to leave. – Unexpected news. Can it be true Buonaparte's in France? As a consequence my departure delayed, yet very little. In the morning conversation with Mme. de St[aël]. She touched me, and I felt that, angry though I am, I didn't really hate her. Dined at Mme. de Rumford's [the American ambassador's wife]. Evening with Juliette. Nothing to be done there in the way of love, and as friendship it's hardly worth the candle with so dry a soul.'

Now it's Tuesday,

'7 March: News confirmed. Will the government make approaches to us [liberals] at last? What's certain, I'll no longer be an unwanted [*désavoué*] volunteer. Dined with Mme. de St[aël]. She's all upside down. I'm afraid her being paid [the two million francs she is owed[16]] may not suffer as a result of this.'

He finds 'there's a lot more Bonapartist joy than I'd have thought possible'. But this morning, like other Parisians opening their copies of the official newspaper *Le Moniteur*, he reads:

'Napoleon Bonaparte is declared a traitor and a rebel for entering the department of the Var by force of arms. It is incumbent upon all governors, commandants of the armed forces, National Guards, civil authorities, and even

private persons, to hound him down [courir sus, *literally to 'run at', a med-*
iaeval term used for dangerous common criminals], *arrest him, and immedi-*
ately bring him before a council of war which, after confirming his identity, will
impose on him the penalties of the law.'

Anyone, be he merely a 'simple citizen', who '*after eight days from this pub-*
lication of the decree aids or abets the said Bonaparte exposes himself to the same
penalty,' *ie* the guillotine or the firing squad. The whole 'given at the château
of the Tuileries, 6 March, 1815, in the twentieth year of our reign.'

Few if any responsible persons, it seems, want the Tyrant back. Certainly
not Soult, who next day fulminates in the *Moniteur*.

'This man, Bonaparte, who abdicated a power he had usurped and put
to such fatal uses, has landed on French soil, on which he should never
again have set eyes. What does he want? Civil war. What is he looking
for? Traitors! Will he find them among the soldiers he has so many
times deceived and sacrificed, [but who are now] in the bosom of
families which his name still fills with terror? This man, as his latest
demented action at last reveals, is nothing more than an adventurer.'

After despatching a column under General Miollis to Sisteron to take him in
the rear, Masséna writes from Marseilles:[17]

'Bonaparte's in the mousetrap. It'll be the end of his crazy enterprise.'

Old Marshal Jourdan declares him 'a public enemy.' And General Maison*,[18] once declared by Napoleon to be 'worth two marshals' and now the
Paris military governor, points out that it had been Bonaparte who, as a
result of the Treaty of Paris, has finally lost Belgium, Holland and the Var,[19]

'all conquered by French valour before he was even heard of in our
ranks. He even laid France and the capital itself open to the foreigner.
Not one of us but feels animated by the greatest indignation against
him.'

Sentiments shared no doubt by the father of Napoleon's *officier d'ordonnance*
Captain Raoul, who's 'never forgiven Napoleon for not having fought with
the Army of the Sambre and Meuse.' And at Nancy, Lieutenant-General
Pacthod – commanding the ex-Chasseurs of the Imperial Guard – declares
he 'regards Napoleon's landing as an act of madness' and, assembling his
officers, reads out Soult's proclamation which, so he assures Soult, has

'the greatest effect on them. Each sees in it the line of conduct he must
follow, and is penetrated with the indignation every Frenchman
should feel for the man whose project, at once atrocious and insensate,
of carrying civil war into our beautiful country must render him odious
to any being gifted with reason.'

What does the rest of the capital, 'France's opinion-factory', think? Not
always out at her château at Charenton, *Mme. de Staël* is also occupying the
ground floor of the Hôtel Lamoignon, a large private mansion in the Rue de

Grenelle. Occupant of the first floor is Napoleon's devoted ex-Postmaster. One of Lavalette's reasons for lying low is that hidden under the floorboards of his country house, stashed away in what look like quarto books and which have survived the unsuspecting Prussian officers who'd been billeted there last year, are 80,000 gold francs Napoleon had confided to him on the eve of the Russian campaign.

'The day after the Emperor's landing had become known, Mme. de Staël invited me to come down to her. As I entered her drawing room she came up to me, her arms crossed on her bosom, and in a feelingful but loud voice exclaimed: "There you are, you see, monsieur, he's back!" – "He's not here yet. It's a long way, and I'm afraid the obstacles..." – "He'll be here. He'll be here in a few days. I've no illusions on that score. Oh, my God! There's freedom gone for good! Poor France! After so many sufferings, despite all the ardent, unanimous wishes... Since his despotism's going to triumph I'm leaving this country, and [pointing pathetically to her daughter Albertine, newly engaged to the 'stiffly unattractive' Victor de Broglie, scion of one of France's bluest-blooded families] leaving it for ever, no doubt.'

What does Lavalette think will become of her? Or of those two million francs her father, Necker the banker, had once lent the Republic? She needs them so urgently as Albertine's dowry. Gone for good!

Lavalette: 'You've nothing to fear from the Emperor. Misfortune and public opinion will have great influence on him...'

But again she interrupts, deploring the Bourbons' extraordinary failure to take her good advice, or even receive her at the Tuileries. Then, looking him in the face:

"I don't want to penetrate into your secrets, M. de Lavalette, nor know what part you've played in this scheme. But I'm counting on you that I shan't be ill treated. The persecutions may start even before he gets here, because all this seems to me to be so well prepared..."

And indeed everyone – except the Bonapartists themselves, who know better – is quite sure the Man from Elba's return is all part of a widespread Bonapartist conspiracy, hingeing on Hortense. Mme. de Staël offers Lavalette a quid pro quo: "If I hear of anyone wanting to maltreat *you*, you'll find my doors open at all hours, with means for you to escape by the garden."

Meanwhile Constant, against all his friends' advice, has spent the day penning a fiery press article inveighing against

'this Attila, this Genghis Khan ... this fallen tyrant who's trying to seize the sceptre again ... this enemy of mankind who after enticing the nation's elite to the end of the world, abandoned it to the horrors of famine and icy rigours. Today, coming back poor and greedy to snatch from us all we have left, his appearance is a renewal of all our

misfortunes. And for Europe a signal for war. No nation can depend
on his word. If he rules, not one of them can remain at peace with us.'
Rounding it off with a little flourish on his own behalf, the Bourbons, he
writes, had

> 'thought to find one nation, but found nothing but a herd of perjured
> slaves. Such will not be my language. I've sought liberty in various
> shapes. I've seen it's possible under a monarchy. I've seen the King
> rally to the nation. I'm not going to be a miserable turncoat and crawl
> from one power to another,'

– so neither must the 'warriors who for twenty-five years have covered France
with boundless glory'. This same evening, after a 'brief visit to Juliette' who's
been 'very cold' to him, Constant too comes to Mme. de Staël's; only to be
preached 'another political sermon'. At the same time his keen eye for
ambiguities notes that the Bonapartists, paradoxically, won't be all that
upset if their hopes of a military revolt are nipped in the bud.

Nor will Fouché. Not behindhand, of course, in hearing the news, he has
instantly tumbled to the situation's various possibilities. If Bonaparte's
captured, he calculates, the immense flurry will be optimal to the success of
the generals' plot. At least it can hatch a new government, headed of course
by himself. If not, and in the unlikely event of Bonaparte's reappearing in
Paris, then he, Fouché, his former and incomparably efficient Police Minister, will be able to claim to have facilitated His Majesty's happy return.
(There are of course other possibilities, all exploitable should they arise.)
But the moment has certainly come to act. And, before the elder Lallemand,
who happens to be in Paris, even has time to hear the news, he sends him off
to d'Erlon at Lille, with the agreed signal.

Officialdom may have shrugged off Bonaparte's landing as a 'mad enterprise', but everyone who is anyone becomes worried. The Bonapartists are
terrified of a Bourbon purge. And Hortense (as she'll claim afterwards) is
above all worried for the royal family, 'whom I feared would be the first
victims of popular vengeance'. Flahaut and Caulaincourt come and visit her,
and are no less

> 'amazed and worried. We were so used to seeing the Emperor succeed,
> we relied so on his capacities, that in our mind's eye we already saw
> him as having carried out his project. But what would happen then?
> What would be the outcome if he thought he'd found the nation in the
> same state as he'd left it?'

Another visitor to the Rue Cerutti is Ney's wife Aglaé. Like her fiery-tem-
pered husband, this daughter of one of Marie-Antoinette's chamber-
maids,[20] now Princess of the Moscova, has every reason to feel resentful

towards the régime. At her first appearance at the royal court the Duchess of Angoulême had kissed her on the cheek and welcomed her with a patronising: "Ah yes, our dear little Aglaé!" On at least one occasion she'd come home in tears after a courtly snub – so that Lavalette, walking one day in the Tuileries gardens, had heard Ney burst out into a furious tirade:

"You're lucky to be set aside and far from this mess! How happy you must be not to have to suffer either insults or injustices! This lot don't understand the first thing about anything. Don't they know what a Marshal Ney goes for? Or are we going to have to teach them?"

Deeply upset, Aglaé tells Hortense that Ney's been ordered to his headquarters at Besançon

'to assemble troops and march against the Emperor. She was in despair and burst out passionately against "this wretched landing". She knew her husband, how he was always spoiling for a fight. Not for a moment did she doubt that the Emperor would fall victim to his foolhardy scheme.'

For her part Hortense doesn't for a moment doubt Napoleon will succeed. Her only private hope in the event of him doing so is that she'll be allowed to retain wardship of her boys. 'Irritated by these expressions, I put it to her that she and her husband perhaps misunderstood the spirit of the army and the nation's ability to think.' From this Aglaé assumes Hortense is secretly hoping for Napoleon's success,

'and she reminded me of all we'd suffered during the Emperor's everlasting wars, and how I'd always loved and longed for peace. I interrupted her: "This isn't a matter either of hopings or wishings. I'm as amazed as you are at the sudden turn things have taken, but I'm sure the Emperor will succeed."'

Aglaé also knows quite a few of Ney's younger officers of course – the 'exalted feelings', for instance, of Labédoyère.[21]

Now Fouché, Hortense's next-door neighbour, has himself announced. They've never been friends – he'd had altogether too much to do with Napoleon divorcing her mother. But Hortense realises that 'in critical circumstances all advice is good, particularly if it comes from someone who'd so long been at home in the political mazes.' So she admits him.

First and foremost, he says, he's afraid he'll be arrested, and she, suspected as she is of having corresponded with Elba, is in no less danger. Should an attempt be made to lay hands on him, can he have her permission to flee via her garden? But of course. Hortense lends him a key into the little door out into the Rue Taitbout. But that isn't his whole mission. Her brother Prince Eugène, everyone knows, is on intimate terms with the Tsar in Vienna. Because of their 'innumerable mistakes' the Bourbons' cause (which the Tsar has never cared for anyway) is hopelessly lost:

'Even if perhaps we must reckon with a brief civil war, the Emperor will easily gain his ends – perhaps too easily, so we shan't be able to impose certain terms for again placing power in his hands. For he can't be the same emperor as before. Most urgent of all is to know the attitude of the foreign powers.' Won't she contact the Russian ambassador, Boutiajin, and fetch Eugène back to Paris? Hortense contacts the Tsar's ambassador, who asks her to make him a memorandum of Fouché's ideas, which 'without even making a copy' he sends off to his master.

So he, Fouché, has taken his dispositions. If Bonaparte brings off his hair-brained project, well and good. Lefèbvre-Desnouëttes will meet him at Fontainebleau, and it will seem he, Fouché, has backed it up. If it fails, so probably will the insurrection. And he'll have already denounced Lefèbvre-Desnouëttes to the government. He'll have demonstrated, to either government, his unique qualifications to be a minister of state.

As usual, he has placed his bets not merely both ways, but in all possible ways. Heads or tails, Fouché wins.

As for Ney, for weeks now he's been out on his estate at Coudreaux, more and more convinced it's time for him to retire.

He has diffuse political notions which add up to a passionate loyalty to France, and to the army. His ADC *Octave Levavasseur* sees him above all as
'a patriot, in the true sense of the word. A soldier of the Revolution, since the monarchy's abolition he'd only seen his fatherland and his country. In his eyes, who headed the government was a secondary matter. Always he served France. The voice of France was his only oracle. He obeyed it like a slave.'
Whenever Levavasseur has got steamed up about the new régime's whole-sale
'manufacture of generals and improvised colonels who'd sat comfortably by their firesides while we've been suffering cold and hunger and spilling our blood, and who're daily replacing old officers in the finest commands,'
Ney, 'without contesting these ideas, had remained silent' at the thought of 'so much glory being wiped out by the stroke of a pen'. Certainly it has pained this man 'whose education had been exclusively military'. But what to think or, above all, do about it is beyond him. As for Napoleon ever coming back, young Levavasseur's only had to moot the idea for his marshal to declare hotly:
'The Emperor *can't* come back! He has abdicated. And if he were to land, it'd be every Frenchman's duty to fight him.'
And now he has! Clearly Ney – basically at a loss in civil or political situations, but 'of all the marshals the one who most possesses the army's

131

confidence' – is the man to deal with him. At 6:00 pm on 6 March Levavasseur and he have just been sitting down to dinner when

'one of the War Minister's ADCs arrives bringing the marshal orders to
go immediately to his command area. Like himself, he tells us, a great
many other ADCs have left in all directions. Though what's afoot he
hasn't the faintest idea. He'd left Paris on the 5th, having come out
from a ball.'

Finishing his dinner, Levavasseur leaves with Soult's ADC for Paris. Neither
of them can make head or tail of their 'mysterious orders'. They get there at
6:00 am and Levavasseur's just passing the bronze column in the Place
Vendôme, when he bumps into 'a comrade, who told me the Emperor had
landed!' Hurrying to the Rue Saint Dominique, he tells Soult that Ney will
'soon be at the King's orders'. And only an hour later Ney in fact arrives at
his town house, embracing on its doorstep his new-born son in the arms of
his nurse. It's then he hears the dramatic news from his lawyer, a M. Batardy,
who advises him to see the King. Soult tries to prevent it, saying the King isn't
well. What's worse, he refuses to give him any instructions. He'll 'get them at
Besançon'. But Ney, fancying he 'sees in the consternation of Paris an index
of the repugnance inspired by Bonaparte', insists. Collects his uniforms and
other military belongings. And goes straight to the Tuileries, where, at 11:00
am, he's immediately received.

Does he really burst out that he'll 'bring back Bonaparte in an iron cage'?
And when he's gone does Louis quip: 'I didn't ask him to bring me such a
dicky bird'? Or does Ney only say that 'he deserves to be put in one'? Witnesses will afterwards vary.[22]

For Ney, like many a redhead, is also in high degree a hothead. Often and
often, says Levavasseur, his secretary has saved him from his impetuosity
getting him into trouble, by cooling the tone of many a missive to Napoleon.
Alas, Secretary Cassaing has just left his employment.

Next day, breathing fire and slaughter against the Man from Elba, he
leaves for Besançon, some thirty-six hours away, 'with the firm determination to fight the Emperor, whom he still supposed to be rejected by public
opinion.'

So much for the east. But what about Macdonald? After participating in the
anniversary celebrations at Toulouse he's believed to be on his estate at
Bourges. The effective military man behind the princes who're already en
route for Lyons, Vitrolles has sent him a courier, ordering him – also without
any explanation given – to make tracks for Nîmes, which lies in the heart of
passionately Catholic-royalist Provence.

Summoning the ambassadors of the foreign powers to the Tuileries, Louis
tells them: 'Gentlemen, I ask you to report to your courts that you have seen

I'm not in the least uneasy. I'm sure this will no more alter the tranquillity of Europe than of my soul.'

Sometimes it seems to Vitrolles nothing can.

CHAPTER 6
'IF ANY OF YOU WANTS TO KILL HIS EMPEROR...'

'In the departments of the 7th Military Division,' Colonel *Charles Jubé* of its gendarmerie at Grenoble is glad to report,

'everything was as calm as could be. Everywhere order reigned. Taxes were coming in without difficulty. Deserters were being pursued energetically and we were arresting great numbers of them. Few crimes were being committed. At long last everything seemed to promise a durable peace for a France so-long agitated. True, the new proprietors of nationalised property, intimidated by writings that were circulating, were trembling at the thought of the feudal régime being restored. Commerce was still timid, and people were worried about the outcome of the Vienna Congress.'

For the officers of the garrison of this fortified city of 50,000 inhabitants the winter has 'passed most agreeably'. Lieutenant-Colonel Guiraud, too, second-in-command of the 2nd Engineer Regiment – he who'd been so coldly embraced by Artois – has been among the guests at 'the many *soirées dansantes* given by the town's pleasure-loving nobility, to which they hadn't failed to invite us.' But now, this Saturday 4 March, at about 7:00 pm, Jubé and his wife are quietly if not happily (they're mourning the death of their only son) having dinner, when a summons comes from the prefecture. Going there, Jubé's ordered by Prefect Fourier – an eminent mathematician who'd been with Bonaparte in Egypt and has held this post since 1801 – to arrest an individual whose correspondence, intercepted by the Black Chamber, has shown him to be conspiring against the state's security. Well yes, Jubé says, he can do that, if it's all kept strictly hush-hush. And goes back to his dinner. Hardly has he fixed his bib round his neck than here comes a second, more urgent summons.

This time Fourier isn't alone. With him are other officials, notable among them Grenoble's military governor, Lieutenant-General Count J.G. Marchand*. 'A gentleman of the *Ancien Régime*, elegant and chivalrous, the very type of the benevolent gentleman,' Guiraud has seen him 'perfectly doing the honours of his position'. What's the matter? Without a word he hands Jubé an open letter dated '2 March at Fréjus, in the evening' announcing that Napoleon, with between 1,000 and 1,200 men of his Old Guard, has landed, and is marching on Lyons via Grasse, Castellane, Digne, Gap and Grenoble.

What to do? Much water has flowed under the town bridge since Marchand had been elected captain of the 4th battalion of the Isère Volunteers and gone out to fight for the Revolution. Today, a Grand Eagle of the Legion of Honour and Count of the Empire, he has an income of 80,000 *livres* to look after; and, like so many other top brass, has been in a hurry to transfer his loyalty to the Bourbons, which has 'lost him the sympathy of the troops'. To Jubé he seems utterly at a loss:

'Knowing the roads, I assured them Bonaparte couldn't possibly have any guns with him. And that the promptest way to hold him up would be to move on Sisteron and seize the bridge over the Durance. But since that place didn't lie inside the 7th Military Division, my observation enjoyed no success.'

Marchand's own conviction is that the troops mustn't be allowed to have the least contact with Bonaparte. 'So strongly did he feel this,' his nineteen-year-old nephew and ADC Captain *Randon*[1] sees,

'that he'd have liked to evacuate all his troops, and most of the matériel, from Grenoble and retire toward Fort Barrault and Chambéry. He was sure the best way of keeping the men faithful to the royal government was to keep them away from the neighbourhood and presence of the Emperor. This opinion, though the wisest of all, was doubtless regarded as due to timidity. Some perhaps even cried treason.'[2]

Neither now nor later does Jubé get any orders from Marchand. But other letters from his police colleagues at Valence and elsewhere soon confirm the alarming news – one even assures him Bonaparte has from four to six guns with him. Others just ask for instructions. Assembling his officers (at least one of whom, a Captain Paris, is a surreptitious Bonapartist), he reminds them of their loyalties and duties. As for the town and the garrison, neither of which know anything as yet, they're to keep the sharpest possible eye on their attitudes.

But this same Saturday evening Guiraud (presumably keeping his hat on to hide his fractured skull), is one of many music-lovers attending a concert given by

'the famous violin virtuoso M. Mazas. Suddenly a whisper spreads through the hall. People murmur in each other's ears. Stifled exclamations are heard. Each of us tries to make a secret of what in a few moments has become common knowledge.'

Not waiting to hear more trills, cadenzas or arpeggii, Guiraud and his colleagues hurry to Marchand's office, only to find the conference is already over. They're to come back in the morning.

It's Sunday, 5 March. Gap, only sixty miles away, lies in a wide plain between distant mountains. Its prefect, after issuing his energetic but futile orders against 'the adventurer' and trying to put the town in a state of defence, has had to flee. And entering the town Ali's glad to see

'a little more enthusiasm on the part of the population. A few military men came out from their homes to augment our little army slightly. Which was always something.'

Napoleon himself sees it all (or anyway will remember it) in rosier, perhaps exaggerated, colours:

'I spoke with everyone, as if at a minor reception in the Tuileries. The peasants were overjoyed, saying of the nobles "They want to harness us to their carts", they pulled out five-franc pieces and shouted: "It's him, it really is!" Everything assured us that the common people and troops were for us, and that the Bourbons were detested'

even to a frightening degree. Naturally the countryfolk's rapturous reception is gratifying – the peasantry, after all, makes up over 90% of France's population. But if there's one thing he hates and fears it's mobs, and he has no desire at all to 'become a king of a jacquerie'. But if Grenoble is to be Antibes all over again, then it's all over with his 'crazy enterprise'. Fortunately the signs aren't pointing that way. At Antibes they'd been in the deep Catholic south. Here in the Dauphiné the popular mood is all for him, and can hardly fail to affect the military. And here comes an officer by name Regnault, who has deserted from Grenoble, saying 'the troops were divided, and no one knew what to do'. Which, however, isn't enough to reassure Bertrand.

Napoleon commandeers all the carts and carriages in town. Peyrusse pays out 1,400 francs for a *calèche*, roomier than the *coupé* he's been travelling in since Digne. And the night is spent at Gap.

Grenoble's fortifications, says Colonel Noël[3],

'though not up to standing a long siege, do permit a certain resistance. The lower part of the town is regularly fortified with bastions in the shape of orillons[4] with half-moons, except for the two right-hand fronts, which aren't covered at all. Nor is this part of the fortress terraced and has neither counterscarps nor a glacis. The ditches can be filled at will with water. The right bank, up to the summit of the mountain dominating the town, is covered by an old stone entrenchment, neither terraced nor with banquettes.[5] On this summit is a kind of fort called the Bastille. But the eastern part is weak and can easily be enfiladed and destroyed. The place is armed with sixty-three cannon.'

If properly served, these are certainly able to nullify the efforts of a small force without artillery. Marchand's first measure has been to order the guns to be hauled out onto the ramparts, certain faulty embrasures to be hastily repaired, and a wooden palisade to be erected outside the suburbs on the left bank of the Isère, the side from which Napoleon is approaching. At the same time he has sent off an urgent despatch-rider to Brigadier-General Devilliers, in command at Chambéry, a day's march away through the mountains (where Labédoyère has at last arrived to take over the 7th Line which comprises so many veterans from his former 112th). If ten days have gone by and he still hasn't sworn his colonel's oath of fidelity to Louis XVIII, either it's because his new duties haven't given him time to, or, more probably, because he's loth to. Did he, at Hortense's place, before leaving Paris, really tell Flahaut he'd 'come over' to Napoleon, and has Flahaut really 'sent word' to him to that effect? Napoleon certainly knows more about the regiments' dispositions than Fleury de Chaboulon has supposed; and perhaps (as he'll afterwards claim) has been 'asking about the where-abouts of the 7th'.[6] Anyway, at Chambéry, out of the blue, Devilliers – on receipt of Marchand's despatch – has immediately sent for Labédoyère and ordered him to march his regiment to Grenoble.

"May I ask why?"

"Bonaparte has landed in the south."

Though Labédoyère has heard rumours to that effect, he refuses to believe it. "The whole thing's a mystification," he declares, over and over again, perhaps half-hoping it is, half that it isn't. But of course carries out his order, so that next day 'toward 11:00 am' Jubé sees

'the 7th and 11th Line regiments arrive from Chambéry and draw up in the Place Grenette. The general [Marchand] presented himself there, harangued these troops, had copies of his order of the day of 5 March distributed to them. They took them, but said they wouldn't fight [so loud that] the general himself must have heard it.'

Jubé 'studies this new unit's mood,' and, like his gendarmes, realises that townsfolk and garrison are

'in perfect agreement. The cafés, the bars were packed. Each citizen took one or two soldiers aside, some more, some less, and were standing them drinks. The 7th Regiment was there almost in its entirety, by whose orders I don't know. Whole companies had been placed out at intervals along the ramparts. The townsfolk were bringing them something to drink and eat. The Béaune Gate, the one the Emperor would arrive by, was open. No one had shut the others. Nothing could be better proof that everything was disposed and pre-pared to give the Emperor a warm welcome.'

Yet everything's quiet – or would be if the comings and goings of Jubé's mounted policemen weren't 'beginning to worry people'. Notified that Émery's in town, Jubé orders his gendarmes to find him. Perhaps the squad detailed off is commanded by his Captain Paris and doesn't search glovemaker Dumoulin's house too thoroughly? In the morning Jubé hears that General Mouton-Duvernet,[7] governor at Valence, has passed through last night in the mail coach, en route for Gap.

But at Marchand's headquarters everything's at sixes and sevens. Prefect Fourier keeps sending Jubé orders to provide his carriage with an escort of gendarmes in case he has to leave town 'on urgent business elsewhere'. And Marchand has invited all superior officers to the castle to sound out their attitudes. Naturally there's only one topic of conversation. Everyone condemns the Man from Elba for his foolhardy enterprise. Most declare their loyalty to the Bourbons. Only a few beat about the bush. Some, like Lieutenant-Colonel Guiraud, definitely harbour ambivalent feelings about Great Men, and privately

> 'thank Heaven for so rarely giving the earth beings so superior to human nature as not to identify themselves with it. Placed at a peak of intelligence, they plunge beyond the limits set by the Eternal One and although they're the amazement of the world, are too often the scourge of nations.'

Only Marchand's nephew Captain Randon argues eloquently that a single round of grapeshot will suffice to put paid to the whole drama. And offers to fire it. As for Labédoyère, everyone notices his silence. Does no one smell a rat? Hasn't the War Ministry privily notified Marchand of his politics? It seems not. And hasn't Labédoyère just married into an impeccably royalist family and received his regiment entirely thanks to his brother-in-law's intervention? Hasn't he just spent a few days with Governor Damas at Lyons? His fellow-colonel Durand of the 11th Line, who has a regicide father-in-law, by name Réal, invites Labédoyère there to a private dinner:

> 'Taking Durand aside after dinner into a window niche, he tells him he's resolved to go and meet Bonaparte. Durand, horrified, makes vain attempts to dissuade him. Afraid his plans may get known, Labédoyère immediately goes out and assembles his regiment.'

Meanwhile Marchand, inspecting his map, has noticed that just on the far side of the small market town of Lamure the Gap road passes over a wooden bridge, 200 feet (sixty metres) above a torrent and known in fact as *La Haut Pont*, The High Bridge. Hoping at least to gain time, or even deflect the enemy's thrust from Grenoble ('if time could be gained, perhaps the hurricane would take another direction,' General Marchand has thought), he decides to send forward a party of pioneers equipped with barrels of gunpowder, and protect them by a battalion of the 5th Line under its reliable Major Delessart. Having blown up the Haut Pont, Delessart is to retire again to Grenoble. Jubé, hearing of the plan, is sceptical.[8] 'It was too late.'

Doubtless somewhat reassured by the attitudes of the Gap populace, Napoleon, as his newly bought cabriolet – already 'so covered in dust you couldn't see what colour it was' – rolls on along the winding hillside road, is certainly aware that the crisis is approaching. 'All day', says the valet Louis Marchand – and Ali sees it too – 'the Emperor was very tired and had a cold'.[9]

Everything now depends on how well or ill Governor Marchand has his troops in hand. The die is well and truly cast; and Masséna will almost certainly have sent a column forward from Toulon to Sisteron[10] to cut off his retreat – of which anyway, deep in the interior of France as he is, there can be no question. As the cabriolet and its trotting horses carry him onward, with an immense wide valley rising to more mountains to his left, he certainly has other things to think about than the beauty of the landscape.[11] Doubtless his fatalistic streak, combined with his shrewd assessment of the probabilities, is calming his apprehensions as he reaches the next overnight halt at the little hillside town of Corps.[12]

Pushing on with his chasseurs and his forty Poles, Cambronne must have spotted the Pont Haut on his map as a possible obstacle; and may even have feared an attempt to blow it up. Is this why he has outmarched Major Delessart's battalion? Crossing the gorge, with its 200-foot vertical rock walls, his advance guard enters La Mure, a small market town with a single long, sloping main street, a couple of miles further on.

In Grenoble, meanwhile, General Marchand is certainly nervous for the outcome. Anxious to know what's become of his expedition, he sends Randon – who, young as he is, is obviously an exceptionally good horseman and has an unusually swift horse – to find out. On some high ground just outside La Mure, known as La Pontine, Delessart tells him its townsfolk absolutely don't want their bridge to be blown up, and have intervened. Faced with such massive popular resistance, he's felt it wiser to withdraw to this spot, within sight of the town, where he's nevertheless planning to billet his men for the night, and has sent forward his quartermaster to see the mayor about it.

Meanwhile Cambronne's quartermaster Captain Laborde, too, has gone to the town hall, for the same purpose. And the two men bump into each other. As it happens, they're old acquaintances.

"I see we're wearing different cockades," says Laborde. "But tell me with a soldier's frankness. Are we friends or enemies?"

"Two former comrades in arms will always be friends," says the other, evasively. But holds out his hand.

"Then let's do our billeting together."

But of course this is no moment for frankness. And the friend slips away, reports back to Delessart. As Laborde does to Cambronne, who's at his dinner: just then a peasant comes and tells him some of Delessart's men are making for the bridge in the dark, probably to blow it up. Leaving his soup to get cold, Cambronne sends Captain Raoul back to the High Bridge at top speed, telling him to secure it. And then, to protect his small advance guard against being taken by surprise or circumvented – quite a small nocturnal party of the miners' company with a barrel or two of gunpowder will be quite enough to blow the bridge up and cut him off from the main column – Raoul is sent galloping back to Corps to tell the Emperor what's going on, and warn him that the 5th Line may well be as firmly in the hands of its officers as the Antibes garrison had been. Then, ordering his men to form a *grand'garde* outside the town's northern entrance,[13] he sends forward an officer, inviting Delessart to a parley. Delessart refuses. And upon Cambronne himself riding forward, an officer commanding a small outpost shouts at him that if he doesn't fall back he'll fire on him.

Clearly the head-on collision is at hand.

What's Delessart to do? He has been given two orders, either of which, taken by itself, is unambiguous. But taken together they aren't. By now he should have blown up the High Bridge, if necessary defending his sappers by 'meeting force with force', and, mission accomplished, be effecting a peaceful withdrawal to Grenoble. After all, his expedition has only been a gesture to gratify royalist opinion and gain time. But the energetic Cambronne has been too quick for him and public fury at La Mure has foiled the coup. What shall Delessart do now?

In Grenoble it had been obvious that his men share the townspeople's sympathies. With such unreliable troops, and fearing Cambronne will out-flank him, he decides to fall back to a more easily defensible position than La Pontine. Such a position he, an experienced officer of the Imperial Guard, has noticed during his advance. The approach to the village of Laffrey, at the brow of the very long steep slope that descends to the town of Vizille,[14] passes between the hillside and a lake, forming a narrowish defile. And it's here, a couple of hundred yards in front of Laffrey, that Delessart, after sending Randon back to Grenoble for further orders, halts his retreating battalion. During its night march not one man has defected to the enemy. Which is encouraging.

From Gap the march order is

'forty Corsican gendarmes first, the grenadiers by platoons at considerable distances. Carts carrying the grenadiers' packs are being urged on. The Poles advancing on the flank.'

Not once since landing at Antibes has valet Marchand taken his clothes off. And now, at Corps, he's

'lying down fully dressed in the Emperor's bedroom, as I'd been doing throughout the journey, when Saint-Denis [Ali], who was sleeping in the room outside it, knocked at the door and told me the Grand Marshal was asking to speak to him. I opened it and announced him to the Emperor. He read General Cambronne's report.'

It tells him that Delessart's advance guard, consisting of

'a battalion of the 5th Line, a company of pioneers and a company of miners, 700 or 800 men in all, has taken up a position close to the village of Laffrey, barring the main Grenoble road in a defile between the lakes and the hill.'

So it's here the crucial confrontation is to take place!

'The Emperor asked whether his grenadiers had caught up. The answer was yes. "Let them rest up, and tell Cambronne to wait for me to get there before doing anything." At daybreak the Emperor dressed and got going, the Guard after him.'

'From then on,' Ali says, 'we marched with order and prudence. En route we caught up with Cambronne, who'd tempered his march with frequent halts.'

The news that Bonaparte has crossed the La Mure bridge reaches Jubé at between 9:00 and 10:00 pm. 'So nothing could prevent him getting to Grenoble.' Can't it? Before daybreak of this eventful day (7 March) Delessart has drawn up his men in front of Laffrey, and at 7:00 am has again been rejoined by Captain Randon. 'He showed me,' Randon resumes,

'an enormous parcel of proclamations he had under his greatcoat which he'd so far managed to prevent being distributed. His unit was calm, there'd been no desertions during his night march. Doubtless it was his men's apparent attitude that had made him decide to suspend his retreat to Grenoble which, at this moment, could have been carried out without the least difficulty. I thought it my duty to remind him of the text of his order: that if anything should prevent him from carrying out his mission, he couldn't do better than come and give his own account of it, bringing his unit back to Grenoble. Unfortunately, he thought he could afford to wait a while longer, and his position was every moment becoming more and more critical.'

'Toward midday,' Randon goes on,

'an imperial advance guard of a score of horsemen appeared on the horizon. Soon they were drawn up in line of battle to the left of the road, at 500 metres from our position.'

An hour or so passes. 'Around midday' Ali and his comrades see

'the advance guard opposed to us. The Emperor had his Guard draw up in line and approach as closely as possible, and placed his few cavalry on the wings. I don't recall having seen the Corsican battalion; I believe it hadn't yet caught up.'[15]

In six days the column has covered nearly 200 miles. The ill-disciplined Corsicans, 'small of stature and ill-equipped', are certainly footsore and probably no little dispirited. ('If I'd only had Corsicans I certainly shouldn't have succeeded. It was my Guard's bearskins that did most; they brought back so many memories.') But neither can the Guard battalion be in perfect trim, though it's rested up at Gap and since then has been travelling in the post coaches commandeered there.

On the other hand, how well in hand are Delessart's men? As well as Ornano had managed at Antibes? Another officer, deserting from Grenoble, comes and assures Bertrand that 'all the troops are for us. Guns are guarding one of the city gates, but he's sure of their [gunners'] attitudes. The troops certainly won't fire; but the Emperor must walk forward with his grenadiers, with reversed arms.'

This cheers everyone up.

Now the long hour's waiting is over. Randon, standing beside Delessart with the 5th Line's voltigeur company, its advance guard, and still watching Cambronne and his twenty troopers drawn up in line, sees Napoleon get out of his carriage, mount his horse. 'When within suitable distance,' Louis Marchand goes on, 'he ordered the battalion to halt and to form column of platoons. To the right was a little plain' – a small very uneven area of grassy hillocks[16] overlooking the lake and descending gently ahead towards the village, a couple of hundred yards beyond Delessart's men, drawn up there in line and barring the road. On the other side the 'plain' rises steeply 350 feet to a wooded skyline, about 200 yards away. The First Valet goes on:

'Seeing the success of his advance guard, the Emperor made haste to arrive. He told the Poles, some Mamelukes and every person in his suite who had a horse to go down into it,'

(*ie* the meadow) 'the forty Corsican gendarmes first,' Napoleon himself will add, describing the event a year later. 'Then the grenadiers by platoons, each at a very large distance from the next. We hasten on the cart carrying the grenadiers' packs.' Probably it's now that the bearskins, hitherto carried in their leather pouches, are taken out. As for Treasurer Peyrusse, though he's been through the Russian and 1813–14 campaigns, his habits haven't accustomed him 'to such hostile dispositions' and he feels he's becoming 'an embarrassment. Placing myself to one side of the road – I'm not afraid to admit it – I anxiously awaited the outcome of this confrontation.'

'Then Napoleon [the First Valet goes on] sent Colonel [*sic*] Raoul, his *officier d'ordonnance*, to tell the battalion [of the 5th] he was there. Its commander [Delessart] told him [Raoul] he'd been forbidden to communicate, that his hands were tied. Raoul came back and informed His Majesty of the [5th's] attitude, which couldn't be doubted. It was just a matter of getting them to recognise him and of speaking to the men.'

Through his spyglass Delessart sees 'the Man from Elba agitatedly taking big strides on the road'. But the whole scene is confused by masses of peasants, some of whom actually approach Delessart's voltigeurs and proffer them Napoleon's proclamations, though of course he sternly orders them away. The voltigeurs don't budge. Louis Marchand, certainly in close attendance, sees one of the Vauthier brothers 'sent to warn the man in command of the battalion that the Emperor would hold him responsible to France and posterity for what orders he might give.'[17] Randon:

'The Emperor appeared on the road and halted beside his troopers. Some 100 grenadiers of his Guard who were following him placed themselves off the road to his left, in line with the cavalry. It was the most emotional [*pathétique*] moment of the encounter. The Emperor appeared to us amidst his rays of glory, untarnished in the men's eyes by any setback. More than ever, Napoleon was the idol of the army, the man of the people. All these feelings exalted minds, set hearts violently beating. Never, one could say, was military obedience more rudely tested. The two bodies had been facing each other for an hour or so. The sight of the Emperor, of that historic costume and of his person, shook the fidelity of the men of the 5th Line. Silence had been followed by talk. One man spoke of his war memories, another of what he was feeling just now. All, it must be said, asked nothing better than to justify themselves by ranging themselves under his banner.'

Again Randon urges Delessart to retreat, as he should have done all along:

'But from his agitated replies it was easy for me to see what violent conflicts he was prey to. In this way time passed without anyone noticing it. We were in the position of two friends who've had a row and are waiting for the other one to take the first step toward making it up.'

Now it's nearly 2:00 pm.

'The Emperor sent an officer to the battalion's advance guard, where I was, as was also Delessart: "Voltigeurs!" shouted the officer twenty paces away from the men. "Since you don't want to join the Emperor, he's going to come to you. His Guard will have its muskets reversed under their left arms. If you fire, the first shot will be for him. But you'll answer to France for so dear a head."'

Still, after twenty years, Randon goes on,

'those words ring out in my ear and remind me of the perturbation they threw me into. When the officer got back we saw the Emperor dismount, the cavalry break into a trot by fours and come on ahead of

him down the road,[18] while the infantry followed on behind him in
column of sections,'

'at the double,' specifies the always sharply observant Ali. Delessart, hoping
at least to avoid desertions from his voltigeur company, orders: 'Right about
turn. Quick march!', saying to Randon: 'How can we start a fight with men
who're trembling in every limb and pale as death?' The yellow-collars retreat
toward the fusilier companies, closely followed by the advancing Poles.
Again Delessart, to prevent a rout, orders: 'Halt! About turn! Lower bayonets!' And is obeyed. The lancers turn their horses' heads and fall back in
line with the advancing battalion. Meanwhile Napoleon has in fact told
Colonel Mallet, the Guard's CO, to order his men to place their muskets,
muzzles pointing to the ground, under their left arms. Mallet, worried, asks
him whether he really wants them, virtually disarmed, to approach an
apparently firm body of troops, whose attitude they can't be sure of. A single
volley will be their death.

'Mallet,' says Napoleon, 'Do as I tell you.'

Then the national colours are unfurled and the band strikes up with
Rouget de l'Isle's stirring melody.

'Everyone, both in the [Elba] battalion and in the Grenoble troops,
was electrified. Clad in the little grey overcoat which so often had had a
magical effect on the men, and accompanied by Drouot, Cambronne
and the Grand Marshal, he came forward to within pistol range ['two
or three fathoms,' Ali specifies – twelve to eighteen feet].'

Then 'taking two or three more paces forwards', halts. And there's a sudden
silence. Peyrusse, from his bolt-hole, thinks he hears him say in a hoarse and
– on account of his bad cold – just now not very resounding voice:

"Here I am. Soldiers of the 5th Line, recognise me ... If there's a soldier
among you who wants to kill his Emperor..." – unbuttoning his grey overcoat – "he can do so."[19]

'It'd be impossible [Randon confesses] to express the feelings this
march [sic] threw us into, or to exactly report my words in these circumstances. But it seems to be well-established [constant] that I'd
urged Delessart to order the men to fire; which wasn't done, and (I
don't hesitate to say so) couldn't have been, not in the state of mind
the soldiers were in. They were in such a paroxysm of mental distress
[trouble], they couldn't have taken a pace forwards or backwards. This
tense [violent] state of affairs lasted hardly two minutes. The cavalry-
men, sabres sheathed, reached the men of the 5th Line, began parleying with them, broke them up; and almost instantly shouts of Vive
l'Empereur! rang out on all sides. As if by an electric chain [reaction] the
[5th's] state of exaltation passed through the ranks of the battalion,
and in the twinkling of an eye shakos were on bayonet points, and all

chests breathed out that vivat![20] ... In an instant the tricolour cockades they had in their packs had supplanted the white ones ['and were soon on all the shakos']. The men knew their old cockade had only been whitened over, a layer a little water soon washed off.'

One old soldier, tears in his eyes, comes up to the Emperor and rattles his ramrod in his empty musket barrel:

"You can see whether we wanted to kill you."

Peyrusse's courage comes back:

'I emerged triumphant from my battlefield and joined in the common rapture. His Majesty's face was radiant with joy. Men and officers, all listened in an intense [*urgent*] silence to all the circumstances of our departure, our landing, our march. All felt the enthusiasm His Majesty's presence among the populations we'd marched through had aroused. This scene took place just before the village of Laffrey.'

Delessart, in tears, surrenders his sword to Napoleon, who graciously returns it. The excitement dies down and order is restored. His voice isn't so reduced he can't give the 5th Line – or anyway such parts of it as can hear him – one of his shrewdly judged pep talks. He has come back, he says,

"with a handful of brave fellows because I've been counting on the common people [*peuple*] and on you. The Bourbon throne is illegitimate because it's contrary to the national will, to the country's interests, and exists only to serve those of a few families."

They've only to ask their fathers to know the fate that's being planned for France. Then, turning to the crowd of peasants, many from Laffrey, who've by now come out to see him: "It's true, is it not, that in your communes they're threatening to bring back tithes, privileges, feudal rights and all the abuses your successes had rescued you from?"

'Yes, Sire,' shouts someone in the crowd. 'Our curés have already been building tithe-barns.'[21]

'The brave fellows of the 5th's battalion asked to be the first to march against the division covering Grenoble. But before setting off, a drum roll was ordered, and His Majesty had the Guard's proclamation to the army read out. This is his how he'd conceived it:

'*Soldiers, comrades! Despite all the ambushes set for him we have preserved your Emperor. We bring you him from across the seas, amidst a thousand perils. We've landed on the country's sacred soil with the national cockade and the imperial eagle. Trample the white cockade underfoot. It's the sign of the shame and yoke imposed by the foreigner and by treason.[22] If we allow those we've defeated to lay down the law to us we'll have shed our blood to no purpose!!! During the few months the Bourbons have been reigning they must have convinced you they've forgotten nothing and learnt nothing. They've always governed by prejudices inimical to our rights and those of the people. Those who've*

146

borne arms against their country, against us, are heroes; you, you are rebels, pardonable only until the formation of an army corps of émigrés has been consolidated, a Swiss Guard has been brought into Paris, and your officers have been replaced successively in your ranks. Then one will have to have borne arms against your country to claim honours and rewards. To be an officer, to be of birth in conformity with their prejudice.'

Enumerating other griefs – notably the cheapening of the Legion of Honour – the proclamation winds up:

'Soldiers of the Great Nation, soldiers of the Great Napoleon![23] *Will you agree to be those of a prince who was France's enemy for twenty years, and who prides himself on owing his throne to the prince regent of England? . . . Soldiers, we're beating the fall in, we march on. Run to arms! Come and join us, join our Emperor and our tricolour eagles!'*

The proclamation had been signed by all the returning officers, and, finally, by Drouot. The reading is hardly over than Peyrusse hears more shouts of *Vive l'Empereur!* And at the same moment an individual in the uniform of a captain of the National Guard is seen galloping up, with a huge tricolour cockade in his hat. Dismounting, he says to Napoleon:

'Sire, I'm glovemaker Jean Dumoulin. I've come to bring Your Majesty a hundred thousand francs and my arm.'

Napoleon tells him to get back on his horse. Though his military experience is no more than befits a captain in the National Guard, he's appointed *officier d'ordonnance.* 'Handshakes were exchanged,' Peyrusse goes on, 'and we got going again'.

'A grenadier of the Guard,' Napoleon will afterwards recall, 'presented his father to me, a nonagenarian. I tossed him a purse and took his name for a pension. What a fine subject for a painting!'

As they leave the spot Louis Marchand notices the ground's littered with white cockades, 'marking the position the 5th Line had occupied.' But young Randon, having turned his horse's head about, is riding hell for leather for Grenoble. Both Marchand and Peyrusse see 'some officers set off in pursuit. They tried to catch up with him; but he had a better horse and eluded them.' Hardly has Randon

'left the village of Laffrey behind than, hearing horses galloping after me, I looked back and saw a superior officer and three or four men on horseback close at my heels, energetically inviting me to join them. Thus escorted, I flew down the hill that leads from Laffrey to Vizille. When I got there I was well ahead of my pursuers, and not wishing to seem terrified as I rode through the little town, I put my horse to a trot. This slowing down almost had nasty results for me. A considerable sum had been promised to anyone who brought me back, so the horsemen were all the more determined to pursue me.

Now they'd gained on me and were only a few paces behind me as I emerged from Vizille. I took a short cut, known locally as the Jarrye Ramp. It was imprudent. Halfway up that slope my horse stopped dead in its tracks.'

Only energetic use of his spurs and riding crop can 'make it go on up to the top. For more than ten minutes it could only go on at a walk. Happily the pursuit had ceased.' He goes on his way...

Once again Peyrusse is 'placed in the rear' of the column.

'My baggage was nothing to write home about. The Poles were advance guard. His Majesty marched in the midst of the 5th down the long steep hill to the little walled town of Vizille where the first revolutionary outbreaks had occurred in 1789. It distinguished itself by its enthusiasm as we marched through. Tired though he was, the Emperor wanted to enter Grenoble that evening. He knew the size of the garrison, which that day had been reinforced by the 7th and 11th Line, from Chambéry, and by the 4th Hussars, from Vienne. But His Majesty was trusting in his lucky star.'

Now the 5th Line, marching as the column's advance guard, meet

'Major Rey of the artillery, who put our minds wholly at rest. He was most ardent and assured us we only needed whips to chase away those who might appear in front of us and that the Grenoble garrison was on our side.'

Which it certainly is. On the south side, from which Napoleon's suddenly doubled force is approaching the town and where its suburbs are,

'the ramparts had been confided to the two regiments from Chambéry. The 4th Hussars were posted on the Place Grenette. The 3rd Engineer Regiment was in its barracks, in reserve in the citadel.'

But since neither citizens nor garrison have the least intention of defending the fortifications, the prospects of holding him up are negligible. 'It must have been about 2:30 pm,' Jubé goes on,

'when we heard a loud babble of voices and saw a tremendous mass of people running across the fields toward the Ebens road. On the Place Grenette, where more people were assembling than anywhere else, I met many soldiers running in the direction of the Beaune Gate, to take up arms and with their packs on their backs. Some were saying as they ran: "Hurry up, they're beating the charge!" Ordering a picket of gendarmes to follow me, I push my way with difficulty, so huge was the crowd, to the Beaune Gate. I'm told that the 7th Regiment, which was there, has just left at the double [*pas de charge*] shouting *Vive l'Empereur!* and that at its head the colonel [Labédoyère], after drawing a pencil plan of the gateway, had broken open a side drum[24] and taken out the eagle, which had been immediately placed on the standard's lance head. Tricolour cockades had been distributed to the men and, at the order to march, the column, at virtually the same instant, had done so.'

But not before Labédoyère, in his 'very fine resounding voice', has told them he's going to join the Emperor and uttered magic words that stem from the days of mediaeval chivalry: "Who loves me follows me [*Qui m'aime me suit*]."

'Followed by an innumerable populace shouting *Vive l'Empereur!*', he leaves the city. 'You can imagine our situation,' Guiraud of the Engineers goes on:

'Our regiments wanted to follow the 7th. The gunners were charging their cannon with the fleurs-de-lis [the very medals, perhaps, Artois had been so lavish with!]. The hussars were tearing their white cockades to pieces with their teeth. I personally barred the door of our barracks to prevent the men from leaving it. Officers and men, all, were burning to go out and meet Bonaparte. In vain I reminded them of their oath.'

Only General Devilliers, Labédoyère's superior, is determined to save that young man from his folly. Galloping after him and catching up, he pleads with him to think of his own interests. Labédoyère's only reply is to invite Devilliers to address the regiment. Which he does. And in fact some sixty of its men choose to march with him back to Grenoble. The rest, 'in a hardly describable state of exaltation', march on with Labédoyère on foot, a drawn sword in his hand.

'On the slope between Eybens and Brié' Randon sees coming toward him 'the 7th Line, its colonel at its head. I was taken for an officer from the Emperor's suite, and at the sight of me enthusiastic shouts shook the air. But when I'd drawn even with the first platoon and been recognised as an ADC of the general commanding the division, the colonel ordered me to be arrested. Thanks to my horse's vigour this couldn't be done.'

Again his horse's swiftness saves him. All along his road he sees 'a crowd of the inhabitants pouring out into the plain from all sides, armed with muskets, forks, hayforks, all kinds of implements. An unheard of spectacle, bizarre of aspect, yet terrifying because of the energy of the elements making it up.'

In Grenoble itself Napoleon's proclamation is being read: 'The soldiers were reading them openly.' Jubé even sees General Marchand with one in his hand. 'At length night came down, the gates were closed [at 8:30] and the populace spread out through the town without the least disorder.'

But now Peyrusse sees something else:

> 'We were two leagues [eight kilometres] from Grenoble when we saw Squadron-Leader Jerzmanowski and four lancers coming flat out toward us. It was 7:00 pm. They'd sighted a rather deep column[25] marching along the road in line of battle. We closed our ranks. Each man fell in as he should. We waited. And still the column from Grenoble was coming on. We could hear the clicking of its bayonets and the tramp of its men. Our lancers, falling back onto us, halted a musket-shot away. To the shout of *qui vive?* came the reply: "7th Line!" At the same moment we saw an officer marching at its head. Preceded by a drummer, he was carrying his regiment's former eagle on the tip of a branch.'

Soon Peyrusse also recognises

> 'the 7th Line's colonel, Labédoyère. Coming up to His Majesty, he broke his drummer's drumskin and presented him with the eagle of its former flag.[26] ... The Emperor took the eagle, kissed it and after congratulating the young colonel on his patriotic courage, embraced him.'

The elated Labédoyère, it seems, takes the opportunity to harangue Napoleon on matters of political principle – the importance, in a word, of a more liberal régime, the first of many injunctions he'll be receiving on that score:

> 'The 7th was drawn up along the roadside. He reviewed it, and passed on. This regiment of 1,800 men doubled the Emperor's forces; the crowd of inhabitants quadrupled it. The shouts of "*Vive l'Empereur! Down with the priests! Down with indirect taxation [les droits réunis[27]]*" accompanied this triumphant march.'

Ali notices no shortage of 'refreshments'. Now Napoleon has 'no more doubt the enterprise would succeed.' His anxieties prior to Gap have vanished.

Not so those of Prefect Fourier, that eminent Egyptologist. He's off while the going's good. Earlier in the morning, Jubé says without further comment, he'd

> 'required Captain Saint-Mars to place six gendarmes and a mounted corporal at his disposal, to go with him, he said, into the department, whither he was summoned by crucial business.'

But not before he has exacted a promise from General Marchand not to open the gate until he's gone. Jubé, who has only fifteen mounted and six unmounted gendarmes in all, seven of them already busy elsewhere, thinks such an escort preposterous in the circumstances. But his protest only elicits the same order, 'stronger than the first time, and insisting that the captain himself shall go with him.'

It's now that Colonel Jubé's agonies begin. To refuse to obey orders is to compromise himself. So he obeys. But now General Marchand, too, is preparing to leave; and Jubé, with no alternative but to do the same, orders his quartermaster to get hold of a carriage for his company's cash box and papers. At 7:00 pm Fourier leaves with his escort. 'I waited, ready for anything.' But Guiraud has quit the Engineers' barracks already an hour ago and gone to Marchand, to report on the situation there and to ask for his last orders,

'to which I intended to conform myself, even if I was the only one to do so. He gave me a written order to leave town when Bonaparte arrived and, if the men refused to fight, to follow him to the Barraux Fort.'

Another hour passes. At 8:00 pm it's Jubé who goes to headquarters, where he hears

'General Bouju, head of the artillery school, protesting to Marchand that everything that had been done in the fortress had been done without any orders from him. "Well now, what have you decided to do? It's time we knew!"'

Hearing Marchand speak mysteriously of leaving at 2:00 am, Jubé – still without any orders – suspects him of intending to abandon him, and says: 'No, *we'll* leave at 2:00 am.' Bouju demands a written order to that effect. But Marchand replies that all such details can be arranged later: 'We'll leave together at 2:00 am. All that can be regularised afterwards.' Coming out from the meeting, Jubé hears from an infuriated officer (who takes him for the governor) that 'the colonel of the 7th is at the Beaune Gate with several companies and is trying to break it down.'

As for firing grapeshot, officers commanding the sixty-three guns daren't order even the single volley recommended by Randon, 'for fear of being chopped to pieces on top of them'.[28]

'At 8:00 pm we were approaching Grenoble without having encountered the division General Marchand had ordered to march out from the fortress. Already an advance guard of our Polish lancers had presented itself at the Beaune Gate. They found it closed. The Emperor and his troops marched into the suburb and followed the line of the ramparts. The gunners, with lighted matches, were at their guns. Some cries of *Vive l'Empereur!* made themselves heard. The population of the suburb greeted us with the liveliest acclamations, opened their smoky taverns. A colloquy began between the gunners and our grenadiers.

"'How're your plum-stones? You won't be sending us any, will you?"
"'No risk of that!"

'The garrison's *cantinières* were singing: "*We've got some apples, For the King of Rome*".'

151

By now it's 9:30 pm and

> 'very dark. The crowd was dispersed around him. Though tired, the Emperor wanted to round off the remarkable day with his entrance into the town. The soldiers inside were talking to those outside [namely eight Polish lancers under Jerzmanowski], saying they'd nothing to fear from them, that they'd open the gates. If some of the inhabitants of the district where we were showed any light, several voices were instantly heard shouting: "douse those lights!"'

Now Napoleon's in the suburb. The group around him, Ali notices, is 'silent, anxiously waiting for this scene to end.' Though 'the gates were still shut, which astonished us,' in the uproar Napoleon, 'his riding whip in his hand', is sending a summons to General Marchand to open them:

> 'Colonel Roussille of the 5th, in charge of the post, made him wait.
>
> "'What's this now, Roussille?" he shouted to him. "Are you refusing to open up, whom I made captain at such a time, major at such another?"
>
> 'The grenadiers didn't wait for the colonel to reply. Shouts of *Vive l'Empereur!* by soldiers and inhabitants from the top of the ramparts left no doubt as to the sentiments animating them. The soldiers were shouting that the gunpowder had been wetted. On all sides torches were being lit despite orders to douse them.'

After half an hour Governor Marchand sends a request which, in view of what he must know of his former master's refusal ever to waste time, is a very strange one. Can he please have until tomorrow before deciding? At this Napoleon, according to himself,[29] orders the drums to beat and 'assures them that from this moment General Marchand is cashiered. Then they said: "Oh well, if he's cashiered, then that's another matter."

> 'From time to time shouts of *Vive l'Empereur!* were heard. Finally some voices shouted: "Smash the gates!" "Yes, yes! Axes, axes!" the answer came back from many others ... Captain Raoul, aided by some sappers, soldiers and wheelwrights from the suburbs, smashed in the gates with their axes.'

Jerzmanowski realises axes are also being fetched and applied from the other side. 'The first blows had scarcely fallen than they opened up':

> 'The keys were sent just as the gate was driven in; and the advance guard went in and was met by a crowd with torches. In torchlight all the citizens came running, and, almost at once the Emperor, alone, appeared at the head of his army ... walking some paces before his troops. The crowd rushed upon him, threw themselves before him, seized his hands and knees, kissed his feet, and gave way to every demonstration of unbounded transport. The mayor and many of the municipality would have accompanied him to the town hall, but he

slipped aside into the inn kept by a certain Labarre, an old soldier of his Guard.'

Ali finds himself caught in the jam

'to thousandfold shouts of *Vive l'Empereur! Vive Napoléon!* Swept up on the wave, the Emperor and those who were with him found they'd passed through the gate without even noticing it. The 4th Hussars, who were in the street leading to the gate, served as his escort and accompanied him to the inn where His Majesty dismounted.'

In the inn he's

'for a while completely lost to his staff, who became so much alarmed that Jerzmanowski and Bertrand, after many efforts, pushed their way into the room, and found the Emperor, unaccompanied by a single soldier, in the midst of a crowd who were thronging about him on all sides to see, to speak to, and to touch him. The officers succeeded for a moment or two in clearing the room, and placed tables and chairs against the doors, to prevent another irruption, but without success; for the crowd burst in a second time, and for nearly two hours the Emperor was in their hands, unattended by a single guard.'[30]

Poor Jubé!

'So there I was, in spite of myself, shut up in the town, in the most painful situation, caught between my honour, my duties, my oaths, and the hard necessity of perhaps having to betray them. Worn out by fatigue and needs, even more by worry for the future, I went off home.'

But he's not too tired to write a report. His colleague Guiraud too, 'my orders in my hand, a portmanteau behind me, ready for whatever might ensue', has galloped back to the citadel:

'I read out my order. My officers refuse to carry it out. Colonel Isoard is in tears. I urge him to leave with me. His hesitation doesn't permit me to wait for him. I leave the citadel...'

At his wits end, Jubé too struggles to get back through the crowd to his own headquarters 'via the Rue Montgorge, which I found all lit up.' As for Guiraud, in this chaos he'd soon found himself 'in the Emperor's cortège, two paces away from him.' Ali:

'The street or streets we'd just passed along were so narrow compared with the multitude forcing itself into them that we'd only been able to move on very slowly. The knees of those who had horses were so squeezed by the crowd it was a suffering they had to put up with until they were able to dismount. It hadn't been without difficulty the Emperor had been able to get down from his horse and mount the stairs leading to the apartment set aside for him. He was carried up to it. Reaching the sitting room, he was at the end of his tether. He'd

153

almost been stifled. At moments I don't know how the staircase had been able to resist the considerable weight it had had to support. What a day! What an extraordinary day! It was, as best I can remember, about 10:00 pm.'

This time there's no shortage of municipal enthusiasm:

'Several functionaries presented themselves at once and wanted to take His Majesty to the Prefecture. But the Emperor had set up his headquarters in the home of one of his former Guides [Chasseurs à Cheval of the Guard], a man named Labarre, who kept the *Hôtel des Trois Dauphins*.'

Colonel Guiraud's lodgings, as it happens, are immediately opposite it. At last he manages to extricate himself:

'Already the Lancers of the Emperor's Guard were surrounding *Les Trois Dauphins*. I got out by the Saint-Laurent gate, whose lock General Marchand had just had blown off.'

Jubé, on the other hand, hasn't quite been quick enough off the mark. And when he, back at his police headquarters, orders his fifteen gendarmes to leave town, he finds all the gates have been closed, and 'that Marshal Bertrand's orders no longer allowed anyone to go out'.

'Hardly had we installed ourselves [the First Valet goes on] and had the Emperor had supper, than, to the sound of fanfares, the inhabitants came to deposit the debris of the Beaune Gate under the balcony of the Town Hall. Since they hadn't been able to offer the Emperor the keys of his good town of Grenoble, they said, they were bringing the gates instead. The town was spontaneously lit up.'

But out in the murky countryside Colonel Guiraud and other fugitives, officers all, are making for Governor Marchand's country residence at Saint-Himier. There he finds Marchand himself,

'his ADC, his chief-of-staff Pétiet,[31] Colonel Génin of the artillery, Lieutenant-Colonel Etschgoyen, Staff-Captain Carvalho, artillery captain Alexander and myself, the only unit commanders who hadn't rushed out to meet Bonaparte. Lambert, one of our captains, had quit the regiment in the morning.'

Jubé realises he's not the only senior officer who hasn't been able to leave: 'General Bouju, the artillery colonels, the sappers of the 5th Line, and several heads of the military administrations were in the same quandary.' One of his gendarmerie officers, none other than the Bonapartist Captain Paris, asks him what he's going to do now. 'Having no reason to distrust M. Paris, I said I'd no intention whatever of presenting myself to the Emperor.' Neither, says Captain Paris hypocritically, has he. No more has another captain who's come back from escorting Prefect Fourier to a place of safety.

Jubé advises them to lie low, go home, and say nothing. If they like, he'll even have it put about they've left town.

During the night, Guiraud will hear, one more officer, sub-director of a depôt, escapes

'by sliding down from the top of the ramparts to the ditch. Intendant Rostaing, too, had left (later he'd be an ardent persecutor of everything that hadn't followed his example at the time). The colonel of the 11th Line and his major got back to Chambéry with a force about the size of a battalion.'

Tomorrow everyone knows there's to be a great parade, 'at which the Emperor would be replacing absent officers'. Particularly anguished news for the absentees out at Saint-Himier! Colonel Isoard sends his brother to Guiraud to let him know

'he'd decided not to appear before the Emperor unless I myself was with him. He put it to me that I'd done enough to prove my intentions and feelings to the King, and must think about my future; and that Bonaparte's comeback had apparently been prearranged with Austria.[32] And since everything seemed to conduce to a belief in the enterprise being a total success it wouldn't be wise in one instant to lose the fruit of twenty years of service.'

Together they all hold counsel in front of Marchand, who tells them that he, in his own elevated position and at the end of his career,

'can't set an example of infidelity and become a target for accusations. As for you, gentlemen, you're lost in the crowd and have a long future ahead of you. And by yourselves you can't make the King's cause triumph. It's true you've been almost alone in having followed the path of honour; but doubtless the entire army will soon deviate from it, and you've no obligation to base your conduct on mine. Anyway, I'm no longer your superior officer. You're free to do whatever you think best.'

After this somewhat ambiguous utterance his listeners 'hesitate a long while'; but in the end, 'rather than act alone and in the sole interest of a party that detested us', they decide to go back and 'rejoin the army as a whole, all our old comrades-in-arms. Sadly, with heavy heart, we took the road back to town.' What kind of reception they'll get they can't even guess. Reproaches? What can Napoleon reproach them for? When he'd abdicated hadn't he ordered the army to swear fidelity to the House of Bourbon? And what use is an oath, anyway, if it doesn't hold good in a crisis?

Now it's 8 March, and in the inn Ali, throwing back the apartment's shutters to admit the morning light, sees 'the population early on its feet, the national colours flying on all sides and everything of a military nature or representing the government wearing the tricolour cockade.' At 2:00 pm there's a 'protracted' parade. But though Ali, 'not being on outside service that day [doesn't] know what was said or done,' Peyrusse does:

'The Emperor reviewed all the troops, more than 7,000 in number, with the same easy manner, dignity and freedom of mind he'd had at the Tuileries. Enthusiasm was at its peak. An advance guard of 4,000 men was formed. As he took command of it Cambronne asked for cartridges. "You won't be needing any, General," the Emperor said. "All along your way you'll only meet with friends."'

'After the review several units set off for Lyons.' And Peyrusse has himself announced

'to tell His Majesty about my accident at Digne and take his orders as to how to increase my funds – work he postponed until he'd entered Lyons. That day we bought a carriage for His Majesty. I took a wagon for my baggage from the vehicle park.'

Afterwards both Marchand and Ali will vividly recall how some time that afternoon 'the Emperor's former mathematics teacher emerged from inside the inn and asked whether he mightn't be allowed to receive his former pupil.' Ali announces him,

'a big thin man, in a wig. He seemed to be about seventy or seventy-two years old, but still holding himself straight. He was very modestly dressed ... The Emperor was in his bedroom. He came to the door to receive him ... and the two of them, throwing their arms round one other, embraced effusively, exchanging such words as an old and affectionate friendship might suggest. The door being closed, I couldn't hear the two friends' conversation. They spent a long time together. So deep had been the former headmaster's feelings during their colloquy that when he came out his face beamed with joy and he had tears in his eyes.'

It's one of the occasions, Ali adds, 'when I saw how tender the Emperor's feelings could be [combien l'Empereur était sensible].'

The quarrelsome Raoul is a native of the Grenoble district. Now he presents his father, an old general of the Army of the Sambre et Meuse (who, it will be recalled, had 'never forgiven Napoleon for not having fought with it'). Promising to look after the general's son, Napoleon gains one more convert; but is deeply upset that Prefect Fourier, whom he has done so many favours, should have made himself scarce. And when Bertrand sends for Guiraud and the others who'd quit, he's affability itself:

'No serious reproaches, just jokes accompanied by any amount of caresses. The Emperor's policy and interest was to return to power by general consent and without opposition.'

Local Bonapartists draw up an address, full of high-flown sentiments and classical allusions, but no more devoid of liberal warnings than Labédoyère had been. They want to see

'no more foreign troops in France. Let us renounce world empire, but be masters in our own home. Sire, your magnanimous heart will overlook weaknesses. It will pardon error. Only traitors will be driven out, everyone else's happiness will be their punishment. Your Majesty will give the French people protective and liberal laws.'

All this is fine. But poor Jubé's in for even worse trouble than he fears. 'The Emperor soon knew we were in our homes. Perhaps I could tell how he knew it,' he adds bitterly, 'but this isn't the moment to make trouble for anyone.' The fact is, his Captain Paris is a snake in the grass who wants his superior's job. Hearing that Napoleon has summoned General Bouju, the colonel of the 5th Line, and has 'even written to the colonel of the 4th Artillery regiment and his major, who'd left the town, to come back', Jubé assumes he too will soon be getting an order to present himself. His Captain Saint-Mars says he's heard that

'the Emperor was most surprised not to have seen any officers of the gendarmerie. From now on I could only regard myself as a prisoner, and I saw no means of refusing such an order without uselessly exposing myself.'

But what advice shall he give his fifteen gendarmes, their officers and their weeping wives, who've come to him and are begging him for orders, or least counsel?

'If I persisted in my resolve, they'd find themselves without jobs and reduced to poverty. They added that I'd be no more guilty than all the others who'd just submitted.'

'I confess,' he'll write a week later,[33] 'this has been the cruellest moment of my life. Happy are those who've never been in command in such a circumstance!'

Finally he decides that if and when they're sent for, they shall all go to *Les Trois Dauphins* together. And in fact, 'some half-hour later', one of Napoleon's staff officers comes with a message from Bertrand, saying the Emperor's asking for them. But though they all go together and wait till 7:00 pm to be received, Bertrand tells them they're to come back tomorrow. Which, so to speak, puts them in their exact place. 'By 11:00 pm the streets were free, one met no one on them.'

But now it's Thursday 9 March. And at 6:00 am here comes M. Paoli, 'a lieutenant of gendarmerie I'd left on Elba in February 1814 at the time when Tuscany had been evacuated'. Flatteringly, he tells Jubé the Great Man has 'often spoken about him, has a high opinion of him, but he'd shown himself most upset at not yet having seen me since he'd been in Grenoble. To this I said nothing.' And at 9:00 am here's Bertrand's ADC again, come to summon him and his officers. Getting to *Les Trois Dauphins*, he's surprised to see that Captains Paris and Bonnoit, 'afterwards captains in the army', are already there. And again they have to wait, this time for about three hours. 'Then we went in. The Emperor received us kindly and gently, asked each of us which army corps we'd served in, to which we replied.' At this moment Bertrand chips in.

"You've a captain here who used to be in command in this department, but has been destituted by the King."

And when Jubé, amazed, says he knows of no such officer, Bertrand points to Paris and Bonnoit, saying they're members of the entourage. Yes, says Paris, with bare-faced effrontery, that's how it is, but the prefect and the whole department is wanting him back. 'Which is tantamount to saying : "I ask you to give me my job back, and dismiss the man nominated to replace me [*ie* Jubé], seeing as how people don't like him."'[34]

Such treachery! Poor Jubé almost explodes with indignation. Worried to death for the outcome 'I instantly adjudged us lost.' Only with difficulty can he restrain Captain Saint-Mars – 'loyal, a good comrade, a man of probity and honest, but so vivacious he can't put up with an injury' – from challenging Paris to a duel, right here on the spot, on the cobblestones outside *Les Trois Dauphins*:

'I saw him turn pale. A glance from me restrained him. We had to avoid a nasty scene there in the street, in the midst of an immense crowd, under the Emperor's very eyes. I made haste to prevent it by ordering my squadron-leader to promptly take Saint-Mars home to my place. To keep them apart I grabbed hold of Captain Paris, and remained with him several paces behind.'

Getting home, he finds Saint-Mars there, still in a towering rage:

'I did all I could to calm it, and in the end ordered him expressly never to speak to that officer nor have any disputes with him. He swore on his word of honour to execute this order, and up to this day he has kept his oath.'

Alas, this isn't the end of Jubé's tribulations.

Napoleon has been calling for an intelligent officer to carry an important despatch. 'Captain Bonnoit offered to go; but the Emperor, thanking him, said he wanted an officer on the active list. No one replied, no one came forward.' And at 2:00 pm Jubé is again sent for. He's to go to Vienna with a despatch for Marie-Louise. 'M. Bubna,' says Bertrand, 'will let you pass through the outposts.' Guiraud sees

'Jubé give a start, at first horrified by his mission. Then took it as his duty to obey. But whether his head was turned or he tripped over his spurs, we hear him roll from top to bottom down the stairs.'

Jubé records that

'as I'm coming down the staircase from Marshal Bertrand's I miss my footing, and, in the presence of a huge number of people and the guards, roll down it from top to bottom.'

Guiraud sees Bertrand 'run down the stairs, snatch the letter. "It's an express," he shouted. "Someone else shall take it."'

'I thought I was dead [recalled Jubé]. I was taken to my own place, where my wife, death in her soul and already ill after the very recent demise of our only son, received me. A surgeon was sent for. He ordered the instant application of several leeches. My boots and trousers had to be cut, so swollen were my foot, leg and thigh.'

Guiraud: 'An hour later Jubé was cashiered.'

In bed for several days, the shock of his fall is as nothing compared with the anguish of having found himself trapped in the 'most terrible situation any honourable man can find himself in.' However he consoles himself that he has nothing to reproach himself with: 'I did my duty up to the last moment, and am resignedly awaiting my fate, which can't be more terrible than what I've been through.'

Guiraud gets off much more lightly, albeit at the cost of a few scratches. 'We paid Bertrand a formal visit and chatted with him quite familiarly.' Bertrand says he'd "rather be pounded to pieces in a mortar than consent to all the things done since 1789 being plunged into oblivion." Drouot, too, tells him the Emperor's going to recall all officers to his Guard who'd been serving in it when he'd left for Elba.

At 3:00 pm 'the Emperor appeared on parade, as if it were happening daily in the courtyard of the Tuileries. Everyone came close to him, the populace touched him, pressed around him. "Surely he's being protected," they were saying. "How can he expose himself like this? One determined man can put an end to him." But among all Grenoble's many royalists there's no such man. The devil bears a charmed life, many of them must be thinking as they contemplate the wreckage of the *Café Bourbon*, where Guiraud's been in the habit of meeting up with his like-minded associates these last eleven months.

Nor are the Grenoble ladies so ready to forgive Guiraud as Bertrand and his officers have been. When he meets them again – with his hat on, as always – he has to

'put up with the liveliest of scenes and defend the cockade I'd found it so repugnant to wear. It was wrenched from my hat, and only with difficulty could I defend myself against their scratches.'

His lodgings directly opposite *Les Trois Dauphins* are with a certain Mme. Gruau ('Gruel'!). And it's from her window he witnesses the astounding and continuing popular enthusiasm: 'Acclamations under the Emperor's windows fit to make your head burst, throughout his stay.'

But if the Grenoble populace[35] think he loves them they're under an illusion:

'Though the acclaim redoubled whenever he appeared, he didn't seem satisfied at the kind of people who were so curious to see him. "All I can see," he said, "is the dregs of the populace.[36] These crowds are essentially revolutionary."'

'His Majesty,' Gourgaud will note in his diary on St Helena, 'was afraid it was only the mob that was siding with him'.

CHAPTER 7

COLLAPSE OF A CONSPIRACY

The great artillery depôt of La Fère, in Picardy, is in one of France's second-line fortresses. Besides the town's regular defences, it stands in the middle of flat open countryside and is further protected against an invader – or, for that matter, a political coup-de-main – by a system of sluices, which can be opened to flood the surrounding countryside.

Major Pion des Loches, second-in-command at the artillery depôt, has 'never liked Napoleon' and is now a convinced royalist. Even before news of the Antibes landing had reached him he's been having trouble with his officers. Notably so with the younger Lallemand, whose elder brother, the general (likewise a blatant Bonapartist), is in command at nearby Laon. To Pion's disgust Colonel Lallemand has been 'making all the halls echo with his complaints and hopes'. The mayor is an ex-émigré, and at one of his dinners Lallemand has openly declared that the army isn't devoted to the King and is just waiting for an opportunity to mutiny,

'even hinting that the moment was soon at hand. The burden of his complaints was always the suppression of the Guard Artillery, in his eyes the army's most distinguished unit.'

Not that Pion des Loches regards Lallemand, in himself, as all that bright. Though he dines with the battalion commanders 'he didn't even have enough intelligence to win them over. He put everyone off by his arrogance and vanity, and in the end they'd left him to eat by himself.'

Now, in early March, Pion, far from suspecting the conspiracy that's been hatched in Paris, doesn't even realise the Lallemands have been plotting under his very nose. But then, 'one afternoon in the first days of March', his friend the mayor has summoned him and told him the terrible news. Bonaparte had landed in the south:

"*Eh bien*, Monsieur Pion, so we've a civil war in France!"

"I'll bet he's already been arrested," Pion had replied indignantly. "He won't find any partisans in Provence, where he was almost assassinated last year."

On the other hand he agrees that if the army does go over to him all is lost: "But he won't have time. There aren't many troops on the Alpine frontier[1] and the garrisons will at one and the same moment hear the skirmish has begun and ended." But the mayor isn't so easily reassured. And Mme. des Loches, on the contrary, is sure it's all been combined with a conspiracy within the country and that all is now lost in advance.

A day or so afterwards Colonel Lallemand, back from Paris, where he should be, approaches Pion, and in a desultory way begins talking to him about the ex-Guard Artillery's accounts. This is only a pretext, as Pion realises. But, he asks bluntly, what about the great event? What are they saying in Paris? And what's he, Lallemand, doing here anyway? Why isn't he at his post in the capital? Has he brought any orders?

"No. Everyone, as you know, sees these things the way he wants to."

Pion noticed his great embarrassment as he said this. 'He didn't dare raise his eyes.'

"When did you leave Paris?" asks Pion, suspicious.

"The moment I knew the Emperor had landed – I stopped off at Laon to see my brother."

'Here [says Pion] his embarrassment redoubled. At the least advance from me he'd have let me into his secret.'

Only when they're in a dark spot at the foot of the staircase does Lallemand ask him 'in a low voice, in broken phrases': "What's the feeling in your regiment? What did it say when it heard the news?"

"The regiment didn't say anything, but it'll do its duty." 'I tried to look him in the eye, but didn't succeed."

They part company – for good, as it'll turn out, apart from a brief glimpse in the street at the crisis of the affair that's now brewing.

Already Bonaparte's failure to suborn the Antibes garrison is known. And that he's marching on Gap.

On 9 March, General Lallemand, at Laon, sends for Colonel Rapatel of the ex-Dragoons of the Guard, and 'tells him of his projects for seizing artillery at La Fère. Urges him to join him with his regiment.' But Rapatel isn't having any: "If you weren't my old friend," he tells him, "I'd pass my sword through your body." Which Pion des Loches (who'll afterwards hear about it from Rapatel himself) thinks isn't enough: 'He should have reported it to the Minister of War. Did he? I don't know.' But certainly it's his own duty to warn his superior, General d'Aboville, the military governor at La Fère. But for some reason doesn't. Who's on which side? The subalterns' sentiments, it seems, are quite clear. But quite a lot of superior officers are obviously sitting on the fence, waiting to see which way the cat'll jump.

That evening Pion has turned in quite early when, at 10:00 pm, someone comes and 'hammers on my door. I recognised the voice of Squadron-Leader Michel of the 5th Artillery Train'. D'Aboville, says Michel, wants to see him instantly.

'The night was pitch black and it was raining cats and dogs. Yet a certain agitation seemed to be reigning in the town and lights were burning at several windows. Crossing the Rue des Vaches ['Cow

Street'] I met a horseman leading his mount by the bridle. It seemed to me I could make out a colback and a jacket with a yellow collar. "Trooper, who are you?" "A King's chasseur, monsieur. We've come from Cambrai today and are waiting for orders.'"

Now what the hell can the former Chasseurs of the Imperial Guard be doing here at La Fère? And why, in weather like this, have they marched by double stages? Is Bonaparte 'such a threat in Provence that garrisons in Flanders are having to be set in movement?'

After doing garrison duty at Tours, Saumur and then Le Mans, the Grand Army's senior and most prestigious cavalry regiment, during the years of its glory always in attendance on the Emperor himself, has ended up at Cambrai, in muddy Picardy. Lieutenant *Chevalier*, whose gaze last year, like his comrades', had filled with tears as it followed the carriage of 'the immortal Napoleon' until it was out of sight down the Fontainebleau road, has been among those who, in the early days of March, had mounted their horses and trotted despondently off toward Saint-Quentin. Only en route had their colonel, Lefebvre-Desnouëttes told them why.

'Napoleon had landed in Provence with his little unit from Elba and was marching straight for Paris; that the Bourbon family was trembling and getting ready to leave; the Imperial Guard was reassembling itself; the Horse Grenadiers had left Arras already and were following us; in a word, we were marching on Paris! At that moment the whole regiment was seized with joy, delirium, each of us was weeping with pleasure. And in a jiffy the silver fleurs-de-lis given us by the Duke of Angoulême were sent flying off onto the road and got broken. And the name of the hero we so revered flew from mouth to mouth.'

Only a few of their officers are dubious. Isn't the whole movement premature?

Pion finds d'Aboville 'sitting by his fireside, dreamy and worried.' Can he understand, the governor asks him, why the Chasseurs are here, 'unannounced, without any travelling warrant?' He'd been at the theatre when a commandant had come and told him one of their officers had come with his quartermaster, asking for billets; but when asked to show his warrant had replied that doubtless their colonel had it 'but in any case he'd soon be here and after such a long ride it'd be disagreeable not to have any billets ready for them.' To this d'Aboville had replied that he'd no authority in the matter; but even if he had, he'd refuse to let the regiment into the town. But though he offers Pion an artillery picket to guard the gate, he finds the whole Chasseur regiment already inside the town. Sending for the commandant, he severely reprimands him, saying it can cost him dear. The latter, upset, protests that he'd only given in to extreme pressure, and assures him it's all happening by orders of General Count d'Erlon at Lille.

"Oh well, it's late. We'll look into all this tomorrow."

Next morning, 10 March, Pion's in his office when two of his captains, Bonafous and Bosquet, appear with decidedly premature news:

"It's all over. Bonaparte's been recognised again in Paris. The King's been assassinated. And a provisional government's been organised under Carnot until the Emperor gets there."

That's all very well, Pion replies dryly, and doubtless it'll smooth Bonaparte's path. "But *Le Roi ne Meurt pas* ['the King Never Dies'[2]]."

"Artois and his sons have been assassinated too," the two Bonapartist captains assure him "The [working class] suburbs are in insurrection against the central districts. The Chasseurs are here to get some guns and march on Paris to put an end to this revolution."

Really? Who's told them all this?

"Colonel Lallemand. He's ordered us to load the ammunition wagons. During the night a big detachment of the Chasseurs has been commandeering remounts in the neighbouring villages. In the course of the morning they'll be joined by infantry. His brother the general is on his way from Laon with a squadron of the former Dragoons of the Imperial Guard."

D'Erlon, he'd added, would be leaving Lille today

"at the head of his division, 10,000 men strong. He's expecting to meet up with us on the far side of Senlis at the *Patte d'Oie* Inn, the general rendezvous. This whole coup has been prepared a long while. We were expecting the Emperor, but a week later. He's got the jump of us. But the contretemps has been made good."

Pion (or so he'll claim afterwards) is sceptical:

"Don't you believe a word of this supposed revolution," he replies. "Lallemand's announcing as facts things that still remain to be done. Go to your quarters, await my orders, and keep your mouths shut."

'Lallemand was taking it for granted we'd perjure ourselves, as he had. He wasn't expecting a major he'd known in the Guard Artillery to stand up to him, nor yet a regiment he'd been seeing throughout the winter and where he knew there were a lot of malcontents.'

But why, Pion wonders, has Lallemand been so frank with Captain Bosquet, who he knows 'hated him as much as I did?' Why hasn't the older Lallemand, their superior, simply sent d'Aboville a regular order to march for Senlis or Compiègne? It's all too transparent.

But d'Aboville's a cautious man. Very cautious indeed. Is Pion sure of his men? 'Let's resist, but not attack. Don't let's start a civil war in the streets.'

'But, general, we must force the Chasseurs to leave town.'

'No. We'll keep them shut up in the arsenal. Then they'll be forced to withdraw of their own accord.'

For a quarter of an hour they argue. Pion wants to take all the Chasseurs' bridles 'and even their saddles' out of the stables: 'All that can be done silently in ten minutes. Maybe there'll be a few shots fired on one side or the other, but who knows what effect such a good example may have on the army?'

No. The most d'Aboville will consent to is for the mayor and superior officers to come and hold a council of war as to what measures are to be taken.

Said and done. Pion consigns all his 'subalterns to the mathematics hall and the troops to barracks'. Two officers support d'Aboville's passive scheme. Only Captain Baud supports Pion des Loches, and offers – 'it not being right for a regiment's CO to do such a thing' – to himself go and arrest Lallemand. But even he gives in. Pion goes to the mathematics hall and tells his officers about Lallemand's and Lefebvre-Desnouëttes' plans. He's sure he can rely on their swords, he says; but being new to the regiment he's by no means sure how far he can count on its gunners:

> 'There was no enthusiasm. Several captains replied rather coldly that they thought their men would obey orders. Obviously, if I'd tried to carry out my first plan I'd have had to be very careful in selecting my agents. Contrariwise, if I'd been one of the conspirators I'd only have had to say the word for everyone to join me.'

Even when he declares, heroically, the regiment will have to pass over his dead body before it joins the Lallemands, his *Vive le Roi!* rouses only a mild echo. Neither from his narrative nor from his portrait does Pion des Loches seem to have been a man to awaken enthusiasm in his subordinates. Know-alls who're always in the right and never fail to point it out rarely are. At the same time there's no doubt of the sincerity, even staunchness, of Pion's new-found royalism.

Much too late he realises he should have sent someone to close the town gates in time, before the Chasseurs could get in. All he can do is send one of his officers to reconnoitre a unit that's drawn up outside the town hall. The man comes back laughing, saying it's only a company of grenadiers. As for the Chasseurs, they haven't stirred. But their horses are already saddled up in the stables. With d'Aboville's approval Pion draws up his half-regiment (the other half is in Paris) and the regiment of the Train, each on its own barrack square; stations his gunners at various points in the town; and then, taking up his own position in front of his lodgings on the esplanade, with his six companies to the right, the Train squadron to the left, sends for an ammunition wagon loaded with cartridges.

'Two cannon were aimed at the exit from the street that enters the town from Laon. Two at the exit of the Rue des Vaches. Four on the town. The others I left drawn up in battle order, ready to be sent wherever they might be needed. The ammunition wagon arrives. I open it myself; but inside, to my great amazement, find only infantry cartridges in lieu of grapeshot.'

However, he puts a good face on it, and distributes the cartridges to his men, 'd'Aboville prescribing that they were only to use them if attacked.'

But who's that 'coming out, alone, in parade uniform, from a house at the end of the Rue des Vaches', if not Lallemand himself? What does he want? 'Seeing us, he abruptly retraced his steps.' A moment later a retired major in the La Fère accounts office, by name Charpentier, wearing the uniform of a captain of clothing supplies of the Guard Artillery – 'who seemed to have just breakfasted with those gentlemen' – comes up to d'Aboville and says Lallemand has something to tell him. Will he join them at his lodgings or, if he prefers, at the Post Inn? 'Could it be,' Pion des Loches wonders, 'that the Dragoons squadron has refused to march, and the conspirators, seeing their coup has failed, want to parley with us?' D'Aboville, for his part, is about to accede to the invitation and has already put one foot in front of the other to follow Charpentier, when Pion checks him:

'Where are you off to, general? You're at your post. If these gentlemen need you, they can come here.'

What's more, if d'Aboville insists on going, then he, Pion, won't obey any orders he may send him, for fear he may be acting under duress. What's more, if he isn't back in a quarter of an hour he'll march on the Post Inn and forcibly interrupt the conference.

'Charpentier turned pale. I looked him between the eyes. He didn't dare look at me. The mayor came up to me to prevent d'Aboville going. And Charpentier was sent off. A moment later Captain Marin [a Bonapartist relation of the mayor's] came up, in full uniform, so drunk he could hardly stand.'

Pion tactfully lets him take d'Aboville aside for a private chat,

'but if he'd addressed the men I'd have arrested him. But they couldn't help laughing at this man, hat askew, a big sabre between his legs, likely at any moment to fall over and pass out with his nose in the air.'

Pion wants d'Aboville to arrest Marin, saying he deserves to be shot. But blood's thicker than water. D'Aboville refuses to arrest a man who's the mayor's cousin, and Marin disappears, only to be replaced a moment later by a squadron-leader of the Chasseurs, who asks d'Aboville to let them leave La Fère.

Certainly. Why not?

'But the gates are guarded. Are you intending to keep us here?'

'Instead of replying in the affirmative, as I'd have done in his place, d'Aboville, faithful to his defensive plan, replied: "Monsieur, you may leave whenever you like. What route are you going to follow?" "The Paris road."'

Though sure that 'since the Chasseurs had entered the town without authorisation we should have kept them there until the Minister of War had decided what their destination should be,' and that 'having them in our hands, we shouldn't have let them go and join their accomplices', Pion has to order Captain Bosquet to let them out through the Paris Gate. But when the complaisant d'Aboville even grants a request that the rest of the Chasseurs, who're out in the countryside, shall be allowed into the town to rejoin their comrades, he jibs:

'I refused to tell Baud to open that gate. Perhaps the request only hid a trap, and would be followed by an attack instead of a retreat. D'Aboville saw my point, and I hurried to the Laon Gate, where the squadron-leader was already parleying with Baud: "No, gentlemen," I said, "this gate isn't going to be opened. The general's changed his mind."'

And when the squadron-leader wonders just where the Chasseurs who're outside the town are going to cross the river to rejoin their comrades, Pion tells him:

'Wherever they like. That's their business. What have you come here for anyway?' And to Baud he adds: 'Remember your orders, Monsieur Baud. If they try to force their way through, do your duty. Your arms are loaded.'

The Chasseurs' squadron-leader goes back to d'Aboville, but gets nowhere.

'A quarter of an hour later Bosquet came and told us the Chasseur regiment had presented itself at the Laon Gate. Lallemand had ordered it to halt in front of the guard, whose four companies were under arms. Cursing Bosquet and Captain Vallier, he swore they'd never be promoted. Then, exhorting the gunners to follow him, took off his fleur-de-lis and threw it on the ground. The ones that followed him did the same, and the regiment trotted out shouting *Vive l'Empereur!* The gunners were so indignant Bosquet could hardly restrain them. Only one of them went off with his former comrades. It wasn't yet 11:00 am.'

Unlike the populations at La Fère or Grenoble, the population of Lille isn't Bonapartist. But the garrison is. And it was at Lille that General Exelmans had recently been resoundingly acquitted of a whole list of alleged crimes against the régime by a court martial presided over by Marshal Mortier, in command of the 16th military district.

After receiving Fouché's message, d'Erlon has just been making his last dispositions for his 30,000-strong division to march on Paris and even sent off several regiments in that direction when, quite unexpectedly, who should turn up if not Mortier, his immediate superior. The big jovial marshal ('the big mortar,' Napoleon has joked, for that's what his name means) is certainly not a man to deviate from the strict path of duty:

'Meeting a unit led astray by two conspirator generals he'd halted them and by his reproaches made them go back to their posts, in the name of discipline and honour.'

Nor is d'Erlon a man for bold initiatives – and certainly not one to defy his superior; least of all a Marshal of France. Rather, if anything, one to take orders from whoever's closest to hand.[3] And he promptly countermands the whole project. Mortier becomes suspicious. Looks into what's been going on, tumbles to it that what he has under his nose is a nascent military revolt, and orders d'Erlon's arrest.

These developments, however, are as yet unknown to the La Fère garrison, and certainly to Pion des Loches. What is more serious, for them, is that they aren't known to the Lallemands either. Riding on for Noyon at the head of the Chasseurs, the older of the brothers orders a halt at the village of Channy, where the former Dragoons of the Imperial Guard have their barracks:

'Going up into the rooms, he ordered the troopers to pack their portmanteaux, and a trumpeter to sound the *To Horse!* Their other squadron, he told them, would be arriving from Laon, together with their colonel.'

Again the project is foiled:

'The commander of the Channy squadron appeared on the scene, declared his squadron wouldn't march except at its colonel's orders. Lallemand flew into a rage – his only recourse when he failed to get his own way.'

Though he sends two chasseurs to grab the Paris post and any despatches it may contain, these men, assuming it'll arrive in a big post coach, allow 'the wretched cart bringing it from Noyon to pass, and we [at La Fère] received the *Moniteur*, where it was a question of Bonaparte's march on Grenoble'. Lallemand and Lefebvre-Desnouëttes have no option but to order the Chasseurs to remount and ride on. Nearing the village of Farguier, they see, coming in the opposite direction, preceded by a corporal, a convoy of 'six or seven guns loaded on gun carriages, being sent to La Fère for repairs.' Turning back, the corporal – seeing the impressive cavalry column approaching down the road – suggests to the Train officer in charge that he leave the main road and halt in some village to its right or left. 'Before he had time to obey, he'd run into the Chasseurs.' Ordered to turn back, he refuses. Whereon Lallemand seizes him 'by the collar and maltreated him, while several chasseurs made the vehicles turn round and suborned several of the men.'

So now Lallemand at least has some guns, 'albeit without any gunners or ammunition'.

Back at La Fère, Pion des Loches wants to visit the younger Lallemand's rooms and 'seize his papers'. But finds it

'a useless precaution. After his brief appearance at the barracks he'd rushed back to his lodgings, had all his effects put into his *calèche* and left the town after the Chasseurs.'

Nor does Pion even manage to get Captain Marin arrested – d'Aboville is too considerate of the latter's wife, his own cousin, who's most indignant at such an idea. Anyway, she tells him, her husband is gone. He has fled the arsenal, let himself down over the ramparts and made haste to catch up with his fellow-conspirators – all, no doubt, greatly to the peaceful-minded, or possibly pusillanimous, d'Aboville's relief.

But Pion is still worried. What'll happen if d'Erlon, instead of marching his division straight from Lille to Paris, comes and tries to succeed where Lallemand has failed? What to do to prevent him? An engineer captain by name Gleizes is all for

'opening the sluices to the right of the Paris Gate, preparing to flood the countryside, cut the bridges and open the gun embrasures in the curtain wall near the gate. After dinner all this was done. The advanced posts were placed, and by evening we had guns in battery. The town was declared in a state of siege. It was important to follow the rebels' progress. We heard they were making for Noyon.'

More and more troubled, the Lallemand brothers and Lefebvre-Desnouëttes are pushing on toward their rendezvous with d'Erlon's men. How far away the Emperor still is! Is there no hope of joining up with him? Early in the morning on 11 March they're approaching Compiègne.

It's here the former 6th Chasseurs, together with their former adjutant-major Henckens,[4] are installed. Taken over last year by Berry as 'his' regiment and brilliantly fitted out as the 1st Chasseurs-à-Cheval, its effectives have been raised from a pathetic residue of a mere five officers, eighty-nine men and ninety-four horses (on 1 January 1814) to 800 picked men. Its young, aristocratic but already seasoned Colonel Talhouët had been given 'the pick of all the mounts' so that each squadron 'has horses of a distinctive colour'.[5] Unfortunately for Henckens, Berry had had an émigré nominee of his own and has refused to confirm the plebeian adjutant-major in his well-earned rank.

Still limping from his wound but no longer actually needing a stick, Henckens has had various other astonishing experiences at Compiègne. Notably, acting as usher at a grand ball Berry had thrown in the château for Artois and the Duchess of Angoulême: 'Sparkling with diamonds of all lustres, she had a disagreeable face and a jerky voice – but what of it, after all she'd been through?' Of all outdated garbs this son of Brabant peasants had to don knee-breeches and silk stockings:

'Since the weather was icy [*faisait un froid de loup*] each time the double doors were thrown open it was like receiving strokes of canes on the calves of our legs, above all for those of us [*ie* the real officers] who were in the habit of wearing long trousers with big boots.'

Afterwards Berry, who 'behaved very decently' toward 'his' regiment, had given Henckens a sword with the fleurs-de-lis engraved on its silver hilt. Though regarding Berry's manner as perhaps a trifle too easy-going (*dégagée*) for a prince, Henckens, at least, has nothing against that ebullient and otherwise much-criticised personage. Evidently it's been Berry's idea that in point of prestige, at least, the former 6th Chasseurs shall replace Napoleon's premier cavalry regiment, the Chasseurs-à-Cheval of the Imperial Guard.

For Henckens, that hyper-efficient ex-NCO, a military life is 'not so much a profession as an art, in which I was always trying to improve myself'. And this particular morning, it being his duty week, he's as usual up bright and early at the stables and just making sure the élite company's horses are properly fed and watered,

'when I was very much astonished to hear that the Chasseurs-à-Cheval of the Guard, whom we knew to be garrisoned at Béthune, were advancing along the Oise and on the point of reaching Compiègne. I immediately informed the colonel, who ordered me to sound the *To Horse!* for the regiment. The elite company always being quicker on its feet than the other companies, I quickly had this one to hand, and the colonel ordered me to place myself at the bridge over the Oise and halt all troops whose arrival hadn't been announced.'

Henckens and his comrades know the Emperor is back – they've been reading about it 'and a reversal of political attitudes' in the newspapers. And already there's been 'electricity in the air'. Getting to the bridge, he finds there an advance guard, under

'a captain I'd known during my time at the Equitation School at Versailles. We rode up to each other and I said: "Where the devil are you off to, Captain?" "I've no idea, but I believe the Comrade has landed." "And who are you calling the Comrade?" "The Little Corporal, who was probably bored on Elba."'

At that moment Talhouët rides up, at the head of the rest of the regiment and 'reaches the bridge at the exact moment when Lefebvre-Desnouëttes and the Lallemand brothers present themselves at the head of the Chasseurs of the Guard. Our colonel parleyed at length with them. I don't know what about. But what's certain is that the colonel ordered me to allow the Guard Chasseurs to pass, do them the honours, and come and rejoin him in the barracks after they'd passed through.'

Henckens can hardly fail to notice the striking difference between his own men's smart appearance and these others with 'clothing and equipment that hadn't been renewed since the Restoration and which had done service in the preceding campaign.' Whether the 'Mamelukes ride past at the regiment's head, wearing a crescent on their turbans' (as Orléans will see them do a week or so later) Henckens doesn't say – anyway none of them are authentic Egyptians. Only when the regiment has ridden by does he hear they're 'on their way to join Napoleon'.

But it's here at Compiègne, where the château's masonry is still pock-marked by last year's Prussian musket-balls, that the conspiracy finally comes unstuck. The Chasseurs' officers, not having been explicitly informed that they're in open insurrection against the government, have realised they're out on a limb, and a very dangerous one at that. Nor have the countryfolk along the route responded in the least to this mysterious march across northern France. Neither has the regiment been joined, as promised, by any troops from Lille. And now their officers, headed by a Major Lion, and faced by a resolute colleague, refuse to go further. Next morning Lefebvre-Desnouëttes and the two Lallemands 'deserted the Chasseur regiment and made off for Soissons.' And Major Lion ingloriously but prudently despatches a letter of submission to the King and leads his men 'back to their own garrison town. As for the cannon, they were left on the public highway.' But back in barracks at Cambrai, 'sad, hopeless, but not discouraged', Lieutenant Chevalier and his comrades are 'expressing sincere wishes for the great captain.'

At La Fère, neither Pion des Loches nor d'Aboville nor, probably, anyone else, realises the whole insurrection has already fizzled out. At 2:00 pm yesterday the bridges there have

'already been cut, when an officer who said he was one of d'Erlon's ADCs demanded entry with orders for La Fère. It didn't so much as occur to him that his comrades weren't masters of the town, for he didn't even ask for any information. We hastened to let him in, hoping to seize his orders to the rebels. Here's his dialogue with d'Aboville:

'"Who are your orders for?"

'"Lieutenant-General Lefebvre-Desnouëttes."

'"Written ones or verbal?"

'"Written."

'"Show me them."

'"But they're for General Lefebvre-Desnouëttes."

'"No matter."

'The officer presented a letter whose seal was already broken. "This letter's been opened already. Who by?" No answer. D'Aboville opened it and we read:

'"Dear General – The sudden arrival of Marshal Mortier has upset all our projects. I can't come to our rendezvous. I'll try to be at Péronne on the 13th, try to get there that day. – Signed: Count d'Erlon."' What, d'Aboville asks the ADC, had been the Lille garrison's attitude when he'd left?

"Favourable."

"To whom, the King or Bonaparte?"

For a moment d'Erlon's ADC stands there tongue-tied. Doesn't know what to say. But then recovers his presence of mind:

"It's the King who gives orders in France, not Bonaparte."

Dismissing him until further orders, d'Aboville turns to Pion and says he fancies sending both the man and his letter on to Lallemand. Good God no, says Pion. Do no such thing! "This letter's proof of d'Erlon's complicity, we must attach it to our report this evening. It's also proof that the Lille conspirators, too, have failed." To send on the letter, on the contrary, may give the Lallemands a chance of meeting up with d'Erlon at Péronne on the 13th. And he, d'Aboville, will have helped them do so!

Naturally neither Pion nor d'Aboville know that d'Erlon, all his plans scotched, is already behind bars. So the ADC is duly arrested, and 'next day went into hospital, where we kept an eye on him.'

Now here too comes Captain Charpentier, obviously extremely anxious, trying to excuse himself to Pion for even so much as talking to Lallemand. As an accounts officer, he was after all his subordinate. Yes, he even admits to having carried a despatch to the sub-prefect at St Quehe at 9:00 pm last night at Lallemand's request. But as to what it was about, he assures Pion he's been completely in the dark. Pion looks sceptical. Charpentier swears he's telling the truth – surely if he'd been in cahoots with the conspirators he'd have left town with them? And now here he is, come to take Major Pion's orders.

"Thank you, monsieur,' says Pion dryly, perhaps grimly. 'I congratulate you on having turned back in time. I've none to give you."

After dinner there's a meeting at d'Aboville's place. If he possessed the necessary funds, he says, he'd open the sluice gates and flood the surrounding countryside. Pion offers him the regimental funds (12–15,000 francs), its contingency savings chest (20,000 francs) and the artillery funds (almost 40,000 francs), yes, even his own purse (6,000 francs). 'But above all I insisted on the urgency of sending a report to the King.'

Though two officers are detailed to write one, it turns out to be such a lot of generalised waffle that a disgusted Pion insists on dictating a replacement for d'Aboville to sign, in which he gives him all the credit for having saved the La Fère arsenal,

'intentionally omitting all reference to myself and doing my best to palliate the writer's clumsiness. D'Erlon's letter was appended to the report. It's not the first time I've ascribed to generals things not done by them but by their assistants.'

One copy's sent off to the Duke of Berry, another to Soult.

'To secure the arrival of the first missive I had at my disposal a courier who promised to be in Paris tomorrow midday. I recommended he avoid Noyon and, once in Paris, present himself at the foot of the Grand Staircase at the Tuileries, get the sentry to call the officer of the guard, and insist on handing it to him in person. I gave him fifty *écus* and promised him as much again if he got there.'

D'Aboville has an elder brother at the War Ministry, under General Évain, so the other report goes via him.

Though Bonapartist at heart, the citizens of La Fère have all this time remained passive. Only the mayor and three officers, one a retired colonel, are actually applauding d'Aboville's and Pion's loyalty to the crown. Others, like Marin, are furiously critical. Also a certain Mlle. Anna de Flavigny, 'his sister-in-law and the chief among the women of that party. Already she saw reappearing around her the courtiers she'd already had among the Guard Artillery.' Her lover is a second-grade captain called Merlin, son of Merlin de Thionville, the regicide.

Pion records that 'in the morning of 11 March his [Merlin's] mother had come to me saying how virulently Merlin was attacking d'Aboville and myself, and urging me to arrest him.'

Pion says he can't arrest everyone of doubtful loyalty. But he urges d'Aboville to pretend an order has arrived sending Merlin to the War Ministry. The day's courier can take a message to General Évain at the Ministry "who won't blame you and will send him to prison or somewhere else." D'Aboville takes up his pen to write the letter. But again his nerve (as Pion sees it) fails him:

"I'll just inform Évain of Marin's conduct."

And contents himself with that. What an exasperating general!

On his way to the Paris gate Pion sees a retired gunner of the Guard Horse Artillery who's donned his old imperial uniform and is carrying his port-

manteau under his arm. Suspecting him of being on his way to join Lallemand, Pion halts him and asks where he's off to.

'I'm going to join Colonel Marin, who used to be my captain. I want to
fight for the Emperor.'

Sent back to d'Aboville, who asks him the same question, the ex-gunner
gives the same answers. D'Aboville 'tore off his decoration with the imperial
effigy on it and had him put in prison. He should instantly have been court-
martialled. But nowhere did any authority exert itself.' Though 'admired
and honourably rewarded for his conduct', in Pion's eyes d'Aboville has
'shown himself weak and irresolute.'

Meanwhile more and more news is coming in. Also something much
more gratifying:

'On the morning of 12 March a horse artillery officer announced
himself as attached to the artillery staff in Paris. He'd brought a little
packet of waxed cloth containing his despatches. Under a layer of
cotton covering his despatches I saw the great decoration of the Order
of Saint Louis. In a transport of joy I threw my arms round the general's neck.'

Like General Coursin at Antibes – he of the picnics – d'Aboville has
been made a commander of that exiguous Order, with a pension of
2,000 francs.

"It's thanks to you, Pion, I've been given it," says d'Aboville. The royal
letter also asks for the names of other deserving officers and men. 'First we
embraced the general, and I took out of the packet the ribbon which I hung
round his neck.' Here's another letter, from Évain, congratulating him. A
third, also from the Ministry, orders him to send eleven companies of the
regiment to Paris, with all the guns that can be harnessed up, as quickly as
ever he can. Pion is to designate which companies are to go:

'The rewards already granted presaged others to come. Our minds
were electrified. I opened the contingency cash chest to cover the cost
of going on campaign. The detachment left on two successive days.'

But d'Aboville has insisted Pion shall remain at La Fère, where he's wondering what's become of the Lallemands and the former Chasseurs of the
Imperial Guard. In fact the regiment, its criminal faux pas (in this
increasingly anxious situation) overlooked, has traipsed all the long way
back to its barracks at Béthune. As for the Lallemands and Lefebvre-Desnouëttes, after taking refuge in the country house of a former colleague
they've been arrested by the local gendarmerie, commanded, unfortunately
for them, by an officer or strong royalist sympathies. Their future looks
grim.[6] None grimmer. Unless, that is, Napoleon arrives in time to rescue
them from the firing squad. On 8 March Soult writes peremptorily to
Mortier at Lille, referring to Napoleon as "the infamous usurper

174

Bonaparte", and orders him to have d'Erlon "court-martialled and shot within twenty-four hours."

As for the 1st (ex-6th) Chasseurs, Henckens can't tell whether its colonel has 'received any orders, but everything was done to place us on a war footing, and to leave Compiègne for good. That same day he left for Senlis with the regimental staff, leaving orders with its captains to join him as soon as they could leave their garrison duties.'
Berry's crack regiment is one of the many being concentrated on Paris, to defend the Bourbon throne and altar.

As for the abandoned cannon, Pion and d'Aboville send a picket to fetch them in to La Fère, their original destination.

CHAPTER 8

FRANCE'S SECOND CITY

Everywhere the weather's appalling. All over France it'd been pouring
down. The *calèche* Napoleon had bought at Gap is going generally 'at
a foot pace', and is frequently

'impeded in its route, not only in the towns but along the roads, by the
crowds, who pressed at its side and loaded it with flowers and con-
gratulatory addresses and petitions. At times the carriage was attended
by half a dozen hussars, and at others was without a single guard, and
generally three leagues distant from any body of troops.'[1]

He's in 'a most jovial mood. At nightfall [now it's Fabry, relating local
reminiscences, apocryphal but not necessarily untrue] he reached a village
called Rives, where he halted for dinner.' As usual he interrogates the mayor
about local sentiments – which are anyway quite obvious – and that notable's
personal affairs:

"Have you a wife?"

"Yes."

"Any children?"

"No."

"It seems," quips Napoleon, "*M. le maire* busies himself more with deeds
[*actes*] than with making children!"

'Passing on to other matters, he observed, anent the Treaty of Paris,
how ridiculous it was to have to pass over Piedmontese territory to go
from Grenoble to Chambéry. "But we'll arrange all that," he went on,
turning to his officers. "We must just give the women four years rest to
make children and the mares to make foals."'

An association of ideas doubtless to his officers' taste, it's not to Fabry's, who
sees it as 'most worthy of him who called conscripts cannon-fodder.'[2] On
Monday 6 March every horse in Grenoble had been requisitioned. Assembled at 5:00 am at its arsenal, they'd 'left for Lyons pulling six cannon and
their ammunition wagons'. 'On 9 March,' Louis Marchand goes on,

'the Emperor, preceded by the 4th Hussars and followed by the entire
Grenoble garrison, went on to pass the night at Bourgoin. Despite the
day's rain and bad weather the crowd and enthusiasm continued to
grow. Ever since he'd landed the shouts of "Down with the priests!
Down with indirect taxation!" had accompanied him, but he never
replied to them.'

'Having accompanied him some part of the way,' Ali will always remember,
'the townspeople were successively replaced by the countryfolk who'd

lined the road and, in their turn, accompanied him singing songs suited to the circumstances. I remember the peasants had lit bonfires at distances to illumine the road.'

Napoleon still has his 'bad cold, in his carriage, tired and together with Bertrand'. And on getting to Bourgoin goes straight to bed:

'He needed to rest up and cure the cold he'd caught the first or second day after landing, which had left him very hoarse, almost extinguishing his voice. He needed it for replying to the authorities in all the places he was passing through and to harangue the troops which were coming over and joining him. Happily his cold gradually passed over.'

On his country estate at faraway Bourges, still without an inkling of what had happened, Macdonald had just got back after taking part in the Angoulêmes' anniversary visit to Bordeaux, when

'in the night of 7/8 March a despatch rider brought me the order to proceed instantly to Nîmes, where I'd get others from the Duke of Angoulême, from whom I'd just parted. Before doing so I was to direct all the troops in my district to Villefranche, in the Rhône department. No motive was given.'

He racks his brains. What can have happened? His orders, he concludes, must have to do with the demonstration of military strength on the frontiers demanded by Talleyrand in Vienna. 'I assumed similar concentrations were being made in the North. But I was far from the mark' – as he understands later in the night when a report sent to the Bourges commandant by his subordinate at Nevers brings the news of Napoleon's landing. 'This news confounded me, and even then I foresaw the miseries that were going to fall on France.' The report also tells him Artois is en route for Lyons, which he'll have to pass through if he's to take the most direct route to Nîmes.

A few hours later he sets out, and at the village of La Charité hears that the Duke of Orléans, too, has just passed through on his way to join Artois at Lyons and had 'a head start over me of twenty-four hours'. Macdonald and Orléans had known each other in their youth, when they'd fought as subalterns in the Republic's first campaign. Unfortunately the Duke, 'travelling with three carriages', has taken all the post horses. Luckily he stops for lunch at Pougues, where Macdonald finally catches up with him:

'He told me everything that had been known in Paris before he'd left, about Napoleon having landed and his rapid march on Grenoble, which it was thought would certainly put up a resistance. "At least," I said, "we can count on General Marchand. He hates Napoleon personally and is his declared enemy."'

They drive on as far as Moulins; where once again there's a difficulty over horses, and the marshal – who is likely to be the effective element in any resistance to Bonaparte in the South – has to 'wait for his to come back before I could go on, thus giving him a start of several hours over myself.' While changing horses at the last relay before Lyons, a letter comes to him from Artois, who's heard from Orléans that a real live marshal's coming to the rescue and urges him to make all possible haste.

> 'His position was most disquieting. Napoleon's march had been so swift that by now he was only one day from Lyons. The garrison was showing such bad attitudes that he couldn't count on it to defend the Rhône passage.'

The letter is top secret, but everyone seems to know its contents:

> 'I'd gone into the postmaster's house to read it and send an answer. Coming out again to hand over my reply, I saw a lot of curious persons assembled, who were hearing all about the garrison's attitude from the courier, which was being confirmed by the postilion.'

Again Macdonald sets off post-haste. 'But before reaching the suburb one of my carriage's axle-trees broke. It turned over. Though I didn't suffer from my fall, I had to do the last bit on foot. It was 9:00 or 10:00 pm 9 March.'

Lyons, on the Rhône, is France's chief industrial city, and has 500,000 inhabitants, half as many as Paris. In his huge struggle to exclude British and colonial goods from the Continent, Napoleon had always supported its manufactures, notably its silk industry. And knows he is extremely popular there. Even so, when he'd passed through last year en route for Elba it had been in a dead silence, watched by Cossacks.

Just now, ravaged by unemployment, its manufacturers are resentful at having to pay taxes on sums they aren't even earning – all in contrast to the heyday of Empire, when other countries had had no option but to buy Lyons silk. In its suburbs are the beginnings of an industrial proletariat.[3] And here of course both unemployment and resentment are at their height.

Since Grenoble most of the initial anxiety has gone out of the 'crazy enterprise'. After entering Bourgoin close on midnight of 9 March, Napoleon, before going straight to bed, has received a Squadron-Leader Moline de Saint-Yon. Saint-Yon (who also writes opera libretti and military histories) has been 'sent by General Brayer, in command of the 20th and 24th Line and 13th Dragoons' at Lyons to tell him

> 'feelings in that great city weren't in doubt. But the presence of d'Artois, who'd just got there, was preventing them from exploding, and its inhabitants from coming out to meet him. He [Brayer] would even bring me the princes as prisoners if I liked. I thought he was fooling me. I didn't know Brayer yet.'

Artois' and Orléans' military talents are nugatory and can be discounted. But Macdonald, one of the marshals who'd made Napoleon abdicate, is a commander to reckon with. What's his standing with the army now?

The same day as the princes have turned up, the city's governor, Count Roger de Damas, has come back from a fruitless trip to Paris. He'd gone there to tell Soult the town is denuded of guns, and beg him for more armaments. Now, getting back to Lyons, the first thing he does is send forward his nephew of the same name with some dragoons to the village of Verpillière, halfway between the city and Bourgoin. Running into the 4th Hussars' advance guard, the young man has 'almost been taken prisoner. However, the dragoons hadn't abandoned him and had returned with him to Lyons. Not a shot had been fired nor a sabre blow struck.'

All that's available to defend France's second city, Damas tells Orléans, are 'two 3-pounder guns, without limbers, left behind by the Austrians last year. And even they're out of service.' Anyway, there's 'not a single round-shot' in all Lyons to fire from them. So what are they to do?

If Artois' military capacity is nil and his popularity zero, Orléans' standing is a good bit better, at least with the army's higher echelons. After all, he'd fought for the tricolour in his youth, and ever afterwards steadily refused to fight against it. Among his six ADCs is Colonel Athelin of the horse artillery, formerly *officier d'ordonnance* to Murat. If Orléans is here at all it's so that Artois can keep an eye on him and make sure he shows solidarity with the régime. During his journey with Macdonald, whom 'he'd invited into his carriage' (something Artois would never have done), the latter had been glad to see 'he wasn't seeing things in as dark a light as I did, and didn't despair of holding up Buonaparte.' But though there'd been 'plenty of *Vive le Rois*' from the populace, 'dragoons we met along our way were obviously of another disposition' and the closer they'd come to Lyons the less royalist the population had been.

At 4:00 pm on 9 March the Duke has at last entered the city, and is immediately struck by the 'inhabitants' gloomy, despondent and even agitated attitude'. Going straight to the Archbishop's palace, he finds Artois, 'in the National Guard uniform, as usual, with the blue cordon over its coat', already installed. Grenoble, Artois tells him, has fallen, with its 130 guns (*sic*), 'all ready for action, all kinds of ammunition, I don't know how many muskets'. All the troops in the Dauphiné have gone over to the enemy:

"Here we haven't one cannon, not a musket, not a musket ball, and, what's worse, not a penny. That's our position, Monsieur, in a nutshell."

Orléans says he thinks the best thing Artois can do is retire gracefully with as many troops as he can get to go with him.

But imagine, ripostes Artois irritably, the effect on public opinion all over France!

Doesn't alter the fact that they haven't a single gun, says Orléans, and that Bonaparte has 130. As for the ones Artois has sent for from Auxonne, they'll doubtless be useful to Bonaparte, but to himself none at all, "unless you've had them sent you by post." Artois shows him a proclamation he's drafted:

"Brave men of Lyons, the brother of your king has come to entrust you with his person and share the glory and dangers of defending your city ... etc, etc."

Oh, for goodness sake, says Orléans, don't have that posted up, even if you've still time to. Dangers certainly! But there's no glory to be got here. Well, says Artois, it's already posted up all over town...

At this moment Damas enters, tells them Bonaparte's at Bourgoin. And where's Macdonald? Haven't they brought him with them?

"All the marshals put together," Orléans observes, "couldn't defend a town that has no means of defence." Both Artois and Damas, he sees, are 'torn between a fear of leaving too soon and leaving too late.' Already, in fact, all the post horses have been requisitioned for Monsieur's departure. But surely they'll at least wait until Macdonald gets here? Leaving the room, Orléans orders his ADC, too, to hang on to his riding horses which have brought him from Savigny, the last staging post. Now the regimental officers, as in duty bound, come and pay him a courtesy call. They prefer his ADCs – men who'd actually done some fighting – to those of Artois, 'all émigrés'. But otherwise seem little favourable. As for Governor Damas, he too an ex-émigré, he 'isn't being gracious enough toward them to wear the Legion of Honour'.

Having got rid of all his ready cash trying to bribe the troops, Artois is indeed without an *écu*: 'He was sending [after cash] in all directions, to the bank, the receiver of taxes, business people. Everyone was finding pretexts for not sending him any money. It was painful to see his perplexity.' At 6:00 pm both princes go to Damas' official residence for 'a grand dinner that was dreadfully dreary. Marshal Macdonald' – we've seen why – 'didn't turn up until 9:00 pm.' Immediately Artois takes him to his office, tells him he can't go on to Nîmes, 'all the roads being blocked', and summons Orléans and all lieutenant-generals, 'General Brayer, in command at Lyons under Damas, General Digeon, General Partonneaux*, and my ADC General Albert. He also wanted to see the commander of the engineers and artillery.' But when Orléans tells Macdonald that Lyons has neither fortifications nor guns, 'he replied cheerfully:

"That'll greatly simplify its defence."

What about the two 3-pounders? Can't they be placed on the Guillotère

Bridge? During a three-hour discussion Macdonald tries to convince them that the only way of

> "making Buonaparte lose his taste for the idea of halting there is to get some of the Lyons troops to fire on his men if they try to force their way across the bridge. And that if they can't be prevailed on to do so, something the generals regard as impossible, at least they must be got to leave the city and fall back without joining him."

On this point the colonels, too, are sceptical. Anyway, it's decided to hold a parade at 6:00 am tomorrow morning on the Place Bellecour. Meanwhile the town's evacuation and Artois' departure are suspended:

> "We'll always have time to resume the idea," Macdonald consoles them. "Even if Napoleon is only a day's march away, no matter how diligent he is he can't appear before 1:00 or 2:00 pm tomorrow, at the head of exhausted troops."

Meanwhile all communications between the Rhône's left and right banks are to be forbidden, all boats to be brought over to the town side, and both bridges put into a state of defence as far as time and means permit. Artois himself is to go to the riverside and satisfy himself as to the state of affairs there. And patrols are to be sent out. 'Finally, a ration of brandy should be issued before the parade.'

At 3:00 or 4:00 am, during the course of a troubled but busy night, Brayer appears at Macdonald's lodging. The two men had served together in 1813 and 1814. 'He'd come to tell me the troops refused to be reviewed by the princes but would see me, their former general, with great pleasure.' Macdonald, amazed, asks angrily who has set them up in this state of mind? 'Are we at the beginning of a new revolution?' No one has, says Brayer. It's their long list of grievances against the régime, and the officers share them:

> "'So many stupidities have been committed! So little interest has been taken in the military, so many injustices committed to lavish promotion, honours, distinctions showered on émigrés, Chouans, Vendeans!'"
>
> "'From your way of expressing them," I said, "you lead me to think you share these views."
>
> "'Yes," he said, "I'm of their way of thinking. But I'll do my duty up to the end.'"

Meanwhile, says Brayer, time's running out. *M. le maréchal* just has time to advise Artois not to appear on parade if he doesn't want to be insulted. So Macdonald and Orléans go to Artois' headquarters in the Archbishop's palace, where they find the door locked. The Duke shakes

> 'his drawing room door rather roughly. It opened, and I found two officers of his bodyguards lying on mattresses on the floor, already

rather shocked at our brusque manner of introducing ourselves. Recognising us, they both exclaimed at once: "Oh, my God, Monseigneur, what's up?" "Nothing," I told them. "The marshal and I must both speak immediately to Monsieur." '

Well, they can't. The officers don't have the key to his bedroom. It's with their captain, Count Descars. Where's he lodging? They don't know:

'So we had to wait quite a while. In the end we found a valet who had the key to Monsieur's wardrobe, through which we entered his bedroom. He was deeply asleep in a bed with drawn curtains. I half drew them apart and told him the marshal and I wanted to talk to him about important and urgent matters.'

He's just beginning to tell him what they are when the exasperated Macdonald explodes:

"But Monsieur, do get up! This is no joking matter. Perhaps at this very moment Buonaparte's arriving in the Guillotère suburb. Call your people together instantly, harness up your horses and leave! You haven't a moment to lose."[4]

As Artois, grumbling and mumbling, gets out of bed and dresses they try to make him realise the state of affairs. At that moment Damas comes in and confirms that he's himself been to the bridge, and that Bonaparte's hussars are reported to be entering the suburb. Macdonald insists on Artois leaving at once. Orléans takes his cue, says he'll leave too. Artois, angrily:

"Very well, Monsieur, leave if you like.[5] But where are you going?"

"Faith, Monsieur, back to Paris," rejoined the Duke.

But first the all-important parade must be held. Not exactly giving Brayer's reason for him not taking the march-past, Macdonald tells Artois it'll be easier for himself to get at the men's true sentiments if they aren't inhibited by his, Artois', presence. Macdonald suggests that he alone, 'being one of them', should address the troops without either of the princes being present, and so judge their attitude, which they'll no doubt feel freer to express if their royal highnesses aren't present: 'We'll appeal to them as a point of honour, always so ticklish with Frenchmen. We'll show them the evils that must arise from a civil war and the no less great danger to France to see all Europe in arms once again fall on her.' Artois agrees, saying he'll 'be ready to mount his horse as soon as I advised him to. I went back to my place to wait for the troops to assemble on the Place Bellecour.'

The weather's foul. Nor has any brandy been issued, 'neither, during the night, had the war commissary been found so he could accept the units' vouchers, nor any storekeeper to make the issue.'

In pouring rain, on a horse found for him by Brayer, Macdonald appears on parade, entering from the units' right. Ordering them form up in square, he reminds them of the care he's always taken for their welfare, and how, despite their honour and loyalty, it had taken all the armies of Europe, plus 'grave errors', to overcome them. But now there's a new government, and they must be no less loyal to it than to the previous one:

'The troops listened to me in silence. I was most animated. All I wanted of them was to follow my example and shout *Vive le Roi!* [Which he does, several times.] Not a single voice fell in with mine. All remained most gloomily silent. I avow I was disconcerted. My efforts with the other squares were no happier. The troops seemed to have had some order given them.'

Even so, while addressing the dragoons, the furthermost unit, he sends word to Artois to appear, hoping at least he'll be politely received. He isn't:

'The prince went up to an old sapper, who'd been decorated, spoke graciously to him, praised his courage, of which he wore the proof on his chest. The dragoon, whom I can still see, his eyes fixed, mouth agape, remained motionless, impassible. His colonel, several officers who like ourselves shouted *Vive le Roi*, called to him by name, exhorted him, urged him. He remained unshakeable. It made "Monsieur" turn red with fury, though he was wise enough not to let it explode.'

Dismissing the troops without a march-past but with orders to defend the bridges (which he sends Artois to inspect and judge the situation for himself), Macdonald assembles all the officers: 'They were so numerous my apartments couldn't contain them all, the stairs were packed.' Again 'for almost two hours' he appeals to their loyalty; promises the King will amend all objects of grievance. All to no avail.' They were determined not to fire on the corps that had defected at Grenoble. At least I got them to agree, with very poor grace, to stand to their posts and even to reply if attacked.'

Though Artois visits the bridgeheads he finds no measures at all have been taken to defend them. Macdonald again implores him to leave town. Orléans, despite Artois' objections, says he'll stay on, and only gives way in the end when Artois – certainly dubious of his loyalty – positively orders him to leave. But Macdonald, 'having nothing to fear from my men', is going to stay on. Getting back to their inn, the Duke finds

'a party of voltigeurs that had been given me as a guard of honour had already torn off their white cockades and thrown them in the mud.
Though not showing any ill humour they didn't present arms to us.'

As for how they'd been received at the parade, Orléans remarks scathingly to Artois: 'A few isolated shouts of *Vive le Roi* didn't convince me of their attitude, and the dragoons' elite company literally pulled faces at you, as I pointed out at the time.' Orléans and Artois finally leave at 7:30 am. Macdonald feels

'relieved of an enormous weight. If they'd been captured by Napoleon or arrested by the garrison they'd have been hostages for his personal safety, and if any such thing had happened, royalist opinion wouldn't have failed to hold me responsible, could even have gone further and accused me of handing them over.'

Yet he's

'far from calm. The state of mind of the soldiers, the officers, and, I must say, the generals of the 19th military division seemed to be becoming more and more exalted the closer the crucial moment approached.'

He sends off a message to the War Ministry. But only its address gets there. Why? (It won't be the only occasion the Lyons telegraph fails to send an ungarbled or complete message!) 'Soon someone came to tell me the prefect had left town. Only the mayor appeared.'

Since his column may meet with more resistance than it expects and it's not impossible Macdonald, if not Brayer, may succeed in cutting the Rhône bridges into the city, Napoleon gives orders for all boats to be brought over to his side of the Rhône, the basic idea being to initially circumvent Lyons and cut off the princes' retreat. Now the imperial *calèche*, followed by his riding horses – not once, Ali notices, has he mounted his favourite – is trundling along in the midst of his troops; and Napoleon, cold or no cold, is on horseback at their head. More and more people are coming out to meet him. One tells him how

'the populace was awaiting the word to break down the barricades on the bridge. Even the troops didn't want to defend them. How "Monsieur" [*ie* Artois] when reviewing his troops had exhorted an old dragoon of the 13th to shout *Vive le Roi!* And the veteran had replied gruffly: "*Non*, Monseigneur, I can't. We're not going to fight against our father." Turning to Brayer, who was standing by him, Artois had said: "There's nothing left to hope for," and left with his gentlemen and accompanied by the mounted [*ie* aristocratic section of the] National Guard.'

From the moment the officers had told him they won't fire unless attacked Macdonald has prepared a scheme:

'In so large a population as that of Lyons, I told myself, it should be easy to find twenty or thirty men, either devoted [to the King] or avid for gain or recompense. All I had to do was to get them to don National Guard uniforms, place them out at advance posts, ahead of the troops, put myself at their head and myself fire the first shot.'

Once the firing has started, a mere nothing can suffice to change the troops' minds:

'So far Napoleon hadn't run into any opposition. Only a few battalions and squadrons had joined him. But far though he'd advanced into the centre of France, unexpected resistance at the entrance to a town of this importance and with the Rhône to bar his way should give him food for thought and recall to his memory the valiant defence it had so long put up against the army of the Republic.'[6]

But to his amazement the mayor, young M. de Fargues, tells him 'he wouldn't be able to find a single one of the men he was asking for'. Not one? 'The mayor shook his head and made a negative gesture. I dismissed him.'

So what to do now?

Macdonald gets on his horse and 'together with the governor, with Viscount Digeon, Count Jules de Polignac, one of Artois' ADCs he'd left with me, with some other generals and staff officers', goes to see whether his orders have been carried out. Of course none of them have. 'At the bridges the ill-will I everywhere ran into giving me justified fears of defection and catastrophe, I secretly sent an order to harness up my carriage and take it to the entrance of the Vaise suburb,' where both routes northwards meet, so that, if the worst happens, he can escape by the more favourable of them:

'No barricade had been put up at the Morand bridge, no more than anywhere else. It was closed by a grille. No one knew where the keys were. I handed out ten *louis* to go and buy chains and padlocks. My money went the same way as Monsieur's had done.'

Macdonald has another plan to try and unleash hostilities:

'My idea was to reach the bridgehead with the staff officers who were with me, arrest the first men who presented themselves, seize their muskets and open fire. The crowds gorged the quays. Boats were coming and going, taking curious people who couldn't cross by the bridge, filled as it was with our troops, over to the left bank. As I got to the end of the bridge cries of *Vive l'Empereur!* burst out from the other side. The crowd on the quays vociferated so it stunned us.'

The whole length of the bridge is taken up by troops formed up in column.

'"Come, gentlemen, let's go!" I shouted. "On foot!" And there we are, marching at top speed. But we've hardly got a quarter of the way than the hussars of the 4th regiment, scouting for Napoleon's troop, appear at the entrance to the bridge. At this sight, officers and men mingle their acclamations with the shouts of the crowd, shakos are agitated on bayonet points, the weak barricades are forced. Everyone surges forward to bring the newcomers into the town. From that moment all was over.'

Going back to his horse he meets with two more infantry columns arriving at the bridge:

'The crowd had to break up to make way for them. I profited from this to walk past the column, making gestures as if to show it where to place itself. There was so much noise one couldn't make oneself heard.'

Dashing along the quay toward the Morand Bridge he finds there's no more resistance there than at the other. And makes for his carriage, parked in the Vaise suburb:

'General Brayer, who was still with me, having heard me give the order to evacuate Lyons instantly, had suddenly let his mask fall, and said: "No point in it, *M. le maréchal.* All measures have been taken to prevent you from leaving."'

Macdonald says he'll fight his way out at sword point. Brayer doesn't reply, walks away, rejoins his men.

Napoleon, 'surrounded by officers and generals of all degrees who'd come out to meet him', crosses the Guillotère bridge. Night's falling. It's 7:00 pm. The delirium is unparalleled. It's Grenoble all over again, on a vastly greater scale. 'Though still young,' writes one young Lyonnais who'll play a part in all this,

'I'd more than once seen manifestations of popular delight and enthusiasm; but never had I seen anything to compare with the transports of joy and affection to which the people of Lyons gave way. Not only the quays, the squares near the palace, but the streets, even the most remote, were echoing the unending shouts. The only disorder took place on the Place Bellecour, where the common people smashed the windows and tables of the Café Bourbon, known as the ultra-royalists' meeting place. Workmen and their masters, the common people and the bourgeoisie, were going arm in arm to and fro through the town singing, dancing. People who didn't even know one another stopped to shake hands, embraced and congratulated each other on the Emperor's return. It was as if he'd given them back their luck, honour and life.'

Everyone, Marchand sees,

'wanted to see and hear him, make sure it really was he and not some imaginary being, that he was really the object of their hopes and not some disastrous illusion. It's impossible to imagine the crowd of men, children, and old men who rushed out onto the bridges and quays at risk of being crushed. Shouts of "*Vive l'Empereur!* Down with the priests! Down with the émigrés! Down with feudalism!" resounded in the air like a drum roll.'

Only next year will local royalists assure Fabry what they saw that day was 'a suborned populace, the numerous class of silk workers, gathered from all four quarters of France and even from abroad, pillagers come down from the mountains of the Dauphiné with sacks and carts to carry off the city's riches, hoping to pillage it. Lastly, a drunken licentious soldiery, vomiting blasphemies against Heaven and addressing invocations to Napoleon, whom they adored as a divinity, with shouts of "Long live death! The Bourbons to the scaffold! Down with Heaven! Down with virtue! Long live Hell!" Uttering these words they threw stones at windows, entered cafés. There you see what hands the town of Lyons found itself handed over to by Bonaparte's entry into its walls.'

Napoleon, with Brayer at his side, goes to the Archbishop's palace 'so recently watered by Artois' tears', 'where everything was ready to receive him. He entrusted his own person to unmounted National Guard.' As for the mounted one, 'made up of the purest and hardest and most ardent of the opposite party', it alone didn't come to solicit the honour of guarding his person. 'Gentlemen,' he says, 'your conduct towards the Count of Artois [ie first honouring, then deserting him] tells me only too plainly what you'd do to me if luck should abandon me. I certainly shan't submit you to this new trial.'[7] And dissolves the mounted guard, on the pretext of no such unit being stipulated in the regulations.[8]

Once clear of the crowds and making for the Bourbonnais road, Macdonald meets on his way various loyal officers – among them, on the Place Belle-cour, Damas, whom he advises to beat it as fast as ever he can. 'He was most confident and hadn't taken the least precautions'.[9] A little further on, see-ing some dragoons coming back into town after escorting the princes, he orders their officer to turn his men around and follow him, 'adding that his regiment was coming on behind us.' But here suddenly, in the suburbs, coming from the Morand Bridge to bar his way, is a corporal and four of the 4th Hussars,

'all more or less drunk. The corporal came forward to grab my horse's reins shouting: "General, surrender!" The hussars had appeared so suddenly we hadn't had time to draw our sabres. He hadn't finished what he was saying before I launched my fist at his ear and drove him back into the street he'd just emerged from. Upon a hussar throwing himself at General Viscount Digeon, the latter said: "What's this? You miserable fellow, daring to arrest your general!" "Oh, it's you, General Digeon. You must be one of our lot."'

Though Digeon's intervention enables all three top brass to get away, Macdonald looks back over his shoulder and sees the dragoons are still after them:

'They'd left the hussars behind without taking them prisoner; from which I concluded they were in connivance with them and that if they caught up with us we'd be arrested. We forced our pace still more.'

But where's his carriage? For several hours now it's been waiting for him, with his ADCs and secretary:

'But the postilions had got down and were doubtless in some bar, couldn't be found. I threw a sad glance at my carriage, with a considerable sum in gold inside.[10] I thought all was lost. Actually, one of my ADCs held out a portmanteau through the door, but we went past so quickly none of us had time to grab it.'[11]

At the Archbishop's palace Mayor Fargues presents himself to a triumphant Napoleon:

"You're very young to be mayor. How old are you?"

"Sire, I'm thirty-six."

"That's very young. How did you come to be made mayor?"

"I believe it's due to my devotion to the King."

"So you're very devoted to him?"

"Yes, Sire, and always have been. I imbibed those principles with my mother's milk."

"Good. You're a fine fellow. You've served the King well. You'll serve me in the same way. I entrust the town to you."

He says he'll receive the municipality tomorrow. Napoleon's words to Fargues, Fabry goes on, weren't superfluous. He's above all been accompanied by the silk workers. The mob.

Out on the Bourbonnais road, Macdonald and 'poor General Digeon' are still being pursued by the dragoons, who they are sure are hostile. They'd even gained on them, but at length they slowed down. And their own horses are dead beat. 'A little way ahead I saw two gendarmes' horses tied up. They were fresh. We could signal for them to be untied and run after us, who were no longer running.'

Soon both pursuers and pursued are going at a walking pace. A quarter of an hour from the first post-house outside the town they see a 'General Simmer, with whom I'd done the 1813 campaign and who'd served with great distinction.' He has already got the marshal's order to turn back his two battalions at Clermont, and is on his way to Lyons for fresh instructions. Amazed to see Macdonald there, he's still more amazed when the marshal breathlessly asks him:

"Have you got two fresh horses to lend me?"

Yes.

"Well, go back and get them saddled up." Simmer gallops off. With the dragoons still after them, they reach the post-house, where the two battalions present arms. Macdonald sees no sign of tricolour cockades. Taking Simmer aside he tells him what's happened, tells him to about-turn his troops. "They'll certainly not obey me." "Very well, leave them here." Simmer remains, and Digeon and Macdonald gallop off northwards, Digeon obsessed with the notion that Macdonald's white plume will be their undoing. To please him he takes it out of his hat and 'still at the gallop in the rain, I ripped it out and tore it to shreds.' At that moment Digeon's horse falls, luckily without more than scratches to its rider.

Now their companions, the other generals, are far behind. By and by Digeon, who's short-sighted, fancies he sees his own horses being led along ahead of them. 'We dismounted at once and saddled them ourselves.' The others, hot from their long gallop, make off to a stream. 'We let them go.' And away they go again, still galloping, and Macdonald gets a stitch in his side. 'It would have been still worse to trot.' At a village where a peasant, leaning against his door, salutes them with a *Vive l'Empereur*, they hear that Artois must by now be halfway up the long incline ahead. But though Digeon, 'still shocked by the way he'd been treated by the hussars', wants to go on, Macdonald, who hasn't had a bite to eat since yesterday, insists on sending for some bread and cheese and a glass of wine, telling his companion to keep a sharp lookout: who are those horsemen they can see in the distance behind them? Then they change places, and 'despite the steep slope and at cost of winding the horses', they gallop on again. 'The main thing was to catch up with the carriages.'

Which they do at the summit. Realising what's happened, Artois invites the marshal into his carriage, despite Digeon's panicky protests that they'll certainly be caught, the carriages going so slowly. "No matter, we'll force the pace or share their fate." At the next relay Digeon, dead-beat, at last consents to take a seat in Artois' ADCs' carriage. 'His Royal Highness gave me one beside him, in that, I believe, of the Duke of Fitz-James. Count Cars, and the Duke of Polignac, his equerry, made up the carriageful.'

Hour after hour they roll on, talking. Macdonald rehearses all the régime's mistakes, notably toward the military. Artois and his officers concede the point. 'Were they in good faith? I think so. Fear had made a big impression.'

And here, among persons announced at the Archbishop of Lyons' palace, is Fleury de Chaboulon. He'd got as far as Turin, much preoccupied by his various secret missions in France, when he'd been astounded to hear his idol is back. Now, admitted to the imperial presence and no doubt more than a little peeved to have been sent on a wild goose chase, he's received with a smile and a

"Well, I wasn't expected back so soon, eh?"

"Only Your Majesty can offer such surprises," bows Fleury diplomatically.

There follows (according to the 'intrepid ex-prefect') a long almost hail-fellow-well-met conversation.[12] Does Napoleon really ask him about the state of Parisian opinion (as if Fleury knew any more about it than he does)? Or confess his annoyance with Hortense for having 'begged' Louis XVIII for the title of Duchess [*sic*] of Saint-Leu and for trying to get wardship of her two sons? "She's committed a great stupidity in making a spectacle of herself in front of the courts. Whoever's been advising her are fools. Why ask for such a title as duchess?"

"But Sire," Fleury (says he) objects. "She didn't ask for it. It was the Emperor Alexander..."

"It makes no odds. She should no more have accepted it than asked for it. She should have called herself Madame Bonaparte. That's a name as good as another. What right did they have to make her son a Duke [*sic*] of Saint-Leu and a Bourbon peer? Louis [Bonaparte] was right to object. If Josephine had been alive she'd have put a stop to that fine project!"

Does Fleury think the Paris National Guard will declare for him? Fleury says he can't be sure, "but that at least it won't act against us." All this and much else Fleury affirms having jotted down in his verbatim notes at the time.[13] Since his devotion and pen may come in useful he's added to the office staff, as Fourth Secretary. And it's to him Napoleon dictates eleven radical decrees – abolishing 'royalty'[14]; exiling the Bourbons and those émigrés who'd returned with them, and wiping out all their emblems, orders and decorations; abolishing the nobility and all feudal rights. All changes and appointments made during the eleven-month interregnum are to be *non advenus* – 'as if they'd never happened'. Both the Chamber of Peers ("partly made up of persons who have borne arms against France and in whose interest it is to re-establish feudal rights and annul sales of national property") and the Chamber of Deputies ('whose powers have expired and most of whose members have made themselves unworthy of the nation's confidence') are suppressed, and two new chambers are to be elected via the imperial electoral colleges and meet in May at a '*Champ de Mai*' – a concept going back to Merovingian times.

The tone of these edicts is less democratic than their content. Has the old imperial ring to it: 'As far as Grenoble I'd been an adventurer,' Napoleon will concede at St Helena.[15] 'At Lyons I was a sovereign.' Has the leopard begun to show its spots, the eagle to show its claws? The people at Grenoble had been 'citizens'. These swarming crowds at Lyons – also '*une mandille*' – are 'subjects'. 'To the shouts of "*Vive l'Empereur!*" and "Long live the mayor!" Napoleon, who has no love for mobs, turns to the mayor and asks him "why he only saw men in waistcoats [*gens en veste*] in this mob." The mayor replied: "Because only that class of individuals love revolutions. They're always ready to applaud social upheavals. They'll applaud your fall as they do your triumph."'

191

"I know them," says Napoleon. And 'with a gesture of his hand: "I'll contain them[*Je les tiendrai*]."' Noticing how popular the mayor is, he says he'll surround him with great respect: "You need that, to be mayor of Lyons." Among other topics he discusses with Fargue is last year's Treaty of Paris, which had placed France back within her pre-Revolutionary frontiers, but which he says he'll respect. Their conversation, Fabry will afterwards hear, 'lasted an hour and a half. He interrupted it to go and review the troops.'

Marchand sees him 'accompanied by a few generals and a hussar picket, go to the Place Bellecour, to review Brayer's division.' A vast crowd, no less enthusiastic than it was yesterday, surrounds the square. Factitious enthusiasm, Fabry assures us sourly in a footnote,

'regularly subsidised, morning and evening during the three days Buonaparte spent at Lyons. As soon as he'd appeared at the window, people shouted *Vive l'Empereur!*, put their hands behind their backs and received a 100-*sous* piece. These were distributed twice a day, at midday and in the evening.'

The parade lasts two whole hours. And immediately it's over Napoleon orders Brayer to leave with the Lyons garrison for Paris. The footsore Elba battalion – already Peyrusse is calling it 'the Old Guard' – is to embark northwards on the Saône. Then he goes back to the Archbishop's Palace, where he finds 'the great gallery packed with generals, colonels, magistrates, administrators of every rank and kind – one could have been at the Tuileries,' thinks an ecstatic Fleury de Chaboulon. 'He paused a few moments, embraced Generals Mouton-Duvernet,[16] Girard and other officers who Paris was assuming were at his heels. After having distributed a few smiles and many compliments to right and left,' he received the local and regional authorities,

'beginning with the King's judges. Buonaparte did a lot of talking, or rather beat about the bush, declaimed against the nobility, tying up the thread of his ideas, often interrupted, with the text of his proclamations at the Golfe St Juan, which he developed with a commentary suited to the circumstances.'

In his *calèche* – now to be exchanged for a proper travelling *bastardèle* (the *calèche* he gives to Marchand[17]) – he has certainly been doing some political thinking. To be deliriously welcomed back by pitch-forked peasants as the champion of popular liberties (in their case from aristocrats and priests) and now no less deliriously by the townsmen and middle classes of Grenoble and Lyons as champion of intellectual liberties, freedom of the press and elected assemblies – all this is the exact opposite of what he has always stood for. And has certainly come as no small surprise. Doubtless he has listened, at least with one ear, to Labédoyère's advice. Far more than any putative resistance on the part of the Bourbons, it must be his political options that are preoccupying him. An entirely new role; whatever he's thinking privately, the actor in him[18] is up to playing it for the time being at least. Realising he must trump Louis XVIII's Charter, whose main vice in liberal eyes is that it's been 'granted', he tells the assembled company:

'I've no wish, like Louis XVIII, to foist on you a constitution I could then take away. I wish to give you one that's inviolable and will be the joint work of the people and of myself.'

Not, of course, of *le peuple*, in the narrower (*viz* broad) sense – everyone present understands that. But a 'correction and modification' of the Constitution of the Empire, to suit *la nation* – that ambiguous word, again, which is all things to all men, but is at least by implication anti-royalist and will confirm 'the interests established by the Revolution' – those so well represented here by the propertied members of the Lyons town council. Notably (according to Fleury[19]) he concedes that he'd been

"diverted into a false path by the force of circumstances. But, having learnt from experience, I've abjured this love of glory, so natural to Frenchmen, that's had such fatal results for them and for myself. We've had enough glory, and need a rest. I'd have preferred the repose of Elba to the worries of a throne, if I hadn't known France to be unhappy and in need of me."

He has come back, he goes on, 'after a few insignificant replies by his listeners',

"to protect and defend the interests arising out of our Revolution. I've come to agree with the nation's representatives a family pact that will for ever preserve the freedom and rights of all Frenchmen."

Neither Fleury de Chaboulon nor anyone else, he's sure, 'doubted the sincerity of Napoleon's promises and resolutions.' Fabry observes that upon one of the vicinity's mayors

'addressing him now as monsieur, now as Sire, says: "Call me whatever you like, even Consul." And tapped him gently on the cheek. Afterwards the Chief Judge, a M. Vouty, felicitates him, saying: "I'll have to kiss this blessed cheek a thousand times that's been touched by the hand of my saviour."'

Anyhow, with 12,000 troops to command and many other units hurrying to join him, if often commanded only by their NCOs, he's again in the full panoply of real military power. And that's the main thing. Makes all the difference.

Hearing he's sent for, Peyrusse, who's just paid out 3,700 francs[20] for the bigger carriage, hastens to the prefecture. On his way there he recalls how, less than a year ago, he'd passed through

'this same fortress town escorted by Cossacks, and how a few stifled

shouts of devotion had hardly made themselves heard on the same
bridge as His Majesty had just crossed in triumph.'
But now the boot's on the other foot:

'I'd had two millions in gold. This sum wasn't enough if we were to
manage while on campaign and pay such troops as might join us. His
Majesty ordered me to obtain some resources. I explained to him that
all the public funds had been ordered to leave Lyons, that the only
money was in the Bank. "If there's no other way out," His Majesty said,
"tell Jerzmanowski to take a 4-pounder." I replied at once that I
wouldn't need to have recourse to so violent a measure. I presented
myself at the Bank. We drew up a protocol, stating that private property had been violated [*une violation de domicile*]. And I took 600,000
francs in silver or notes,'

– all to be repaid in Paris. Peyrusse hears that the towns of Mâcon, Chalon,
Dijon and Tournus have just declared for the Emperor,

'who the Paris newspapers were saying was a vagabond and a fugitive,
abandoned by his soldiers and sowing consternation and fright
wherever he went. The *Moniteur* said: "The enemy is surrounded on all
sides. He can't escape the punishment he deserves, and it's because he
is not hiding his irrevocable loss. It is because he can no longer either
march on or retreat, that this great captain, once so active but whose
faculties have so greatly fallen off, is amusing himself at Lyons
reviewing his little force"',

rolling rhetorical sentences that betray the jitters behind them.

None of the local ladies, Fabry – at least refraining from telling us they'd all
fainted – will hear, 'wished to present themselves that evening. Only one
who, summoned, introduced herself in a mysterious manner.' This is a
certain Elénora Denuelle de la Plaigne, one-time *lectrice* to his sister Caroline. In 1805, after Austerlitz, she'd been summoned briefly to share his bed
at the Tuileries.[21] Now she brings with her her eight-year-old son, whom he
has never seen.[22]

More importantly he 'has a letter written to Marshal Ney, who was at Lons-
le-Saulnier with his army, to march out and come and join him.' And
another to elder brother Joseph, ex-King of Spain, now in Switzerland,
telling him to inform the Austrian and Russian ambassadors to the Swiss
Confederation, whose 'protector' he'd once been, that he'll respect the
Treaty of Paris. For the Lyonnais he dictates in true imperial style a rhetorical 'souvenir of the beautiful moments they'd given him':

*"In the moment of leaving your town to enter my capital I feel a need to let you
know the feelings you have inspired in me. You have always been in the forefront
of my affections. On the throne or in exile, you have always shown me the same*

sentiments. The elevated character that specially distinguished you has merited all my esteem. In more tranquil moments I shall come back to busy myself with your needs and the prosperity of your manufactures and your town. – Lyonnais, I love you."

Clearly, since leaving Grenoble the old Napoleon has surfaced. What the locals – of various shades of opinion, republican, liberal, royalist – really thought of it we don't know. But men like Labédoyère must be having their private thoughts. At 1:30 pm, Monday 13 March,

'he mounted his horse and rode out of Lyons, escorted by horse artillery and men from the 4th Hussars, and accompanied as far as the barrier by the populace, whose vociferations redoubled as he left.'

As the Elba battalion leaves, the Lyons National Guard presents it 'a flag with a golden eagle.'

But in Vienna on the other side of the Alps, 575 miles away as the crow flies (or some 840 by road), the secretaries of eight of Europe's 'legitimate' sovereigns and their representatives are just now dipping pens in silver inkpots for their masters to sign Talleyrand's final ferocious Declaration.[23] Bonaparte's escape, it reads, being

'an outrage upon the social order by which, in breaking the convention that had established him in the island of Elba, he has destroyed the sole title to which his existence was attached. In returning to France with intent to cause trouble and disturbances, he has deprived himself of the protection of the laws and has manifested in the face of the universe that with him there can be neither peace nor truce. In consequence, the Powers declare that Napoleon Bonaparte is placed outside all civil and social relations, and that, as the enemy and perturber of the world's peace, he has delivered himself to the public vengeance.'

Never before have all the powers of Europe declared war on one man.

CHAPTER 9

CHANGING SIDES AT LONS-LE-SAULNIER

Now here's Ney, in a very bad temper indeed, arrived at Besançon, near the eastern frontier. With him he has his two ADCs, Levavasseur and Devaux. But no orders. Where's Berry? No one knows. Where's his artillery? He hasn't any. Where are his troops? Strung out in cantonments throughout the Franche-Comté; only 400 men are in the Besançon fortress. Only one thing's clear. He's going to put paid to Napoleon, once and for all. In a towering rage, he's breathing fire and slaughter against his former master, whom he doesn't like, and who knows it, and who, whatever glittering epithets he may have bestowed on his name, doesn't like him either. Isn't it he, Ney, who, with the fatal words 'We've had enough, the army will obey its generals', had forced him to abdicate? Now he declares in the presence of no fewer than seven witnesses:

"It's a good thing the Man from Elba has attempted his crazy enterprise. It's going to be the last act of his tragedy. I'll fix Bonaparte. We're going to attack the wild beast. That raving lunatic'll never forgive me for making him abdicate. Before six months are out I wouldn't put it past him to have me beheaded."

But when he repeats his words about taking Napoleon back to Paris in an iron cage, the sub-prefect demurs:

"Wouldn't it be better dead in a tumbril?"

"No, the Parisians like a spectacle."

All the time, as the Burgundian countryside had rolled by, young Levavasseur had everywhere noticed the inflamed state of public opinion. One colonel, Prince Carignan of the 1st Hussars, had told Ney frankly he couldn't rely on his men to fight Bonaparte; whereon the marshal had told him to march them to the nearest town, with secret orders to its mayor to shut the town gates after them and not let them out. Finally, reaching Besançon on 10 March, Levavasseur has found everyone in a panic. And almost no troops or ammunition: 'The artillery lacked teams and most of his guns weren't even mounted.' No orders have come, either from Soult or Berry.

As his second-in-command Ney has a certain Breton aristocrat and former Chouan leader, by name Lieutenant-General Auguste-Victor Count de Ghaisne de Bourmont,

'a little fellow with a not very remarkable face, a very gentle voice and air, small eyes and something polite and affable about him that at the time seemed more due to natural benevolence than to long familiarity with court life.'

197

Bourmont, very much the *grand seigneur*, is – as events will show – the very epitome of a Mr Facing-Both-Ways, but at heart (and Rumigny assures us he has one) a royalist. Like most of his ilk he's used to living beyond his means.[1] A reasonably good general, his only notable military exploit so far[2] has been to defend Nogent in 1814 'with 1,200 men against 15,000 Allies for two days,' before himself being wounded (whether severely or lightly was a matter of opinion). Whereupon, in the general dearth of officers,[3] though he'd once likened him to 'a grass-snake' and scribbled 'not to be employed' on his papers, Napoleon had promoted him general of division. Just now Ney's second-in-command, more a snake-in-the-grass than a mere grass-snake, is keeping a wary eye on his extremely tense and excitable marshal.

The 6th Military Division is made up of two line regiments (the renumbered 60th and 77th), the 8th Chasseurs, and the 5th Dragoons. Perhaps feeling the need for someone more of his own ilk to command his 2nd division, Ney sends Levavasseur to fetch in a former comrade-in-arms from revolutionary days cashiered by Napoleon for alleged 'immorality' but in fact for having been a partisan of Moreau. Here at Besançon people are saying – and doubtless hoping (as people are also doing in Vienna) – that Bonaparte will throw his army across the Alps and join up with Murat in Italy, and General Lecourbe, who'd been the Republic's foremost expert on mountain warfare, is just now, reinstated in his rank by Louis XVIII, living on his estate nearby. So Lecourbe seems the very man to bar Napoleon's way through the Alps. Brought to Besançon, Levavasseur hears Ney say:

"Lecourbe, I know you. You love your country. Bonaparte abdicated. He only has 4,000 men with him. You owe him nothing. If he exiled you to your estates it was because he wanted all services to be done to him personally. You're a patriot. Join us. You can't refuse your country this service. Bonaparte has come to bring us a civil war."

Lecourbe says he harbours no bitterness against Napoleon. But accepts.

Besançon is the centre of a Catholic royalist freemasonry and local opinion is split violently between the haves and the have-nots. But already, all over the Franche-Comté, where Ney's units are scattered, the peasantry is declaring for Napoleon.[4] How many men, how many units, has Bonaparte got with him by now? Why isn't Berry sending him, Ney, his orders? But Berry's in Paris, and none have come. What, for the matter of that, are Artois and Macdonald doing down at Lyons? Ney has no news. What *is* happening down at Lyons? In Paris? In the other military districts? He writes to Berry:

"We've no news here of Bonaparte's activities. I think this is the last act of his tragedy. I should be much obliged if Your Royal Highness can give me some information, and if, above all, you would deign to make use of me."

No reply.

But here, from Moulins, to the south-west, comes one of Artois' ADCs, the Duke of Maillé. Inviting him to dinner, Ney suggests he join forces with Artois between Besançon and Auxonne. Has Bonaparte really been acting in concert with his father-in-law in Vienna? If so, then the Bourbon cause is really in danger. Not that Ney believes anything of the sort: 'It's just his usual boasting.'

But though by universal acknowledgement he is the most brilliant and prestigious of all field-commanders "Bonaparte by himself is nothing."

On the other hand Ney's own resources are utterly inadequate. And even those he can muster, his unit commanders tell him they don't think they can rely on unless they're confined to barracks and kept away from the populace. Ney studies his map, takes all these matters into consideration. Likewise Bonaparte's probable route. And decides to order both his divisions to concentrate southwards at Lons-le-Saulnier. From there they can perhaps act as Artois' left wing, and, if properly supplied, attack Napoleon's column, either in the rear or in flank, according to circumstances. But certainly this can't be done without artillery, so he orders eighteen guns to be brought in from Chalon. Then, after sending on Levavasseur to set up his headquarters at Lons and taking Bourmont with him in his carriage, he sets out along the road that winds along the foothills of the Jura mountains.

At Geneva, just beyond them, the news of the Antibes landing, received on 5 March,[5] had at first been greeted only as a bad joke. But the Genevans, who've had their fill of being a French 'protectorate', have quickly tumbled to the new danger. One of them is the well-educated young Captain *Jean-Louis Rieu*.[6] 'Everyone around me, beginning with my parents, was utterly furious with the *Usurper*, as he was then being called.' And it must be admitted, he goes on,

'we Genevans had some reason to tremble for our nascent liberties.
But I, as a French officer, couldn't just stand there with folded arms. I had to take sides. And I sided with the allegedly legitimate monarchy.'

Last year, after 'a very cheap journey to Russia which, we being burdened neither with money nor baggage, hadn't cost us a penny (the Cossacks having been so obliging as to put us out of reach of thieves)', he'd finally got back to Paris and been granted extended leave to visit his parents in Geneva. And now here he is, travelling by post-chaise through a snowstorm in the Jura mountains to report for duty in Paris.

With him he has two fellow officers. One, de Vincy by name, is an officer of the newly reformed Swiss Guard (*Les Cent Suisses*[7]); the other a fellow Genevan lieutenant by name *Frédéric Rilliet-Constant*, formerly of the 1st Cuirassiers, now transformed into the Cuirassiers of Louis XVIII's Guard.[8]

En route they've run into two compatriots, both royalists, who'd reached

Lyons at the same time as Napoleon. One of them had 'stood on a barrel' ('on a mail-coach', his comrade politely corrects him) to see 'the Emperor' (no longer the 'Usurper') enter the city. 'Despairing of the sacred cause of the throne and the altar (as the phrase went in those days)' the businessmen are bolting back to Geneva.

Finally the three officers, after pushing on through thick snow, see 'at the foot of a steep hill, the last of the Juras', the little town of Lons-le-Saulnier.

Here, at 2:00 am on 10 March, Ney has taken lodgings at the modest *Pomme d'Or* Inn, just off its main square, where Levavasseur has already set up his headquarters for him.[9] But though he invites his second-in-command to share his rooms, Bourmont chooses to find other accommodation in the town.

From all along the edge of the Jura mountains Ney gets busy assembling every unit for fifty miles around. No question of his determination to fight the invader. Concerts his plans with the prefect, the Marquis de Vaulchier, summons all his senior officers, sends off despatch riders to hasten on the concentration, and writes to Soult to tell him that as soon as he has some artillery he'll concentrate his force at Bourg, so as to manoeuvre toward Mâcon. But now it's the night of 12–13 March, and Ney, in his room at the *Pomme d'Or*, gets a nasty shock. In fact two.

Not only has Napoleon already entered Lyons and disposes of at least 14,000 troops; but both Macdonald and Artois are safely back in Paris – and here he still is without any orders! Immediately on getting to Lons he'd held a quick review of his men. And when he'd exhorted them to remember their oath of fidelity a schoolboy by name *Gindre de Mancy* had noted there'd been 'a few murmurs, perhaps, but no cry for revolt was heard, and the populace, for its part, remained an impassible and silent witness.' Seeing his regiments lack cartridges, Ney sends back one of his staff officers to Besançon to forward 50,000 as fast as possible by mail-coaches. One of Artois' ADCs, the Marquis de Saurans, having 'arrived at Lons at the same time as we had, breakfasted and dined at the marshal's table.' More importantly,

'a businessman called M. Boulouze, returning terrified from Lyons, had brought the famous proclamations dictated at the Gulf of St Juan, in which the Emperor said "victory will march at the *pas de charge*, the eagle will fly from steeple to steeple with the national colours till it alights on the towers of Notre Dame".'

It really looks as though Napoleon's words as reported to Ney by Boulouze – "We shall walk to Paris with our hands in our pockets" – are coming true. Yet Ney doesn't give much for Boulouze's statement that the Man from Elba has the support of the Austrian government, or that the British navy had eased his passage:

"Oh go along with you," he'd said. "He's just boasting."

Boulouze had been impressed by his firmness:

"*M. le maréchal,* you've already saved France once when you made him abdicate. You'll save her again."

Ney, thoughtfully: "Yes. If I can make the King's cause prevail I'll be the country's liberator."

The Marquis de Soran tries to put a good face on things by describing His Royal Highness' flight as a tactical withdrawal toward Moulins. "The worst thing that could possibly have happened," Ney writes on 12 March:

"His Royal Highness should first and foremost have marched on Grenoble to attack Bonaparte there. If he'd done so, our predicament would probably be over by now. Macdonald seems to have no confidence in his men. But it isn't by making them retreat you find out whether they mean to do their duty."

By now Ney's beginning to realise he's fallen foul of a highly problematic situation. His troops aren't to be relied on. And at most he has only 7,000 of them, as against how many of Bonaparte's, advancing swiftly and every moment gathering size and momentum? And here's the prefect of the Ain department, M. Capelle, an ardent royalist, who's just been driven out by the populace. Introduced by Bourmont,[10] he tells Ney:

"*M. le maréchal,* between Bourg and here there's nothing but disorder and violence. Everywhere I've seen the revolutionary madness bursting out among the dregs of the populace, and among the military."

It's reminded him horribly of "the first period of the Revolution", when the peasantry had burnt down châteaux and massacred aristocrats.

Ney: "It's unheard of! Here am I, left without any news or orders since I left Paris. I don't even know where my regiments are. In the old days when I'd sent my orders for horses to be sent to such or such a place I slept sound at night." Where does Capelle think Bonaparte is now? How many troops has he got with him?

Capelle: "By now his advance guard, at least, is at Mâcon. He left Lyons with 5,000 men, but the 76th Line has just defected, probably other units too. By now he can't have less than 12,000 men."

Silence. Then both Capelle and Bourmont hear Ney mutter:

'What do you expect? I can't stop the sea with my bare hands!'

Capelle: 'We can still count on the Swiss.'

Instantly Ney's on his feet, furious: "Monsieur! If foreigners set foot on French soil, the whole of France will be for Napoleon!"[11] Flushing scarlet, he shows the two men the door: 'This'll reverberate all the way to Kamchatka!'[12] Going downstairs Capelle takes Bourmont's arm. Asks him in a low voice:

"General, are you still counting on the marshal's loyalty?"

Bourmont, always evasive, says he thinks so. "I'm counting on his good faith."

To assess the grim realities further south Ney sends for Colonel Xavier de Champagne, commander of the Lons National Guard. Can he find him a reliable spy? Champagne sends for his quartermaster Monnier, who finds Ney

'in a state of perplexity hard to describe. Having placed himself between his duty and the instincts of his entire life, he hardly wished to be seen or approached in so false a situation. The marshal was lying fully dressed on his bed, its drawn curtains hiding him from his visitors. There the great warrior was heaving deep sighs that to me seemed to indicate a most painful anxiety. Gently drawing back the curtains, M. de Champagne presented me as one of his officers he could count on. "Leave at once for Chalon-sur-Saône," the marshal said to me in a curt tone of voice, as if we'd been with the Grand Army. "Find out how much matériel the Emperor disposes of, and find a way of letting me know at the earliest moment." At 10:00 pm I was given a passport, and at 11:00 pm I left in one of the vehicles of the departmental receiver-general of taxes.'

This night of 12–13 March Ney's already on the horns of an existential choice, an anguished dilemma. Yet next day, when each regiment's officers, headed by its colonel, are ordered to present themselves at the *Pomme d'Or* to receive his orders, he exhorts them:

'Gentlemen. We're all brave fellows. We've all served the Emperor honourably and faithfully. The Emperor has abdicated. Louis XVIII reigns over France. For our honour's sake we must serve him as faithfully as we did the Emperor. I'm counting on you. You'll see me at your head. But if anyone among you, for personal reasons, finds it repugnant to fight this war, let him frankly say so. Orders will be given for him to go home, because I don't want anyone beside me except brave men I can count on. That, gentlemen, is what I had to say to you.'

Out amidst the crowd on the stairway Levavasseur, observing the officers' attitudes, hears

'murmurings, showing the marshal's words weren't altogether to their taste. From this moment all the aristocrats of the town and countryside encumbered the sitting rooms, saying they doubted whether we'd be able to stand up against the trend. Ney knew the Bourbons' partisans lacked energy. "We don't need any cry-babies, male or female," he said.'

Yet neither Levavasseur nor Devaux, his fellow ADC, doubt the outcome:

'The Marquis de Grivel, commander of the department's military police, came and told the marshal that some grenadiers from Elba had been sent to suborn the men. Ney ordered me to look into the matter, which I found to be correct. In one group I myself arrested a grenadier who was wearing a greatcoat with eagles on its buttons.'

One of the two infantry regiments under Bourmont's command, as we've seen, is the 77th Line, which 'in the first days of March,' has heard 'a vague rumour announcing the Emperor's landing on the coasts of Provence. In our garrison,' says Sergeant-Major Larreguy de Civrieux, of the former 116th,

'the joy had been electric, couldn't be repressed by General de Bourmont's severe order of the day, which had confirmed this piece of news and proclaimed Napoleon an outlaw. A meaningful silence had reigned in our ranks. We understood each other by glances. We squeezed each others' hands, and this mysterious pressure revealed that each man's joy was in everyone's heart.'

One of Ney's first acts having been to imprison an officer for shouting *Vive l'Empereur!*,

'our regiments viewed the Prince of the Moscova with great distrust. Such coolness toward the Bourbon cause astonished him. He'd hoped to change our feelings by the prestige of his glorious reputation. More than once he came and mingled with our groups of NCOs and men on the town square, to be pleasant to us and sound out our dispositions.'

Tall and temperamental, never given to mincing his words – though just now he'd do well to do so – any rebellious word has been causing the redhead

'to become animated in word and gesture. With fiery brush strokes he painted for us the miseries Napoleon was bringing back on our country, the sacredness of the oaths binding us to the standard of the lily. "I'll set the example," he cried. "I'll march at your head. And if need be it'll be I who'll fire the first shot!"'

But he has also threatened: 'I'll run my sword through the first man that budges!'

At which, says Larreguy de Civrieux, 'the group had melted away', to go on muttering its 'discontent and impatience inspired by the prince's dispositions, so little in harmony with the army's mood.' Next day Ney had written to Suchet, his fellow marshal at Strasbourg:

'We're on the eve of a tremendous revolution. The only hope lies in cutting the evil at its root. Everybody is thunderstruck at the swiftness of his progress, and it must be said there is a certain class of people who've helped him. There's a fear the troops will be infected. I hope, my dear Marshal, we shall soon see the end of this crazy enterprise, especially if we put speed and concentration into marching our troops.'

But gradually the news from Lyons – mainly brought by persons who seem oddly uncomfortable in civilian clothes – begins to seep through.

His resources may be small, but there's still been no lack of determination in Ney's attitude – or loyalty to the government. On the other hand there's something hectic about his mood that's making his more insightful subordinates feel apprehensive. Not, however, Levavasseur:

'Night fell. I remained in attendance on the marshal, who went to bed. His secretary Dutour was in another part of the house. Generals Bourmont, Lecourbe, Mermet and Jarry were in lodgings in the town. Around 10:00 pm an officer of the National Guard brought a despatch. I took him in to the marshal, leaving a candle on the bedside table, and went out of the room, leaving the officer alone with him. After a quarter of an hour he came out again, and I went in saying: "*M. le maréchal*, have you no orders to give me?" "No," he replied. And, taking the candle, I also picked up the letter beside it.'

It's from the prefect at Mâcon, who writes:

"A colonel of gendarmerie by name Jameron, from Lyons, has just entered this town, announcing the Emperor's imminent arrival. Great enthusiasm has just broken out at this news. The tricolour is being flown everywhere. Triumphal arches are being raised, and I find myself obliged to leave the prefecture."

Indignant, Levavasseur, who knows Colonel Jameron personally, takes the letter to secretary Dutour's room to show it to him. Again, around midnight, the same thing happens. And again he picks up the new despatch lying beside Ney's candle. This one is from the mayor of Chalon-sur-Saône, who has the honour to inform Ney that

"a battalion of the 76th Line, which was escorting your artillery park, has just entered Chalon to shouts of *Vive l'Empereur!* The town has instantly revolted. The troops say they want to present this artillery to the little corporal, etc."

So much for his eighteen guns. Picking up this letter too, Levavasseur notices in Ney

'a great agitation, an impatience and a displeasure that struck me. He was stamping his feet [*trépinait*] in his bed and muttering to himself. Soon afterwards, another officer, sent by General Pelgrin, came to tell the marshal that the regiment of hussars commanded by Prince Carignan had adopted the tricolour cockade, forced the gates of Auxonne, and was marching on Dijon,'

which also has gone over. It's getting on for 4:00 am when a fourth officer follows, confirming the news that Carignan has in fact entered that important town, whose 'fine National Guard', too, is now sporting the tricolour:

'I noticed that Ney, though still in bed, was in a state of great perplexity. At about 5:00 am the Marquis de Grivel appeared with some papers and took them in to the marshal. He was accompanied by two men in civilian clothes, who stayed by me a moment. I questioned them, and they told me they'd come from Lyons and were greatly surprised to have been arrested.'

They are two officers of the Imperial Guard, both personally known to Ney.[13] They've brought him two letters. Attached to the first is a march order for his divisions and a note in Napoleon's own handwriting:

"*Mon cousin.* My chief-of-staff is sending you your orders. I don't doubt that on hearing of me getting to Lyons you've made your troops resume the tricolour. Implement Bertrand's orders and come and join me at Chalon. I shall receive you as I did on the evening of the Moscova."

– *ie* Borodino. That's the promise. Here (obviously also dictated by Napoleon) is the stick. The Emperor's peaceful success, Ney reads in the other letter (supposedly written by Bertrand), is now certain. If he, Ney, should oppose it, he'll be responsible for shedding French blood in a civil war.

His conversation with the Guards officers lasts an hour or so. The Emperor, so they also assure him (and certainly they believe it), is acting with the assent of his father-in-law the Emperor of Austria. Marie-Louise and the King of Rome will be returning shortly, and the British navy had connived at His Majesty's peaceful voyage from Elba to Antibes. He'd even dined on board a British ship. How otherwise could he have made it? 'Then,' Levavasseur goes on, 'the marquis took away his prisoners. Going in to the marshal again, I saw bundles of proclamations that had been seized in the two travellers' carriage.'

For a long while Ney, in extreme agitation, paces his room, where a Colonel Saurans hears him mutter over and over to himself: "Victory will march at the *pas de charge*. The eagle with the national colours will fly from belfry to belfry to the towers of Notre Dame...", language which Ney, the ostler's son, understands. He also bursts out with criticisms of the way Artois has acted at Lyons. Artois, 'who's never deigned to invite a marshal of France into his carriage', has left him here with neither troops nor orders. He also reverts to Louis XVIII's disdainful rejection of his advice to adopt the Old Guard. Not that he's any less furious with Napoleon: "That lunatic'll never forgive me for having made him abdicate! The first soldier that budges I'll pass my sabre through his guts, the hilt'll do to plaster him up. But the soldier always marches toward the sound of the guns, and my ADC Levavasseur knows perfectly how to use them." And to Bourmont: "Our numbers will be fewer, but we'll give him a drubbing."

Levavasseur:

'At dawn [14 March] the marshal opened the door to the room where I was and said: "Levavasseur, send for Generals Lecourbe, Bourmont, Jarry and Mermet." I carried out his order, and one after another they turned up during the forenoon. Soon my room was packed, as it had been yesterday, with the men who were most devoted to the King. Their audience with the marshal lasted a long while.'

Apparently Ney moots the question of loyalties, for Bourmont tells him: "How do you think I could serve under that b——? He has done me nothing but harm, and the King only good. And anyway, I'm in the King's service; and you see, *M. le maréchal,* I have my honour."

To which Ney blazes up:

"And I, too, have my honour! That's why I don't like being humiliated. I don't want to go on seeing my wife come home with tears in her eyes from the humiliations she's received at the Tuileries. It's obvious the King doesn't want any part of us. It's only with a man of the army, such as Bonaparte, that the army can be respected."[14]

'My head was bowed over that fatal proclamation,' Ney will relate afterwards:[15]

'Both of them were standing with their backs against the fireplace. I was facing them. I summoned Bourmont, on his honour, to tell me his thoughts. Without answering, Bourmont takes the proclamation, reads it, tells me he approves of it and adds: "*M. le maréchal,* you can read that out to the troops." Then I turn to Lecourbe, who reads it, says nothing, hands it back to Bourmont. "Has this been sent to you?" Lecourbe said to me after a moment's silence. "There's been a rumour to that effect. For a long time we've been able to foresee all this...".'

A distressed Levavasseur goes on:

'Finally Ney half-opened the door and ordered me to assemble all the troops on the esplanade. General Bourmont went out to assemble the troops. He'd had two hours to think it over.'[16]

Is it really Ney, as Levavasseur will remember, who orders the troops to assemble? Or Bourmont? Because certainly Bourmont doesn't raise any objections, nor does Lecourbe. In the town Lieutenant Rieu, the Swiss officer of the Royal Guard, hears

'the drum ordering the fall-in for him to review the troops. One could see at a glance that, so far from being an obstacle to the ex-Emperor, they'd serve him as an escort. Everywhere the soldiers were uttering Bonapartist shouts and insulting the Bourbons.'

Which, however, isn't quite how his more royalist-inclined comrade Rilliet sees the situation. Bumping into an old friend, one of Bourmont's ADCs, he too has seen

'the town full of troops wearing the white cockade. They seemed animated by a good spirit, except for a regiment of dragoons whose horses were occupying the stables of the hotel where we'd got down. These troopers were singing highly meaningful songs in honour of *Father Violet*.'

Just as they'd come out from the prefecture, where they'd gone to get passports, 'much easier to obtain than horses', the three Swiss had again seen Ney about to enter it with Bourmont and Lecourbe. And it had been while waiting for some horses that Rilliet's royalist friend had told him:

'We're leaving this evening. Tomorrow we'll meet Bonaparte. And we'll soon put paid to him. Ney's as resolute as a lion.'

Just then their horses had been brought around, and they'd set off again for Paris. And therefore do not witness what follows. Which is a pity. For to Larreguy and his fellow sergeant-majors, ordered to assemble their companies under their officers within the hour 'on a vast esplanade near the town, in full uniform' it's 'obvious a great event' is at hand. 'We ran to arms with indescribable emotion. We went out from Lons-le-Saulnier and formed an immense square, one of its faces closed by the cavalry.'

In the group of officers around Ney only young Levavasseur isn't anticipating anything out of the way. While he'd been trying to keep up the courage of the mass of timorous royalists huddled in the *Pomme d'Or* and Ney had 'half-opened' his door and given his order for all the troops to assemble on the town's esplanade, Levavasseur had pointed out that neither he nor the marshal have a horse between them; and Bourmont had just told him to go to his own ADC and get two saddled up for them. All the time Levavasseur's praising Ney's firmness of character and imperturbability. 'Then he came in to us, and asked us to leave him alone a moment with his secretary.' So they all go into another room:

'Neither Bourmont, nor Lecourbe, nor Mermet, nor Jarry attempted to give us the least idea of what was afoot. I still seem to see them, seated, silent, while I energetically expressed myself about our forthcoming triumphant entrance into Lyons, to shouts of *Vive le Roi!* and with Marshal Ney at our head.'

So far is Levavasseur from expecting what's going to happen that he admires the courage of this handful of officers who're prepared to stand up to their obviously mutinous men, and is even praising Ney's firmness in these impossible circumstances. But then, just as everyone's sprucing himself up for the parade, Bourmont, with Lecourbe, Mermet and Jarry, go off on their own. 'He behaved very cleverly,' Ney will remember:

'I'd implored him to lodge with me. He'd not wanted to. He went off

207

and took refuge at the house of the Marquis de Vaulchier, where they together formed some coteries to be on their guard against events and arrange a backdoor for themselves whatever happened.'

All of which sounds entirely credible and in line with Bourmont's character.

Now the gilded procession is leaving the *Pomme d'Or* for the esplanade called La Chevalerie. Only a couple of hundred yards away, it lies outside the town's east gate. The commanders have been joined by the local authorities, royalists to a man. Levavasseur and Devaux are bringing up the rear. Against the sombre background of the distant Jura mountains local schoolboy Gindre de Mancy, who's among the spectators, sees the Chevalerie esplanade is only partially filled with Ney's troops, over which the white Bourbon flags are flying. An advance-guard has already left for Bourg. Otherwise there's only the 60th and 77th Line,

'recently joined by a squadron of the 3rd Hussars, commanded by the son[17] of our illustrious compatriot Marshal Moncey. They'd formed up in several ranks in an elongated square, one of its sides against the Chevalerie buildings. The opposite side was still open when we and our comrades, coming out of school, and other curious persons, came and placed ourselves there. But almost immediately the squadron of hussars emerged from the Rue du Jura. The troopers dismounted and came toward us. And the marshal – I was struck by his worried air – told a sentry:

'"Get these youngsters out of the way."

'So we found ourselves placed behind two or three ranks of soldiers.'

Ney:[18] 'When the troops were assembled, Bourmont and Lecourbe came to me at the head of the officers and accompanied me to the centre of the square.'

To Larreguy, the marshal, 'without any cockade in his hat – something that wasn't noticed until later' – seems

'pale, wan, all-in [*défait*]. He was followed by General Lecourbe, the Count de Bourmont, that former Vendean leader. The marshal draws his sword, orders a roll of drums, and all the cavalry's NCOs to dismount. After the drum roll, which sent everyone to his post, followed a most solemn silence. Then, in a stentorian voice, holding his sword in one hand and a paper in the other, the marshal summoned all the superior officers to the square's centre. A tremor of impatience passed through all the ranks. The men's elbows were pressing each other electrically.'

Levavasseur, who otherwise seems sharp-witted enough, can't be all that sensitive to his marshal's mood, nor to the turn things are taking. For he's utterly amazed when his colleague Devaux, hearing him going on in the same vein as ever, murmurs in his ear 'in a very low voice':

'"Levavasseur, it seems to me things..." and makes a wavy gesture with his hand. At that moment I leave the side of the Marquis de Grivel, and hear the marshal's stentorian voice reading out the proclamation.'

What, Sergeant-Major Larreguy is wondering, will become of Ney should he 'pronounce an anathema on Napoleon?' More than one anxious observer is remembering the critical days of the Revolution, when troops had massacred their officers. But Levavasseur, hearing the marshal read out (in what to Larreguy seems 'an emotional and jerky voice') the first words of his proclamation, is

'so far from expecting a reversal of opinion, that hearing the words "*Officers, non-commissioned officers and soldiers, the cause of the Bourbons is lost for ever...*" I expected him to add "unless you stand by me." But what was my surprise when I heard the rest of the proclamation?'

Which goes on – startlingly:

The legitimate dynasty adopted by the French nation is going to reascend the throne. Only the Emperor Napoleon, our sovereign, has the right to reign over our beautiful country. What do we care whether the Bourbon nobility chooses to expatriate itself or consent to live among us? The sacred cause of our independence and our liberty will no longer tolerate their disastrous influence. They have wanted to vilify our military glory, but they've deceived themselves. This glory is the fruit of works too noble for us ever to lose the memory of it. Soldiers! The times are past when peoples were governed by suppressing their rights. In the end liberty triumphs, and Napoleon, our august Emperor, is going to confirm it for ever ... Soldiers! I've so often led you to victory. Now I'm going to lead you toward this immortal phalanx Napoleon is leading to Paris and which will be there in a few days time. There our hope and our happiness will be realised for ever. Vive l'Empereur!'

All of which the schoolboys, 'too far away from him, rather gather from the ensuing effect than hear.' 'The first words,' Larreguy goes on,

'had petrified us. We couldn't believe our ears and eyes. The shout of *Vive l'Empereur!* set our hearts, so long oppressed, on fire. An undefinable explosion from us all responded to the marshal's shout. The ranks were instantly broken, the troopers abandoned their horses, and we threw ourselves at the Prince of the Moscova to embrace him, press his hand, touch his clothes, his sword. It was a magnificent disorder in which all hierarchy dissolved in a moment. In ecstasy we went up to men we didn't even know, embraced them. A drummer kissed his colonel! We laughed, we wept. The *vivandières*, exalted by so much enthusiasm, were no longer selling their brandy, they were giving it away, thus fanning the flames. One saw officers and men prick their hands to mingle their blood with the liquor and so swear to shed it to the last drop for Napoleon's cause. All packs had been spontaneously opened, and each soldier, with few exceptions, had taken out his tricolour cockade, so carefully hidden away since a year ago. The white flag, the Bourbon cockade, were trampled underfoot. And to huge delight and everyone's surprise an elderly NCO exhumed from his pack the Imperial Eagle which had once rallied his regiment on many a field of battle. This glorious relic ran from hand to hand, each of us wanted to see it, kiss it.'

'It was truly a delirium. The officers,' so much at least as Gindre de Mancy can see, are

> 'waving their swords in the air or embracing each other, tears in their eyes. The men were ripping the white cockades out of their shakos and the fleurs-de-lis from their lapels, to shouts of *"Vive l'Empereur!* Down with the white trash! Down with the lobsters!"'[19]

Even Ney throws himself 'into the arms of the officers and men. He went along the ranks like a man in delirium, embracing even fifers and drummers.' Levavasseur is stunned by the shouts of enthusiasm 'unleashed among the soldiers, who thrust themselves into our midst saying they'd never had any doubts about our patriotism.'

The schoolboys, too, 'giddy youngsters, brought up in the cult of Napoleon and burning to avenge the disasters of 1814, we madly mingled our acclamations with those of the soldiers.'

What a painful situation, though, for a staunch royalist like the Marquis de Grivel.

> 'Complimented like ourselves by the men, he couldn't hide his indignation. At length the ranks slowly reformed. The cavalry horses were running hither and thither, bounding about the countryside. The sound of the warlike trumpet recalled them to their squadrons. Then, when silence had been re-established, we were witnesses to a scene worthy of antiquity.'

Grivel, the colonel of the Jura National Guard,

> 'an old knight of the Order of St Louis who'd emigrated with his Prince's staff, stepped forward into the middle of the square, broke his sword, threw the pieces on the ground and said to the marshal in a firm voice: "Prince, this sword cannot and shall not serve any but the children of St Louis!" He saluted, and walked away, protected by everybody's esteem and admiration.'[20]

Larreguy himself picks up a section of Grivel's sword and puts it into his knapsack as a kind of talisman.

Next to step forward is Colonel Dubalen of the 60th Line. Who tells Ney:

"I judge no one's conduct, but I regard myself as bound by my oath. Prince, I ask you to authorise me to go home."[21]

Permission granted.

But Larreguy sees how Ney, 'to efface these transient impressions, went past each regiment, one by one, and it wasn't hard for him to revive the enthusiasm momentarily suspended by these fine and courageous lessons in rectitude and fidelity.' All the time Bourmont is

'present, pale and silent. Great was the amazement of the population of Lons-le-Saulnier. A revolution had just happened outside its gates, and it knew nothing of it! That morning we'd marched out with the Bourbon cockade and flag. We re-entered the walls with the imperial eagle and our national colours. As Marshal Ney went back to his lodgings the population scattered to let him pass, shouting thousands of *Vive l'Empereurs!*'

Following the troops back to the main square, Mancy hears one of his more sophisticated comrades remark coldly: 'This is all very well. But afterwards...'

'At these words exaltation gave place inside me to dejection. Suddenly, by some kind of foreknowledge, it gave me a glimpse of the fatal consequences of so glorious a return from exile that would be so fatal for our unhappy France'

– the same distressing vision, no doubt, as had assailed Captain Gazon at Antibes. A few disorders follow: Larreguy will afterwards seem to recall 'the emblems of the monarchy on a mass of establishments' being smashed up; and Mancy, looking out over the main square from a bookbinder's upstairs window 'opposite the Café Bourbon, kept by M. and Mme. Rodet, and the rendezvous of the town's royalists', sees it invaded by 'a mob of maddened soldiers' – grenadiers evidently, because they have

'sabres in their hands. They smashed mirrors, window panes, tables, chairs, plates and dishes, in a word, anything within reach. All this because they'd been told – a wicked calumny – that the cafe's mistress had sworn to wash her hands in the blood of French soldiers! I've never heard that any officer took part in this ignominious act of devastation. On the contrary. We even saw generals rush into the café to bring the men to their sense of discipline and duty.'

But Larreguy, though he too sees how 'for a moment anarchy triumphed,' sees it

'suppressed almost immediately by our chiefs and by the army's good morale. We were in too great a hurry to join the Emperor, who was already at Chalon, and tomorrow would be at Autun – only three days' march from Paris.'

But if Ney, in a blend of regret and bewilderment at his own action, walking back to the *Pomme d'Or*, has 'perhaps believed his staff, [that] all the generals and officers are going to follow him and compliment him', he's in for a grievous disappointment. For by the time he gets back to the inn Levavasseur sees he's

'quite alone. Each one of us, reflecting on the responsibility incurred by this new situation, had collected his thoughts and withdrawn. I went to my room. The marshal, who'd left his door open, said to me:

'"Well, Levavasseur...?"

'I went slowly up to him, tears in my eyes.

'"*M. le maréchal*," I said. "You're lost! How can you, in one day, tarnish so high a reputation and so much glory?"

'"I couldn't do anything else," he exclaimed. "The country before everything, my friend. France has had enough of the Bourbons. We must obey the country."'[22]

And he goes on to rehearse all the talk of Napoleon having landed with the connivance of the foreign powers. But Levavasseur interrupts:

'*M. le maréchal.* Bonaparte'll never forgive you for the way you acted at Fontainebleau. Is he going to forget it was you who made him abdicate?'

'It's not him I've been thinking about in this matter,' says Ney, 'it's France. And I'll let him know it. If he's still counting on leading us into the depths of Poland, he's fooling himself. I'll tell him he's abdicated and that it's the King of Rome we're defending.'

What Ney *ought* to have done, Levavasseur makes so bold as to observe, is to have gone back to Besançon and awaited events.

'I couldn't. It would have been to trigger off civil war everywhere, it must be promptly extinguished. I'll never be a brand of discord. What? To march against Bonaparte I'd have had to march over 40,000 French corpses.'

And when Levavasseur goes on arguing the toss, Ney loses patience:

'That's enough! You're no longer my aide-de-camp.'

'*M. le maréchal*, you won't lack for aides-de-camp.'

As his new chief-of-staff Ney temporarily takes on a Major Genetière, who's been assistant to Bourmont's. Having sent off 'five or six officers to Oudinot [at Metz], Suchet [at Nancy] and the other marshals with troop commands' he invites all his generals and unit commanders to dine with him. Too deeply devoted to Ney, who'd been a second father to him, to abandon him, Levavasseur decides he'll go on obeying his orders. But when Ney dictates to him a letter to Besançon taking over the town in Napoleon's name and ordering preparations for its defence and orders the arrest of its royalist prefect and fortress commander,

Levavasseur gets up from the table. And a 'new altercation' breaks out between them.[23]

Though Ney offers to let various officials stay on in authority here at Lons, they decline. "I can't serve two masters," declares Prefect Vaulchier. And resigns. "Then all I can say,' says Ney, using a thumping 'military expression", "is that you must be pretty stupid [*borné*]. Don't you see that for three months now everything's been prepared for the Emperor's return?"[24]

Similarly with 'the brave General Delort'.[25] Though he offers him the command of the Jura, Delort asks him whether he does so 'in the name of the King who's sent you here, or of the Emperor you've just proclaimed. Until I know, allow me to decline' – a reply 'little to the marshal's taste.'

A gloomy dinner follows. 'It didn't at all come up to the marshal's expectations.' The conversation runs on the one hand on the faults of the Bourbons; on the other on the need to 'order Bonaparte' from now on to occupy himself exclusively with French affairs and 'forbid' him foreign wars. 'He'd be reminded he'd abdicated in favour of the King of Rome, and be told it was to assert the rights of Napoleon II that France had risen again.' Levavasseur's neighbour at table is an infantry colonel called Marchal. Though as reserved as himself, he confides him his decision not to fight the King's troops: 'I'd rather leave the army.'

As for Ney, he sits troubled and depressed. Seems only now fully to realise what he's done. And what it must imply.

But his men, Larreguy goes on, are ' impatient to make haste to catch up with Napoleon.' And next morning [15 March] at sunrise Ney tells Genetière to order Bourmont and Lecourbe to march their divisions to Dôle. Evidently – and all too justifiably – he's unsure of Bourmont. Perhaps also of his new chief-of-staff. So he also sends Levavasseur to Bourmont, who finds that gentleman in bed: 'He received me rather indifferently.' But says he'll obey Ney's orders. Leaving the *Pomme d'Or*, Ney tells Levavasseur to get into his carriage, and a few more words of the same kind as yesterday are exchanged between them.

Everywhere, as the carriage rolls on westwards through the Bresse district en route for Chalon and passes between the quaint mingled timber, brick and stone arcades of ancient Louhans, they see the population's in revolt.

"Isn't that the nation's feeling?" asks Ney. "Isn't it what the country wants?"

Levavasseur agrees: "But that doesn't mean you'll be any the less blamed for that."

Silence.

That night they lodge at Dôle in the house of a Count Valdahon, whose portrait 'in the brilliant uniform of a [royal] musketeer' hangs in the dining room. All of a sudden Ney's former chief-of-staff Colonel Clouet[26] turns up. A Vendean, a freemason, but also a royalist *agent provocateur* and a close friend of Bourmont's,[27] Clouet had first heard the news on 12 March at Tours, where business and the population had been beginning to flourish again, as everywhere in the West. Subscriptions are even being raised to pay anyone who'll assassinate the Usurper:

'The fury at the first news of Buonaparte having come back was universal, unheard of. People came running from all quarters, armed themselves, joined their regiments. When we went to the theatre the whole audience sang in chorus some couplets in honour of the Bourbons,'

– all except 'the local commandant. Today for the King, tomorrow for Buonaparte,' Frénilly adds, 'only he was dumb.'

Violently anti-Bonapartist, Clouet has been travelling day and night to rejoin his marshal, and heard about his defection en route. Now, rushing in, he demands to see Ney; and Levavasseur, introducing him into a room apart, hears the two men having a loud altercation. Rushing out again, Clouet seizes a scrap of paper, scribbles on it the words: "My ADC Clouet is ordered to proceed to Paris at once with my cook and a servant. By order of the Marshal, signed. . .". Seals it with Ney's seal. And leaves. After a moment Ney comes out.

"Where's he gone? He's mad. Go after him. Just imagine, this officer for whom I've done everything! Try to make him calm down. He'll do something stupid."

All to no purpose. Already Clouet has joined Lecourbe and Bourmont, disguised as a doctor and his valet, and taken the road to Paris. 'Hearing of Bourmont's flight, Genetière also thought he ought to quit his post and expatriated himself to Switzerland.'

Pressing on westwards, Ney and Levavasseur have a violent quarrel about a letter Levavasseur has undertaken to deliver to the Countess Valdahon's husband in Paris, and which Ney, 'without even unsealing it, tears up' and throws down on the carriage floor. Passing through an insurgent village, Levavasseur, 'swollen with resentment', so far forgets himself as to tell Ney: "Only the mob can approve of you."

'The word exasperates the marshal. He orders the carriage to halt, and says. "I've had enough. Get out!" I get down, the marshal drives off, and I'm left alone on the road. Half an hour later the second carriage arrives, with Dutour in it.'

Naturally the secretary, amazed to see him there by the roadside, asks him what's happened.

'Nothing, nothing. I think he's lost his head.'

They catch up with Ney at Dijon, where the marshal, after destituting the mayor and 'at sound of drum' appointing a Bonapartist to replace him, attends a grand dinner. Nothing more is said of their dispute. More than twenty times the indignant ADC has to write Ney's orders to mayors to 'immediately fly the tricolour'. On one such occasion Ney's so exhausted he can't even appear in person, and Levavasseur, obliged to represent him, is careful not to say a nasty word about the royal family.

Meanwhile Rieu, Rilliet and Vincy, the three Swiss, pushing on through the foul weather, have stopped at a wayside bar, where they hear that Mâcon and Chalon are in insurrection:

> 'By and by we heard the galloping of a horse. It was a gendarme bespattered with more mud than I've ever seen on a man's back, who was coming from Lons-le-Saulnier. Extremely agitated, he demanded a horse. Forced like the rest of us, and despite his official status, to wait for one, he told us that the troops we'd seen assembling three days ago at Ney's invitation and example had just adopted the tricolour cockade. He'd been sent by the prefect to carry the news to Dôle,'

where everything had as yet been quiet. But at Dijon,

> 'as we passed through, half the inhabitants were sporting a white cockade, the other half a tricolour one. The prefect had had his postchaise harnessed up, ready to flee. In a word, nothing could be more precarious than the state of people's minds in that town. This made the direct road to Paris too chancy; so once again we had to change our itinerary, and go via Langres,'

where Napoleon's influence has as yet been 'weak'. All along the road the three Swiss see how prudently people are trying to square impending events with their personal interests. Enthusiasm, it seems to these neutral observers,

> 'counted for nothing. At each relay we were surrounded by a crowd of local political wiseacres, anxiously asking for news of Napoleon's march. The poor fellows didn't realise they'd had to do with pitiless jokers who cold-bloodedly told them the tallest tales, diametrically opposed to the facts. All this they swallowed with gaping mouths, and as we got back into our post-chaise we laughed at it as far as to the next staging post.'

Suddenly their post-chaise overturns into a deep ditch; and they have to spend the night in a peasant's cottage near Auxonne. Naturally, events are discussed:

> 'This fine fellow didn't in the least hide from us his joy at the Emperor's return. He seemed to see him bringing back the Golden Age – by way of a beginning he'd surely indemnify him for his losses during the siege of Auxonne last year. Upon our raising some doubts

as to this pleasant picture, and especially our fears that conscription would be reintroduced, he replied without batting an eyelid that conscription was most agreeable to the poor because, apart from the advantage of ridding a numerous family of useless mouths, it provided a means of earning a little money by supplying substitutes.'

By 1814 the price of sending one to the army instead of one's son had risen to an exorbitant, virtually unpayable 10,000 francs.[28] 'The views of this poor agricultural worker, who knew nothing about any political question, was probably that of a great number of his like; perhaps even of those who only a year ago had been trembling at the very word conscription!'

Next morning the Swiss push on for Paris.

But back at Lons-le-Saulnier the National Guard's quartermaster Monnier, Ney's royalist spy, has arrived in the afternoon of the 14th with by now completely superfluous information from Chalon, where he'd 'several times seen Napoleon come out onto the balcony of the Hôtel du Nord to show himself to the enthusiastic inhabitants' and had found it hard to distinguish between the local garrison and

> 'the old soldiers from Elba, all equally enthusiastic. On my way I met General G—— and several other superior officers with huge tricolour cockades in their hats, an obvious token of their defection. Their horses were going flat out on the muddy highway. It was a question of which of these gentlemen would be the first to arrive in front of their master.'

Monnier finds the scene at Lons-le-Saulnier 'void of actors. Everything had become Bonapartist again.'

Meanwhile, across the rolling plains of Burgundy and its famous vineyards, the 60th and 77th Line, laden with 'all the countryside's requisitioned carts and carriages' and followed by the squadrons of the 3rd Hussars, are bumping and lurching onwards towards their tryst at Auxerre.

> 'Orders had been given to relay us onwards, so that we could travel day and night. A proclamation of the marshal's had enjoined on all municipalities and the inhabitants to bring us food along the way. You can't imagine the imposing, picturesque spectacle of this great convoy,'

Larreguy de Civrieux will one day tell his grandchildren.

> 'All the time the road was lined with waves of the populace replying to the patriotic songs intoned by our 10,000 voices. Our night march was lit up by myriads of torches and bonfires with girls and boys dancing around them. What delirium! Nothing less than our feverish state of mind could make such a march possible after so many fatigues.'

Many years afterwards, 'softened by the gentle pleasures of a happy life', he'll

'scarcely be able to grasp how I, still so young and with my frailish constitution, didn't collapse under the weight of all I had to carry. But Napoleon, that genius, angel or demon, he was dominating us all!'

CHAPTER 10

PARIS TALKS, THE OLD GUARD MARCHES

Instead of being settled on gory battlefields, as they've so largely been these last twenty-three years, France's affairs are again being found to be manipulable at elegant Parisian dinner tables. At first, says *Fanny Burney*, the English novelist who's one of the diners,

> 'a species of stupor utterly indefinable had seemed to envelop the capital with a mist that was impervious. Everybody went about their affairs, made or received visits, met, and parted, without speaking, or, I suppose, thinking of this event as a matter of any importance. This inactivity of foresight was universal.'

To save her from 'even the shadow of any unnecessary alarm' and to spare her 'any evil tidings', the 'first and constant solicitude' of her ex-émigré husband General d'Arblay, though he commands the artillery of the *Maison du Roi*, is to take her out for her usual morning drives in the Bois de Bologne. Hadn't she 'for the last ten years lived under the domination of Bonaparte and known many of his closest associates and his character by narrations the most authentic and documents the most indisputable'? Afterwards she'll find her 'own participation in this improvident blindness incomprehensible.'

Suddenly the liberals think they can see which side their bread's buttered on. And there's been a massive reaction in favour of the régime. Albeit *octroyé* ('granted') by the King instead of accepted by him,[1] even Louis XVIII's royal Charter of liberties is found infinitely preferable to Bonaparte's military tyranny. All day on 8 March, it will be remembered, Benjamin Constant's pen had been busy denouncing him as

> 'claiming to want peace, but in fact wanting war. He reappears, this man steeped in our blood. He reappears, this man formerly pursued by our unanimous curses ... This Attila, this Genghis Khan, more terrible, more odious, who's putting all in order to regularise massacre and pillage.'

Only to have his vitriolic article turned down by the censor. Caught between Juliette Récamier's coldness and Germaine de Staël's 'political sermonisings', he's beginning to feel the political situation is no less ambiguous than the lovers' passions so subtly depicted in his still unpublished and epoch-making novel *Adolphe*, which he delights in reading aloud to the ladies. Next day, however, his article, submitted to the *Journal de Paris*, is accepted.

> '10 March: Immense news! The collapse is terrifying. My article of tomorrow will put my life in danger. So here goes! If I must perish, let's

do it properly. What cowards these royalists are, making me out to be an enemy of the government. They're trembling, and I alone dare propose we defend ourselves. Shall I perish? We'll see a lot clearer tomorrow evening.'

'11 March: More and more news, though as yet everything's obscure, except that everyone's sure all is lost. I persist in believing everything can be saved. It's *time* that's being lost.'

That day he, also to no purpose, has gone out to Germaine de Staël's châ-teau at Charenton, but found it all closed up. Already he's been shocked to see how 'thin' her once so opulent figure has become (she has cancer); how 'pale' her features are, and how visibly worn out by ill health her whole talkative person is. Perhaps also by her long struggle against the dictator. He'd found her 'distrait, almost dry, thinking only of herself, hardly listen-ing to anyone else'. But now he jots in his diary: 'Mme. de Staël gone. Dined at Juliette's. Visit to Dessolles [the general Napoleon had dismissed the army at Smolensk, now in command of the National Guard]. All's lost, because everyone's saying so.' As for the Parisians at large, always sceptical, they're beginning to see through mendacious press reports. In vain the *Journal des Débats* comforts its increasingly jittery readers that though Bonaparte

'left Lyons on the 13th for Mâcon and Chalon, the combined dis-positions which we have already revealed made it rather obvious that this movement was foreseen. Marshal Ney, who has been watching it, is marching in strength on his tracks. Within fifty miles of Paris there is an army of 35,000 men filled with the finest morale. Buonaparte is dismayed to learn of loyal troops everywhere, and that Paris remains quiet.'

Aren't these very reassurances alarming? Surely the newspapers are pro-testing too much? Even Mme. d'Arblay *née* Burney (so-termed in her hastily issued passport), who's been assuming that 'Bonaparte had of course been either stopped at landing or taken prisoner, or saved himself by flight', realises that, on the contrary, he's 'pursuing unimpeded his route. The project upon Paris,' she thinks has at length become 'obvious; yet its success was little feared, though the horrors of a civil war seemed inevitable. M. d'Arblay began to wish me away. He even pressed me to depart for England.'

Only Louis XVIII, with his 'maddening calm', remains to all appearances royally imperturbable in the Tuileries. On the arrival of a despatch from Artois (who at the time of writing hadn't yet heard of Labédoyère's defec-tion) saying it's above all the Usurper's peaceful progress that's making the population go over to him, Vitrolles has to

'awaken the King in his little very narrow iron bed with green silk curtains. His huge corpulence filled not merely the bed's width but even seemed to overflow from it. A white night-cap covered his head and gave him the appearance of a colossal child'.

Louis tells Vitrolles to read out the 'big pages filled with Monsieur's very cramped handwriting'. Which Vitrolles does, very slowly, repeating the crucial passages. But though Artois has written that his troops, though 'restrained by their sense of duty', have 'neither affection nor enthusiasm for the royal cause', and though Vitrolles sees Louis listen 'without visible emotion', he also sees the King 'has to overcome himself'.

On 11 March the court has been reassured by the news of the collapse of the generals' conspiracy; and not only lavishly rewards such generals as d'Aboville at La Fère and Coursin (but not of course Ornano) at Antibes;[2] it has even magnanimously forgiven the ex-Chasseurs à Cheval for their outrageous march to Compiègne. But when the news comes in of Ney's defection, confirmed on the 17th, it seems to open up an abyss. And, not least, throw a dark shadow of suspicion on all the marshals. Particularly so on Soult. Isn't it he who, as Minister of War, has been responsible for all the dispositions being taken against Bonaparte? Hadn't he – Davout apart – been the very last marshal to rally to the royal régime? Who has been giving all these orders for so many regiments to march south, ostensibly to fight Murat in Italy, but actually to go over to the Usurper, if not he? Prime minister Abbé Montesquiou, with 'his long, pale sallow face' and ridiculous lisp, detests Soult and, quite sure of his treachery, is busy fomenting suspicions of him in the Chamber of Representatives. So to Vitrolles it's obvious that it must be against Soult the hubbub is

> 'the most ardent, the blindest, the most violently expressed. His treason, it was being said, was flagrant. Officers, generals and others he'd received at the moment of their leaving for the army, had gone over to the enemy the moment they'd got there. No question about it! From his private office he was giving orders contrary to those being despatched by the bureaux.'

None of which, Vitrolles is sure, is true. Isn't General Brun, Soult's closest friend and immediate aide at the War Ministry, married to a niece of the Count of Bruges? If it *were* true, too many officers of undoubted loyalty would have twigged it. And doesn't Dessolles regard the detestable Bonaparte as 'the most crooked and wicked of men'? And isn't Soult himself coming 'twice or thrice a day to our office in the Pavilion de Flore, bringing all his correspondence and submitting every order he's sending off each day to our decisions?' Yes yes, but Blacas, too, is sure he's a traitor. At 7:00 am in the morning of 15 March Vitrolles enters Blacas' salon:

> 'Even more solemn than usual, he asked me what I thought. "Keep a sharp eye on him, M. de Vitrolles," he said. "Everyone says he's

betraying us. And public opinion is openly condemning our inconceivable blindness, saying we're letting ourselves be fooled under our very noses."'

Nothing Vitrolles says can reassure Blacas, who never sees anything, least of all reason. No no, he, the Minister of the Royal Household, has decided to have it out with Soult, personally:

'I've his resignation in my pocket, I tell you. Would you like to see it?'

'With these words he took a great long pistol out of his pocket.' He must be joking?

'"Certainly not," he said in a comic-heroic voice.'

A weird scene follows, 'more amusing,' Vitrolles assures us, 'to those who've known M. de Blacas' stiff, cold, impassible face.' As the other Councillors turn up, Blacas launches out into a tirade against the absent Soult, ending it by flourishing the same melodramatic pistol. 'Instead of the burst of laughter I'd expected,' writes Vitrolles, 'the discussion began in earnest. The others spoke in much the same sense.'

Vitrolles is ordered to instantly summon Soult. Just as he's taking up his pen to do so, the door opens and who should the usher announce, if not Monseigneur, His Excellency the Minister of War, the Duke of Dalmatia, Marshal Soult:

'No one was prepared for this sudden apparition, and everyone was disconcerted. As usual he'd brought with him his most important despatches and the little map with coloured pins marking the positions of the marching troops, both our own and the enemy's. Likewise a note of the orders he was going to send off. Hardly had we listened to him than the Abbé Montesquiou picked up his hat and left.'

One by one the others follow suit. In the end only Soult, Blacas and Vitrolles are left:

'I was determined to remain behind if Blacas began his great showdown, if only to prevent the drama from reaching its climax. But as he didn't say anything, I thought only my presence was hindering him. After all, I told myself, he doesn't need a witness to blow out the brains of a marshal of France.'

And leaves, he too. But who knows what a fool can get up to? Not altogether quiet in his mind, Vitrolles decides to go and speak to the King about it. Just as he's entering 'the long wooden gallery which had been built for the King to be able to walk straight into the chapel, I saw Blacas going along it in the same direction.' In such a situation, as Brun is thinking, it would have been 'madness not to have resigned.' And that's exactly what Soult, with or without the benefit of Blacas' pistol, has just done. Entering the King's bedchamber, Vitrolles sees him 'standing to the King's left. I'd entered the office at the same moment as the marshal had left it. His Majesty told me what had just happened.'

Tendering his sword-hilt to the King, Soult has asked to be put on trial, so that no shadow shall fall on his conduct. Accepting his resignation, but saying he's sure he'll never draw his sword except in his service, Louis has blandly handed it back to him:

'Leaving the King's office, the marshal found himself at the top of the grand staircase facing the immense crowd that daily filled the châ-teau's courts and vestibules. Raising his hat with the white cockade, he shouted three times: *"Vive le Roi!"* 10,000 voices replied with the same enthusiastic acclaim.'

But at the War Ministry Brun de Villeret sees his patron has had his fill of politics, anyhow for the time being. And promptly leaves with him for their homes in the South. As for the Ministry, the King, 'with much indifference', replaces Soult with another ex-Bonapartist top brass, the Duke of Feltre, alias General Clarke, who'd held the post between 1807 and 1814, but has rallied to the royalist cause. Not that Vitrolles thinks it makes the least odds:

'I attached little importance to ministers chosen *in extremis.* To me any change only seemed to be one more stone falling from a ruined building on the verge of total collapse. These great military reputa-tions we'd been so dazzled by were worthless to us at political level.'

As for Louis XVIII, Vitrolles sees very clearly it's

'not from him we could expect any great resolutions. As he saw royalty, it wasn't his business. Above all he was busy defending himself against anything that might touch him [personally];'

something Louis XVIII is

'clever at. During the first days after the news of the landing he'd reassured himself, confident it'd have no consequences. But when the enemy had put Lyons behind him, he had two or three days of inquietude, where his anxiety went so far as to bring his blood to his head and redden his eyes. This emotion lasted at most two or three days. These being over, he, with the most sublime indifference, had made up his mind to go along with whatever might ensue. This gave him a serenity of mind perfectly suited to his royal attitude.'

Everyone's saying any defensive measures must be concerted with the Chambers. But Vitrolles, a man of action, is sure that 'nothing ever comes of the deliberations of political bodies and the ground was about to open up under our feet. I felt time was being lost.'

Absurdest of all the various schemes being propounded, as one might expect, is that of Blacas: an 'idea that smelt of his taste for the fine arts and was more like a painting than a political thought.' In all seriousness he proposes to the Council that

'the King shall calmly wait for the Emperor to arrive, and when he
knew he was only a few leagues from Paris, get into his open carriage
together with the First Gentleman of his Chamber, the captain of his
guards, and himself, Blacas. The carriage should be surrounded by the
Chamber of Peers and the Deputies, on horseback. All this procession
should go out to meet the Emperor and ask him what his business was.
Bonaparte, embarrassed, would retire!'

All the plan lacks, jokes Vitrolles at the Council meeting, is that 'the cortège
should be preceded by the Archbishop of Paris carrying the Holy Sacra-
ments, like St Martin of Tours had done when he went out to meet the
Visigoths.' Tut tut, reprove the Councillors, this is no time for joking. 'Which
barrier should they go out by?' – the Porte de l'Italie or the one on the
Fontainebleau road?

'I assured them they wouldn't so much as encounter the Emperor,
who wouldn't embarrass their pompous promenade by his presence.
He'd enter by the Barrier of the Throne or that of Saint-Denis, go and
calmly install himself in the Tuileries, and the King and the Chambers
would probably spend the night under the stars.'

Marshal Marmont, exempted (though he as yet doesn't know it) from
Napoleon's amnesty, has another, more belligerent idea. Why not fortify the
Tuileries? He'll undertake to defend the palace[3] for several weeks. Surely
Bonaparte won't go so far as to attack an aged crowned gentleman in his
own palace? No, says Vitrolles acidly. He'll simply establish himself in the
Luxembourg Palace, seize all the government offices and

"have no difficulty in getting himself obeyed in Paris and throughout
France. Then, when all the château's provisions are exhausted and the
besieged are on their last legs, the King will have to capitulate
unconditionally."

Whereupon one of the Emperor's ADCs would put the old monarch, the
princes and his entire family into the best carriages, 'accompany them with
all possible respect to the nearest frontier, and that'd be that.'

In sharp contrast to all these fatuities Vitrolles has a plan of his own. A
bold and far-reaching one. Proposed in the teeth of everyone's else's
objections ('no one is so good at criticising ways out as those who can't think
of any') his plan is that all royalist volunteers, speedily enrolled and taking
with them all available arms, artillery and ammunition, shall be given rendezvous at Orléans, Tours, Blois, Saumur or Angers. There they'll defend
the line of the Loire and organise the intensely royalist West and South and
also part of Normandy. Finally the

"fifty or sixty millions in the Treasury must be secured. Then if, as
seems probable, Paris proves impossible to defend, the King shall
retire to La Rochelle [together with both Chambers]. Any army

attacking La Rochelle will find itself surrounded by hostile populations, be immobilised and unable to provision itself, and thus in an untenable position."

At worst the King can always re-embark for England. The navy[4] at least is loyal.

But though Vitrolles batters away at the King with this idea and Louis seems 'to listen with interest and raise no objection, I couldn't ever get a word of approval out of him.' Artois, Vitrolles' patron, is more favourable. But, alas, to this prince who makes no bones about declaring that he has 'no other ideas than those he'd been born with', etiquette is everything. And it prevents him from acting without his brother's consent. In a word, Vitrolles, that man of bold enterprises, is finding the whole situation utterly exasperating. Only Beugnot and Dessolles, while regarding his scheme as being 'on the gigantic side', take any interest in it. As for Montesquiou, currently trying to whip up the opposition's enthusiasm for the royal cause, he furiously attacks it. Surely it'll cause the King of France to be regarded as a mere 'king of the Vendée. Only a Chouan minister could propose such a thing.' Better that, replies Vitrolles, annoyed, than a foreigners' king, if Louis has to flee the country. 'After which Montesquiou,' who seems to be having some success with the opposition, 'only referred to me as "the Chouan minister".'

12 March, Constant's diary:

> 'The royalists [are] making up to me. Saw Juliette. She received me nicely, to encourage me. Went back to Lainé's.[5] Terrible news. Idea of a peerage. If it succeeds I'll consecrate and gladly risk my life to repulse the tyrant.'

> '13 March: Attempted a thousand things to organise resistance. Everything falling to pieces in my hand. Session of the deputies. What weakness and what poverty of spirit! Advances from the Bonapartists, same as yesterday. Saw Juliette. She refused to receive me – to give a rendezvous to M. de Forbin.[6] Infamous creature! It made me very sad, but I've a lot else to do.'

So has the Council, though it doesn't seem to be doing it. Or indeed anything at all. Abbé Montesquiou even suggests they all resign en bloc. Finally it's decided to convene the Chambers for a Royal Session – tomorrow, 16 March.

Fanny Burney's husband is a close friend of Jarcourt, who's acting as Foreign Minister during Talleyrand's long absence in Vienna. *Tout Paris* is applying to him for passports; and that evening he puts his signature to one

> '*for Madame d'Arblay, née Burney,* avoiding to speak of me as the wife of a general officer of the King, lest that might eventually impede my progress, should I be reduced to escape from Paris.'

This same day, 16 March, at getting on for 9:00 am, Vitrolles goes to the King, whom he finds

'holding a little square piece of paper in his hand. He read out to me the discourse he was intending to pronounce to the Chambers. Without flattery I found the sentiments in it admirable, as well as his way of expressing them. Nothing more noble ever came from the pen of a king.'

Reading it out aloud to the Council

'he was so sure of his memory that he gave me his slip of paper to have it printed and published during the actual séance.'

Alas, it's pouring with rain, and all the troops lining the royal route to the Palais Bourbon, just across the river from the Place de la Concorde, are getting drenched through. Just as King Louis is about to lift his enormous weight into his state coach he notices Macdonald, back from Lyons. 'As he passed me he showed me the order of the Legion of Honour he'd been advised to wear. No one noticed it, and certainly no one was touched.' Least of all Artois or Berry or the Duke of Orléans. As they all get into the royal coach, Orléans remarks dryly:

'Wouldn't Your Majesty have done well to have adopted it earlier?'

No reply.

The royal session is to be held amid all conceivable pomp and circumstance. The route is lined by

'troops who were complaining at having to do it. It was raining in torrents. They were wet through. And to pass the time they were shouting: "*Vive le Roi! Vive le Roi!*" at the tops of their voices,'

but adding sotto voce, so Count de *Lamothe-Langon,* a noted gossip, thinks he hears "*...de Rome, de Rome.*" All the way along the riverside to the Invalides guns are booming, crowds cheering, drums beating, a military band playing. Hurrying into the Palais Bourbon, Lamothe-Langon gets perhaps the last seat:

'The crowd filled both the galleries and the first four rows, only leaving the Peers, seated on the right, and the Deputies, on the left, such places as were strictly necessary for them. The superb apparel, the opulence of their clothes and, still more so, an almost universal feeling of love, interest and concern,'

promise to give 'this solemn occasion a character all its own.' If the usually punctilious monarch is nearly an hour late, it's probably due to a last-minute rehearsal of some amateur theatricals designed to make the scene affecting. Now, inside the Palais Bourbon,

'a deputation, composed of twenty Peers and twenty Deputies, go out to receive His Majesty at the outer doors. Then, with an unusually

226

loud crash, the two leaves of the inner door were thrown back and the troops drawn up in line presented arms. Finally a powerful voice proclaimed: "The King, gentlemen! The King!" In the sudden silence everyone turned and gaped, with eyes fixed, half-open mouths, stretched necks and bent torsos. First to file by were the Chamber's ushers, the State messengers, the ushers and lesser officers of the King's Bedchamber, his heralds of arms, his pages, equerries and gentlemen.'

The first real personage to enter, senile and enquiring pathetically what all this fuss is about, is the father of the executed Duke of Enghien, the aged Prince of Condé. 'The King,' Macdonald goes on, 'was received with acclamation.' As for Artois and Berry, it's their first appearance in the Chamber of Deputies, and Lamothe-Langon's sure Orléans' 'demeanour proclaimed that he was expecting a catastrophe'. Supported to the throne by Blacas and the Duke of Duras, Louis, to loud cheering, 'walked slowly. Suffering marred his features. But his eye was calm and his forehead radiated that majesty which never deserted him.' But the throne, as he seats himself on it, seems to the otherwise enthusiastic Lamotte-Langon to totter – probably because it's never before had to support so massive a monarch:

'The air was filled with harmonious fanfares. The ladies waved bunches of lilies and white handkerchiefs. The Peers and Deputies shook the elegant plumes of their Henri IV-style hats, like a heavy snowfall, a singularly graceful effect.'

The King personally bids the Peers be seated. But only Chancellor Dambray can bid the Deputies do the same – the very same insulting distinction between blue and ordinary blood that had precipitated the Revolution twenty-six years ago. Seated on folding chairs on either side of the throne are Artois, Berry, Orléans and poor old Condé. 'Without losing any of his noble serenity' Louis puts on his hat, and 'in a strong clear voice' holds 'a most touching discourse', saying how he has

"worked for the well-being of my people. In this moment of crisis which, arising in one part of the kingdom, menaces the liberty of all the rest, I've come into your midst to draw closer those bonds which, uniting you to me, are the strength of the State. Could I, at sixty, better end my career than by dying in its defence? I fear nothing for myself, but I fear for France. He who comes among us to light the torches of civil war also brings with him the scourge of foreign war. He comes to place our country under his iron yoke. He comes..."

– and here comes the political bit –

"to destroy the constitutional Charter I have given you, my finest title to glory in the eyes of posterity; that Charter which all Frenchmen cherish, and which I swear to uphold..."

'Here all the four princes extended their hands and, joining themselves to the King's, cried: "Yes, Sire, we too swear to uphold it."'

And still the amateur theatricals aren't quite over. Louis' speech being ended, Artois asks, as an unusual favour – and against all royal protocol – to be allowed to speak. A nod from Louis graciously permits it. "Let us swear, on our honour," Artois exhorts the assembly, "to live and die loyal to our King and to the constitutional Charter."

It's the first time Artois has ever been heard even to refer to it.

Sensation. The whole assembly rises and swears.

'Throwing himself at the King's feet, Marshal Mortier, Duke of Treviso,[7] swore everlasting fidelity to him, and was embraced and thanked for his prompt intervention at La Fère [sic].'

Even Benjamin Constant finds the scene 'touching'.

'What struck the population most,' Macdonald thinks, 'were the almost frantic demonstrations of the troops lining the King's route.' And Rilliet, who's just arrived in Paris with his two fellow Swiss officers, is also forcibly impressed by the

'deafening shouts of Vive le Roi! of a regiment of cuirassiers that was providing detachments for the escort, which resounded on the banks of the Seine – shouts echoed by all the troops that were on their way to the army out at Melun. Paris seemed to present a spectacle of the liveliest enthusiasm for the royal cause. A man had just been killed by umbrellas in front of the Tuileries for shouting Vive Napoléon! At the theatre, which I attended, the actors had to sing the song, again newly popular, of Vive Henri IV, the pit spontaneously joining in, while the ladies in their boxes fluttered their white handkerchiefs.'

The Royal Session is rounded off by the Deputies' president Lainé – a man of certain integrity who last year had led the opposition to the imperial dictatorship – exhorting them to unite against 'the common enemy'.

Is author François-René de Chateaubriand the only person present who, amidst all this loyal oratory, 'in a moment of silence' fancies he can hear 'Bonaparte coming closer with giant strides'?[8]

But that evening, at a dinner held in Blacas' apartment, only Montesquiou's in seventh heaven. 'Thuperb théanthe!' he declares ('the difficulty he had in pronouncing his s's made his words a trifle ridiculous'). That, rejoins Vitrolles, will depend on what results it has. If any. At which Montesquiou mutters something

'between his teeth. Then, more clearly, said I spoke of such matters like a blind man of colours. To which I replied very calmly that it was a great advantage to wear a clergyman's collar, but he shouldn't abuse it.'

Blood pressures rise. But Blacas intervenes, and they all sit down to dinner:
'Everyone was glum. Only spoke to his neighbours. And all this
apparatus of a grand household and power contrasted painfully with
the thought that it was all about to vanish like a dream.'
Even Dessolles, 'a cold man of calculation rather than feelings,' tells
Vitrolles 'almost with tears in his eyes' how awful it feels to see 'these
unhappy princes overthrown by an audacious Corsican. If you only knew
him as well as I do! Of all men he must be the most crooked and malignant!'

Unjustly suspected of being in cahoots with her stepfather, Hortense's
situation is daily becoming more critical. On 8 March her private catastrophe has become a fact – the law courts have granted Louis Bonaparte
wardship of her two sons. And now here comes a police official to notify her
privily that the King's drawing up a list of persons to be arrested. One of
Berry's officers too, Lieutenant-General Girardin, comes and tells her it's
being said she's sold her diamonds and is 'running about the barracks'
bribing the troops to mutiny.

Meanwhile Artois, it seems, has been acting behind his brother's back. For
at 10:00 pm on 15 March something almost beyond belief has happened.
In the courtyard of the left-bank town house of Mme. de Vaudémont, a
friend of Fouché's, first one, then another unidentifiable carriage, from
which the royal arms are notably absent, has drawn up. And who should
descend from one of them but Artois? And from the other the man he, not
to mention the Duchess of Angoulême and the Ultras, loathe beyond all
others. Fouché. At long last – the mere thought of having him in the government's been unthinkable – even the Ultras have tumbled to it that this
immensely wealthy ex-terrorist, sitting on all possible political fences and
every conceivable bit of privy information, is in himself a major political
factor. And it's Artois who has asked for this hush-hush meeting to be
arranged *chez* Mme. de Vaudémont. What it must have cost Louis XVIII to
agree to it – if he really has – may be imagined. In front of them in her
drawing room Artois and the two officers who've come with him see before
them a man of a stature
'hardly above the ordinary, extremely thin. His strange facial pallor,
peculiar to itself and hard to define, isn't the lividness that betrays a
perpetual repression of bile; nor the sickly pallor that reveals poor
blood and an etiolated constitution. It's a tone cold but alive, such as
time gives to monuments.'
Fouché, determined to charm the heir to the Bourbon throne, turns his
heavy-lidded eyes on the handsome prince, his almost exact contemporary.
Eyes

'very light blue, but altogether without that light in their look which reveals the movement of the passions and even the play of thought. [A regard] of a curious fixity, demanding and profound but immutably lustreless, which nothing could avert from a question or a man as long as he chose to occupy himself with it or him.'[9]

Well?

Two equally cynical men. But strangely they seem to hit it off much better than either can have expected.[10] And Artois, in some 'noble and touching words', offers Fouché the Police Ministry.[11] It's the Duke of Otranto's moment of triumph. Yet he doesn't allow it to throw him out of his calculations. 'Feigning sorrow' but certainly laughing up his sleeve, the ex-terrorist replies:[12]

'It's too late. I can no longer serve the King's cause.' But adds ambiguously: 'You, Monsieur, save the King, and I'll save the monarchy,' leaving Artois and his two aides to climb mortified back into their carriage, and return, humbled, to the Tuileries. And Fouché to exclaim to his henchman Gaillard:

'Those imbeciles! I told them in advance what would happen, and now has.[13] If they'd followed my advice they wouldn't be where they are. They've played cock-of-the-walk and not wanted to believe me. And now, when the situation can no longer be remedied, they've come to me, supposing me to be so stupid as to want to bury myself with them. You've no idea of the stupidity of this Count d'Artois. I was ashamed of it on his behalf. Apart from Louis XVIII they're all cretins.'

And by now the government's doings are in fact so bewildered and aimless that next day something else, almost more absurd, will happen...

Receiving proof from the Russian ambassador (still extending the Tsar's friendship to her) that she's being regarded at the Tuileries as at the heart of a Bonapartist plot to bring back the Usurper, Hortense is most of all terrified she and her two sons will be taken as hostages. And when she also hears that 'royalist gangs from the revolutionary time' have gathered in Paris, are being given 'large sums to organise a revolt', and are aiming at certain houses, among them that of Savary (who in 1810 had succeeded Fouché as Police Minister), 'which was next to mine', she decides to go into hiding.

The time has come for her to flee from 18 Rue Cerutti:

'At ten o'clock, wearing Mlle. Cochelet's[14] hat and cloak, I left the house and, to make myself less recognisable, allowed her brother to offer me his arm instead of M. Devaux, my old stablemaster,'

this to deceive the police spies 'posted in every doorway, who looked a bit surprised but let me pass'. It's not so much the police she has to fear as the royalist gangs of ten or twenty young dandies who're roving the streets on the lookout for a victim. Haven't three such gangs just flung themselves on a half-pay officer at a corner of the Rue St Honoré and, to the applause of two women from a fashion shop, slowly killed him with kicks and whiplashes, left him a mangled corpse? No more than with the *demisolde* who'd dared to shout *Vive l'Empereur* outside the Tuileries and been stabbed to death by respectable umbrellas, have the police intervened. But more than any such danger, Hortense is impressed by the reflection that she's never before in her life been 'out in the street alone, on a young man's arm and without any ladies attending me. Luckily it was raining, and the umbrella served still further to hide my face.'

Her cavalier is terrified lest her lace-bordered skirt, peeping out from under the cape, will give her away. But though 'the street seemed endlessly long' even the longest street has an end; and at last they've taken refuge in an apartment in the Rue Duphot, amidst 'our family portraits and a thousand little things' piously preserved from her Martinique childhood by Eugène's old nurse, who welcomes her with open arms. From her hiding place she writes to the head of the police department, protesting against all the rumours 'which anyone who knows her must see are false, and asking him to put a stop to them'. Shown to the King, her letter only makes her seem even more suspect. Looking down on the boulevard from her window, Hortense witnesses

> 'rather strange behaviour. Sometimes it was groups of royalist volunteers, made up of young enthusiasts and old servants, the former grim and threatening, the latter breathless and already exhausted by having to carry their heavy weapons, the whole lot equally useless for military service, all equally keen to fight.'

Count *Louis Gobineau*, though he's one of them himself, thinks they're

> 'the most ridiculous and unmilitary body of men you could possibly imagine. Old men, but also boys rigged out in uniforms with epaulettes of every rank, hardly able to carry their packs, muskets and cartridge pouches, led by a corporal with a *sous-lieutenant*'s epaulettes.'

But down there, much more impressive, Hortense also sees

> 'one of the old army's cavalry regiments, whose troopers were sitting their horses like statues amidst the excitement people were trying hard to infect them with, listening scornfully to the empty phrases and declamations. Calm, detached, their thoughts seemed to be more with the man they were being sent to defeat than with those they were to defend. Meanwhile the crowds, exactly as if they were at the theatre, knowing perfectly well who'd win in the end and whom they'd applaud, silently awaited the end of the drama.'

Meanwhile, while Artois had been making Fouché his vain and belated offer, the council has removed the Police Ministry from Beugnot's even more inept successor and given it to *L-A.F. de Bourienne,* Napoleon's one-time secretary and boyhood friend. Disgraced at Hamburg, where he'd been his satrap,[15] for scandalous peculation of 680,000 francs' worth of public funds, he has become the inveterate enemy of his former friend and protector; and Lavalette knows only too well that 'the Emperor's friends realised what they had to fear from this man, who was very well acquainted with their persons and habits.' He's especially worried for Hortense and her children should the Princes decamp.

When it's a question of arresting the prince of all policemen, however, Bourienne's efforts turn out to be inept. At 11:00 am on 16 March, the morrow of Fouché's meeting with Artois, just as his carriage is turning into the boulevard from the Rue d'Artois, Gaillard spots a police posse posted at the street corner. No little embarrassed, its commander, Police Inspector Foudras, steps forward, halts it, and shows his warrant:

"It's false," exclaims Fouché. "This warrant's not in order!"

Oh, but he's just a moment ago seen M. de Bourienne sign it, Foudras objects.

"I put it to you," asks Fouché calmly; "does one arrest a man who all last night has been in conference with the King's brother? This warrant is invalid. Fetch the National Guard."

A picket of twenty-five National Guardsmen is fetched from the nearest post. Perhaps, its officer suggests timidly, he should send one of his NCOs to the Tuileries, to look into the matter? Well, of course, Fouché blandly approves. A very good idea. And in the meantime invites them all into his palatial residence, the opulent creation of two successive bankers. Everyone admires its magnificence. But here's the NCO, back from the Tuileries.

'Not daring to lay hands on my person, these men who'd so long obeyed me limited themselves to handing me the warrant they were acting under. I take this paper. I open it. And hardly have I pretended to glance through it, than I say with self-assurance: "This warrant isn't according to the regulations. Stay there, I'm going to protest against it."'

Who better a judge than Fouché, who has issued so many, of whether a warrant's in order?

'Leaving the door open I go into my office. I sit down at my desk and I write. Then I get up, a paper in my hand, and suddenly changing course...'

he leans against a secret revolving door in the panelling – and vanishes! Where's he gone? Locating the secret door, the policemen smash it in with the butts of their carbines, and find themselves in a dark chamber. Out in his garden Fouché finds 'a ladder propped against the wall to Queen Hortense's house. Despite his fifty-six years

'I climb it lightly. One of my people lifts up the ladder to me, and I let it fall on its feet on the other side of the wall. Quickly I climb over and, even more quickly, go down it. I arrive as a fugitive in Hortense's house, who welcomes me with open arms and like a miracle in *The Arabian Nights*, am amidst the pick of the Bonapartists, in the headquarters of a party which I find in a state of hilarity, and where my presence brings inebriation.'

No story is so true it can't be improved in the telling. In reality[16] he, in his haste, had broken the key he'd borrowed from Hortense, from her garden into the Rue Taitbout. And had taken refuge in the house of a friend, Lombard-Taradeau, ex-secretary general of police. In Hortense's house – precisely because the police know its proprietress has fled – there's only one noted Bonapartist: Lavalette. Instead of accepting Mme. de Staël's proposal he has taken refuge in its attic; and if there's any merriment among its frightened occupants it's at his 'disguising' himself with her majordomo's wig.[17] Reunited with Gaillard, Fouché says:

'Anyone who's been Minister of Police for ten years isn't such a fool as to let himself be nabbed by half a dozen cops [*argousins*].'

Napoleon, hearing of the incident, will comment: 'He's certainly the smartest [*le plus malin*] of us all.'

As for the marshals, they've all been ordered to their military districts. Which in Oudinot's case means Metz, most important of all the northern frontier fortresses and seat of the two regiments of the ex-Grenadiers of the Imperial Guard. So precipitate has been the move that he and his wife Eugénie, the one-time Mlle. de Coucy, now Duchess of Reggio, are put to considerable expense to find adequate furniture for the necessary receptions. She goes on:

'The marshal decided to throw a grand ball, which doubled my activities as mistress of his household. I was just finalising the arrangements and was going up to get dressed, when I was brought some unheard of news. The Emperor, it was being said, had landed at Cannes and was marching on Paris! I was still doubting it, when the marshal comes upstairs and confirms it. He'd just received the news via a courier from the War Ministry. A courier! When the telegraph could have informed him twenty-four hours earlier! A courier who'd travelled less swiftly than the Emperor's emissaries! His ex-Guard had known it before my husband did!'

Even so, the ball must be held – even if a 'mutiny was being calmly and methodically prepared.'

"You will dance, my dear," the amiable marshal says. "You'll keep up appearances, you'll know nothing and not let anyone else do so either, not in your presence. I need the ball to be an animated one, because while it's going on I'll be holding a council of the generals and colonels and the district's notables in my office" – one of the colonels being Victor Oudinot*, his son by his first marriage, now commanding the 1st Hussars.

The ball is held. 'Tons of punch' circulate. And when at last its 'physically, spiritually and mentally exhausted' hostess, who's not even had time to get over her strong emotions at the news and still knows nothing of what's been decided downstairs, is about to go to bed, her husband comes up. Yes, the Emperor's marching on Paris. And he, Oudinot, has just received orders[18] to send some of the Grenadiers and Chasseurs (stationed at Nancy) to Langres, to oppose him. Not that he has any illusions about their sentiments. But with the prospect of a new invasion he must above all make arrangements to secure Metz against a Prussian coup.

Next morning – by now pathetically out of date – comes Ney's first letter from Besançon.

When and how have the two Grenadier regiments heard about their idol's return? For they have. Now the column, 'made up of detachments of all arms' and, for its size, certainly the most formidable in Europe,[19] forms up. And Oudinot orders General *Roguet*, its commander, to march it to Toule. There they'll be joined by the Chasseurs from Nancy, where he this evening, after depositing *Madame la maréchale* en route at their château at Bar-le-Duc, proposes to join it. 'In all haste,' Eugénie goes breathlessly on,

'I handed my keys to Mme. Gouy, and made ready to accompany the marshal. Just as we were getting into our carriage, a King's courier handed him an urgent message, wholly in the Duke of Berry's handwriting. Tardy and useless, vainly solicited by the marshal at a more opportune time, it authorises him to rename the corps 'the King's Grenadiers and Chasseurs' and tell them "the rank of second lieutenant is instantly to be conferred on all rankers of the former Imperial Guard".'

"Let's march to Toule," says Oudinot dryly. Stuffs it into his pocket.

Among the column's sergeants, at his station beside the 1st battalion of the 2nd Grenadiers, is Hyppolite de Mauduit: 'Two battalions fully ready for action had been called for from our regiment, and on 14 March we leave Metz to go and meet Napoleon and oppose his passage.' At Toule, Eugénie Reggio goes on,

'night had fallen when we got out at a hotel on the town's main square. It was packed with officers. The largest room had been kept for us, but it was the only one. Not a corner I could retire to. Soon the generals were turning up, as ordered. Without explaining exactly what he was going to tell the troops, my husband asked these gentlemen how they'd receive a speech ending with *Vive le Roi!* "Just try," General Roguet told him, "try." The others were silent. "Very well, then, pass on my orders," the marshal said. "Tomorrow at dawn I'll hold the review and speak to them."'

The officers leave. But a moment afterwards General Trommelin enters.

'He'd just been seeing and hearing the Emperor's emissaries in the town's cafés, and collecting unequivocal proofs of the plans that had been drawn up by officers of all ranks.'

Oudinot feels he must instantly clarify the situation: "Go and tell the generals to immediately send me all the officers, from second lieutenant to colonel. I want to speak to them. We must put an end to this situation."

'A few moments later a triple rank of these gentlemen came pushing itself into our room, drew up in a circle with the marshal in the middle. He let them form up in silence, then expressed himself more or less like this: "Gentlemen, in the current circumstances I appeal to your loyalty. We're marching under the white cockade. Before leaving tomorrow I must review you. What cry will you respond with to my *Vive le Roi!*?" These words were followed by a dead silence.'

Eugénie herself – a woman of course has no business in such an assembly – is hiding behind a curtain:

'Never has anything more striking happened under my eyes. Hidden behind my curtain, I was forced to witness this unique scene. Two of the inn's torches illumined it sufficiently for nothing to be lost; but their pale light on these rough and sombre faces produced an indescribable effect. The marshal couldn't take their silence, no matter how expressive, for an answer. I saw the storm was about to break. Each second was a century. "Well, *messieurs?*" At this a young officer of inferior rank stepped forward and said:

"'To your cry of *Vive le Roi!* the men, and all of us, will reply *Vive l'Empereur!*'

"'Thank you, *monsieur,*" replied the marshal. Saluted. And, without another word uttered, they all went out.'[20]

'Roguet, who commanded us,' Sergeant Mauduit goes on,

'refused to obey Marshal Oudinot's orders, and openly, in the presence of the two Grenadier battalions, on the public square of this little Lorraine town, declared for Napoleon. From this moment our two battalions marched independently under this general's orders, and did so in full military fashion, as if in the presence of the enemy.'

Only two or three officers, part of the royalist

'cadre which, even though they'd never served in the French army's ranks, by a maladroit, impolitic and anti-military measure had been placed in each of our two regiments, refused to follow under the new flag.'

Though a few other officers, Mauduit stresses,

'sympathised noisily, thus associating themselves with the criminality of our general's abrupt breach of his oaths, our old Grenadiers preserved the calm and impassibility of military obedience. Not a word injurious to the Royal Family passed their lips, no matter how ignored their former glorious services had been.'[21]

Leaving Eugénie at their country house at Jean-d'Heure, Oudinot joins his column. At Chaumont, however, the storm bursts.

'Just as my husband was receiving the news and positive details of Ney's defection, his Grenadiers had the word passed to him that if they so far, out of respect for him personally, had worn the white cockade, they should forewarn him that they were going to adopt the tricolour cockade and march under those colours toward the Emperor, not to fight him but to support him. And they begged him not to leave them.'

Oudinot doesn't reply. Leaves for Jean-d'Heure to pick up Eugénie and go back to Metz.

At Nancy the Chasseurs' CO, General Pacthod, 'doubtless regarding Napoleon's landing as an act of madness,' had replied to Soult's orders by saying he was convinced 'the Chasseurs de France' were sincerely devoted to the King and were filled with indignation at the 'atrocious and senseless action of bringing civil war into our beautiful country', such as must make it 'odious to any being gifted with reason.' All this is very well, and couched in resounding phrases. But the Chasseurs, even so, had marched for Toule, leaving their general, Curial, behind. Only after catching up with them at one of their halts does he enter the bistro where they're refreshing themselves and ask them whether they still regard him as their colonel. Certainly, they say, if he'll join them under the Emperor.

Back at Metz, Oudinot collects the rest of his troops, which are

'still showing the same colours as himself. For if – no doubt about it – insurrection was in all hearts, not an outward sign of indiscipline had given the commander-in-chief reason to think his men belonged to the opposite camp.'

In the King's name he instantly proclaims Metz in a state of siege.[22] This proclamation, 'posted up at all the street corners', causes 'part of the garrison and part of the town to boil over.' Once again Eugénie, 'pressing her nose against her window' – people are accusing her husband of trying to preserve the city as a bolt hole for Berry – is witness to a mass demonstration. But when the crowd tries to break down the door, the intrepid, many times wounded marshal, goes out, addresses it, 'and is listened to.' His son Victor still has his 1st Hussars in hand and manages to disperse the crowd, 'measures facilitated by the bad weather and the lateness of the hour.' But when next morning Eugénie, still at her window, sees the tricolour break from the highest tower of the cathedral, she realises 'everything was over! The marshal's authority was rejected. There was nothing for us but to leave' – which they do, escorted at a walking pace beyond the glacis by Victor's hussars. Not another word has come from Paris. In this respect Oudinot has been just as isolated at Metz as Ney had been at Besançon.

But Oudinot's stance is going to be quite different from Ney's.[23]

CHAPTER 11

AN ICY RECEPTION

And now Napoleon's at the big river port of Auxerre, only two days march from Paris. Leaving Lyons on 13 March, 'a large number of wounded military men' had been presented to him at Villefranche, the little town last year 'littered with corpses' after the Austrian incursion, but now

'packed with the curious. A lot of eagles had been placarded on the houses and several trees of liberty planted in streets and public squares. He dined on a chicken whose bones were bought by two peasants,'

two, that is, of the '60,000' who'd dropped their work to accompany him on his way.[1] At Mâcon he'd received a municipal deputation from Dijon. On the 14th he'd been at Chalon-sur-Saône, where five days ago the populace had prevented an artillery unit from reaching Artois. On the 15th at Autun – where a M. Pignon, a staunch old octogenarian, had heroically stood his ground against local insurgents, and narrowly escaped being beaten up by the 16th Dragoons' long straight swords as Brayer's cavalry had come galloping in. After which the column had bivouacked on its immense market place, and the Emperor had bawled out the local authorities for governing only in the interests of a 'clique of nobles' (and Peyrusse had time to go sightseeing among the historical relics). On the 16th he'd reached Avallon, in the idyllic winding valley of the Cure. Riding on in his newly-bought carriage and followed by valet Marchand in the discarded *calèche*, at times almost without an escort, he's everywhere being deliriously greeted by the working and middle classes, albeit the latter are terrified of being pillaged by the mob. Certainly he's more popular with the masses[2] than he'd ever been during the last years of the Empire. Everywhere

'the population of the countryside, women, children, soldiers and retired officers, came running toward us along the highway, making the air ring with their shouts of *Vive l'Empereur!*'

But all the time Marchand's noting that he 'never replied at all to the shouts of "Down with the clergy! Down with the *droits réunis!*"' Had he not himself restored Catholicism with his Concordat? Likewise the unpopular indirect taxes? At Avallon his self-justificatory monologue lasts an hour and a half, so that Mayor Raudot and his councillors

'ten times tried to take our leave. But the Emperor still retained us, introducing gaiety, abandon, a great lack of constraint, a familiarity carried to excess'.

Each day Brayer's dining at his table, and Marchand certainly doesn't guess for a moment that this man he's waiting on will one day be his father-in-law.[3] Napoleon finds Brayer 'a most distinguished man', though he has 'never known anyone so anchored in his own opinion':[4]

> 'He'd fooled Artois up to the last moment, retained his confidence, offered him lots of advice, and even sent his men chasing after him. All the time he kept telling me: "Go on. You've nothing to fear, I know the troops well, they're all for you." When I heard about the d'Erlon affair he exclaimed: "Go straight ahead, they've made a mess of things, but it's of no consequence."'

All (it'll seem to him afterwards) in sharp contrast to 'practically all the other generals along the way', who'd seemed 'morose and unsure of themselves, or even hostile, having merely gone along with their men's impulse'. As well they may have. What'll happen to them, these generals, if it all goes wrong? And some no doubt are suffering from the qualms of divided loyalties. Young Moncey*,[5] for instance, colonel of the 3rd Hussars and son of the Marshal, though he puts his regiment at the Emperor's disposal, sends word that 'though he'd never fight against him, he was bound by an oath he couldn't ignore', a message which, Marchand notes, 'astonished' Napoleon. But many officers, both commissioned and uncommissioned, are turning up. Seven generals have even left Paris to join him.

And now he's at Auxerre.

It had been as a vague rumour 'among the regulars who talked politics at the *Café Milon*' that little Coignet had first heard his idol was back. 'Coming up to me, they asked whether I'd heard the news.' And when, surprised, he'd said he hadn't, they'd taunted him:

> 'You don't want to say anything for fear of compromising yourself.'

> 'How so?'

> 'It's being said a Capuchin monk has passed through in disguise, together with another top person the prefect wanted to arrest.'

Coignet still doesn't get it.

> 'One of the old men said: "This is what he's been keeping his horse for. He's been waiting for the *grey overcoat*." I was beside myself with joy. Already I thought I saw my Emperor arriving.'

Soon all Auxerre had buzzed with the tremendous, terrifying news,

> 'joy for some, sadness for others. Certitude exploded when early one morning a Line regiment[6] arrived, headed by Marshal Ney. It was said he was on his way to arrest the Emperor. "That's impossible," I told myself. "The man I saw take up a musket at Kovno[7] and hold up the enemy with five men, this marshal the Emperor called his lion, just can't lay hands on his sovereign!" I trembled at the idea. Finally, the

marshal went to the prefect. A proclamation was published throughout the town. The police commissary, strongly escorted, announced
that Bonaparte was back and the government had ordered his arrest.
Shouts of "Down with Bonaparte! Long live the King!" God, how I'd
suffered!'

But now, on 17 March, here he is at last! As his approach is announced the
crowds rush out 'along the Saint-Bris road to see the Emperor arrive, well-
escorted, in his carriage'. Among them a youngster by name Robineau
Desvoidy, who shouts *Vive l'Empereur!* 'with all the effusiveness of my youthful
lungs' as Napoleon's carriage passes in through the new gateway – the one
Davout had erected in 1810, the mediaeval one being too narrow for his own
to pass through. Also in the crowd, and of course no less delirious, is
Imperial Headquarters' former Quartermaster: 'The snowball had grown.
Seven hundred old officers formed a battalion and troops were turning up
from all quarters.'

When Napoleon alights at the prefecture he finds, for the first time,
a prefect is at his post. The more surprising as Prefect Gamot is one of
the few prefects recently installed by the King to replace an imperial
appointee. On the other hand he's Ney's brother-in-law. Entering the
prefectorial drawing room Napoleon's gratified to see Gérard's 'full-
length portrait of himself clad in imperial robes, likewise the bust of
the Empress and his son.' The King's – one never knows – has
replaced it in the attic.

His first action is to send for Abbé Viart, vicar-general of the cathedral,
who's been preaching against him. A staunch royalist, Viart has to be summoned three times, the third time 'with threats', before he consents to
appear: 'M. de Viart,' Fabry tells us,

'had said he'd come, but the moment for a public service in the
church was approaching, and the worthy pastor didn't want to disturb
it. Tired of not seeing him move, they order him to come instantly. But
he replied "God before men" and went to the church.'

The service over, Viart tells his clergy to accompany him:

'Many of them asked to be excused this visit. M. de Viart left them free
to do as they liked. Some went with him. Getting to the prefecture, he's
told His Majesty is giving no more audiences. Delighted, M. de Viart
goes off home. But the prefect hurries after him and fetches him back.
After waiting half an hour he's introduced. Viart, not wanting anyone
to think he'd come to honour the idol, had neglected to put on his
long coat. As he entered, he said. "We're summoned. We present
ourselves so you can inform us of your wishes."'

Bonaparte upbraids him: "All priests are trouble-makers."

Viart: "I know of none who could seem so."

Bonaparte: "All the peasants detest you."

Viart: "If you interrogate the superior classes of society you'll find that we, at least there, enjoy some confidence and esteem."

Bonaparte: "All you talk about is tithes."

Viart: "This is perhaps the first time they've been spoken of here, and it's not from the mouth of a priest the word comes."

Bonaparte: "Priests, priests. Yet it was I who was their good fortune."

Viart says the benefit (of the Concordat) hasn't been forgotten, but is insufficient.

Bonaparte: "Nowhere else in Europe are the clergy better off."

An argument begins as to whether their salaries are adequate. Napoleon says the Gospel enjoins detachment from worldly things. Yes, says Viart, and it should apply to everyone else too.

Bonaparte: "Enough! Enough!"

Viart: "You yourself permitted us to have recourse to supplements [*ie* fees for weddings, funerals, etc]."

Bonaparte: "Get out! Withdraw!"

'At these words,' writes Fabry, who of course is wholly on the side of the vicar-general, 'uttered in anger and accompanied by a gesture of the foot, the curé raised his hand and said: "Blessed be he who humiliates us."'

And that's the end of that.[8]

An officer arrives, announcing Ney's imminent arrival. Well, let him come. At dinner Ali hears Brayer suggest they

> 'fall on Paris with a few hundred men and surprise the Bourbons in their beds. The proposal wasn't accepted. And indeed, what would the Emperor have done with those princes? They'd only have been an embarrassment to him. He much preferred to leave a door open for them. What did he have to fear from them?[9] ... From time to time detachments of cuirassiers, chasseurs, dragoons were coming in and swelling the army,'

one of them being Captain Marin, Pion des Loches' bête noire at La Fère. After a long and exhausting day Dr Foureau has to give Napoleon a 'soporific broth' to help him get some sleep. But in the middle of the night Bertrand comes and knocks on his bedroom door. Marchand opens it. It's to 'announce the marshal's arrival. The Emperor put off receiving him until the morrow.' And some time during the forenoon of 18 March Ney arrives, alone; and enters the prefecture, not by its main entrance,[10] the all-observing, always objective Ali[11] notices,

> 'but by the back way [*par l'intérieur*]. He stayed a few minutes in the room adjoining the bedchamber. His eyes were filled with tears. He was alone. The Emperor didn't make him wait long. I think it was the

Grand Marshal who introduced him into the bedchamber. The door having been immediately closed, I couldn't see what kind of a reception he got, nor did I hear the conversation, at which no one as far as I know was present, unless it was the Grand Marshal.'

What is being said behind that closed door? According to Napoleon himself Ney at first seems 'embarrassed'. As well he may. Hasn't he only the other day called His Imperial Majesty 'a mad dog', 'the wild beast', etc? If Napoleon no longer has confidence in him, all he, Ney, asks for is a place in the ranks of his Grenadiers.[12] 'It's true,' Napoleon will say afterwards,

'he'd been rather nasty about me. But how could I forget his admirable courage and so many deeds in the past? I threw my arms round his neck, calling him the Bravest of the Brave, and from that moment all was as it used to be.'

According to the always intrusive Fleury de Chaboulon,[13] says 'Embrace me, my dear marshal. I'm happy to see you and I've no need either of explanations or justifications,' – heaping, as Abbé Viart would doubtless agree, coals of fire on the redhead.

Which will do for the myth. But the reality? According to Fleury, Ney stands up for himself; holds a long, almost Thucydedeian speech: 'Sire, I'm very attached to you [*Je vous aime bien*], but first of all and before everything to *la patrie*. Your Majesty can be sure we'll support him, because with justice one can do anything with Frenchmen. But there must be no more thoughts of conquest, we must think only of France's happiness.' All of which closely echoes Fleury's own sentiments, even if they're also Ney's.

What is less likely is that Ney makes so bold as to tell Napoleon: "I haven't come to join you by attachment or out of any consideration for you personally. You've been my country's tyrant, you've brought mourning upon all families, you've disturbed the world's peace. Since chance brings you back, swear to me you'll in future busy yourself repairing the evils you've done to France, that you'll be its people's happiness, etc."[14]

Probably he says very little or nothing. Anyway, as far as we know, the gruff always taciturn Bertrand won't ever let on about what is or isn't said behind those closed doors. Or can it be that someone, so to speak, is listening at the keyhole? For a rumour spreads that Ney's reception has been 'icy' (*glacial*) – which Napoleon, above all a stickler for law and order, can certainly be to marshals who betray their sovereigns. But, he says, he 'can keep his command' – a double-edged concession since it means Ney isn't to share his triumphal entry into Paris. Instead he's sent off north-eastwards on a mission to various towns to ensure they're flying the tricolour. By the time Michel Ney, Duke of Esslingen, Prince of the Moscova, emerges from the prefectorial bedroom he knows he's no longer anyone's man: 'Sometimes I wanted to blow my brains out.'

Meanwhile Fleury de Chaboulon has been set to the task, at times frightening, at others amusing, of going through the mails, seized en route at Avallon, where

'the Emperor had ordered his light cavalry scouts to bring him the mail couriers and myself to examine the despatches. I waged pitiless war on the ministerial correspondence, and if I often found in it insults and threats, of which I had my share; at least they offered details no less important than curious.'

Particularly two secret orders 'whose publication, even today, would cover their authors in eternal opprobrium. Many respectable letters' are

'no less revolting. Most of them were dictated by delirious hatred and could legitimately have merited the rigours of the law. But I regarded them as the pitiable work of sick brains, and before returning them to the courier contented myself with appending a *Seen*, which doubtless, like a Medusa's head, must have petrified more than one noble reader.'

More importantly, some letters gossip about 'Vendeans alleged to have left Paris intending to assassinate the Emperor'.[15] One newspaper even says these assassins are disguised 'as soldiers and women, and that the Corsican will surely not elude them.' Even love letters Fleury endorses with his *Seen*.

But if none of this seems to worry Napoleon in the least, it worries his entourage so much the more:

'Up to now when travellers had asked to bring him news, I'd slipped outside to enjoy a few free moments. But from now on I didn't leave him and, my hand on my sword, didn't let the eyes, attitude and gestures of persons he admitted to his presence out of my sight.'

Bertrand and Drouot and the other staff officers do the same. But

'it seemed as though the Emperor made it his task to defy the blows of his murderers. That same day [18 March] he reviewed the 14th Line [from Orléans and still headed by its colonel, Bugeaud] which had formed square on the Place Saint-Etienne,'

where Peyrusse sees and hears him

'chatting familiarly with the officers and men of this old regiment. Seeing an old sapper decorated with three chevrons [sign of seven years service] he said to him, pulling his beard: "How long have you served for?" "Twenty-three years, Sire." "So we were together at the affair at Rivoli?" "Yes, Sire." "I see you're a good soldier, I'll look after you." It's impossible to imagine the enthusiasm of this old warrior, who'd shown what he'd gone for in the wars in Italy and Spain.'

A rapturous Coignet, also present, sees how he

'afterwards had the officers form a circle, and seeing me, made me come up to him: "So there you are, grumbler." "Yes, Sire." "What was

your rank in my staff?" "General Headquarters baggage-master."
"Very well, I promote you my palace quartermaster and baggage-master-general at General Headquarters. Have you a horse?" "Yes, Sir." "Very well, follow me. Go and see Monthyon in Paris.'"

Head of Imperial Headquarters personnel, Monthyon has long been Coignet's patron.[16] As 'the fine circle of officers around the Emperor made a crown out of their swords over his head' Napoleon tells them they've nothing to fear. The Bourbons' only soldier, he says, is the Duchess of Angoulême.[17] Coignet reports for duty to Bertrand. Afterwards Fleury and the staff are at their wits end to protect him as he mingles

'with the populace and the soldiers. In vain we tried to surround him. So persistently and impetuously were we shoved to and fro it was impossible to stick to him for two moments together. He was infinitely amused by the way we were being elbowed. He laughed at our efforts and, to defy us, pushed still further ahead into the midst of the crowd that was besieging us.'

This rumour of assassins is almost fatal to

'two enemy agents. One of them, a staff officer, came and offered us his services. We questioned him. He hardly knew what to reply. His embarrassment was already exciting violent suspicions when, unluckily, someone noticed he was wearing green trousers,'

enough to convince everyone he's one of Artois' guards. A second interrogation seems even more suspect:

'He was just going to be thrown out of the window when, luckily, Count Bertrand came by and gave orders he was to be put out by the door.'

Suspicions also fall on

'a squadron-leader of hussars, his face decorated with a sabre cut, who also came and joined us. He was warmly welcomed and even invited to dine at the big table of the chief household officers. Wine is the cradle of lies. The newcomer, forgetting his role, gave himself away so obviously it was easy to see he was a false brother.'

The Paris National Guard, he declares, is

"'all for the King, likewise the entire Imperial Guard. Each faithful ranker is to get five francs, each officer 1,000 francs and be promoted one degree [this last, quite correctly, as per Berry's letter to Oudinot]. That Napoleon has been outlawed, and that if he's taken...'" At the last words Colonel ——, sitting beside him, seized him by the collar. Everyone wanted to kill him on the spot.'

'I alone,' Fleury braves it out, 'didn't want it.' And makes them a speech! 'The officer was spat at and driven out. We saw no more of him.'

Fleury also has to deal with a hussar officer who comes claiming he has secret news for the Emperor's ear alone; 'but the Emperor, who knew no

245

secret but strength [*force*] didn't want to waste time on listening to him.' Since 'he didn't consider me worthy of his confidences' the hussar officer is sent to Bertrand, to whom he confides a long rambling tale of how last year he'd been ordered by the provisional government to assassinate Napoleon on his way to Elba; had been horrified at the idea, and held his hand. He even provides 'written proof of his connection with the royalist Maubreuil[18] and his gang.' But he too is sent packing.

In the end, Fleury says, Napoleon, 'being entertained to all these plots against him, was painfully impressed':

'I can't imagine [he said] how men in danger of falling into my hands can go on provoking others to assassinate me and put a price on my head. Twenty times, if I'd wished it, I could have had them brought to me bound hand and foot, dead or alive. I've always been so stupidly generous as to despise their rage! And still do.'

And he orders Fleury to write to General Girard, now in charge of the advance guard, forbidding it to fire a shot: 'You'll only meet Frenchmen.'[19]

Bertrand is ordered to collect all boats procurable to

'embark the army, which was already four divisions strong, and to move it that same evening [by the Yonne] to Rossard, so as to be able to get to Fontainebleau at 1:00 am ... Napoleon got busy embarking that part of his army that was worn out by forced marches. Sending for the harbour master, he made him give an account of the number of his boats, means of preventing accidents etc, and went into such detail with him that the man could hardly get over his surprise or understand how an emperor could know as much as a bargee.'

All available water transport has been collected, even by express mail coaches to other ports up and down the river: barges, lighters, 'water coaches' and even coal barges. Several times Napoleon, who's 'in the habit of using everyone around him for anything that passed through his head,' interrupts Fleury's fascinated reading of other people's letters, and sends him down to the quayside to hurry on the operation, causing his votary to believe 'his genius knew no limits. He thought we others, weak mortals, should also know everything and do anything.' And certainly the barges are heavily overloaded, especially as the river's in full flood after the continuous rains.

Late in the afternoon, just as he's leaving for Sens, two despatches arrive. One tells him that Marshal Suchet, General Gérard and other top commanders have declared for him. The other that the Duke of Angoulême has started a royalist rising in the far south and is aiming to recapture Lyons. After 'taking measures' – no eyewitness specifies what they are – to counteract it, he leaves Auxerre for Sens, being 'in a hurry to reach Fontaine-bleau and enter Paris on the 20th':

> 'At Frossard he found a dragoon regiment coming to meet him, without any of its officers. He reviewed them and distributed compliments and commissions.'

The 65th and 77th Line may not be exactly footsore – for four days and nights, relayed non-stop in jolting waggons and farm carts all the way from Lons-le-Saulnier they've 'passed through patriotic Burgundy amidst its inebriated populations. Each regiment's band had taken turns playing tunes appropriate to the circumstances, which our troops repeated in chorus.'

And now they've arrived too late even to glimpse the grey overcoat! What they do hear about before being instantly embarked 'on big coal barges' is Ney's 'glacial' reception.

> 'So impatient were we to get to Paris and see the Emperor, we cheerfully put up with the extreme discomfort of this voyage. We were stuffed into these barges, our feet in water, with hardly room for each of us, his pack and his weapons.'

At the cathedral town of Sens, though its mayor presents himself at Napoleon's carriage door and implores him to pass a few hours in his ancient city, he excuses himself by saying: 'The outposts have come to blows. Only I can prevent bloodshed.' And only halts long enough to change horses. Ali – evidently it isn't his duty day – says he 'doesn't know where the Emperor slept during the night of 18–19 March, nor even whether he slept anywhere except in his carriage.'

But the fact is that close on midnight he arrives 'like a cannonball' at the riverside town of Pont-sur-Yonne, much too late for the town council, who're already sleeping off their libations in the town hall, leaving Mayor Clément's pretty seventeen-year-old wife, heiress to the *Belle Image* inn, to do the honours. Noticing His Majesty's wearing 'an old overcoat with a leather waistcoat containing an ample pocket full of snuff', she wonders whether it isn't a disguise to fool would-be assassins.' And not until she glimpses the green uniform jacket underneath is she sure it's really he. Not only has she put a warming pan in his bed. She has placed her finest porcelain vase on the mantelpiece. Napoleon, stretched out as usual in an armchair, ignores the bed, having ordered every courier coming from the opposite direction to be brought up to him for questioning. And hardly gets a wink of sleep. His brief night is also disturbed by Drouot kicking downstairs a ten-year-old boy he catches peering in through the keyhole.

What's all the hurry really about?

Just beyond Fontainebleau lie the two towns of Melun and Essonnes. There, he knows, Berry has assembled his troops in an entrenched camp. The three divisions are commanded by Maison, Rapp and Kellerman. Over them, Berry's second-in-command, is Macdonald. But though Napoleon can hardly be doubting that these regiments, like all the others, will come over to him, one never knows. There's many a slip 'tween cup and lip. What if some fanatically royalist officer triggers off hostilities? A soldier's a fighting animal. One shot deserves another. Two can instantly become 200, or 2,000, and turn a skirmish into a battle for which his own force, though now four divisions strong, with thirty-five guns, isn't really organised. And anyway, fighting is what he above all wants to avoid.

And in fact something of the sort very nearly happens.

For centuries Montereau, at the confluence of the Seine and the Yonne, has been regarded as the key to the capital. Saved temporarily last year when the 1st Hussars, defying massive Württemberger grapeshot, had charged so gallantly, its twin bridges are now to be held against Napoleon by the 6th Lancers, another specially favoured regiment Berry has provided with new uniforms and new brass helmets, gleaming under furry black crests. However, here comes a counter-order from Bertrand to hold them for the emperor. Their Colonel Galbois, although 'overwhelmed with favours', promptly obeys. Here, now, comes a fifteen-man detachment of Royal Lifeguards under two trusty royalist officers, Javel and Camboulas, sent forward to arrange billets for them in Montereau. Reaching the first bridge, Javel and Camboulas had seen – as expected – the blue-and-white pennons of the 6th Lancers waving in the chilly breeze. But also one of its captains coming towards them:

'Do you realise,' he asks them, 'we've just declared for the Emperor? You can go back to Paris, but only after you've had a word with Colonel Galbois.'

Galbois? Javel knows him very well. Indeed they're friends. So he agrees; but as he comes up to him notices that the Legion of Honour on his chest isn't the royal version with Henri IV's head on it, but the original model. And instantly they're friends no more. Galbois orders his men to arrest Javel and Camboulas; and they, in turn, call on the Lifeguards to rescue them. Seeing a whole crack regiment assembling at the far end of the bridges, the Lifeguards hesitate, as well they may. There's a kind of half-hearted skirmish; which ends with the Lifeguards, worsted, turning their horses' heads and fleeing, leaving Javel and Camboulas prisoners.

Such has been the second – inglorious – battle of Montereau.

How much does Napoleon, stretched out for a couple of hours uneasy sleep, know about it? Whether he does or not, at 4:00 am, he is just about to leave again when suddenly, down at the river, the jollifications aboard the barges carrying the 77th Line are interrupted. And the First Valet hears

'a terrifying noise. By mistake the bargees, either drunk on wine or absent-minded, had steered their heavily laden barge under an arch not meant for navigation and bristling with pointed stakes. And the leading barge had just sunk within sight of Pont-sur-Yonne, right underneath its bridge.'[20]

In the dark cold night the holed and overladen barge instantly fills with icy water. 'With a little presence of mind,' Larreguy de Civrieux is sure

'the 200 men of my regiment packed inside it could have saved themselves. But those closest to the gunwale, clung to by those behind them, couldn't jump for the bank. By not waiting their turn they made it impossible for everyone to be saved. Prompt help arrived, but the night was so dark it was badly organised. Almost the whole of this unhappy fraction of my regiment was drowned.'

In the dawn light their comrades, following on, are saddened to see 'a large number of corpses lying on the banks of the Yonne or floating along beside us.' Coignet, also travelling by water with ten other officers, sees 'the river covered with boats full of troops. Passing under the bridges we saw men under the water.' Some of Larreguy's comrades are so upset they

'at grave risk of severe punishment take the first opportunity to go ashore. We hired a little cart and in this way reached Melun before the regiment did, slipping in among its ranks again as it disembarked – a notable and inexplicable act of weakness on our part,'

so Larreguy will reproach himself many years later. Coignet too hires a 'rickety old coach' to get to Paris as fast as ever he can and report to Monthyon. 'After a few hours rest,' Larreguy goes on, 'the division was ordered to take the Paris road and double its stages, so as to be on the Tuileries square early tomorrow.[21] But at Pont-sur-Yonne there'd been no time to be lost in grieving. When headquarters had left at 4:00 am, catastrophe or no catastrophe, pretty young Madame Clément, entering what had been His Majesty's bedroom, had seen to her horror her vase had been... used for a certain purpose.[22] And exclaimed:

'Oh, the...!'

But the Old Guard Grenadiers and Chasseurs, that formidable column which in Russia had marched through clouds of Cossacks 'like a ship of the line through fishing boats',[23] is still en route for Sens by by-roads, where it's hoping to join the Emperor. After Toule, Mauduit notices, they've been successively crossing

'several of the battlefields where a year ago we'd rendered military honours to so many of our brave companions-in-arms, and which in twenty different fights the Imperial Guard itself had sprinkled with its blood.'

Everywhere the population is sympathetic. Yet not always to be depended on. What about popular sentiments in the large fortified town of Troyes? Last year the inhabitants had shut their front doors on the Young Guard and left its exhausted units to starve in the streets. Mauduit's officer had judged it best to send a party of twenty-five NCOs and Grenadiers under an officer to reconnoitre it: 'Chance picked us out for this perilous nocturnal expedition. In dreadful weather and the darkest of nights we'd set out at 8:00 pm from Vandroeuvre.' At 2:00 am, after a six-hour march, they reach the town gate:

'The situation was critical, for us one of life or death. Our weapons were charged against all eventualities. Prudence dictated careful measures if we were to avoid what had happened to the thirty grenadiers sent under Captain Lamouret to Antibes,'

which they've evidently heard about. But when a sentry challenges them with a *qui vive?* their officer replies 'in a heavily accentuated voice: "Imperial Guard!"' And a few minutes later

'the doors open on their rusty hinges and deliver the town up to us, its inhabitants and garrison, all still deeply asleep, never guessing they're in the power of twenty-six men of Napoleon's guard.'

But soon they're surrounded by 'the whole population, disputing who should receive us and give us some supper' – a very different situation from last year. Mauduit's officer arranges with the mayor to provide food for the two battalions 'who'd be getting there at 9:00 am and, after resting up a few moments, leave again.' This time it's on some of the Bourbon agents the locals take vengeance, 'as if,' reflects Mauduit,

'the vexations caused by the Russians and Prussians had depended on a fleur-de-lis or some man who perhaps hadn't even known the Bourbons existed. But such is the common people in its feverish moments. It strikes out to right and left, often even against its own friends and benefactors.'

Roguet, however, who should know better, has underestimated Napoleon's velocity. When the two Old Guard regiments finally get to Sens it's a day too late. He'd passed through yesterday. After waiting for the rest of the column to catch up, Mauduit and his disappointed comrades of the 2nd Grenadiers leave again for Fontainebleau.

Meanwhile Napoleon and the headquarters party, accompanied by its cavalry escort and preceded by Girard's advance guard, has left the embarked regiments to go on following the windings of the Yonne, and is travelling swiftly on along the long straight road across the north Burgundian plateau. Getting to Moret at

'10:00 or 11:00 pm, perhaps midnight. He installed himself in an inn to wait for the result of reconnaissances that had been pushed into the forest.'

Here, in the old mediaeval town on the fringe of the Fontainebleau forest, Ali rejoins and hears from Marchand how deeply distressed the Emperor's been 'by so sad an event' as the disaster at Pont-sur-Yonne 'which had cost so many brave men's lives'. 'The Emperor was placing his entire glory in re-entering Paris without it having cost a single life.'

Now with a whole army encamped beyond the forest, he can't be too careful, least of all in view of persistent rumours of royalist fanatics lying in ambush. The first man to reach the forest, it seems, is the First Valet. He's been 'sent on ahead and ordered by His Majesty to wait for him there.' Of the '1,100 or 1,200 men' allegedly lurking behind trees he sees no trace. At 11:00 pm, driving into the great courtyard, he's admitted by the concierge, who's 'just been dismissed but was still there,' and is received by a 'M. Deschamps, a former Palace quartermaster':

'Everything had been prepared to receive His Majesty. He'd lingered for four hours at Moret, and didn't leave it [Ali sees it's 'about 1:30 or 2:00 am'] until he'd received the report that the forest had been flushed out, and that strong outposts [grand'gardes] had been placed at all its exits on the Orléans and Paris sides. We were near the royal army, but I'd seen nothing of it en route.'

All Ali, seated on the box beside Noverraz or one of the other coachmen, glimpses are some

'grenadiers and chasseurs of the Guard. Tired though they were, they were pressing on at the double. Shadows, one could say. If they didn't reach the château at the same time as the Emperor, they got there a quarter of an hour later.'

Actually these weary 'shadows' advancing at the double through the night aren't from the Elba battalion, nor from any other Guard units. There are after all limits to what even a grognard can do in the way of foot-slogging for twenty days on end! And Cambronne, to his extreme mortification, has been replaced at the advance guard by Girard. So the shadows can only be one or another of the regiments who've joined en route. But doubtless at Bertrand's orders Napoleon's coach is surrounded by 100 cavalry as it drives through the forest.

'Getting to Fontainebleau at 4:00 am, escorted by a few hundred troopers – Colonel Jerzmanowski, Colonel Raoul and M. Buisson, a palace quartermaster, galloping at his carriage door – the Emperor went to his apartments, where a nice fire had been lit in his bedroom, and took a few moments' rest. After which, to freshen up, he did his toilet.'

Like Ali, Marchand describes the memorable scene:

> 'He sent for the concierge, one of his old servants, who told him how ever since the Bourbons had arrived they'd busied themselves removing all emblems that might remind anyone of the imperial régime. But they'd forgotten to remove the crowned Ns which, for a fact, were still sculpted on the bed.'

Promptly reinstated, the concierge is 'assured of his continuing favours to himself and his dependants'. After which Napoleon takes 'a couple of hours rest':

> 'Though ever since Grenoble he'd very largely been travelling in a carriage, he seemed fatigued. Surely anybody could be for less than that!'

CHAPTER 12

HASTY DEPARTURES

At the Tuileries everything's at sixes and sevens. King Louis may be vexed to have to climb down from the throne. But he has no intention of dying on it, as he'd promised only three days ago. The news of Ney's defection, confirmed by Colonel Sauran on 17 March, has been decisive. Next day

> 'foreseeing his imminent departure but without notifying his entourage, the King confided to M. de Vitrolles the task of packing up the crown diamonds, which he wanted to take with him to the frontier. Similarly, all the funds at his disposal were to be hidden away [*dissimulés*] in some artillery wagons.'

Louis sends for his middle-aged First Valet and almoner, *François Huë*, a man of cool head, steel nerves and total loyalty.[1] Among the crown jewels, worth a total of 7,434,050 francs,[2] is the world's largest diamond, the famous Regent. Louis tells Huë to 'transport this precious baggage' to Calais and thence over to England. The greatest prudence is of course required. But who more resourceful and prudent than Huë?

> 'Next day [19 March] M. de Blacas gave me the needful safe-conducts and passports and a list of the crown jewels, drawn up by M. de Gournay, and ordered me to leave the Tuileries around midnight 19/ 20 March.'

More problematic to transport is the State's disposable cash. 'A reserve of money must be secured,' Vitrolles tells Blacas, pushing him angrily into a window recess. A bewildered Blacas agrees, but how? Now it's the turn of Baron Louis, the Minister of Finance, to ask Vitrolles whether he knows 'how much a sack of 1,000 silver francs weighs. And how many wagons will be needed to carry twenty-five million francs?'

> "Never mind, let them be taken away in gold."

Does Vitrolles really think it's so easy to rustle up twenty-five millions in gold, just now, when a tenth of the country's specie has already been withdrawn from the bank? Or at what rates now, when government bonds, which had stood at seventy-eight francs on 5 March, have fallen to sixty-six francs? In the end they decide to send for

> "Lafitte or some other banker, and see what he can do to supply you with bills of exchange on London or other places abroad. It was done, and [to Vitrolles' great relief] a sum of some fourteen million francs was easily procured."

To his annoyance, however, twenty-two more millions have to be left in the

Treasury for that insufferable bandit Bonaparte to lay his greedy hands on. Can it be, he wonders, that Baron Louis is buttering his toast on both sides?

The King's by no means the only person who's packing up his valuables. For a week at least the city's two top bankers, *Ouvrard* and Lafitte, have been coping with a rush for bills of exchange cashable in London or Frankfurt, or indeed anywhere, in return for cash. It's every man for himself and the diabolical Bonaparte take the hindmost. Two days ago Generals Maison, governor of Paris, and Dessolles, commanding its National Guard, paid Blacas a peremptory visit. To stand by the king, they'd explained, may well cost them their lives. And how about their families? They'll be obliged to depend on royal bounties:

Blacas: 'Messieurs, you mustn't doubt the King's gratitude. He'll know very well how to reward your devotion...'

Maison, turning to Dessolles: 'You can see he's just pretending not to understand us. We must speak more clearly. Monsieur de Blacas: either you can no longer count on our services, or you must give each of us 100,000 francs.'

And at 4:00 pm Gournay, the treasurer, had duly paid out the two huge sums. Clarke, Minister of War since Soult's resignation on 11 March, also indents for 100,000 francs. 'This,' ironises Vitrolles, 'was termed taking precautions.' He contents himself with his arrears of salary – a somewhat vague figure.

Anyone who is, has been, or hopes to be anyone is fleeing.

In the evening of 17 March young *A-F. Villemain**, an aspirant to literary fame who'd been Narbonne's secretary in Russia,[3] had attended one of Mme. de Staël's receptions, and found her wearing

'her usual outfit, at once brilliant and careless [*négligée*], her thick
black hair under a scarlet turban half-enclosing it harmonising with
her eyes' expressive *éclat*. Whether or not she knew what had happened at Lons-le-Saulnier she didn't seem the same person.'

Though he'd seen how she still has her habit of twirling a little twig between her thumb and fingers as she talks, 'almost wholly and always about herself, her face,' he's shocked to see, 'was fatigued, as if sick with sadness' as she'd taken farewell of Mrs Rumford, wife of the American ambassador: 'I've only strength enough to flee,' she'd said. 'It's all too horrible.'

She's sure her new exile must be for ever. As for the two million gold francs her father had lent Louis XVI's government – now she must give up all hope of ever seeing them again. How terrible! Hadn't it been she who'd done more than almost anyone else to overthrow the Tyrant? Yet the King hasn't even deigned to receive her! Well, the Bourbons only have them-selves to thank.

On this morning of 19 March, at 7:00 am, Villemain goes to the house in the Chausée d'Antin of his patron Fontanes, Napoleon's arbiter of taste and literature. 'Having climbed at a run a staircase lumbered with travelling trunks' he finds the great man 'already in his greatcoat', pacing impatiently to and fro in front of 'a fire half-extinguished under burnt papers, anxious to be off. It seemed he'd hardly had a wink of sleep last night.' In his right hand he's holding *Le Journal des Débats*, where he's just been reading Constant's furious attack on Napoleon:

'Let us redouble our efforts against France's enemy, the enemy of mankind, who caused grass to grow in our commercial cities, took away the arms of agriculture, dragged the elite of the nation to the ends of the earth. Stained with our blood this man reappears. Under Bonaparte we'll be submitted to a government of Mamelukes. . .'

As Villemain comes in, he bursts out:

"So that's that! The dice is cast. And that's the end of the first adventure. The Emperor'll be here tomorrow. But I shan't! It's all over between him and me. He's no longer the man I served fifteen years ago, who restored society and put a stop to the Revolution." He, Fontanes, isn't going to "dust off his victorious *calèche* with all the half-pay officers at the Tuileries.[4] This time he's just bringing chaos, and he'll fall before he can put in irons the Jacobinism he's unleashing."

Villemain, naively: "Oh but surely – Constant's article shows everything's not over yet?"

Fontanes: "More heat than strength! The fact is, he's in love and singing for the sirens, the ones who never appeared at Bonaparte's court. It's Romeo singing under Juliet's window. D'you know what's the curse of our age, my dear fellow?" he goes on, pacing agitatedly up and down. "People who make up constitutions, as others do shoes. Bootees that press the legs a little, or slippers – it's all one. I shan't be surprised if in a few days time Constant won't be taking Bonaparte's measurements and working for him."

Villemain admits he's "only seen two revolutions, last year's and now this one", but he can't believe Constant will do such a thing, "not after his furious article calling Napoleon an Attila!"

Fontanes: "There's no strength except in the army, and the army's his. That's what your English ideas have brought us to! He triumphs, and he's lost. Tomorrow he'll be in the Tuilieries, and in six months I don't know where. I've no doubt of it." Fontanes, who has "known Napoleon sometimes posing in front of himself, deflecting his thoughts from his own interests and regarding himself in his cold-blooded imperial way," is sure "he's already feeling he's lost, or soon will be." No no. As soon as ever the post coach arrives he's off. To Normandy, "a sensible country where people are neither strong legitimists nor rabid revolutionaries", where he can stay in a nice château "surrounded by prose and verse"; and, in case things really get too hot for his wife's taste, conveniently close to the Channel. All he believes in is "the force and logic of events". And in Talleyrand at Vienna, with "his iron hand in a silken glove. Just imagine what credit he's enjoying for his useless prescience!"

Staggered, young Villemain totters out onto the boulevard.

At about the same moment as he'd got up, General d'Arblay, Fanny Burney's husband, after spending two successive nights 'armed on guard' – first at the Tuileries 'in his duty as Garde du Corps of the King; the other as artillery captain at the barracks' – but now 'affected by the most gloomy prognostics', had come home,

> 'harassed, worn, almost wasted with fatigue, and yet more with a baleful view of all around him and in a sense of wounded military honour in the inertia which seemed to paralyse all effort to save the King and his cause. He had gone to bed for a few hours, and then, after a wretched breakfast,'

urges Fanny 'in the most solemn and earnest manner' to leave with their friend Mme. d'Hénin,

> 'should she ultimately decide to depart. We knelt together in a short but fervent prayer to heaven for each other's preservation, and then separated. At the door he turned back, and with a smile which, though forced, had inexpressible sweetness, he half-gaily exclaimed *Vive le Roi!* – and then he darted from my sight. In my bedroom ... I ran to a window which looked upon the inward courtyard. There, indeed, behold him I did, but oh! With what anguish! Just mounting his war-horse, a noble animal, of which he was singularly fond, but which at this moment I viewed with acutest terror, for it seemed loaded with pistols, and equipped for immediate service in the field of battle, while Deprez, the groom, prepared to mount another, and our cabriolet was filled with baggage and implements of war.'

Fanny, 'now sufficiently roused for action', gets busy packing up her 'small portion of [silver] plate etc' and paying off 'every bill that might be owing,' including the rent, 'so that no pretence might be assumed from our absence for disposing of our goods, books or property of any description'

But the landlord is 'thunderstruck' – hasn't 'the King reiterated his proclamation that he would not desert his capital'?

Very likely. But is deserting it even so.

Everywhere in the Saint-Germain quarter dozens of private coaches are being loaded up. Among other personages intending to take their jewellery with them is Berthier*, Captain of the Royal Guard. Likewise his beloved Mme. Visconti and all his presents to her in a jewel case.[5] Another departing carriage belongs to the Duke of Richelieu, formerly the Tsar's governor of the Crimea; and yet another to his ADC General *L-V-L. de Rochechouart.*[6]

"All this is going to end very badly," the Duke tells Rochechouart. "At the Tuileries they've lost their heads. I think we're going to have to retreat before the flood. I can't decently abandon the King in his present danger, and I'll stay with him to the end. But at this very moment I'm sending off my secretary with my barouche, my valet and my effects. They're to wait for me at Frankfurt." And he hands Rochechouart "10,000 francs in gold procured for me by M. Ouvrard. I don't doubt we'll be leaving in a couple of hours. You have two horses. Lend me one of them."

After arriving in Paris with Rilliet, his fellow Swiss, Captain Rieu has been enrolled in an improvised battalion. Now in the forenoon, it assembles and is marched to the Place du Carousel,

> 'facing the central balcony of the Tuileries. Soon there appeared on it, walking with great difficulty because of his bloated legs, His Majesty Louis XVIII. He saluted affectionately, but with a very sad air, and withdrew amidst shouts of *Vive le Roi!* from the chests of "pure" royalists.'

Rieu notices the hurrahs aren't 'by any means as loud as the ones that had formerly greeted Napoleon as he'd passed his reviews on horseback on this same spot.' At midday, it's been decided, Louis shall review the *Maison du Roi*, assembled in the Champs Elysées.[7] And then, escorted by it, leave via Saint-Denis and Beauvais for Lille, chosen because it's 'only two relays from the frontier.' The parade

> 'of the whole of the Household Troops, the Horse Grenadiers, the Bodyguards and two regiments of cavalry – upwards of 2,400 superb horsemen, well-mounted, the elite of French youth, all animated by the most sincere and lively enthusiasm for the King's cause,'

takes place on the Quai de Passy and in the Allée des Veuves. A dazzling display of military gold lace that seems, however, not to impress Louis: 'That prince passed in front of us in his carriage. He looked sad and depressed.' As usual his *calèche* just gallops past the ranks. With him he has Marmont, Berthier and Lauriston. Evidently scared by the lack of enthusiasm in the onlookers, he returns prematurely to the Tuileries, even though Macdonald reassures him that the rest of the troops 'have obeyed and left Paris. Your Majesty no longer has any but loyal men about him.'

"How do you expect me to leave quietly just now?" complains Louis from his armchair.

As long as his carriages stand outside waiting, Macdonald points out, the crowds will go on gathering. 'Send them away empty. Everyone'll think you've cancelled your departure and leave. You can recall your carriages during the night, when everyone's dispersed.'

Rilliet goes home to put his effects in order for a nocturnal departure – as he thinks – for Melun. Passing in front of the Tuileries, he sees the Swiss Guards (*Les Cent Suisses*)

> 'under arms, looking worried, silent, waiting for orders. Groups of the populace and army officers filled the streets. The agitation was growing. The appearance of calm from the morning had changed.'

And young Villemain sees people reading the newspaper, 'almost all of them pale, undecided, neither daring to repeat Benjamin Constant's fiery philippic nor give any more news from the army or the Tuileries, in their dreary reality.' But two things everyone now knows.

Ney has changed sides.

And the Emperor's at Fontainebleau.

Besides aristocrats and bourgeois, royalists, Orléanists and Bonapartists, there's another much-feared factor in the situation. *Le peuple.* What will happen, all respectable – *viz* moneyed people – are worrying, if there's an interregnum and the mob breaks loose from the little narrow streets, 'dark, damp and everlastingly lined with thick black sticky mud' around the Saint-Jacques market,

> 'low, badly lit and for the most part looking out on narrow dirty courtyards, infected by the smell from the lead pipes for taking the domestic water from floor to floor, [with their] excessive pile-up of human beings, great numbers of live animals, vapours coming from their corpses left there to rot, the vegetables also rotting, which doubtless help thicken and make even more unhealthy this atmospheric cloaque one breathes and swims in.'

In these quarters, as on the Ile de la Cité, where each house provides a dwelling for twenty to thirty people,

> 'overcrowding is made worse by the layout and smallness of the rooms, the narrowness of doors and windows, the great number of households, perhaps ten per house, and finally, by the crowding in of the lowest class, attracted there by the cheapness of the dwellings.'

Here hatred for the arrogant fops of the court, only a few hundred yards away, not to mention envy of the stupendous Saint-German mansions just across the river, knows no bounds. Few labourers have perhaps lived so long, but the oldest certainly remember the delirious days hardly thirty years ago when the guillotine had daily lopped aristocratic heads in the Place de la Révolution. How much of Napoleon's haste to arrive is due to a desire to forestall such a rising? The last thing he wants is to arrive in Paris as 'king of a jacquerie', as a 'Robespierre on horseback', as Mme. de Staël has called him. Hence his message from Auxerre, sent on to his partisans, to 'remain quiet'.[8] Nor does he want to start his new reign by having to use the army to crush a popular uprising.

Anyway, nothing happens. Or hardly. Only a handful of Charenton workers march in under red flags singing the *Carmagnole* and the *Ca Ira*. But a volley of musketry from a party of royalist Law School volunteers disperses them. Kills five. Otherwise the city 'remains quiet'.

All Vitrolles – muttering as an aside 'we don't need the sun to light up the shame of this flight' – has managed to obtain at the Tuileries is that the royal departure shall put off until after nightfall:

'The King went back into the château with a calm that could make one despair. The ministers were told they should hold themselves ready to follow him. The Minister of War [Clarke] asked me to point out to His Majesty that these preparations and separation from his own people meant for him expenses his limited fortune would not permit him to defray. I immediately spoke about it to the King; and it was agreed with him and Blacas that 100,000 francs be paid out of the Crown Treasury to each minister who'd follow the King.'

The carriages are temporarily dismissed. And the crowds that have gathered around them slowly disperse. It's Palm Sunday. And, even more important, dinnertime, sacred to all Parisians.

Meanwhile Artois, wearing National Guard uniform, has been reviewing 'some of its legions'[9] on the Place Vendôme. Rieu is present:

'The prince did his best to seem to smile, but at the bottom of his heart he must have been sad when, as he passed by, he encountered the malevolent glances of former military men in civilian clothes, muttering decidedly unroyalist opinions.'

Together with the 1st Hussars making up General Talleyrand's light cavalry brigade, Saint-Chamans' 500 men of the 1st Chasseurs are drawn up on the Place Louis XV (ex-Place de la Concorde[10]). Arrived yesterday from Béthune, he'd found 'lots of emotions, lots of shouting, but not a single measure that one could believe would check the torrent menacing us.' Henckens is here too, under Colonel Talhouët, arrived from Compiègne. To Saint-Chamans the *Maison du Roi* seems to be 'hardly in a state to go campaigning. The royal volunteers were scarcely armed.' Vitrolles, looking on, probably from the terrace of the Tuileries gardens, finds the review 'very sad. No one knew what the sovereign's ulterior plans were' – not even the Chamber, in the Palais Bourbon, just across the river. All morning the Deputies have been sitting in secret session, waiting for some member of the government to come and tell them what's going on. But none does.

Told that morale is bad, Lieutenant-General Roussel d'Hurbal, commanding the light cavalry division, orders Saint-Chamans to assemble his officers. He wants to speak to them. Briefly reminded of the royal favours that have been showered on them – the right to wear aiguillettes, for instance – they remain 'cold, but calm'. Only when Saint-Chamans gets off his horse and tells two of the worst trouble-makers to leave the ranks and go back to Béthune do they 'explode':

> 'In a very loud voice they declared they wouldn't; that I hadn't the right to relieve them of their commands without a court-martial; that they clearly saw the intention was to ruin them, but they'd rather be shot on the spot than at Béthune. The moment was utterly critical. The chasseurs were looking most discontented and murmuring among themselves. Some of the populace had gathered. At a moment of such great effervescence, in the midst of troops and men of ill-will, I was afraid to unleash a serious riot at the gate of the Tuileries. I trembled at the danger the King and his family might run, and saw clearly I'd have to give up insisting on obedience to a verbal order I lacked the force to implement.'

So, extracting a promise from the two Bonapartist officers that they'll do nothing against the royal service, he lets them return to their posts. But tells General *Belliard**, Berry's chief-of-staff, how bad his regiment's morale is. It's sheer folly, he says, to send the army, which 'wants nothing better' than to go and greet the Emperor, to fight him. On the contrary, it'd be better to take it into Flanders or toward the Rhine and so scatter it. 'If they get near Napoleon, a unanimous defection is inevitable.' Belliard replies that he'd preached the same policy 'four or five days ago, but no one had wanted to listen to him,' and recommends he speak to Berry direct: 'Perhaps he'll believe you.' Invited to dinner at the Tuileries, Saint-Chamans 'passes through halls filled with courtiers' and finds Berry in the Throne Room. If the troops march against Bonaparte, he tells him frankly, "they'll only be bringing him everything he lacks, fine cavalry and artillery." Why don't they take the army to Flanders or Alsace? It would 'paralyse him'. At table he finds many officers, among them Belliard* (acting as Berry's chief-of-staff) and Rapp*, Napoleon's senior and once-favourite ADC. Berry, who seems cheerful enough, asks him if he can count on his regiment. To which Saint-Chamans, 'not judging it suitable to give any hint of the terrible truth in front of everyone and the servants,' says he can.

After the light cavalry division, 'still wearing the white cockade', has marched off 'toward Fontainebleau against Napoleon', Saint-Chamans lingers, feeling he must have another, franker word with Berry, and going back to the Tuileries is admitted to Berry's office, and ordered 'on his honour and conscience' to say what he really thinks. And has to admit his regiment isn't to be counted on. Even so, he thinks, 'if some unit hotly commenced an affray,' his men would 'fight the Emperor's troops to support those who were already engaged. The prince asked for nothing better.' As for withdrawing to the north, "It's too late," Berry replies. "We've engaged the Household Troops, and must support them."

'In that case,' says Saint-Chamans, 'I must expect to see my entire regiment desert.'

"Should that misfortune occur," says Berry, "don't quit your regiment."

'What, Monseigneur? If my men go over to the Emperor, do you want me to follow them?'

"Yes," he replied. "Go and rejoin your regiment and do as I tell you." And breaks off the interview.[11]

> 'I left the Tuileries with death in my soul, and made haste to catch up with my regiment, which was already on the Essonnes road. In its rear and outside the barriers I came across several chasseurs, mostly drunk, who were talking loudly of the "Little Corporal" and the pleasure they were going to have at seeing him again.'

At Essonnes he catches up with his fellow colonel of light cavalry. Talhouët and he had known each other as prisoners of war in St Petersburg. Both tell the older Exelmans (Count Valmy), in charge at Essonnes, that they don't think their men will fight. But Talhouët is less candid:

> 'Not that he was less sure of it, but there was something in his character more reticent and more political, which I didn't possess. As for the Household Troops which M. de Berry had said were engaged and must be supported, no one had so much as seen or heard of them.'

On the bridge at Corbeil Saint-Chamans falls in with Count d'Affry, colonel of the 4th Swiss. He too is sure his men won't fight.

Among its worst blunders (from its own point of view) – as if there weren't enough of them already – the government has summoned all half-pay officers to report for duty. First they'd been sent out to Melun; but then, 'probably not knowing what to do with us', have all been sent home, only to be ordered out again this morning to Saint-Denis, where they're spending the day in a state of agitated expectancy. One such *demisolde* 'the government thought it could utilise by making us handsome promises' is *Jean-Marcel Routier*, of the 102nd (ex-85th) Line: 'On 18 March had come a new order for us to assemble tomorrow morning at Saint-Denis. We spent all night and the following day in that town.'

Responsible persons are feeling the time has come to take appropriate measures. The headmaster of the prestigious Collège Henri IV, ex-Collège Napoleon, for instance. Recovering Napoleon's bust from the school latrines, he has it dusted off. To at least one of his pupils, looking out from his classroom window, 'an anxious waiting' seems to dominate people's minds:

> 'I can't do better than compare it to what one feels as one watches a huntsman jumping from one rock to another along a path fringed

with precipices. Everyone was holding his breath. There were crowds on the streets, a silent one on the boulevards, sombre faces. Discouraged postures. Eyes animated by a ray of hope. People were speaking two by two, throwing distrustful looks at those around them. The street hawkers seemed to have no voice left to cry up their wares, and the shopkeepers hardly did anything except observe passers-by.'

As on the eve of 21 January and its abortive massacre of Bonapartists and left-wingers, it seems to Carnot's son that Paris offers 'the spectacle typical of a great city when she feels herself on the verge of a catastrophe.'

The prudent – that's to say most people – are changing sides as quietly and unnoticeably as possible. Despite her hostess' warning, Hortense, this morning of 19 March, is still looking out over the boulevard from her balcony in the Rue Duphot, and feeling bored. As one anxious day has followed another she's been watching her neighbour across the street, 'an enthusiastic royalist'. Suddenly she notices 'the huge white rosette he usually wore in his buttonhole had vanished.' And wonders impatiently whether this doesn't indicate a change of régime?

Not yet.

Most despondent of all is the mood at the Tuileries. Every quarter of an hour or so arrives a despatch-rider from the Fontainebleau road, with news of the 'enemy's' progress. Yet the King's imminent departure is still being kept a secret and nothing's being done. Again and again Vitrolles has urged his great plan on the King. About forty departments, after all – about half of France[12] – can be counted on to stand by him. Louis neither agrees nor objects 'but seemed determined not to embrace such a plan unless everyone adopted it.'

And when Marmont, given overall command of the *Maison du Roi*, comes for orders and gets one, it's to 'transport the King to Saint-Denis', written on a 'little square slip of paper, reserving to himself the right to give him further orders later.' Marmont, still in the dark as to his ultimate destination, observes that he certainly won't be able to stop at Saint-Denis. 'The King took another slip of paper, dating it from Saint-Denis, with the order to transport him to Beauvais.' All without any indication of his ultimate goal.

Is he afraid it'll only be another flight to Varennes?

Donning their imperial uniforms again, Planat, Résigny and Briqueville have gone to see Flahaut and decide what's to be done tomorrow. They find him

'walking in his garden. I told him we were going to join the Emperor and asked if he wanted to come with us. To my great astonishment he refused. Though protesting his great devotion to him, he also declared he had a horror of civil discord. I didn't insist and made haste to leave him.'[13]

Instead, Planat goes to see his boss at the War Ministry. Finds General Évain 'packing up his things to follow the King to Belgium,' though his sister Agathe is dead against it. And tells Planat so. They're just discussing how to dissuade him, when Évain enters. His sister says:

"Here's M. Planat. He doesn't think you should leave."

'*Mon général*,' says Planat, plucking up courage. 'You're nothing of a politician, and whatever government establishes itself in France will always have need of your talents and experience. What have the Bourbons done for you to justify such an excessive devotion? You owe yourself to France, she needs your services.' Isn't Drouot his friend? He'll certainly see to it he keeps his job.

Évain reflects a few moments, says: "Very well, I'll stay."

'And you don't mind me resuming my functions as ADC to Drouot?'

"Of course not..."[14]

Which is why, at La Fère, Pion des Loches will soon be noticing how the sentiments expressed in Évain's despatches, though still signed by him, are – without transition – being inverted. Without batting an eyelid, Évain, who's been praising Griois and Pion for their royalism, will soon be praising their attachment to 'our well-loved sovereign the Emperor'. A job, after all, is a job. And most officers and officials without any private fortune – and many who do have one – simply can't afford to sacrifice future promotion or their family's welfare to their political sentiments.

Now it's about 9:00 pm. Just as Fanny 'd'Arblay née Burney', is finishing packing up her effects her friend Mme. d'Hénin sends word 'that we must bring nothing but a small change of linen, as by the news she had just heard, we should be back again in two or three days'.

So she puts her few things into 'a hand-basket, made by some French prisoners in England; swallowed, standing, my neglected dinner', and with another woman friend gets into a cab to 'drive to General Victor de la Tour Maubourg. It was about nine o'clock at night, and very dark.' When she gets there she finds the general's house all topsy-turvy and 'in a state of most gloomy dismay', without even anyone on the door. 'Officers and strangers were passing to and fro, some to receive, others to resign commissions, but all with quick steps, though in dead silence.' Not a servant anywhere. In the drawing room, where people are waiting, 'a dismal taciturnity prevailed'. But La Tour Maubourg brings her a note from her husband. Belonging to the artillery company, he 'could not be spared even a moment.' It reads (in French):

'My dear friend – All is lost! I can't go into detail – please, for Heaven's
sake, leave! The sooner the better. – In life and death. A.. d'A..'
Fanny goes on to Mme. d'Hénin's, where the finds the same chaos and a
message

'brought by a confidential servant, to announce that Bonaparte was
within a few hours' march of Paris! By now almost distracted by this
dreadful prospect of indefinite detention, Mme. d'Hénin instantly
ordered horses to her berline, which had long been loaded. And
calling up all her people and dependants, was giving her orders with
the utmost vivacity, when intelligence was brought her that no horses
could now be had, the Government having put them all in requisition.'

Panic. However, her 'faithful domestic from her childhood' lends her his
horses 'for one stage from Paris'. So her travelling coach, harnessed up to
them, arrives in the gateway, and Mme. Hénin,

'with a sweetness most engaging, suffering the women to kiss her
cheek, and smiling kindly on the men, who kissed her ... we now
rushed into the carriage, averse, yet eager, between ten and eleven
o'clock at night.'

And off they go. What an incredible number of carriage lights must be
glimmering as they jolt northwards along the rain-sodden Saint-Denis–
Beauvais road, running from the modern Attila, and making tracks for
Belgium! But after dining yesterday with *Castellane**, one of his former ADCs,
and spending the evening with Juliette Récamier ('fundamentally she
doesn't love me'), the author of that heartfelt diatribe is sure that 'if he
triumphs and catches me I perish. If the Corsican's beaten my situation here
will improve. But we've twenty to one against us.' So he has taken refuge with
Mme. Rumford at the American Embassy.

Meanwhile unit after white-cockaded unit is marching southwards through
the rainy night along the Essonnes–Fontainebleau road. When Saint-
Chamans catches up with his chasseurs he finds 'the royal army camped on
the banks of the Rungis near the Arceuil aqueduct, guns trained and ready
to fire.' His orders are to spend the night with the rest of his division 'in
cantonments in the neighbouring villages, and be in the camp at 5:00 am',
ready for the impending battle.

But back at his lodgings, Captain Rilliet of the Cuirassiers of the Royal
Guard has fallen in with a friend who tells him bluntly:

'All the Melun troops have turned their coats. This very evening Bonaparte will sleep at Fontainebleau. The King has sent word of it to the
Chambers.' It's 'no longer a moment for hesitation'. Rilliet grabs up a few of
his effects, confides the rest to his two friends, and takes a cab to the barracks
in the Rue de Grenelle:

'It was 10:00 pm. In Paris all was calm. Lights were shining brightly in the Tuileries, no extraordinary stir was to be observed there. I took farewell of my friends. At 11:00 pm we went to the Champ de Mars. The night was pitch black. One couldn't see two steps ahead. We formed up in line in the middle of the Champ de Mars, to the right of the École Militaire.'

Out at Saint-Denis, meanwhile, Captain Routier and 300 or so fellow *demi-soldes* 'of all grades, most unquiet about what was happening and what they were thinking of doing with us', are spending a noisy time in the *estaminets* and bistros. No one brings them either news or orders.

At the Tuileries, Vitrolles is at his wits' end. When he'd asked the King whether he wants him to come with him or try to carry out his plan to raise the West and South, Louis had simply sent word to him that he 'can do as he likes.'

'I was distressed to the bottom of my soul. No one who hasn't been present at one of these extreme moments can understand the situation where, still all alive, one knows tomorrow one will be dead. Passing one of the Tuileries' ground-floor halls, I was struck to see a magnificent dinner laid in honour of the Spanish ambassador, a meal for twenty-five to thirty persons, given in the King's name by his maître d'hôtel. And that was happening only four or five hours before the King was going to leave!'

Seeing Artois and the Chancellor in conversation, he's halted by Artois, who says:

"We were just talking about you, and I was telling M. de Dambray I think it's a good idea the King shall send you to the South. If anyone can do anything there, it's certainly you."

Artois and Dambray go in to the King to tell him so. But when, later, Vitrolles asks Blacas what's been decided, Blacas tells him the King has said again he can "do as he likes". He's always welcome at his side, but, on the other hand, he's sure he'll serve him devotedly in the South.

'The King's reply threw me into despair, as a new instance of his nonchalance and inability to make up his mind.'

Going to Artois, he opens his heart to him. Won't he come with him to Toulouse? If they're going to die, isn't it better "in blood than in mud"? But no. If anything happens to the King, says Artois evasively, and he isn't at his side, it'll be "imputed to him as a crime." But after he's followed the King across the frontier, he says 'several times', he'll join Vitrolles at Toulouse. Privately Vitrolles doubts it. It's after 11:30 pm. Just then a door opens and the First Gentleman of the Chamber announces that the King wishes to see him instantly: 'I found the King in the same calm and his ordinary habits.'

Holding 'a little letter like a visiting card between his first two fingers', he tells Vitrolles to leave for Bordeaux and Toulouse, where he can do whatever he thinks best for his service. And give this letter to his niece, who's to hold out as long as she can, and then do the same as he's doing. When Vitrolles asks for authority in writing, Louis says:

"Authority? You don't need any. As my minister there's no limit to your powers. Anyway, my nephew and niece are there and will empower you."

'After these words the King held out his hand, which I kissed, certainly more moved than he was.'

But now the moment has come. Just before midnight a dozen carriages draw up in the Tuileries courtyard, the one reserved for Louis under the awning of the Flore Pavilion. Servants, National Guards who've taken over from Line troops on guard at the palace, courtiers, officials and bodyguards have collected on the staircase and at its foot. All in a deep solemn silence. The door of the private apartments opens and out comes an usher holding aloft a flaming torch. Then, supported by Blacas and the Duke of Duras, Louis appears on the threshold. Everyone falls to his knees, and a few faint exclamations of *Vive le Roi!* are heard among sighs and sobs.[15] An aged servant murmurs:

'He's wearing a crown of thorns!'

Louis can hardly get through the crowd of individuals kissing his hands and touching his clothes. This is too much.

"I foresaw it," he mutters sotto voce to Blacas. "I didn't want to see them. I should have been saved this emotion." Then, louder: "My children, I'm touched by your devotion. But I need my strength. Please, spare me... go home to your families. I'll soon see you again."

And climbs into his carriage. Vitrolles helps Artois into his lighter one, and, with a numerous escort of mounted bodyguards, the procession departs. Vitrolles throws

'a last look at the Tuileries, which a moment ago had been so brilliant with lights, so heady, so filled with men and movement, that palace so recently surrounded by all the attributes of greatness and power, now sombre, deserted by its masters, ready to be handed over to a Corsican who had no other rights than his audacity and the servility of a troop of janissaries.'

Going home, he finds M. Sauvo, the editor of *Le Moniteur*. Mechanically faithful to all régimes, Sauvo asks him to approve the day's royal proclamation, drawn up by Dambray, 'as if for us this fateful day had a morrow. I smiled at the thought that we'd throw this last word to the public after we'd left.' So he checks over the text:

'Louis, by the Grace of God, King of France and Navarre, to our trusty and well-

beloved friends, the Peers and the Deputies: Divine Providence, which recalled us to the throne of our fathers, today suffers that throne to be shaken by the desertion of a part of the armed forces. We could have profited from the loyal and patriotic attitude of the great majority of the inhabitants of Paris to challenge their entry; but we shudder at the misfortunes of every kind that a struggle within her walls would have brought down on them. We are withdrawing with some brave [sic] *men ... to gather strength in another part of the realm* [among] *Frenchmen more advantageously placed. We have the tranquil presentiment that the mis-guided soldiers will not be slow to acknowledge their errors, and will find in our leniency and bounties the reward for their return to their duties.'*

The Chambers will soon meet in another place in the kingdom – Vitrolles checks over the text of this suave announcement, and tells Sauvo (a man for whom régimes can come and go as long as *Le Moniteur* comes out without any printing mistakes) he's leaving for Toulouse. Sauvo, terrified for Vitrolles' sake, tries to dissuade him; and when he won't be dissuaded, asks in tears to be allowed to embrace him. Fearing the city gates may be closed at any moment, Vitrolles leaves on his grandiose self-created mission,

'alone, with a valet, in the same carriage I'd prepared for leaving with the King. I didn't even have one of those passports the Secretary of State had given people by the hundred. I couldn't give one to myself, and no one was left to give me one.'

As for the four Red Companies of the Royal Household, fuzzy orders have been given for its members to assemble 'outside the Étoile gate', on the edge of the countryside. 'But a great disappointment met us there,' a mortified Rochechouart goes on,

'as the number of officers or corporals or sergeants was far in excess of those of simple guardsmen, most of whom had gone off home, or even to their quarters through the streets of Paris by night.'

But in the Champ de Mars the men of the Royal Guard, Rilliet among them, have been waiting in pitch darkness:

'A few minutes before midnight, entering by the gate next to the École Militaire, some carriages came swiftly toward us. It was the King who, to throw the curious off the track, had followed this route to leave Paris.'

No acclamations, this time, from his Household Troops:

'Just now everything was grave and sad. Louis XVIII crossed over the Iéna Bridge, followed the outer boulevards, and took the Beauvais road. The Swiss Guard had already gone off in that direction. We were young and light-headed. Yet what a deep emotion, what a shiver passed through our veins as we heard in the night's darkness, made more solemn by the troops' silence, the sound of the King's carriages fade away!'

Rilliet's thoughts go to the famous flight of Louis XVI to Varennes, almost thirty years ago, which, had it succeeded,[16] he fancies would have saved Europe from 'so many crimes and revolutions'. At the Étoile, with the four-square pylons of the unfinished Arc de Triomphe[17] looming up into the rainy sky, Rochechouart and Richelieu see the King's cortège go by. To have only seven or eight musketeers in his unit is too small a command for a man who's governed the whole of the Crimea. And Rochechouart, feeling it beneath his dignity to bother with them, hands them over to 'three officers and four NCOs.' After which he and Richelieu 'follow the road the King had taken' and make, they too, for Beauvais.

CHAPTER 13

'IT SEEMED HE'D JUST COME BACK FROM A JOURNEY'

At about 6:00 am on 20 March Ali, at Fontainebleau, sees how 'some regiments of lancers, chasseurs or hussars came and drew up in the White Horse Courtyard' – the very same courtyard where his master had last year taken so moving a farewell of the Old Guard. Since these cavalry are 'wearing new uniforms and each company had horses of the same size and colour' the lancers can only be the same ones (the 6th) as had seized the Montereau bridge. 'Each squadron was numerically few, but so well organised it pleased the eye.' An hour later, 7:00 am, Napoleon gets up, dresses, comes out into the courtyard, inspects them 'at length' and orders them to leave for Paris. Then goes back up to his apartments[1] and breakfasts.

What has happened to the last few days' urgency? It seems he's in no great hurry to leave. On the contrary,

'no sooner[2] had he got to Fontainebleau, than he went through the gardens and the palace with as much pleasure as curiosity,[3] as if he were taking possession of it for the first time.'

Though Fleury de Chaboulon is watching him closely as he follows him about the palace, with its magnificent state apartments dating from the days of François I, and is expecting him to show some emotion at again being at the scene of his abdication[4] last year, or at least to 'be forced to give a thought to the fragility of human grandeurs,' he's surprised to see nothing of this. In his private apartments Napoleon

'affably pointed out to me their extreme elegance. Then took me into his library, and as he came upstairs again said with a satisfied air: "We'll be well off [*bien*] here."'

'Yes, Sire,' echoes Fleury, already no doubt something of a sycophant. 'One is always well off at home.'

'He smiled, and, I think, was grateful to me for my well-timed flattery.'

In Paris, still seventy kilometres away, 20 March has dawned with drizzling rain. Though François Huë should have left with the crown diamonds and the seven millions in gold at midnight,

'certain stirrings among the troops had been noticed to prevent my departure. So I couldn't leave the Tuileries until 6:00 am. Each of the wagons making up my convoy also carried two disguised and strongly

269

armed gendarmes. Myself I left in a post-chaise with horses from the royal stables, and got to Saint-Denis without too much trouble.'

There he changes over to ordinary post horses, and through 'fine icy showers' makes for Beauvais, the next post-house en route for the Channel ports. While changing horses out at Saint-Denis he must certainly have noticed other 'stirrings'. For it's here Captain Routier and the 300 other *demisoldes* have passed the night noisily in the *estaminets* and bistros:

> 'At dawn some of us were already assembled in the square at the end of the Paris road [writes Routier] ... There we were told the King had abandoned the capital and that he'd passed through Saint-Denis during the night, fleeing from Napoleon's impending arrival and making for Belgium. We all clustered together, consulted together. Finally our long pent up feelings exploded, a shout of *Vive l'Empereur!* bursts from all throats. The white cockade is ripped off and trampled underfoot. Lieutenant-General Maison [military governor of Paris], who's present at this scene, jumps on his horse and flees. We resolve on the spot to go to Paris, and form up in platoons. The colonels command them, the majors, captains etc are rankers. Having got ourselves organised, we leave enthusiastically under the most senior colonel, Simon – former chief engraver to the imperial cabinet – to go and conquer the capital.'

Just about then Lavalette has quit Hortense's attic 'in order to go home to my wife, who wasn't well and whom I hadn't seen for a week.' Like Captain Rieu who, 'having slept the sleep of the just', is 'no little surprised' to find Rilliet gone, he finds Paris

> 'as it were, transformed What a metamorphosis! In the streets no more shouts of *Vive Henri IV* and still fewer of *Vive Louis XVIII*, but wildest, maddest shouts of *Vive l'Empereur!* No more white cockades, every-where tricolour ones, and then the compact crowd on the boulevards waiting for Napoleon and his braves from Elba! In a word: to a royalist population, as if by magic, had succeeded a Bonapartist one.'

The ever-curious Lamothe-Langon – he who'd been so impressed by King Louis' heroic Royal Session – has realised that the next act must be played out at the Tuileries and its great Carrousel Square, scene of so many brilliant parades during the Empire, where now other

> 'onlookers – mainly well-dressed people – the populace and the actors had each assembled at a separate post, as if their seats had been designated for them in advance. The first occupied the upper regions and, in general, had access to the walls, so as to be able to retire if the peace were momentarily disturbed. The populace, *ie* a sizeable gath-ering of petty bourgeois, workers and hangabouts, plus a goodish number of pickpockets, sharpers and loose women, clung to the

courtyard railings and filled the vast extent of the square, came and went, laughing and singing rounds, no sooner started than broken off at sight of the first officer with bulky epaulettes to meet their eyes.'

About 9:00 am the sight of thick black smoke coming from the chimney of the Flore Pavilion causes an alarm. "Fire, fire! The château's on fire!" But it isn't, only the chimney, from a holocaust of Artois' more compromising papers in its fireplace. Some of the National Guards who've taken over the palace appear at the windows and reassure the panicking crowd. An hour later there's another, more serious alarm. A lot of potential rioters from the suburbs break into the square shouting "Down with the priests! Down with the National Guard!"; which picks up its muskets, aims at the railings being shaken by these working class men and women. But instead of firing their muskets, the 'armed property owners' of the National Guard counter their shouts with '*Vive l'Empereur!*'

This does the trick. The new arrivals go back muttering, but peacefully, down the Rue Saint Antoine and the Rue Saint Honoré, without even breaking any window panes.

Going through the streets where 'every bird seemed to the workmen to be an eagle,' Lavalette hears that

'the King and the entire court have left during the night and that the town lacked magistrates and military commanders. Emerging from the Rue d'Artois into the boulevard, I ran into Sébastiani* in a cabriolet.'

Yes, says Sébastiani. The King's gone. Has he any news of the Emperor? No, none.

"What I'd like to do," Lavalette tells him, "is to go and see if there's any news to be had at the Post Office."

Sébastiani invites him into his cabriolet, and together they drive to the Rue du Coq-Héron. Ever since the Revolution, and even more so during the Empire, France has been Europe's most highly centralised country. And to all intents and purposes the Post Office is its nerve centre, over which Lavalette, that 'man of extreme probity', had presided for seven years. It's from here in 'the mail coaches, their horses harnessed up from as early as 6:00 am', at a speed of 'sixty leagues [240 kilometres] every twenty-four hours', news and government orders are carried to all major cities and prefects (except Lyons, which is joined by telegraph). Lavalette will afterwards have every reason to be meticulous about his actions during this memorable day.[5]

Entering 'the audience chamber outside the director-general's office, I saw a young man sitting at a desk, and asked him whether Count Ferrand was still in the building.' Ferrand's as impassioned a royalist as Lavalette is Bonapartist, and, so his predecessor has heard, 'an elderly man, sick, and father of a family. I'd never seen him, but I was astonished at him having so long delayed his departure, and by a generous feeling I wanted to protect his retreat and guarantee his safety. M. Ferrand appeared, but without stopping or listening to me, he opened his office door – I didn't follow him in, I went into another room where I found all the departmental heads, delighted to see me again, and prepared to do anything I asked them. Having taken his papers, M. Ferrand withdrew and left his office to me.'

Torn between a desire to hurry out to Fontainebleau to see his sick wife, Lavalette resolves his dilemma by sending off a courier to Fontainebleau with news of the King's departure and asking for Napoleon's orders. At the same time he asks Sébastiani to go to Dessolles to request a picket of the National Guard 'to protect the Post Office's cash boxes' from any mob. More fatally (in royalist eyes, and many of his former subordinates are royalists) he inhibits the despatch of Louis XVIII's last proclamation forbidding his Parisian supporters to fight. Why hasn't it already been sent off to all the prefects? Can it be Ferrand has wanted to unleash a civil war?[6] Instead Lavalette sends out one of his own to France's postmasters:

The Emperor will be in Paris within two hours, perhaps less. The capital is in the greatest enthusiasm. Everything is calm and whatever anyone can do there will nowhere be any civil war.'

And then goes home: 'I was far from thinking this brief action would be imputed to me as a crime.' He sees his wife for an hour. Then, feeling he must consult Cambacérès, goes to his place, where he finds him grumbling about all the medicines he has to take. 'With his usual sangfroid and gravity' Cambacérès tells him:

"Doubtless you've acted very properly. I see very well that disorders can happen in Paris. But for my part I'd certainly not utter a word, nor make a gesture, that might make the Emperor suspect me of anticipating his decisions. I haven't forgotten the reprimands he gave me when he'd come back from Russia."[7]

Going back to the Post Office, Lavalette is amazed to hear Ferrand still hasn't left. Is even asking him to issue him and his wife with a safe-conduct. Whatever for? Surely his own signature is perfectly valid? 'But Ferrand was sure I was part of a vast conspiracy and wanted a piece of paper with my signature on it, above all to protect him in the streets of Paris.' Ferrand's wife too begs for one. Which Lavalette provides.[8]

But if the populace and the military are all aglow, in the highest administrative circles the temperature is hardly even tepid. Nor is Lavalette Cambacérès' only visitor this morning. Two others are Savary, Duke of Rovigo, Fouché's successor as Police Minister; and Mathieu Molé,[9] that sensitive and delicate, not to say hypochondriacal, student of human nature.

At Cambacérès' place the ex-Grand Judge is told that Savary, too, has been there already, but that the former Archchancellor is giving no one any directives. Obviously Cambacérès has no illusions, wants no part of this new "adventure. Only to end my days in repose". They, the former ministers, can form a temporary government if they like, "but a grand dignitary like me has no part to play." Follows a scene worthy of Molìere:

Molé: "Oh but, Your Highness, I don't regard myself as a minister of the Emperor unless he chooses to reappoint me. And that's why I've come to consult you. I feel old and worn out before my time. Please, Monseigneur, help me to get him to agree to me retiring."

Cambacérès, complaining he too is burnt out: "My dear fellow, I'm upset [*faché*] to see you having such sentiments. From the moment when you became a minister of the Empire you must have realised you'd burnt your boats. You can't think of retiring."

Molé: "Monseigneur, I've made up my mind. I've no ambitions. My health is destroyed. Please, support my plan. You'll never do me a greater service."

Cambacérès promises to give Napoleon a faithful account of their conversation, 'but if he asks my opinion I'll tell him he should keep you on.'

Only Hortense and Lavalette, it seems, even if they realise what perils it's going to unleash on France internationally, are overjoyed at the Emperor's return:

'About lunch time M. Devaux came and told me everything tended to show that the Emperor would be in Paris today. He brought a letter from Fouché, asking me to send it on to the Emperor at once. It was important, he said, that it should be in his hands before he made his entrance. I think it contained a warning about disguised royalists who were after his life.'[10]

It's the news he's been waiting for. During the morning 'several couriers' have passed through Essonnes, shouting out that they've been sent by Lavalette. But now it's 11:00 am and none have arrived at Fontainebleau. But now, at midday,

'the news of the King's departure was brought to him simultaneously by a courier from M. de Lavalette, by a letter from [the actress] Mme. Hamelin, and from M. de Ségur*.

Once again Marchand is sent on ahead:

'He summoned me at once. "You're to go on ahead," he said, "and prepare everything." "It's to Essonnes, I suppose, Your Majesty is ordering me?" "No, to Paris. The King and the princes have fled. This evening I'll be at the Tuileries."'

Moments later Ali sees some infantry 'very tired though they were, joyfully put their packs on their backs again. It would be the last day's march they'd have to make'.

He assumes, wrongly, that they're Grenadiers and Chasseurs of the Guard. Actually Marchand has just heard Napoleon give orders that 'the Elba battalion should have a day's rest'; which means that grognards from Elba, marched from their position in the rear to Montereau, where it's to embark for Paris, won't share the Emperor's triumphal entry into the capital. One can imagine Cambronne's mortification.

'When all was ready the Emperor got into his carriage together with the Grand Marshal. Ever since Grenoble it had been post-horses that had been doing this service, and so they still did. Part of the cavalry that he'd reviewed in the forenoon served as escort. The whole army either preceded or followed the Emperor's cortège,'

which, Ali sees, 'goes at a walk or a slow trot, so that everyone was able to keep up. The escorting cavalry rode in single files along the sides of the road.' Between Fontainebleau and Essonnes Marchand's carriage is brought to a halt; and looking out of the window he sees why. Napoleon is reviewing yet another regiment. 'The Emperor asked what carriage this was. When he knew it was mine he ordered me to go on.'

Saint-Chamans has been up since long before daybreak, when he'd heard his officers passing on a rumour of the Bourbons' flight, and that 'the whole Paris garrison' is coming out to Fontainebleau. 'No human force,' he agrees with one of them, 'can hold up the Emperor.' At the Corbeil bridge most of his chasseurs are drunk

'either on regulation issue brandy or on what the citizens who'd come out from Paris or Fontainebleau were making them drink as they told them about the flight of the King and his family. Shouts, if only isolated ones, of *Vive l'Empereur!* were already being heard. By order of their commanders a large part of the royal army we'd met yesterday, like the troops that had left Paris with us, had passed over, arms and baggage, to the side of the disembarked "comrade".'

Now Sébastiani 'and the Paris general staff' come up to his fellow colonel Talhouët and tell him that 'HM Louis XVIII had left Paris and HM the Emperor Napoleon had been proclaimed.' Drawing his regiment up in line, Talhouët calls its officers – Henckens among them – to the front, and says

'distinctly, so that the whole regiment can hear him: "*Messieurs*, a new order of things has been established. I must hand in my resignation because of my poor health. I enjoin you to take your place in the column which is rejoining the Emperor, who has been proclaimed, and always maintain the honour of the unit." He embraced several officers. I too had that honour. And he left for Paris. We had no time for deliberations. The Emperor, in a post-chaise, was at our heels and didn't even ask us whether we were again willing to follow him. He asked after the regiment's number, and we became once more the 6th Chasseurs. He ordered us to move toward the northern frontier and invited the officers to the Tuileries tomorrow 21 March at 10:00 am.'

Realising during the night that the royal cause is lost if the regiments go over to Napoleon, Macdonald has issued a general order to concentrate at Saint-Germain (*sic*, actually Saint-Denis), and left, hoping against hope he'll find his headquarters staff assembled there. The general order reaches Saint-Chamans, who tells his officers his instructions are to march them to Saint-Germain. Will they obey?

'At that moment several officers behind me waved their sabres in the air and shouted *Vive l'Empereur!* And immediately the whole regiment responded with the same shout and with almost insane enthusiasm. Many shouted "To Fontainebleau! To Fontainebleau!" The shout became general.'

Saint-Chamans, disgusted at such insubordination, tries to leave; but some of his officers surround him and say they won't let him. He also sees Colonel Montesqiou-Fezensac* abandoned by his 2nd Line, and sees one of its lieutenants tear off his epaulette and fling it in his men's faces. Caught between his instinct to quit such mutinous troops and Berry's inexplicable order not to, Saint-Chamans wonders whether

'behind his orders there might not be perhaps some secret scheme the prince hadn't thought it advisable to acquaint me with, and to whose success it might be useful if royalist officers remained with their regiments'.

Anyway, he decides to stay with his men, at least for the moment. Only one of his captains leaves. They embrace. And telling him he'll be joining him tomorrow, Saint-Chamans orders "To horse! Mount! March!" Further on down the road, at about an hour's march from Fontainebleau, they meet up with the 4th Chasseurs, who say they're 'falling back according to orders upon Paris.' Some of Saint-Chamans' Bonapartist officers offer to turn them back. 'I positively forbade it. Hoping to keep the 4th Chasseurs loyal to the King,' he orders them to tell their colleagues in the other regiment they're 'making a reconnaissance against the Emperor's troops'. The 4th Chasseurs' colonel, riding along at his side, twits him with looking so depressed. But too many eyewitnesses are present for an exchange of confidences.

Altogether Saint-Chamans is in a very sticky position. For who knows how it'll all turn out? His own loyalty is unimpeachable. But the circumstances can impeach it on the basis of his actions, as having 'debauched the troops to take them to Napoleon'.

Dawn still hasn't broken when out of the darkness one of the Colbert* brothers appears, together with Colonel Jacquinot of the 1st Lancers. Neither, it seems, have heard the King has fled. General Colbert, all sympathy for his colleague's plight, keeps exclaiming: "And this is how they compromise decent fellows!" As a last expedient, hoping to avoid meeting Napoleon, "who couldn't be far off", Saint-Chamans orders his regiment to bear off to the right toward a village, ostensibly to water its horses. And 'worn out and needing a bite to eat' goes

> 'alone into a little inn in a village on the high road whose name I don't know. There I found some troopers belonging to the Emperor's advance guard (some of the 4th Hussars, 6th Lancers and 13th Dragoons). A quarter of an hour ago we'd met a detachment of cavalry from the same army [*sic*], who'd handed our men packets of Napoleon's proclamations and decrees as they'd passed.'

After a few minutes a courier arrives at the inn from Fontainebleau, announcing that Napoleon is close at his heels:

> 'I at once remounted my horse and went back along the Paris road, intending to join my regiment in the village I'd sent it to. But before I could reach the road that turned off toward it I was overtaken by a rather wretched-looking post coach, escorted by some cavalry. I suspected it might be Napoleon; and standing aside looked into the coach, where in fact I recognised the ex-Emperor and Bertrand, seated in its depths beside him. To me the Emperor seemed to have grown fat and looked very brown in the face. He was completely bronzed.'

The coach quickly disappears down the road. And Saint-Chamans slowly goes on his way, burdened with his thoughts,

> 'never doubting but that I'd soon be rejoining him. But at a sharp bend in the road a little more than a mile further on I found Napoleon on foot, reviewing two infantry regiments that had come out that far to meet him. As I got there they were just ending their march-past. I found myself rather close to the Emperor and Bertrand. Bertrand, whom I knew well ever since the Bologne camp [in 1803], saluted me, and coming up to me asked me where my regiment was. I waved my hand in the direction of the village I'd sent it to and which could be seen from where we were. He asked me if it was well mounted, and to my saying it was: "So much the better, today they'll escort us to Paris." At that moment the Emperor, having finished his review, got back into his carriage, Bertrand after him.'[11]

Though nominally making for Melun, few if any of the regiments seem to have got further than Essonnes.

The rumour that the Emperor has already gone by spreads swiftly, and soon the 1st Chasseurs come cantering up, 'hoping to see him. But it was too late.' Though their colonel wants them to spend the night on the Essonnes road, one of Napoleon's orderlies gallops up and hands Saint-Chamans Bertrand's formal order to catch up with him at the trot. 'He was waiting for us'. That the regiment's horses are winded is no excuse:

'Hoping the Emperor, who by nature was always in a hurry, would weary of waiting for us, I continued at a walk. But soon I saw a superior officer arrive, who took command of my regiment, made it double its pace, and very soon we reached Villejuif, where the Emperor, his carriage surrounded by some hussars and lancers, was in fact waiting for us.'

Two of Saint-Chamans' squadrons are ordered to precede Napoleon's carriage and two to follow it.[12] A dispute breaks out among his officers as to who should command the regiment: 'One of them claimed he had the Emperor's order to, another that he'd been given the same order by Bertrand. A third said he'd been sent by Exelmans.'

Nothing Ali, on the box of his post-chaise, has seen so far can be compared with

'the spectacle that met our eyes at Essonnes. Here was nothing but coaches, saddle-horses, officers of every rank, every age, peasants, bourgeois, women, children, soldiers from every unit, all arms. In a word, it was an immense rendezvous where everything was pell-mell. Never had such great variety been seen, and all this multitude, beaming with joy, happiness and enthusiasm was making the air resound with shouts of *Vive l'Empereur! Vive Napoléon!*'

As for the

'several carriages drawn by six or eight horses from Louis XVIII's stables, driven by coachmen, postilions, stud-grooms wearing civvies, all of whom had belonged to the Emperor's household',

Napoleon has no use for them. Asked whether he doesn't prefer to get into one of the gilded state coaches he says he's quite content with the post coach:

'Ever since Grenoble the wretched post coach had been drawn by post-horses, and these went on doing so to Paris. All the grand personages, both civil and military, had come out to salute the Emperor, who welcomed them in the most moving manner. Part of the cavalry reviewed in the morning hours was serving as escort. The entire army was preceding or following the Emperor's cortège. We proceeded at a walking pace or a little trot, so that everyone could keep up. The cavalry of the escort was riding along each side of the road in single file. A multitude of the inhabitants of the villages were accompanying the Emperor, either inside or outside the hedge of troopers. At each instant high-ranking officers and many other personages were turning up who'd come to greet the Emperor and swell his staff, which was already extremely sizeable.'

'General Montholon,[13] one of the most obstinate,' Saint-Chamans sees, is 'extremely over-excited. He was riding a white horse.'

Meanwhile, finding that only Hulot, his chief-of-staff, has turned up at Saint-Germain in response to his general order, Macdonald too has departed for Beauvais.

In the centre of the city a schoolmaster's having a hard time of it to hold his pupils' attention. From their classroom window at the Collège Henri IV Carnot junior and his schoolmates can see at a distance

'the tip of the Vendôme column.[14] We were at our work. But my eyes were more often raised to the window than bent over my books. Suddenly a shout arises from every mouth and spreads through the whole class. The white flag had just fallen. The tricolour waved in its place. We jump over our benches, we upset the tables, the doors are opened, we acclaim, we kiss, we embrace each other. It's delirium.'

What time does this happen? And can the march of the 300 *demisoldes* have something to do with it? Meeting some vehicles outside Saint-Denis being driven by men in royal livery, the *demisoldes* had been

'told they belong to the Duke of Berry. Our superiors halt them and make them turn round and go back, escorted by ourselves. Half a league further on we come across a regiment drawn up in battle order by the roadside. The situation gets tricky. We don't know what this force's attitude is or what it's doing here. However, we halt in front of it, and all draw our swords, forming up in line of battle by the left.'

The superior officers harangue it and say Napoleon will any moment be arriving in Paris:

'Its colonel tried in vain to resist a defection that seemed to him inevitable. A unanimous shout of *Vive l'Empereur!* goes up from our ranks, the men respond to it, tear off their white cockades, put their shakos on the tips of their bayonets. The whole regiment is for us, and its colonel quits it at top speed.'

But the 300 aren't content to share with it the honours of capturing Paris. 'Leaving the converted regiment to sort itself out as best it could, we resumed our march.' Further on their way they meet with a largish artillery park, making for Saint-Denis:

'Still more men to rally to the imperial eagle and a resource we carried off to keep for the Emperor. All the gunners joined us, instantly turning their guns and caissons round, and gaily followed us, repeating our favourite refrain. From this moment our march began to be impressive. Our officer numbers were growing, everything was going well . . . when we found the barrier was closed and were embarrassed by a refusal to open up.'

What to do? 'Open ourselves a passage by gunfire?' They decide against 'such evil means'. At this tense moment, while they're still parleying with the town guards, Exelmans appears, puts himself at their head, has the barrier opened,

> 'and in we went. So there you are! Paris captured by 300 officers dragging with them an artillery park and the carriages of a royal highness who'd taken to his heels!'

Swords drawn, they march by sections down the Boulevard Saint-Denis, turn right, and followed by an 'astounded crowd, peering to see whether Napoleon wasn't in our midst' – actually they haven't a clue to his whereabouts – they go down the Rue Richelieu and debouch onto the Place du Carrousel. Here, at last, they run into resistance:

> 'Two battalions of the Paris National Guard were lined up in the Tuileries courtyard. The grilles between it and the Carrousel were shut. The white flag was still flying on the [central] Clock Pavilion and everything told us there was no intention of letting us take possession of the château.'

But that's not how the 300 see the matter:

> 'We were on the point of delivering battle. We were counting on seizing it, first as a place of safety for ourselves, then as the Emperor's dwelling. He might arrive from one moment to the next and we wanted to prepare his lodgings – singular quartermasters that we were! But the circumstances which had improvised us were also unique in history.'

The National Guard is commanded by a general named Lecapitaine,

> 'a brave senior military man I'd known as a captain in the 102nd. Exelmans asked him to withdraw his men and open the grille. He said he wouldn't. By this time it was midday. We were surrounded by an immense crowd, which was observing us with curiosity. Time was getting on, we couldn't remain in our equivocal position after acting as we had during the forenoon.'

So they draw up all their cannon. And this does the trick:

> 'In order to avoid a fearful collision in such a place and for a lost cause, he [Lecapitaine], who also cherished the Emperor, prudently decided to yield his ground. And we were far from wishing to shed a drop of French blood. The two Parisian battalions withdrew via the gardens.

When they'd gone, all the grilles were opened and we entered the interior to a thousand shouts of *Vive l'Empereur!* So there we were, masters of the château by right of conquest.'[15]

It's agreed, however, that for every sentry posted by them, another would be provided by the National Guard. Meanwhile, still commanded by Exelmans, they take

'all needful precautions for our security, which might be compromised from one moment to the next by events impossible to foresee. Taking the artillery and Berry's carriages into the interior courtyard, we closed all the grilles around us, planted posts of gunners at their gates, in the [artillery] park and around Berry's vehicles, perfectly intact, and which we'd next day restore to the competent authority.'[16]

Officers have been 'posted everywhere within the Tuileries. Then the white flag that was still flying on the Clock Pavilion was removed and replaced by a hastily fabricated tricolour. It was the first of the day to be flown in Paris.'

'Our affair was being bruited abroad all over Paris. Best of all for ourselves, it was bringing to the Tuileries a large number of officers of all ranks who'd until now stayed at home. We took possession of the building on the square outside, facing the grilles, occupied until that morning by Louis XVIII's company of Swiss Guards. There a kind of staff was set up. We still didn't know the Emperor's whereabouts. Everything round us was calm.'

A proper list of all present at that moment is drawn up, both those from Saint-Denis and those who'd joined en route.[17] Whereupon Routier suddenly realises he still hasn't even had breakfast. Rushes off home to his father. Snatches a quick meal.

Villejuif lies more or less half-way between Essonnes and Paris. Here Henckens sees 'shopkeepers selling tricolour cockades at two *sous* apiece, saying as they thrust them under our noses 'surely this is worth two *sous?*' Still more troops and officers have come out to welcome the Emperor. In the morning Planat, Résigny and Briqueville, having bought themselves horses and reassumed their imperial uniforms, had gone to see Gaspard Gourgaud, 'never doubting but that he was ready to join us'. True, their feelings for this highly emotional officer have cooled since his

'conduct, first at Fontainebleau, then in Paris. He was to have left for Elba with the Emperor and had protested his devotion to him in the warmest terms. But on the eve of his departure he'd asked permission to go and embrace his mother and say good-bye to her. He'd gone, but hadn't come back.'

The visit to Gourgaud had turned out to be even more upsetting than the one to Flahaut:

'We found him in bed, saying he was very ill, and with a big bottle of medicine on his bedside table. In a feeble [*languissante*] voice he told us that he "had an inflammation in his intestines, that he envied us our luck and was dreadfully unhappy to be in no condition to show his devotion to the Emperor."'

All of which may be true. Gourgaud's disposition is no little hysterical.[18]

'At which we left him and made for the Fontainebleau road. As soon as we were outside the barrier each of us donned his tricolour cockade, and when we got to the high ground at Villejuif we came upon an infantry regiment drawn up in line. The colonel came towards us and asked us where we were going. In a loud voice Briqueville replied: "We're going to join the Emperor. Here are *messieurs* Planat and Résigny, officers on his staff, and I, I'm Colonel Briqueville." Before he'd finished, the entire regiment had disbanded and surrounded us with shouts of *Vive l'Empereur!*

They tell them to obey their officers until he gets here: 'The men fell in again and we went on our way without the colonel doing anything to prevent us.'

A message from Napoleon has reached Caulaincourt to come and meet him. And Flahaut, after deciding there's not going to be any 'civil discord', has come with him. It's between Villejuif and Courneuve that Planat and his two friends 'meet the Emperor's carriages preceded by a picket of lancers.' When Drouot leans out of the window of his carriage – presumably, as hitherto, preceding Napoleon's – and holds out his hand to him, Planat feels 'stifled with joy, almost ready to faint'. At the same time he's most surprised to see

'General Flahaut on horseback beside the Emperor's carriage. Since our interview he'd received messages from Fontainebleau and [Planat observes scathingly] had become sure there'd be no obstacle to the Emperor entering Paris.'

Obviously, despite the drizzly weather, the hood's been let down, because Ali, on the box of the post-chaise – he doesn't say whether it's Noverraz or one of the Archambault brothers who's holding the whip – can hear

'despite the uproar all round me the Emperor praising me to the Master of the Horse, and for quite a while I was even the object of their conversation. In this circumstance my petty vanity felt the keenest satisfaction, and a few glances from the Duke, which I snapped up as I looked behind me from time to time, let me know how pleased he himself was about it.'

But Napoleon is certainly less pleased when Caulaincourt refuses to resume his post as Foreign Minister. Does Napoleon sense, from what he's telling him, how little enthusiasm there is among his former ministers? Or is Caulaincourt, certainly not in an unfriendly way, telling him about Hortense's unsuccessful lawsuit? High-level matters if so, to which Ali of course turns a deaf ear.

By now it's late afternoon. 'At last we reached the Villejuif barrier' where 'five or six hundred people, all from the mob' have gathered and are waiting to acclaim their hero. The shouting, the yells, the hubbub are extreme: '*Vive l'Empereur!* Down with the nobles! Down with the priests!' is what Ali keeps hearing. Of a regular state entry there is no question, if only because there's no time for one. Is it because Fouché's warning of royalist ambushes and assassins that Napoleon, though 'always in a hurry', 'prefers not to take the shortest route' to the Tuileries? Or because he wants the procession to pass by the Gros Caillou district, with its military population? Anyway the cortège goes along 'the outer boulevards and enters Paris by the Montparnasse barrier', Planat and his two friends are struck by this odd way of entering the city, which they'd been assuming would be
> 'via the Austerlitz Bridge and the boulevards, where an immense crowd was impatiently waiting for him. We followed the boulevard that leads to the Invalides.'[19]

On the box of Napoleon's carriage Ali, too, is struck by this odd way of entering the city. 'All this was taking a long time.'

Lieutenant-General Paul Thiébault had been ordered out to Charenton by Macdonald to command all the troops there, defend the bridge, and, if necessary, blow it up. Though 'certainly no partisan of the Bourbons, but without enough confidence in the Emperor to rejoice in his return', Thiébault, to whom 'everything that has so much as a semblance of a duty has always been sacred' and 'the departure of a sovereign being only the disappearance of a man, not of the authority he represents' had obeyed. And until 6:00 pm he has stayed at his post. But then a 'superior staff officer with the tricolour in his hat' comes and tells him to go home. Which he does.

But it's more than he can do to stay there. 'So electric is the power of popular exaltations, I'd hardly left my place than felt swept up by the current'. After briefly looking in at Macdonald's town house and finding him gone, and no matter how much he prides himself on his 'prudence, reflection and reserve', he can't help being 'drawn to the Tuileries by an irresistible force.'

To Saint-Chamans, still riding despondently on at the head of his enthusiastic but by now hungry and thirsty chasseurs, it seems there's 'hardly anyone in the streets, at least not in those we were riding along.'

Now it's getting on for 9:00 pm. Saint-Chamans, reaching the misty riverside, crosses 'the Louis XVI Bridge [Pont de la Concorde]'; signals a right turn; and rides on down the quay beneath the Tuileries gardens' balustrade toward the palace where Captain Routier, after his breakfast-lunch-cum-dinner, is strolling to and fro with his comrades 'along the length of the building. The clock on the Clock Pavilion had just struck nine' when Saint-Chamans' 500 chasseurs enter the Tuileries courtyard by the Pont Royal gate. Oddly enough Routier doesn't even see them, or anyway won't afterwards remember it:[20]

'Suddenly some very simple carriages without any escort present themselves at the waterside gate and announce the Emperor.[21] It's beyond me to describe that moment. The grille opens, the carriages enter. We all rush to surround them...'

Reaching the Flore Pavilion, Ali sees it's impossible

'even to move the carriage on as far as to the pavement. The Emperor, seeing he could get no further, got out in the midst of the immense crowd pressing around him.'

Routier:

'Oh! Then all heads are delirious. We throw ourselves at him, no order, we press on him, we almost stifle him.'

Thiébault is in the crowd:

'Suddenly Napoleon reappeared. The explosion was sudden, irresistible. I thought myself present at the Resurrection of Christ. The miracle of his return put the last touch to making this man into a being more than human. The transport of joy at seeing him was like a clap of thunder, one would have thought the ceilings would have collapsed.'

Routier:

'In the end, despite anything the generals accompanying him can say or do, we carry him up to his apartments.'

Ali:

'No sooner had he set foot on the ground than he was carried, so to speak, up to his apartments without his feet touching the steps of the staircase.'

Thiébault:

'Prey to the most delirious of exaltations, 20,000 people, at least,[22] were crowding round the approaches to the Flore Pavilion, on the staircase inside and in the apartments, which I thought I'd never reach. As he'd got out of his carriage the Emperor had been surrounded, grasped, lifted up and borne aloft as far as the salons. Those who'd carried him seemed to have gone mad. A thousand others were boasting of having kissed his clothes or merely touched them, and their exclamations were lost in the incredible hullabaloo of shouting and vivats echoing in the courtyard and garden.'

Routier:

'The memory of that moment, unique in world history, still makes my heart beat with joy.'

Spotting Thiébault in the crush, Napoleon, 'reading my emotion in my face', utters his name,

'nods and smiles graciously. Yet only three hours ago I, a soldier of the Bourbons, had been training my guns on him! But now I seemed to have become French again, and nothing equalled the transports and shouts with which I tried to show him my participation in the homage being paid to him. One moment and one man had sufficed to give France back to the French, the French to France.'

But even Thiébault's enthusiasm can't match Lavalette's:

'Crammed together, stifling each other, *demisoldes* were packed together in the vestibule and filling the staircase. The Emperor was wearing his famous grey overcoat. I moved toward him, and Caulaincourt shouted: "In God's name! Get in front of him so he can get on." He starts mounting the stairs. I'm going first, moving up backwards, one step ahead of him, contemplating him with deep emotion, my eyes bathed in tears and in my delirium saying over and over: "What! It's you! It's you! At last, it's you!" For his part he was coming up slowly, his eyes closed, holding out his hands in front of him like a blind man, and only expressing his happiness by his smile.'

Waiting for him on the first landing is Hortense, in black, in mourning for Josephine. With her are Joseph's wife Julie and her sister Désirée. She notes that his entourage 'only consists of two of his former adjutants', meaning presumably Bertrand and Drouot. 'The ladies,' Lavalette goes on,

'tried to come forward to him, but a wave of officers from the upper storey rushed forward, got in their way, and would have crushed them if they hadn't been so nimble. Finally the Emperor was able to get inside [*chez lui*]. The doors, with difficulty, were shut, and the crowd dispersed, happy to have had a glimpse of him.'

Thiébault, having managed to force his way through the scrum and up the staircase, penetrates into the great halls, where there's

'no more shouting, but everyone was talking at once. It was impossible to understand anything. For several hours only the populace [*sic*] formed the court of the man France was putting back on the throne. All their souls seemed to overflow with joy. Any of the officers who'd come back from Elba only had to appear for them to throw themselves on him as if he were a precious relic they were trying to share out. Even the valets were being touched and fêted',

Ali no doubt among them. After handing over the dusty post coach to Noverraz or Archambault, he too has tried in vain to get up the main staircase. 'But it was impossible. I had to give up. Without losing time I went up the one in the Flore Pavilion, whence it was easier to reach the hall of the junior officers.' Pushing his way through into the next one, reserved for senior officers, he sees

'the Emperor at table with several people, one of them being the Grand Marshal, the Duke of Vicenza, and perhaps General Drouot. Around him were standing chamberlains, grooms, generals, colonels and many other people, both civilian and military. Dinner was being served as if the Emperor had never left the Tuileries. Not one of the servants was missing. The superintendent M. Colin, the major-domo Dunant, the carver, the head of the office, the ushers, the apartment valets, the footmen, all were at their posts. The only difference was that most were in ordinary clothes. During the meal the Emperor conversed with those around him, often speaking to them all and recounting what had happened during his journey from Elba etc. Dinner over, he got up from table, saluted everyone present, and went into the drawing room, accompanied by the Grand Marshal, the Grand Equerry and a few other intimates. Shortly thereafter the crowd that had been encumbering the halls and staircase scattered. Calm reigned in the interior of the Palace, as it had in the past.'

Marchand, who's been here since 6:00 pm, sees

'no sign of any other sovereign having inhabited this palace. The services of honour and of the household were at their posts. It seemed His Majesty had just come back from a journey.'

'Thus ended' writes Peyrusse,

'an enterprise that, without running into any obstacle, without burning a cartridge or shedding blood, instead of being judged as an imprudent piece of audacity, should count among the most sublime calculations of the Emperor's life. The march from Cannes to Paris is without example in the history of nations.'

To have done it in a mere twenty days is one thing. To form a government, quite another. And much more problematic.

NOTES

NOTES

Preface

1. Concerning my at times somewhat unorthodox translation method, the reader is referred to the preface of *1812: The March on Moscow*.

2. Just as I was completing this book, Jean Tulard's *Les Vingt Jours: Louis XVIII ou Napoléon?* appeared. I was glad to see that great authority, who penetrates the background of these events' more than I have done, sees them in exactly the same light.

Chapter 1: 'A Crazy Enterprise'

1. There have been various estimates of the number of half-pay officers during the First Restoration. Henri Houssaye's figure of 12,000, in his deeply researched *1815*, is probably the best.

2. See the index to my *1812: Napoleon in Moscow* (hereafter cited as *Moscow*). As in my 1812 trilogy, all persons whose names are italicised at their first appearance will be found in the bibliography. An asterisk indicates that they also appear in the Russian trilogy.

3. During the Empire the profits from the mines had gone to finance the Legion of Honour's school for its many orphans. Pons had provided healthy dwellings for the miners, shared their food, taken an interest in their families and in general cared so paternally for their welfare that they'd called him *il nostro babbo* – 'our Daddy'. On one occasion when Napoleon had ordered him to appropriate to his Elban budget that part of the income from the iron mine that had been allotted to the Legion of Honour to support schools for its legionaries' orphans, l'Hérault had refused. And when Napoleon had tried to come the heavy over him, declaring 'I'm your Emperor!', had stood up to him, replying 'And I'm a Frenchman!' During the First Restoration the Legion's schools

had also been under attack, so Macdonald relates, from Abbé Pradt*, and the property of at least one had been restored to the senile Duke of Condé.

4. For his former subordinate Major *Pion des Loches*'* angry dismissal of Drouot as 'a military Tartuffe', and the Guard Artillery commander Sorbet's scorn for him, see my *1812: The Great Retreat* (hereafter cited as *The Retreat*), p.211. But most of our other memoirists seem to have admired him.

5. Various figures would be given at the time for the exact number of soldiers Napoleon brought back with him from Elba. The consensus seems to have been about 800. For their composition see below.

6. Or so at least he'll claim at his trial. But Napoleon himself, who 'seemed a little angry', would tell Gourgaud on St Helena: 'It was Drouot himself who'd drawn up the proclamation. It's false that he wanted to divert me from the project. Everyone knows I don't let myself be led by his advice' – and this is confirmed, as we see, by Marchand. Unfortunately on the morning of the fatal 18 June he would take Drouot's advice, as an experienced gunner, when he advised him to 'wait until the ground had dried out after the rain for the guns to manoeuvre,' so that Drouot would ever afterwards reproach himself for having lost Waterloo by allowing the Prussians time to come up.

7. See note 3 above.

8. Captain *Jean-Roche Coignet**, who hadn't been allowed to go to Elba because he didn't actually belong to the Guard (Napoleon, he claims, would gladly have promoted him a major in it, but had pointed out that his signature was no longer valid) describes the famous scene: 'He was allowed 600 men for his guard. He made them stand to arms and called for

men of good will. All stepped forward and he had to make them go back into the ranks. "I'm going to choose them. Let no one stir." And passing along the rank he pointed them out himself: "You, come out!" and so on. It took a long time. Then he said: "See if I've got my total." "You need 20 more," said General Drouot. "I'll bring them out." His contingent finished, he chose the NCOs and officers, and went back into his palace, telling Drouot: "After I've gone you're to take my Guard to Louis XVIII in Paris." When all his preparations were done and his carriages ready, he, for the last time, gave the order to stand to arms. All those old warriors having come into that great courtyard, once so brilliant, he came down the flight of steps, accompanied by his whole staff and stood in front of his 'grumblers'. "Bring me my eagle!" And taking it in his arms, he gave it the farewell kiss. How moving it was! All one heard was a groan through all the ranks. I can say I shed tears to see my dear Emperor leave for the Island of Elba. There was only one shout: "So here we're being left to the discretion of a new government." Lieutenant Chevalier and his fellow-troopers of the Chasseurs-à-Cheval had wept as their gaze had followed Napoleon's departing carriage: 'He's done for, this idol of France's glory, this demigod of battles, the first captain in the world... Adieu, immortal Napoleon!'

9. The Polish lancers had first been sent to Marie-Louise at Lucca, but, not wanted there, had subsequently joined the others at Porto Ferrajo, and their horses put out to graze on a nearby islet.

10. Marchand says the 'whole Guard', 600 men, were distributed between the brig, the *Étoile*, the *Caroline* and the four [*sic*] transports. Afterwards the total number of actual troops would repeatedly be said to have been 800 or 900. Marchand's and Peyrusse's accounts don't quite agree on all points. Marchand wrote his fascinating and wholly convincing memoirs many years afterwards for his daughter; Peyrusse, who gives the impression of having based his on a diary, is perhaps more accurate.

Where they agree, I've sometimes fused their narratives.

11. Possibly as a result of a misunderstanding, at least so Constant would claim.

12. Ali's *Souvenirs sur Napoléon,* first published in 1926 and republished in shortened form in February 2000, are in some ways even more impressive than Marchand's. He'd been Caulaincourt's* valet before being recommended by him to Napoleon. Like Marchand, he'd been promoted after Roustan had quit. His memoirs seem the more obviously reliable because as soon as he fears his memory fails him he always says so. He gives, for instance, details from Russia which I wish I'd been aware of when composing my *1812* trilogy.

13. When Marchand had served coffee out of a wrong cup at Porto-Ferrajo, Napoleon had flung it at the wall – but a moment afterwards had forgiven the error, explaining to the terrified Marchand that his absolute demand on everyone around him was that they should *plier* (obey him absolutely).

14. A beauty the sharply observant Ali had nevertheless found a trifle faded: 'She could perhaps have been between 30 and 35. From what could be seen of it her person had all the lovely proportions of the Venus di Medici. All she lacked by then was a little youth, for the skin of her face was beginning to be wrinkled. But the few shortcomings due to age disappeared under a light makeup that lent her pretty features greater animation.' *Souvenirs* (2000 edition), p.72.

15. Normally he restricted himself to five uniform coats (each costing 350 francs), forty-five flannel waistcoats, two hunting coats and a single civilian overcoat worth 200 francs, each of which had to last for three years. For his complete and meticulously regulated wardrobe, see Arthur Halévy's hagiographic but very detailed and still very readable *Napoléon Intime* (Nelson edition, n.d.), p.41. If Napoleon

wasn't wearing his usual green uniform jacket but rather the blue (grenadier) one he habitually wore on Sundays – a point the re-enaction authorities at Antibes should perhaps note for authenticity's sake – it was doubtless because it had been on a Sunday that he'd left Porto-Ferrajo; and since then he'd had other things to think about. Anyway, it doesn't seem to have been his uniform that impressed his contemporaries, but his plain grey overcoat and 'little' hat – little, that is, compared with his generals' gilded and plumed ones.

16. During the Hundred Days the Duke of Berry would hear from a British officer in Belgium that in the weeks before the landing the local authorities had, to his knowledge, detected spies from Elba. It seems only too probable. Napoleon must also have known that the Gabelle Fort (*Le Fort Carré*) had been dismantled, otherwise he'd never have dared land his men on the half-gravel, half-rocky shore beneath it.

17. Today in the Cannes Yacht Club enclosure.

18. So a journalist called *Fabry*, following up these events to provide a sequel to his previous year's best-seller about Bonaparte's exile to Elba, calls him; and gives these details.

19. This may not be quite accurate. As far as we know all of Lamourette's party made for Antibes.

20. In 1816 Fabry would issue a sequel to his *Itinerary of Bonaparte*, about his return. According to him almost every lady along the route would faint on hearing he was back – news that seems to have knocked them over like ninepins. But of course it was *le bon ton* in those days for a well-brought up woman to faint at the least hint of an emotion. Neither Fabry's sympathies and/or interests, nor his interviewees' haste to share them, detract from his crcumstantiality, which often agrees and sometimes contrasts with that of Marchand, Peyrusse, Pons, Laborde etc.

21. When Napoleon had told him they

were going back to France and asked what he thought of the scheme, Cambronne had replied that it wasn't his business to have reflections on his Emperor's plans.

22. During the Hundred Days the exact spot, which lies in the present-day yacht harbour, would be marked with a stone by the men of the 87th Line.

23. Actually five feet two inches four *lignes* in old French feet and inches, equivalent to 1.687 m – *ie* above modern French average.

24. Captain Maitland's portrait on board HMS *Bellepheron*, four months later.

25. In 1815 many observers would be struck by his peculiar bronzed complexion. This being a notable symptom of chronic arsenic poisoning, the Swedish researcher Sten Forshuvud adduces it, together with all the weight he'd put on, as further evidence of his being either a secret arsenophage (arsenic taken in small doses being regarded in those days, and even into the twentieth century, as an infallible specific against poisoners) or already being poisoned – which seems less likely. A psychoanalyst would suspect the rigidity of Napoleon's refusal to take medicine as symptomatic of a *fear* of poison, in his case a very natural one; or perhaps just a soldier's typical scorn for medics?

26. Molé's pen-portrait of him in 1813.

27. The ancient Greeks had a word *prosopopoeia*, by which they meant a middle-aged proneness to re-enact the heady events of one's youth. We shall see many instances of it during the Hundred Days, and by no means only in Napoleon.

28. He habitually said *enfanterie* (which, if it means anything, means 'childishness') for *infanterie, colidor* for *corridor*, etc.

29. See 1812 trilogy indexes.

30. On the other hand one can't help wondering why, with the flotilla sailing back and forth along the coast all morning,

sporting its tricolours, the alarm hadn't been given earlier? Were there no lookouts on Antibes' twin church towers? No telescopes on the lookout for the Algerian pirates who were again beginning to plague the South French coast? Was everyone in Antibes asleep all morning? Nor does the landing seem to have been as efficiently executed as it could have been – why the trip to Saint Marguerite, which surely must have given the alarm all along the coast? Why hadn't the flotilla simply entered Antibes harbour, disembarked its guardsmen, and have them rush the town's open gates? Presumably there are answers to all these questions. History is full of gaps and historians have to make their narratives make sense in spite of them.

31. Entombed in its masonry it contained, and still contains, the remains of General Championnet, hero of the Army of the Rhine, who'd fallen sick and died at Antibes after being put on trial during the Revolution.

32. Napoleon: 'I placed outposts on the roads to halt everything that came along them.'

33. When the Elban battalion had been about to leave Fontainebleau it had been found that it lacked an engineer officer, and Larabit, though he was only twenty-one, had volunteered. Napoleon had supported him in a dispute with Raoul over the fortification of Pianosa Island.

34. Gazon writes '106th Line', the new number given to the 87th in 1814. Napoleon's return would shortly restore its old one. See Digby Smith's *Napoleon's Regiments*, London 2000.

35. According to Paul Sénequier, to whom Gazon would relate all this many years later, it lay just about on the site of today's railway station.

36. See my *1812: The March on Moscow* (hereafter cited as *The March*), p.19: 'As soon as he ran into opposition he unfailingly shifted the centre of argument.' – Caulaincourt.

37. Napoleon seems to have kept this as a kind of fetish. And indeed Marengo, whose history he would successively rewrite in his own favour (see David Chandler's study), had been one of his career's most crucial turning points. Marchand, who seems always to be dependable in matters directly within his cognisance, would certainly know whether the cloak, which would cover him in his coffin six years later, was the one Napoleon claimed to have worn at that battle.

38. A week after Napoleon had left Elba, Pauline slipped away to the Italian mainland, but was detained for more than six months by the Austrians. Ornano says the *Inconstant* was ordered to sail for Corsica. In which case it would have been the *Étoile* that brought Fanny Bertrand and her daughter to Antibes a few days later. Though 'shown all the respect due to the wife of a man so admirable for his constant devotion to Europe's proscript, and given all the help she needed,' she wasn't allowed to land. The vessel went on to Toulon, where Masséna, still adroitly sitting on the fence, took them into custody. Afterwards they were of course allowed to go on to Paris, but that wasn't until April.

39. Examining some members of the Elba Battalion after Waterloo, Macdonald would ask what they'd have done if the expedition hadn't occurred or hadn't succeeded, and they'd replied: 'Gone off home. We'd never undertaken to go to Elba for good.' Back in February seven grenadiers, given indefinite leave, had landed at Toulon and said a great many of their comrades were about to leave Porto-Ferrajo.

40. One of the occasions when Gazon had actually spoken to Napoleon had been in 1813, when Marshal Macdonald's *dormeuse* had carelessly overturned one of his ammunition wagons 'a few days after the Battle of Lützen', luckily without causing an explosion. At that moment Napoleon had come on the scene, asked what had happened; and next day had issued an order of the day that any private vehicle

coming close to a battery should be burnt. *Cf The March* pp.251, 252.

41. Napoleon to Las Cases.

42. A strangely blurred memory! The distance from the olive grove (where Antibes railway station stands today) to the old town is only a few hundred yards and can be walked in ten minutes. When talking to Gourgaud at St Helena he would also incorrectly remember the bivouac as being 'on the road from Antibes to Grasse'. Napoleon's reminiscences are far from reliable. Quite apart from their *tendenz* they contain many errors of detail.

43. Albitte had frozen to death near the Berezina. See *The Retreat*, pp.258–9.

44. On St Helena he'd be even more explicit: 'I was in such a bad way I wasn't running any great risk, only risking my life. If, instead of marching on Grenoble, I'd amused myself by lobbing useless shells [into Antibes] to get my fifty [*sic*] men back, I'd have been lost. I mustn't be outstripped by couriers from Antibes. And then, by marching quickly, I left people ignorant of [the size of] my forces. I wouldn't have succeeded if I'd marched on Toulon, because they'd have formed a correct idea of how feeble they were, and no one likes getting stuck in such escapades.'

45. This doubtless was true of the lower ranks. But with his 'map of France spread out on the carpet' (Marchand) at Porto-Ferrajo on 25/26 February he'd surely discussed his strategy with Bertrand and Drouot.

46. Napoleon to Gourgaud on St Helena.

47. Dictating his memories of the Hundred Days to Gourgaud on St Helena, Napoleon would say that Cambronne's party was made up of 100 men. But the Mayor of Cannes, writing an urgent report to the government at 10:00 am on 2 March, says there were 'about fifty'. In view of Napoleon's penchant for exaggerating figures, the mayor's and Marchand's statements are perhaps nearer the mark.

48. On 13 March a British squadron that had set out on the 8th seeking news of Napoleon would heave to outside Antibes harbour and demand – in vain – that the town hand itself over to its commander as an ally of Louis XVIII. Ornano would refuse. But the same squadron would seize Monaco 'despite its prince's protests', causing Masséna to declare Antibes in a state of siege. A small column still stands in the main square at Antibes attesting to Louis XVIII's gratitude to its citizens after his return for their loyalty to him during the Hundred Days and promising a reward 'which still has to be received' (Ornano). But on 6 May the 87th Line would show its true sympathies by marking the point where Napoleon had disembarked and which, immediately after his departure for Cannes, had been visited by 'thousands of persons of both sexes.'

49. Cambronne, at his trial.

50. To Las Cases at St Helena, p.1247. Napoleon's account of the return from Elba is by and large correct, albeit slanted to give it a 'democratic' tone.

51. Cambronne at his trial.

52. '...and thought he was done for', writes the royalist Fabry, who all the time represents Napoleon as scared and worried, though there's no first-hand evidence for it apart from the 'lively apprehensions' that Napoleon later confessed to Las Cases.

53. This too seems contradictory. How in that case how could Cambronne have known which road the advance guard should take? Certainly Napoleon had also contemplated marching on Toulon and raising the garrison there; but the plan might have failed when people saw how few troops he had with him. The Antibes failure must have still further enhanced the mountainous option.

54. In 1747 Marshal Belle-Isle, command-

ing a Franco-Spanish army, had made the same mistake.

55. See *The March*, p.51. On the eve of his crossing the Niemen in 1812. The Russian expedition, he'd thought, wasn't in the interests of the middle classes. But in 1815 the expression '*la nation*' (like 'freedom' and 'democracy' in our own day) was still profoundly ambiguous.

56. To Gourgaud on St Helena. It's to Napoleon, perhaps also to Goethe, that we owe the cult of the Genius, the superman who 'can't be judged by any ordinary standards', that was to exercise such sway over men's minds in the nineteenth century and, in grotesque caricatures like Hitler and Mussolini, lead to such catastrophes in the twentieth.

57. Fabry says only Napoleon's chicken was paid for. 'The troops [breakfasted on] the victuals which had been requisitioned in Grasse.'

58. 'When he got there,' Marchand will hear afterwards, 'he had to flee from the inhabitants' anger and withdraw to the Continent.' Though at first popular on Elba, Napoleon had become less and less so. See Norwood Young's judicious and deeply researched *Napoleon in Exile – Elba*.

59. Part of it has been preserved in its original condition by the tourist authorities. It's hard going even on a summer's day, let alone in early March.

60. Count Bouthillier, the plump but resourceful Var prefect, was quite sure the column would be taking the main coastal road and had gone to Frejus to bar its progress with some 300 soldiers, gendarmes and National Guardsmen. (Oddly enough the first reports had said nothing about it being Bonaparte himself who'd come back with nearly a thousand men and cannon.) Only in the evening would a reconnaissance sent out in the direction of Cannes report that he was marching for Grenoble through the mountains.

Chapter 2: A Furious Army

1. And the French, as anyone who's ever had anything to do with them knows, are sticklers for principles.

2. She who two years ago had travelled to faraway Vilna to tend her wounded husband. See *The Retreat*, index.

3. Fezensac's memoirs end abruptly: 'Without having contributed to the Restoration, or even having desired it, I'd made up my mind to serve it as sincerely as I'd served the Empire. The command of a brigade of the Paris garrison had been reserved for me, and I took the [tricolour] cockade out of my hat. Already it was no longer mine; but I've preserved it ever afterwards as a precious souvenir.' Unfortunately Fezensac doesn't tell us how he reacted to Napoleon's return from Elba; but a reference to him by Saint-Chamans indicates that he didn't again take service under him.

4. A critic points out to me that, according to Vincent Cronin, Thiébault's memoirs are very unreliable, especially on political matters.

5. Originally he had done so in favour of his three-year-old son. But the reservation, which he'd repeat in his second abdication in June 1815, hadn't been accepted.

6. *Revenant* means literally 'someone who comes back from the dead', a word that would shortly be being applied to Napoleon, back from Elba.

7. Von Üxkull's diaries provide fascinating glimpses of France during the 1814 invasion. In Paris he saw all the sights, enjoyed himself simultaneously with half a dozen mistresses and thought it the most wonderful place of pleasure in the world: 'The Russians are treated very well, but ... made to pay through the nose for everything.' *Arms and the Woman*, p.184 *et seq*.

8. It was in reality only a papier-mâché mock-up, hastily improvised by Beugnot to greet Artois when he'd entered Paris as the

King's Lieutenant-General of the Realm a few days earlier.

9. Noël would collect his diaries and edit them after the 1848 revolution.

10. Later, in the winter of 1814–15 as a consequence of Talleyrand's manipulations at Vienna having almost managed to bring about a new war, some 60,000 men had been recalled to the colours at his behest, to show the Prussians and Russians, particularly, that France wasn't a dead duck.

11. Much less than under the Directory, when the percentage had stood at 4.17.

12. See *The Retreat*, p.169.

13. *The Retreat*, pp.279–87.

14. Like the rest of south-western France, Gascony was solidly royalist.

15. It may seem odd to call an eighteen-year-old a 'veteran'. But it's been calculated (Dufressse and Kerautret, *La France Napoléonienne*, Paris 1999) that in 1814 21% of the army was under twenty years of age.

16. It would be his rigidly reactionary attitudes as King Charles X that would finally put an end to the Bourbon dynasty in 1830.

17. Presumably a relative of the royalist conspirator of the same name, who, though extraordinarily courageous and resourceful, had finally been captured and guillotined.

18. For details of Dupuy's later career I have to thank not only his memoirs but my e-mail friend Christopher Franke, 'chef d'escadron in Brigade Lasalle out of France and in command of the Californian re-enactment group the 7e hussards.'

19. See *The Retreat*, p.371.

20. Coignet describes it in his *Cahiers*. See Chapter 1.

21. Though always careful to stick to the facts, Mauduit, one of the first French historians of the Waterloo campaign, is inordinately fond of multiple exclamation marks, which we, for the sake of local colour, will leave intact.

22. During the Empire, says the future publicist *Désiré Véron* – despite his extreme youth just now attending on the *Maison du Roi* as a surgeon – attendance at church had been obligatory for high officials: 'Prefects and all functionaries had had orders to attend divine service. But it was the Emperor they obeyed rather than God, and one prefect down in the south told me he was most punctilious in attending religious ceremonies, but always took Lafontaine's *Fables* with him in his pocket.'

23. Exceptionally, I quote here from a later source – Henry Houssaye's thoroughly researched and still absorbing book *1815* (Paris 1893), where he, presumably having heard many details *viva voce*, goes into this crucial question in great detail (pp.18–22).

24. One octogenarian businessman who'd given his entire fortune to the Republic's commissioner in exchange for his life had been guillotined regardless.

25. Ever since the Revolution the pavements of Paris had been allowed to disintegrate.

26. Napoleon may be said to have instituted the Age of Bureaucracy. His functioned, in principle, with military precision. See Jean Tulard, *Napoléon, le Pouvoir, la Nation, la Légende*.

27. The old-fashioned feudal title of marquis had fallen into desuetude during the Napoleonic era. But there were many newly-created counts of the Empire.

28. But Maison himself was a royalist.

29. For lack of shakos the 14th Light would fight the Waterloo campaign in fatigue caps. By no means all the cuirassiers – certainly not the 11th regiment, who would storm up against Wellington's squares – would be wearing cuirasses.

30. For Davout's abrasive character, see *The March*, p.64.

31. For his portrait, see *The Retreat*, pp.160–1.

32. 'Without combining anything in advance,' Levavasseur goes on, 'his tactic was to succeed. Often he was victorious, without knowing how he'd done it. Altogether, this man, so great, couldn't account for his own inspirations. He could have conquered kingdoms, but wouldn't have known how to govern them. His education had been exclusively military. It was incomplete. Yet his orders were perfectly conceived. He dictated them with facility. Despite his vivacity he had a good heart. He was never resentful and was always the first to come back and forgive you. Resigned in advance to the chance of battles, if his officers' deaths affected him but little [see *The Retreat*, p.326] it wasn't out of insensibility but from the habit of seeing men die and regarding the death of a man as of scant importance compared with the great interests of the nation. He kept nothing for himself. He paid his men out of his own income. If you told him you needed some money he'd send you to his intendant who'd pay.'

33. See *The Retreat*, chapter 12 and p.395 etc.

34. Notably by Marmont, Duke of Ragusa, who, admittedly in close collaboration with Joseph Bonaparte, had handed Paris over to the Allies last year. '*Raguser*' – meaning to go over to the enemy – was indeed a new word, but very much in the air in that spring of 1815.

Chapter 3: A Chapter of Errors

1. Josephine had died suddenly at Malmaison in May 1814. Napoleon would say the day when he'd heard the news was the saddest in his life. The concierge at Malmaison would always maintain there was something suspicious about Josephine's death, apparently due to pneumonia. Both she and her daughter had been chivalrously protected by Tsar Alexander, who'd prevailed on Louis XVIII – who'd found her 'charming' – to grant Hortense the less provocative title of Countess of Saint-Leu.

2. Disgraced by Napoleon for his disastrous capitulation at Baylen, in Spain, Dupont had spent the rest of the Empire incarcerated in the *donjon* at Vincennes, doubtless in the very same octagonal room where Vitrolles would spend the Hundred Days.

3. 'Chouans' were nominally royalist freedom-fighters against first the Republic and then the imperial régime, who had long terrorised the countryside, notably to the south-west of Paris, robbed mail-coaches, etc. They were not identical with, though they often overlapped and were in sympathy with, the rebels of La Vendée, in Brittany.

4. At the news of the Antibes landing Planat had even fancied one of Drouot's letters had intimated it in advance. But at their first conversation in Paris, Drouot would tell him plainly he'd 'known nothing about it until the last moment, and had even advised against it.' His few surviving letters to Planat witness to his genuine passion for a retired life among his books. Drouot's behaviour in the Empire's last campaigns and his concern for Planat's welfare seem to absolutely give the lie to Pion des Loches' bitter and no little envious view of him as 'a military Tartuffe'. Planat's account of life at Imperial Headquarters and his various missions, notably to Rapp at Danzig, are among the most vivid, not to say well-authenticated, for 1813–14.

5. It will be remembered that the master of one of the ships which had hailed the *Inconstant* en route for Antibes had used the same expression: 'How's the Man?'

6. Reading Lavalette's memoirs, published in 1831, Thibaudeau would be astounded to read that the former Postmaster had regarded him as one of the conspirators. But he assures us, probably truthfully, that

though liaising with the Bonapartists on behalf of the republicans, he was 'never in Bassano's councils.'

7. The *Chambre Noire* was a department of the Post Office that both antedated and had survived the Empire. Its employees were all members of the same family, whose expertise at imperceptibly opening and resealing letters had descended down several generations. When the office was finally abolished in 1830 they protested in vain that their delicate art would be lost for ever.

8. It would be she who, though in a state of advanced pregnancy, would rescue Lavalette from the Conciergerie on the eve of his execution by swapping clothes with him – an intrepid action which, together with her treatment at the hands of his gaolers, would cause her to become psychotic.

9. 'If he'd enjoyed so many favours,' Fleury goes on, 'it had at first been the prize of an unexampled facility for hard work, indefatigable activity, pure intentions, elevated views, unassailable probity; I'd even add an iron health, for in Napoleon's eyes physical energy too was a quality.' For a negative view of Maret, see *1812 – Napoleon in Moscow*, p.111.

10. One day he'd been caught out corresponding with Prince Eugène in Vienna. And Chancellor Dambray – a man for whom 'the French Revolution has quite simply never happened' – had summoned him to the Tuileries to give an account of himself. Entering his office, Fouché had instantly launched into a long, all too pertinent critique of the régime's errors – and then walked out again, leaving Dambray dumbfounded! After which he'd rejoined his long-time henchman *M-A. Gaillard* in the Tuileries gardens and the two of them had laughed heartily at the whole episode.

11. At Louis XVI's trial Fouché had promised his electors he'd vote against the death penalty, but had then voted in favour of it – but in so mumbling a voice that the president of the court had ordered him to 'speak up.' Since Louis XVI's execution had been decided by a majority of just one vote, each ex-conventional who'd opted for it was regarded by the Bourbons as individually guilty.

12. Even Wellington, then British ambassador in Paris, had written to Castlereagh warning him of the danger of a new revolution in France.

13. During the Hundred Days, Fouché, sure that the Bourbons would be back sooner or later, would ensure the destruction of any documents incriminating himself in the generals' plot. So it's difficult to say exactly what part he played in it.

14. He'd stayed at The Briars, where the climate – in contrast to windswept Longwood – is in fact delightful.

15. It was Peyrusse and Cambronne who had rescued the remnants of Napoleon's private fortune. Originally it had amounted to 200 million francs. The same day as he'd abdicated at Fontainebleau, an official – authorised by Talleyrand – of the provisional government, had turned up at Orléans where Napoleon's treasure and Marie-Louise were known to be. 'The waggons of Napoleon's private treasure,' Méneval relates, 'were standing in the public square. They contained some ten million francs in gold and silver coinage, three million in table silver and gold plate, a value of about 400,000 francs in snuffboxes and rings enriched with diamonds intended as presents, the gold-embroidered imperial robes and ornaments, even the Emperor's pocket handkerchiefs marked with a crown ... all this was taken to the Tuileries. One of the casks of gold had been stove in and its contents divided up among those émigrés who were besieging the court of the Duke of Artois, without that prince, at that moment Lieutenant-General of the realm, raising any objections. But when M. de la Bouillerie [Treasurer-General of the Crown] demanded the two million needed to honour Napoleon's engagements in favour of his household officers and servants, guaranteed by Article 9 of the Treaty of Fontainebleau [11 April 1814] "Mon-

sieur" had ordered the débris of the Imperial Treasure (eight or ten million) to be quite simply paid into the public treasury, first as a loan, then definitively.' Cambronne and two battalions of the Guard had meanwhile been sent to protect Marie-Louise, who, however, had left for Rambouillet, whence she was abducted by her father to Vienna. On 13 April Peyrusse, 'whose zeal and fidelity had been momentarily doubted by the Emperor but had proved themselves', had left for Fontainebleau, escorted by Cambronne and his men, with the three million francs he'd been able to save of Napoleon's fortune.

16. As Vitrolles points out, Louis XVIII had not been a signatory to the Treaty. The very same day as Napoleon had boarded Campbell's ship at Fréjus en route for Elba he'd written via Bertrand to Méneval, then and afterwards Marie-Louise's secretary, complaining that 'a treasure of ten to twelve million has been unjustly seized at Orléans and is currently under seal in Paris. There is nothing to be expected of the French government for the two million destined for the upkeep of Elba unless some foreign intervention doesn't attend to the matter.'

17. As Griois had noticed when he'd been stationed there: 'The arable part of the island is divided up into vineyards, fields and olive groves, and even the most arid parts where the soil scarcely covers the rock, producing such elegant shrubs as myrtle, wild pomegranate and superb aloes, almost all forming hedges to a height of eight to ten feet.'

18. In his lucidly researched first volume of *Napoleon in Exile* (1915), Norwood Young, describing the history of the Emperor's finances in detail (pp.210–21), writes: 'From this account it would appear ... he only had just enough to last him till the end of 1815. In reality he could have held out for several more years ... He had more than sufficient to have seen him through a fourth year.' The economic motive therefore seems to have been less important than has been made out.

19. A personal enemy of Napoleon's, Brulart had sworn to kill him in revenge for the treacherous assassination of a friend of his in the Vendée, even though the First Consul had had nothing to do with it. Afterwards, Brulart's ADC would deny that that had ever been in his mind.

20. On St Helena Gourgaud would note jealously that Napoleon would happily dispense with any of his entourage rather than with Cipriani, with whom he would have long confabulations in their incomprehensible Corsican dialect. One day Cipriani, who was also Napoleon's major-domo, would suddenly collapse while waiting at table and die in agony in Marchand's attic bedroom. Napoleon paid for a grave, but Balcombe, the British consul – who would always maintain Cipriani had been poisoned – had it opened for a post-mortem, and found it was empty.

21. A disguise immediately seen through by Mariotti's spy, who wrote in his report of 18 February: 'a few days ago a person of distinction arrived disguised as a sailor, brought by one of Ferici's feluccas.'

22. Unfortunately the garrulous and self-important Fleury de Chaboulon, though he includes important first-hand details in his book (published in England and read and commented on by Napoleon on St Helena) embeds them in a whirl of sentiments and ideas of his own. And he's very much the hero of his own account.

23. The executed Georges Cadoudal, one of the prime conspirators against his life as First Consul.

24. Napoleon's comment: 'There's a clear head for you! Our conversation, which he could have had with himself, changes his dispositions!' Clearly, the monumentally egocentric exile couldn't allow or conceive that anyone, least of all so insignificant a person as Fleury, could have influenced his decisions. On the other hand, Fleury, too, is very much the hero of his own narrative.

25. A departure, likewise Napoleon's

change of mood, duly noted by Mariotti's spy.

26. 'My great mistake was to leave six months too soon,' Napoleon will say. 'I should have waited for the Congress to break up.'

27. A contradiction of what Napoleon himself, less probably, would claim – that it was only outside Grasse that he told them about his choice of route. Here I'm more inclined to believe the valet!

28. Dr Foureau de Beauregard, 'in whom medical science', according to Pons de l'Hérault, 'had disclosed no merit and who in Paris had been physician to the royal stables, was what's vulgarly known as an old woman, and to please the Emperor retailed to him exactly all the tittle-tattle, good or bad, and moreover was too obsequious, in contrast to his vanity towards his subordinates. This had in the end rendered him suspect.' In June, at Malmaison, Foureau would refuse a second exile with his patient.

29. But see Mackenzie, pp.220, 223. He maintains that the flotilla had been ordered to avoid the *Partridge,* and approach the French frigates on the off-chance that they might side with the Emperor. This seems to me highly improbable. Frénilly says the navy was far more royalist than the army.

Chapter 4: Through the Mountains

1. Most Frenchmen in those days spoke with some more or less strong regional accent. Napoleon's own was less regional than 'foreign'.

2. Peyrusse's accounts show that only twenty mules were actually bought during the whole three-day march through the mountains, the rest being presumably rented for the next stage and then sent back with their owners.

3. 'An occupation,' Ali had thought, 'not without certain intentions. At the same time as it threw spies off the scent it brought the men out of their stupor and gave them back their breath.'

4. At Laffrey they would play – all eye-witnesses agree – the Marseillaise; and it seems unlikely they'd have picked up instruments en route.

5. At Waterloo she would be the first of the 1st Grenadiers to be killed by a British round shot. For a most vivid account of her sudden death and improvised obsequies, see Mauduit II, p.291. 'Maria's friend, by bizarre chance, was also hit by one of the first projectiles fired at our squares by the Prussians ... [and] died in the most horrible tortures and was doubtless flung into the common funeral pyre.'

6. In June he'd have a fit on hearing Napoleon had abdicated a second time.

7. The news of the Antibes landing had in fact reached him in much diluted form.

8. Napoleon's spurts of physical energy had amazed Sir Neil Campbell. His passion for hot baths was something of an addiction. His secretary Fain writes that he 'abused them'.

9. *Jean de l'Epée* was one of his men's nick-names for him.

10. Presumably an allusion to his notoriously 'twisted' war bulletins.

11. A feat that even so wouldn't suffice for imperial propaganda. In his official account in the *Moniteur* he would multiply it by four, calling it 'fifty leagues'! Napoleon's memoirs, dictated on St Helena, are packed with such exaggerations in details.

12. The *Guide Napoléonien* gives his name as Mireur, and places Abbé Chiris at Escragnolles. But our eyewitnesses will remember it as having happened at Séranon.

13. Throughout the Hundred Days we shall see him being lavish of such half-promises.

14. According to the verbal account given

'of that memorable night' by the ninety-seven-year-old widow Marie-Catherine Funel in 1887, they'd 'make their triumphal entry into Caille, singing and shouting.'

15. Still following up events a year later.

16. When Pons got there, Masséna – who of course immediately grasped the dangers of the situation – locked him up in prison, saying he did so to protect him from the fury of royalist mobs. Masséna would also detain other arrivals from Elba, *eg* Fanny Bertrand, pending the outcome of the *napoléonade.*

17. The house, truncated to widen the street, still stands in a dilapidated condition in the middle of this singularly depressing village.

18. Probably Désirée, which, however, would afterwards be left in the rear and reach Paris by easier stages than her master.

19. The abrupt firing of questions was habitual with him. No doubt he stored the answers in his computer-like mind. *Cf* The English MP Mr Lyttleton's account of their 'conversation' in the cabin of HMS *Northumberland* in July.

20. 'At this word,' writes Fabry, 'the young lady had a shock which lasted for several days.' He seems to want to suggest that Napoleon had the same effect on the fair sex as a cobra or boa-constrictor!

21. *Mathieu Molé*, that acute psychologist, writes that he 'had the singular weakness of not being able to discern the limits of possibility.'

22. This according to Fleury, who obviously interviewed the Tartansons. It accords with Napoleon's way of ignoring contradiction, as with Gazon at Antibes.

23. 'Three days later,' says Fabry, 'he marched in pursuit of his guest at the head of a detachment of royalist volunteers.'

24. This last according to an account scrupulously handed down in the Tartanson family. 'Ever afterwards when Mme. Tartanson heard Napoleon referred to as the Corsican Ogre, she'd angrily refute it: "I've seen him deeply moved at the thought of his son, whom mine reminded him of!"'

25. Molé too, that notable observer of human nature, had thought not only that Napoleon's speech was '*saccadé*' (jerky, staccato) but his actual mental processes too, a kind of chaos forcing on order and at the same time almost compulsively collecting and storing information of all kinds. Certainly his handwriting is about as chaotic and rushed as can be.

26. Certainly he wasn't. Napoleon was too much the fatalist. No mention is ever made by any of his attendants of him ever having taken any such precautions.

27. One wonders what became of his notes. They should make interesting reading.

28. Jean Tulart, in his *Les Vingt Jour*, thinks that Duval 'at first inactive, then absent' was 'particularly astute. He hadn't compromised himself and had secured the Emperor's support should he succeed in his enterprise.' *Op cit* p.99.

29. All this as Fabry will suitably report it next year for his readers, during the White Terror.

30. Fabry says that Bertrand left behind 'four fusiliers' to take care of the printing work.

31. According to what Napoleon would tell Gourgaud, he'd afterwards heard that though Masséna had 'wept for joy that I was back' he'd told Pons that 'the state of opinion in Marseilles was so bad he couldn't yet declare himself and even, to save him from popular fury, was going to place him under arrest.' Napoleon would think that if Masséna had been more active 'he could have gone to Toulon where attitudes were good and got the troops there to declare for me. But Masséna wasn't light-headed.'

32. Beyond despatching two regiments

under General Miollis to join Loverdo at Sisteron and posting up a proclamation at Marseilles to reassure that ultra-royalist city that he's taking all possible measures to trap Bonaparte, Masséna hadn't in fact taken any extraordinary measures. His prey, as he explained in another proclamation, had a two-day start on him and had passed outside his area of jurisdiction.

33. Las Cases. See also *The March*, p.260.

34. An incident Jerzmanowski would relate to Hobhouse, in Paris.

35. Actually it seems that one had been manufactured on Elba. Perhaps hitherto it had not had a tricolour attached to it, though that seems improbable. See P. Charrie, *Drapeaux et Étandards de la Révolution et de l'Émpire*, Paris 1982.

36. Ali says the troops' marching formation wasn't really re-established until Gap, after Sisteron.

37. He would commit suicide on hearing of Napoleon's second abdication.

38. One notes that in his memoirs Napoleon invariably inflates figures; often doubles them.

39. According to Fabry its proprietor didn't exactly welcome them. When they left again next morning he, like the Tartansons, refused payment 'saying he didn't keep an inn.'

40. Another more circuitous road, by the river's left bank, could also have led Napoleon to Gap. His grenadiers could also have made rafts. But with Miollis' two regiments marching up from Marseilles he could ill afford the delay.

41. Once again, Jean Tulard thinks Gombert behaved astutely, buttering his bread on both sides. By going to meet Napoleon wearing the fleur-de-lis decoration, he's shown himself loyal to the King. According to his own account Napoleon would ask him what part of France he came from; and

hearing he came from the Berry district, jocosely introduced him to Bertrand, who also stemmed from there.

42. Though one of Napoleon's appointees, he issued a proclamation referring to Napoleon as 'an enemy fatal for your tranquillity [*repos*], the man who has cost France and Europe so much blood and tears, who at his abdication bragged mendaciously of his generosity.'

Chapter 5: A Thunderclap

1. It had been Ciappe's brother Claude Ciappe (Chappe is the francophone spelling) who had invented the semaphore telegraph during the Revolution. In 1805 he had committed suicide when his epoch-making invention had been attributed to someone else.

2. Even the usually so scathing Frénilly appreciates Beugnot as 'a man gifted with great penetration, lots of intelligence, and an eminently just mind.' The Jacobin Thibaudeau, at the other political extreme, calls him 'a man of wit and intelligence, gentle-mannered, without character or passions, little capable of devotion, floating between the Court's bad inspirations and liberal ideas.'

3. 'I can't say how long the King stuck with me,' Beugnot goes on. 'But toward the end he began to show signs of impatience and boredom. At the bottom of his soul I fancy he much regretted saying he'd give me all the time I asked for.'

4. 'Gout' in those days meant a variety of neuromuscular, possibly psychosomatic, troubles. During the Hundred Days it would afflict several protagonists at convenient/inconvenient moments. At Beaumont, three days before Waterloo, Mortier would be – authentically – struck down by it.

5. It had taken so long to reach Paris partly because at Marseilles 'it had been entrusted to a courier' who'd fallen off his horse and broken his thigh.

6. The Tuileries, burnt down by the Communards in 1871, lay directly in line with the Pont Royal, which of course still exists.

7. 'The work was exhausting,' Brun tells us: 'Dupont had left thirty-five enormous portfolios for his successor to disentangle. Soult devoted himself wholly to doing so. Though it was in the depths of winter I'd go down to him at 5:00 am and was never finished by lunch time. After half an hour I got back to work again. It kept me until 4:00 pm, when there was a daily audience, of the most wearisome kind, where the marshal received the greatest personages of the old and new régimes.' Not until 11:00 pm has poor Brun been getting to bed for 'scarcely five hours' rest.'

8. See Peter Hayman's *Soult, Napoleon's Maligned Marshal*, London 1990.

9. '...where gaming and sex at every price-level hung out their boards in the street,' *Véron* goes on, 'and with audacious numbers as their ensigns: the 129, the 154, the 113 and the 9, visited and perhaps envied by the whole of Europe, the government authorised and protected the gaming houses' public self-advertisements and challenges to the worker's petty cash as much as the wealthy foreigner's gold coin and the well-bred young man's, the businessman's and the banker's banknote. On the Rue Vivienne side one went down into the Palais Royal by a narrow passage where all sorts of things were being cried up: the Stock Exchange rate, the Paris, Lyon and Strasburg lottery draws, the bulletins of the Grand Army. Since '93 one came quickly on the Rue St Honoré side through those famous and improvised timber galleries by a narrow passage into the vast area that had once served as stables. In these galleries, open to the winds and without any enclosure, a few bookshops were installed that sold *The Muses' Calendar*, various song books, Désaugier's potpouris, the *Picture of Conjugal Love* and the *Address of the Prettiest Women in Paris*. All the other tenants of these shops were modistes who offered their wares at the tops of their voices. The con-man on the prowl, the penniless gamester, layabouts and scum of every class

and age, men and women, crowded into these tortuous cloaques, dazzlingly lit up, its gound often muddy from the rain. The first three stone storeys weren't big enough to hold all the bars, the thirty- or forty-sous restaurants, the cafés (with or without orchestras); nor had one seen everything by stopping at the many boutiques of jewellers, of dressing cases, of ribbon or haberdasher sellers, vast shops selling ready-made clothes and military outfits. It still remained to descend into the cellars to hear the orchestra of the *Café of the Blind*, to hear le Sauvage "blousing" his kettle-drums, or be taken in by some of Fitz-James the ventriloquist's mystifications, he who in 1814 had got himself killed while in a state of drunkenness under the walls of Paris. The god Mars was represented there by a few more or less wine-drunk sabre-rattlers and a mob of queenly Venuses, painted red and white, less impressive for their rags and tatters and their glass trinkets than for their splendid nudities.' How strange it is to imagine all this! Today there reigns on this historic spot only a dead, empty silence!

10. Rumigny's printed text (1921 edition) dates this to 3 March. Examination of the earliest edition would presumably show a misprint for 5 March – the 3 and the 5 of certain nineteenth-century French typefaces are easily confused. And certainly the news hadn't been known in Paris as early as that. Fouché, too, only heard it on the 5th.

11. Rumigny, whose family had been ruined by the Revolution and who'd been adjutant-major of the 2nd Line (only 400 of its 3,400 men had returned from Russia), had been taken onto Gérard's staff at the battle of Viazma after, at Gérard's orders, charging a Russian gun with only a handful of men and quenching its fire. At Montereau in 1814, where Rumigny (still aged only twenty-five) and his horse had received fourteen sword and bayonet wounds, Gérard had embraced him in front of the Guard Grenadiers and obtained a colonelcy for him.

12. No more than Artois did Vitrolles have any use for 'liberal' ideas, even though the

King had formally embraced, and was even to some extent trying to implement them. 'One could say,' he writes, 'that at certain moments there are ideas which spread like epidemics. It's a kind of fever that seizes on people's minds and which no one is safe from. It is, as it were, in the air they breathe. No one discussed it, no one doubted whether this coat, cut to quite another figure than ours, would suit us. No one questioned the difficulty of transplanting the old British oak in new soil.' In the Pavillion de Flore, where once the dread Committee of Public Safety had held its round-the-clock sessions 'in the midst of the luxurious comfort exuded by tapestries, mirrors and furniture inherited from the costly old monarchy', Artois had formed a shadow government of his own, far more reactionary than the King's. Likewise, says Beugnot, the headquarters of his own secret police.

13. Berry did in fact have a kind of rash and wild valour. See chapter 14.

14. This is exactly what they would do, according to Colonel Noël's account.

15. The terrace was a creation of Napoleon. Formerly the whole area had been one immense open-air latrine.

16. Her father, the Swiss financier Necker, had lent the French government two million francs at the outbreak of the Revolution, and she'd been trying to get them back ever since.

17. Miollis had been the general who, together with General Radet, head of his military police, Napoleon had sent to Rome on the eve of the Russian expedition, to arrest the Pope and bring him to Fontainebleau. Though praised by the great Cardinal Consalvo for the tact and consideration he had shown toward the Holy Father, he was decidedly persona non grata with the pious. Masséna's proclamation to the fanatically royalist townspeople of Marseilles, in whose eyes he is deeply suspect on account of his revolutionary and imperial past, has a strongly self-justificatory tone.

18. Together with the indomitable Ney, Maison had been the rearguard's last commander at Kovno on the Niemen. See *The Retreat*, p.446.

19. It was because of this last recovery that the Prince of Monaco had been going back to his restored feudal fief. See chapter 1.

20. Aglaé's mother had drowned herself the day the Queen had been guillotined. Her aunt was Mme. Campans, who in 1814 had been deprived of her position as head of the Ecouen academy for young ladies and daughters of members of the Legion of Honour. Only with the greatest of difficulty had Macdonald, in 1814, managed to rescue the establishment from the greedy hands of Bishop Pradt*.

21. Hortense adds that the marshal's wife had certainly repeated her words to him, and that 'when she afterwards saw I'd been right, took it as certain that I'd been privy to the secret' of the return.

22. Louis XVIII himself will afterwards confirm the milder version, adduced by Ney at his trial, and would always maintain the sincerity of Ney's devotion to the government at that moment. Which, however, wouldn't prevent him from confirming Ney's death sentence in December, despite Aglaé's tears. Nor was the 'iron cage' merely a figurative expression. Dangerous criminals were often transported in them. When Caulaincourt had told Napoleon during their sleigh ride back from Russia that the British wouldn't hesitate to put him on display in the Tower of London 'in an iron cage', Napoleon had laughed aloud, seeming almost to relish the idea.

Chapter 6: 'If Any of You wants to Kill his Emperor...'

1. Randon has left two separate accounts of his own actions at this time. The first is exactly contemporary, in a report to his uncle, and the more vivid and presumably authentic. The second, made thirty years later, is perhaps less so. One day, by then

himself a Marshal of France, he'd be cold-shouldered by Napoleon III.

2. During the ferocious backlash after Waterloo, General Marchand would be tried but acquitted of pusillanimity in not resisting Bonaparte more firmly.

3. In the autumn Noël would be ordered to defend the town against the invading Piedmontese and Austrians, and would do so, for a few days, until many of his men deserted and the inhabitants insisted on surrendering.

4. Orillons were projecting shoulders of a bastion, protecting its flanks from fire.

5. A banquette was an infantry firing-step behind the parapet of a rampart or trench.

6. Napoleon to Gourgaud at St Helena. This isn't inherently improbable, yet it's the only reference, apart from Fleury de Chaboulon's visit and glover Dumoulin's secret correspondence with Émery, that I've been able to find of Napoleon having been directly tipped off before leaving Elba. Though there was no 'plot', as the royalists would stubbornly maintain, there had certainly been other secret communications, eg via glover Dumoulin.

7. At Gap he'd be fooled by Émery, who, again released from arrest, assured him the Antibes garrison had joined Napoleon and that Masséna was now doing the same. Though Mouton-Duvernet would send a messenger to General Marchand informing him of Émery's approach, his gullibility and subsequent activities combating the Duke of Angoulême's military rising in the south would cost him his life. Put on trial, he'd be condemned and executed.

8. It is indeed difficult to see what purpose the blowing up of the Pont Haut could achieve, beyond gaining a little time. Such an obstacle could be easily circumvented since there were shallows up and down stream that the Elba column could ford.

9. Though the exposures of the mountain march would certainly be enough to account for his cold, Napoleon, whose whole constitution, his doctor Yvan tells us, 'was eminently nervous', had a tendency to develop such psychosomatic symptoms in moments of crisis. See *The March*, p.260. Laure d'Abrantès, who knew him well, writes that 'he could never stand the least cold without becoming ill, and couldn't understand that others didn't catch cold, as he did, at the least chilly breeze.'

10. In fact General Miollis' column would reach Sisteron on the 8th, and it would be his despatch back to Toulon that would cause Masséna to assure Paris by the Lyons telegraph that 'Bonaparte is in the mousetrap', *ie* between Sisteron and Grenoble.

11. It's a curious fact that in all his own memoirs, dictated at St Helena, Napoleon – who, after all, had seen the whole of Europe (which, Caulaincourt tells us, lay spread out in his mind 'like a map') – never once mentions the aesthetic appearance of any place or district. This does not, of course, mean he was impervious to such impressions. Merely regarded them as irrelevant.

12. There is traditionally disagreement at Corps as to where Napoleon spent the night. But the best authority is sure it was in a house on the former narrow winding main street. Today an old folks home, it can't be visited.

13. Site of today's traffic roundabout, in front of the hotel there.

14. It had been here, in 1789, the Revolution had first broken out. Today its big château is a museum of the French Revolution.

15. Ali was wrong. See below.

16. The commune of Laffrey has signally, one might almost say scandalously, failed to protect or exploit this super-historical site, but instead has placed upon it a modern camping site with lampposts, electric sockets, etc. One can imagine what

it looks like at the height of the summer season! Nor has the faded notice by the car park any word to say about what happened here, apart from outlining the Route Napoléon. If ever there was a site that cries out for re-enactments one would have thought this was it!

17. All of which is good psychological warfare. As a revolutionary on Corsica the young Bonaparte had used exactly the same formula – a favourite with twentieth-century terrorists – on Louis XVI's governor.

18. It's at this moment, Randon says, he'd afterwards been alleged – falsely – to have 'repeatedly given the order to fire.' According to Houssaye, whose well-researched and well-composed account I am partly following, Randon did in fact shout 'There he is! Fire!' If so, it wasn't his duty, as a mere ADC, to do so, Delessart being their commander.

19. Eyewitnesses give different version of these memorable words – *eg* Louis Marchand: 'Kill your Emperor, if you can.'

20. Which, he adds sadly, 'would afterwards prove so fatal to more than one brother-in-arms.'

21. There is no doubt but that in post-revolutionary France even the parish clergy were almost incredibly unpopular. They were also rare. See Jean Tulard, *La Vie Quotidienne des Français sous Napoléon*. In fact there was little danger either of feudal rights or confiscated pre-Revolutionary properties being restored, though proposals to that effect had been made in Louis XVIII's parliament.

22. Another main theme of Bonapartist propaganda – as in Germany in the 1920s after World War I – was that the French armies hadn't been defeated, but had been betrayed by Marshal Marmont's 'treason' in surrendering Paris to the Allies. Actually his troops had been hopelessly outnumbered and his capitulation had been authorised by Joseph Bonaparte, effectively in charge of the government. It's true that

if Napoleon had had two more days he might have turned Paris into a battlefield. Yet he never accused Joseph of 'betraying' him. As we shall see, the notion of 'treason' among the top brass would turn out to be lethal to the Waterloo army's morale.

23. The proclamation – as we know from Marchand's admiring testimony – was Napoleon's own work on board the brig.

24. '*Une petite caisse*' can mean either a side drum or a small cash box. Historians have usually inclined to the former translation, as the more dramatic! This legend thus seems to have been born minutes after Labédoyère left.

25. By 'column' a much broader formation is usually meant than the three-abreast of a route column of those days.

26. Did he? Or is this an echo of the myth established at Grenoble? Always we must have a certain scepticism about the relative value of the sources. Our eyewitnesses aren't telling us what they saw, but what they'd afterwards remember having seen. But Peyrusse, who'd have his own accountant's honour to defend, is usually reliable.

27. The unpopular *droits réunis* consisted of 'rights on beverages, authorising cellar rats [*ie* customs officers] to break into the exploiter's house, imposing a tax of twenty centimes per kilo of salt, a monopoly of the purchase, manufacture and sale of tobacco in favour of the management of the *droits réunis*' – Jean Tulard, *op cit* p.131. Originally feudal, such indirect taxation had in fact been introduced during Republic and Empire.

28. One such witness at Marchand's trial would defend his failure to give the order to fire by saying an officer shouldn't demean himself by giving an order he knows won't be implemented.

29. To Gourgaud on St Helena.

30. All this Jerzmanowski would later tell Hobhouse in Paris.

31. Not the same Pétiet as will later appear in our narrative.

32. This lie, obviously put about verbally by Napoleon himself, is nowhere to be found in his official documents.

33. Jubé wrote down his narrative on 14 March, still evidently prey to remorse and anxiety as to his and his wife's future. His account therefore has first-class source value.

34. '*Attendu qu'on n'est past content de lui*'. This could also men 'seeing you're not pleased with him.'

35. As has been said before, Napoleon was least of all a friend of *le peuple*. His reference in his will, leaving his body to 'the French people I've so loved', or his statement to Las Cases that he understood the common man because he himself had such origins, must be taken in a most general, not a particular sense. Intentional misinterpretation of the word to mean 'the mob' must have gratified his royal and aristocratic enemies, who'd persisted in regarding him as 'the people's' champion, not as what and how he saw himself: as a barrier between the propertied and unpropertied classes.

36. '*La mandille*', a now archaic word – originally Spanish but perhaps still used in Corsica – meaning 'men with short-tailed jackets', *ie* waiters and suchlike. 'Lower-class scum' would perhaps be rather a bold translation.

Chapter 7: Collapse of a Conspiracy

1. The assembling of troops at Chambéry, as a demonstration in force to please Talleyrand, had been kept secret and evidently wasn't known to the La Fère garrison.

2. It was exactly for lack of this tradition, as applied to himself and his infant son, that Napoleon had realised (when the news of Malet's conspiracy had reached him in Russia) his régime must collapse under the weight of military defeat. 'If I'd been my own grandson it'd have been different.'

3. As his behaviour on 16 June, between Quatre Bras and Ligny, will exemplify.

4. For this hyper-efficient cavalry subaltern and one-time Brabant peasant who after eleven years' incessant service had risen from the ranks to be the 6th Chasseurs' adjutant-major, then lieutenant, see indexes to *Moscow* and *The Retreat*. Henckens had been severely wounded in the heel at Leipzig, his Achilles tendon being almost cut through. Needing to convalesce, he'd insisted on returning to his native Eygelshoven, where his family had been astounded to see him, 'a French officer, but hopping about on crutches. For a moment I thought my mother was going to faint,' as well she might at the sight of his new 'cartridge pouches, sabre belt, shako, cords and epaulettes, all in massive silver', and all a free present from his colonel! 'I'd always been her favourite. She said in our Limburg dialect: "You're not leaving us again. This French game is over, or shortly will be." But 'I had another family. When you're a soldier, you don't look around for subterfuges to desert your flag. I only had one country. It was France.' Rejoining the remnants of the 6th Chasseurs after Napoleon's last victories at Montmirail and Brienne, he'd seen 'Prussian, Austrian and Russian prisoners made to march past along the Paris boulevards under their officers and generals – a sad spectacle, not at all to my taste and which anyway didn't have the success expected of it.' At Falaise, in Normandy, after the abdication, he'd received the Legion of Honour, still with Napoleon's effigy on it, 'the happiest day of my life'. And it was there Berry had adopted the regiment, mainly, it seems, because its young Colonel Talhouët*, Henckens' friend and patron, was both an aristocrat and had been an imperial page, and often been at the Tuileries under Napoleon. Renumbering them the 1st Chasseurs, Berry ordered the regiment to be brought up to strength, gave them the pick of all available horses, and sent them to Compiègne. En route they'd halted at Malmaison, where Henckens and his fellow-

officers had seen the dead Josephine 'lying on her death-bed, still beautiful, but surrounded by Prussians.' The Countess Talhouët, his colonel's mother, had 'heard a lot about him in Russia', and warmly welcomed him to her Paris town house, even invited him and all his fellow-officers to the Opera.

5. Can it have been this regiment which 'Ali' Saint-Denis would notice on the Fontainebleau road? Such equine luxury was certainly by no means common in the ruinous state of French finances in 1814–15.

6. With Napoleon on HMS *Bellerophon*, the older Lallemand would go in terror of a Bourbon firing squad, as indeed Gourgaud must have done. Not allowed to go to St Helena with his idol, Lallemand, with Planat de la Faye (ousted by the hysterical Gourgaud), would be sent to Malta, whence they would in due course be allowed to escape to Trieste. Lefebvre-Desnouëttes, also condemned to death, would die in a shipwreck off the coast of Ireland while returning from Alabama to Holland in 1822.

Chapter 8: France's Second City

1. Jerzmanowski to Hobhouse in May.

2. Whether Napoleon ever used this expression I don't know. But he had certainly boasted of having 'an annual income of a hundred-thousand men'. Horses had been harder to come by, and would also prove so in 1815. See *The March*, p.48.

3. It would be this Lyons proletariat which in 1831 would rise against the new bourgeois régime and be bloodily crushed by Soult, once again Minister of War, and by Oudinot and the army.

4. Orléans' and Macdonald's accounts of what happened then don't tally. But the latter is much more detailed and therefore perhaps the more reliable. The higher the social rank of the narrator, the more

sceptical one must be, their accounts – written down quite a long while afterwards – still having political implications and being inherently self-justifying.

5. According to Macdonald he 'ordered him to leave'. Even the faintest prospect of him going over to the enemy of course was terrible to the royalist cause. Once again, we must remind ourselves to be cautious of the higher ranks' memoirs, written in later political situations. Research has shown Macdonald's to be often unreliable.

6. During the Terror, in 1793, Lyons had rebelled against the Jacobin government. It had been after its defeat that Fouché and Couthon had been sent to inflict terrible reprisals on its citizens and 'demolish the city for ever. Lyons has rebelled against the Republic One and Indivisible. Lyons is no more.'

7. Fleury tells a tall story about Napoleon (who indignantly denies it) having given the Legion of Honour to a trooper who, alone, had stood by Artois in his flight.

8. All according to Fleury, who says he refused to have it as escort because of its failure to escort Artois out of the city, as its duty would have required. 'A fable', Napoleon scribbles angrily in the margin.

9. Actually he had. Only a couple of weeks earlier he'd been to Paris to implore the Ministry to provide him with more weapons etc.

10. Macdonald had been intending to stay for some time at his château at Courcelles. Hence the large sum of money he had with him when he'd been ordered to go to Nîmes.

11. On 13 March Macdonald would get back to Paris, half-crippled by having ridden so many bad horses: 'I hadn't taken my clothes off since 8 March. We didn't waken the King.' Next day, to his amazement, his ADCs turn up with his carriage, his effects and his gold, all intact. Though Louis XVIII, who'd heard of its loss, proffered him compensation he says he refused it.

12. Which Napoleon, in his copy of the book sent to him at St Helena, will categorically deny having had, at least as reported by the self-important Fleury. 'False!' he'd scribble in the margin, 'What nonsense! The Emperor might open himself to Cambacérès, to Lebrun, to Bertrand. But a young secretary of only 25 he hardly knew!'.

13. At St Helena Napoleon's sharp pencil will categorically deny it.

14. A sharp distinction was made, especially by Bonapartists, between 'royal monarchs' and Napoleon's imperial claims, based, at least nominally, on popular plebiscite.

15. The hostile Fabry puts it vividly: 'He'd crossed the departments of the Var and of the Low and High Alps as might have done a band of robbers, following smugglers' paths.'

16. Mouton-Duvernet would be tried and shot by firing squad for going over to him.

17. He would lose it in the rout at Waterloo.

18. It is, furthermore, the role he'll play, more and more unwillingly, throughout the Hundred Days, and con brio when talking to Las Cases at St Helena, thus founding his own myth as an apostle of freedom. 'The trouble with Napoleon was he never for a moment ceased playing the great emperor' – Caulaincourt.

19. But again denied by Napoleon's pencil at St Helena, which draws an angry ring around these pages. Can Fleury's account be dismissed entirely? Whose memory is at fault? Whose imagination is overdoing things? A case perhaps of no smoke without fire? History is made up of extant relics and shards, not of what has vanished for ever!

20. The sum also includes charges for relays of horses between Lyons and Fontainebleau.

21. Yet not briefly enough for her own liking. She'd told all and sundry how, as André Castelot puts it (*Napoléon et les Femmes*, Paris 1998), 'while Napoleon was

occupying himself with her, she'd looked up at the clock hung over the bed and managed to push the minute hand forward by thirty minutes' so that Napoleon, lifting up his eyes, had exclaimed 'Already!' and quickly pushed off. Napoleon's prowess in bed seems not to have compared with what he could deploy on battlefields. Afterwards she'd let *tout Paris* know she'd borne him a son on 13 December 1806 – a statement which, if true (she'd also shared other beds, notably Murat's), would have been crucial since up to then, in view of Josephine's infertility, he'd not been sure he could have children, and thus consolidate his 'Fourth Dynasty'.

22. There was, in fact, no doubt of the future Count Léon's 'legitimacy'. From photos taken in 1860 the facial resemblance is striking.

23. 'It's very strong,' Talleyrand wrote to Jaucourt, sending a copy to Paris. 'There's never been so strong a document.' Its preamble assures the King of France that only if, against all expectations, he should be unable to cope with 'the brigand' Bonaparte's 'criminal and insane enterprise' will the foreign powers come to his aid. Actually drafted by his intimate assistant La Besnardière – Houssaye calls him his '*âme damnée*' – one can hardly escape the reflection that its virulence was also personally inspired. Men, even diplomats, aren't machines. Hadn't Napoleon himself said that an insult is less easily forgiven than an injury? And hadn't he in an hour-long tirade which Talleyrand had listened to leaning against the mantelpiece, publicly called him to his face 'a shit in a silk stocking'? Whereafter his Foreign Minister had limped out, murmuring not quite sotto voce to someone near the door: 'What a pity so great a man should have been so badly brought up!'

Chapter 9: Changing Sides at Lons-le-Saulnier

1. After an interview with Bonaparte in 1800, Bourmont ('the traitor of Waterloo')

had been arrested at Fouché's orders on the very steps of the Tuileries for his involvement in the Infernal Machine plot, been imprisoned in the Besançon fortress, but escaped with the aid of his Chouan friends. But in 1808, having a large family to support, he'd rallied to the Empire, and thereafter been paid handsomely by Fouché to spy on aristocratic salons in the Faubourg St Germain.

2. Apart, that is, from the not inconsiderable one of capturing Le Mans from 'the Blues' – but even then his colleagues had suspected him of treason to the Vendean cause.

3. The same dearth that had caused the War Ministry to peremptorily order Montholon, another drawing-room general, to the front, where he'd promptly stolen his brigade's funds.

4. It's typical that Stendhal should describe his hero in *Le Rouge et le Noire* as coming from this part of France.

5. From there it had rolled on across Europe like a seismic shock wave. Reaching, for instance, Saxe-Coburg – whose 'little contingent' to the Grand Army, though twice annihilated (once in Spain in 1810 'and again in 1812 near Vilna'), had 'had to march out again' in 1813 – two days later, it had terrified the kindly Duchess Augusta*, who writes in her diary: 'What startling news today's newspapers contain! Napoleon has escaped from Elba! It's inconceivable that such a dangerous man shouldn't have been more carefully guarded.'

6. Rieu's adventures in 1813–14 are as vivid as any. Originally enrolled in the French naval artillery, in 1813 Rieu, like many other naval men, had been detailed off to join the army in Germany, where he'd received a Prussian hussar's sabre cut over his right eye at Leipzig, the same blow severing his right thumb and part of his forefinger. Taken prisoner at Leipzig, still covered in blood but having lost – apart from his thumb – only his shako, Rieu had been marched with some sixty other offi-

cers, 'twelve from my regiment', via Berlin – where a kindly émigré lady of his acquaintance, a Mme. de Tremblay de Ribaupierre, had at least been able to notify his family that he was still alive; and, amidst the insults of the population, where they'd had to ignominiously beg arrogant Prussian officers for '*noch ein wenig Brod*' (which was usually refused), and on one occasion see his own no less arrogant major have his backside publicly kicked – northwards 'about 1,270 leagues' (3,000 miles) into the interior of Russia, 'the country where the cold had devoured a French army' but where the Tsar at least had 'generously ordered each prisoner to be given a grant of sixty francs to buy warm clothing and thereafter a daily wage of about five French *sous* to get food'. This grant had enabled Rieu at last to delouse himself. For six weeks his convoy of officers, 'escorted by a Russian officer and three Bashkir cossacks [*sic*] a decent lot for whom we only had praise' and who, among other things, 'provided us with sleighs and where necessary protected us from the population's insults, which fortunately were rare,' had been billeted on Jews at Witebsk where they'd enjoyed sauna baths, all in the same extreme cold that, following on the summer's extreme heats, had a year ago destroyed the Grand Army. A day's march from Smolensk – where he'd seen 'an immense park of vehicles, caissons, wagons and gun carriages abandoned during the retreat and which covered a vast square and reading the names of generals and army corps etc they'd belonged to and still on these vehicles, and seemed to have strayed into another world' – he and another merry lieutenant from his own regiment had been put up and invited to supper by a local grandee, who'd told them Geneva had been occupied by the Austrians – 'news that didn't give me the least pleasure. The idea of my country being set free simply didn't occur to me, so deeply had I identified myself with the French name.' Passing on through Doroghobuí, Viazma and Mojaisk, they'd crossed the Borodino battlefield ('still indicated by half-destroyed redoubts and a small debris of weapons') where their initiated guide had been 'an infantry captain whose singular fate it had been to have been present safe and sound at the battle and during the retreat of 1812, only to come and get captured at Leipzig, and his footsteps begin the long journey all over again.' On 1 May 1814, outside burnt-down Moscow, they'd seen 'the innumerable domes of the great city' before passing through it in carts, escorted to protect them from the populace, and through the Kremlin 'which the French bulletins had blown up, but was still in reasonably good health.' Swiftly though they'd passed through, he'll 'never forget the impression made on me by those Moscow streets lined by charred ruins, amidst which some beautiful buildings, rebuilt or saved from the fire, stood out like oases. It seemed to us we could see them still populated by the shades of that beautiful French army which the cold had petrified.' Thinking their journey can only end in Siberia, it had gone on eastwards in stifling summer heats and on their carts' squealing unlubricated wooden axles, until they'd found no more signs of war, and their daily allowance more than adequate to feed them and repair their footwear. Though it was here, beyond Moscow, the peasantry had been most insulting and scornfully told the 'French dogs' that Paris had fallen, they'd finally stopped at Simbirsk, on the Volga, about 160 leagues east of Moscow, where they'd met up with other French prisoners taken during the 1812 campaign 'a sign we'd be going no further.' In mid-July they'd been allowed to undertake the long trek back to France. Joined by some officer prisoners and rankers from the Great Retreat, the very same Bashkirs and the officer who'd brought them to the Volga had escorted them to Bialistock, on the Polish frontier, a journey that had taken fifty days. There, in early September 1814, they'd found a political split between 'royalists' who rejoiced in the newly restored régime and others 'who couldn't get rid of the idea of Napoleon's invincibility and, refusing to believe he'd abdicated, called themselves Bonapartists. If the journey had been longer I believe we'd have been at fisticuffs.' For twenty mortal days they'd had to hang about waiting for their papers; then 'we left, joyous and as light-headed as a bird that's got

out of its cage.' Only back in Paris 'when they saw French troops wearing the white cockade and the Order of the Lily in officers' buttonholes' had 'our incredulous Bonapartists' at last been convinced Napoleon really had abdicated. 'What changes in our absence! Our amazement equalled that of sleepers in fairytales who wake up after centuries.' On foot and penniless in Paris, Rieu had been delighted to find letters and money waiting for him from his well-to-do family in Geneva. Though most foreign military men were being sent back to their own countries, thanks to her intimacy with the wealthy de Noailles family Mme. de Tremblay had got him invited to dinner: 'When it came to the dessert the Duke, with a solemnity that almost set my heart thumping, took me into his study. Signing a diploma of the Order of the Lily, of which he had a pile of blanks, he apposed my name to one, adding to it the Lily itself in silver, dangling from a white ribbon. The good duke thought he was giving me the height of happiness and I, suppressing a grimace, politely offered him my thanks. Officers of the old army were regarding it more as a mark of humiliation than of honour.' More importantly, Rieu had been allowed to keep his position in the naval artillery, on three-quarters pay, while being free to spend half his time in Switzerland. Ecstatically reunited with his family in Geneva, he'd found the memory of the Napoleonic occupation utterly detested there, and everyone talking their heads off – 'as a first contribution to restoring Swiss liberties'.

7. Louis XVIII's re-establishment of *Les Cent Suisses*, massacred because of his brother's feebleness during the Revolution, had also contributed to the army's discontent. Already, on his way to Paris in 1814, Levavasseur tells us the King had been escorted by 'some Swiss troops in the French service he'd fallen in with en route' under their colonel and at Ney's orders. At a dinner given at St Ouen on 3 May 'we were at table when an officer of the Guard came and complained that all the posts of honour, notably at the doors of the dining room, were occupied by Swiss, whilst our

brave grenadiers were complaining that they'd been fobbed off with the entrance gates and the courtyards. The marshal shared this discontent. In a loud voice he ordered me to see to it the service was shared between the Swiss and the Guard. I instantly carried out this order by placing one of our old *grognards* opposite a little Swiss infantryman. The Guard wasn't less discontented to see itself placed on the same level as such pitiable troops.'

8. Rilliet had hardly left school in 1810 when, 'by taste or caprice', he'd applied to Napoleon's Geneva prefect for a place in the socially prestigious Saint-Germain cavalry school. All his time there he'd only had one free day, but, as a special privilege, had lunched with ex-Empress Josephine at nearby Malmaison. Given his commission, he'd been sent to Metz to join the 1st Cuirassiers. 'Of the handsome regiment of 1,000 men who'd gone to Russia and its stragglers in Germany they, with great difficulty, had made up one feeble company.' Veterans had told them of their monstrous experiences in Russia – one had been captured and stripped by Cossacks near the Niemen but been cared for by an NCO who'd fled with him into the forests 'still without clothes for several days, trying to get to the Niemen, which they'd succeeded in crossing, and with another man, each of us only covered by a blanket' had got to Koenigsberg. Sent forward in charge of a party of twenty recruits into Germany where he'd found his lack of German a liability (no foreign languages were being taught at Saint Germain), Rilliet had written naively to his mother: 'From this moment we're lodged, both ourselves and our servants, at the inhabitants' expense, which makes life cheaper.' For him, yes. But not for their hosts! 'In a friendly country allied to France I was billeted on a townsman, and while I drank wine and ate meat, the poor man, at the same table together with his whole family, drank water and ate potatoes. He was having to work to nourish us.' Even so, war had so far 'seemed to us a pleasurable outing.' At Fulda they'd had news of the battle of Lützen and keenly regretted not having been in time to take part in it. Near Jena

they'd passed over the battlefield, with veteran officers as guides who'd taken part in the battle; and so on to Dresden across a ruined countryside where they'd nonetheless been amiably received by the locals, and entered the capital of Saxony just as Napoleon had been leaving for the battle of Bautzen. 'The King had just returned and so had its inhabitants, who'd fled from the Russians, now in retreat. The capital's animated air contrasted with the countryside's profound desolation; in whole villages there wasn't one piece of bread.' And so on into Silesia, where, after endless marches and countermarches of the 1st Cuirassiers, under General Saint Germain and Ney, Rilliet's troop ('though that's no business of heavy cavalry') had formed the extreme rearguard. Then they too had fought at Leipzig, and afterwards cut their way through Wrede's* Bavarians as they'd tried to intercept the French army's retreat to the Rhine. Finally the 1st Cuirassiers, after taking part in the evacuation of the Netherlands, had been dissolved into the Cuirassiers of Louis XVIII's Royal Guard. Rilliet, still only twenty-one, had applied for leave to return to Geneva to 'tend his wounds and repair the fatigues of war'.

9. Anyone hoping to visit this historic site will be disappointed. After various vicissitudes the building has been turned into an American-style hamburger bar.

10. Who'll afterwards claim to have kept a suspicious eye on Ney ever since his arrival at Besançon.

11. Bringing in foreign troops to quell a rebellious populace had been regarded by the Ancien Régime as perfectly normal. At Toulouse, a fortnight later, Vitrolles, raising the royalist standard there, would regard it as the most natural thing in the world to send for Spanish troops to support it. An idea that was anathema to the post-revolutionary mind, with its cult of patriotism. No man with a heart in his breast (*homme de coeur*) would do such a thing.

12. In remotest Siberia. In 1812 the Tsar had threatened to withdraw to Kamchatka

rather than give up the fight. To Europeans Kamchatka meant 'the end of the world'.

13. But at his trial he would loyally refuse to give their names.

14. At Ney's trial for high treason, Bourmont (quite unnecessarily, since he himself was by then in high favour with the King) did everything he could to incriminate him.

15. When held in isolation and interrogated prior to his trial.

16. Ney's defence at his trial would be that his action had been unpremeditated. Which it certainly was. 'I lost my head.' Louis XVIII would declare he was sure of it; yet find it politically impossible, as Wellington did, to save Ney from the firing squad.

17. See *The March* and *The Retreat*, indexes.

18. At his trial in December.

19. Literally 'crayfish'. 'Crabs' would perhaps be the better translation, since crabs have the reputation of scuttling backwards.

20. At the Second Restoration young Larraguy, thanks to his commitment to the military life but also, one feels, to his family connections, would be accepted for the Royal Guard. One wonders just how idealised this last comment is in the inflamed situation? Gindre de Mancy says Grivel's shout was 'lost amidst all the others'. But adds that after Louis XVIII's second restoration Grivel would *three times* write to that endemically ungrateful monarch asking 'as the only grace, a new sword to replace the one I broke in his service.' No reply was ever received. Probably Louis simply didn't like to be reminded of the painful occasion.

21. Dubalen would command his regiment at the Battle of Wavre.

22. Levavasseur sums up his convictions about what had happened: 'It has been

vainly maintained that the marshal was swept off his feet by the influence [*entrainement*] inspired in him by the Emperor. The only thing that determined him was the sympathy for the Emperor's cause which he thought he saw in the country. The language of the two prisoners brought in by the Marquis de Grivel had made a hundred times more impression on Ney than all the imperial proclamations. In these two men he thought he saw the true voice of the country ... and was also swayed by the silence kept by Bourmont, Lecourbe, Mermet and Jarry when he'd consulted them on the proclamation. Finally, Napoleon inspired in him less affection than fear ... If Ney, that day, had calculated, he'd have ceased to be himself.'

23. Afterwards Levavasseur would hear the order hadn't been carried out and that when an officer had reached Besançon to warn the persons concerned he'd found the town gates closed against him.

24. Words that would be used against him at his trial. 'In this way the poor marshal still further aggravated his wrongdoings,' writes Mancy, 'making it seem that what we like to believe were the effects of his being carried away, so to speak, irresistibly by the circumstances were premeditated.'

25. 'Invited to dine at the Elysée by the Emperor, a better judge of his conduct, he would afterwards command [one division of] the heavy cavalry at Ligny.'

26. Clouet had been captured by a Prussian colonel at the battle of Dennewitz (1813), where Ney had been resoundingly defeated by von Bülow's Prussians, under Bernadotte.

27. Ney, himself so one-dimensional, seems to have had a knack of collecting double-bottomed subordinates – *eg* Bourmont, who, with Clouet, would go over to the enemy on the eve of Ligny; and Jomini, who'd done so in 1813.

28. After doing a flit en route for the regimental depôt, such 'replacers', loth to do military service themselves, would often

return to make a new deal with some other bourgeois family. It had become a profession in itself.

Chapter 10: Paris Talks, the Old Guard Marches

1. As Frénilly sarcastically puts it: 'In one night he'd been brought to bed of a Charter.' The theoretical distinction between the King having 'granted' his Charter instead of accepting it from the Senate as the nation's inherent right, had been an important arguing point throughout the First Restoration. As anyone who's ever had to deal with a French delegate knows, the French mind can't help splitting theoretical hairs in purely pragmatic situations, sometimes paralysing them.

2. Antibes was promised a monument for its staunchness both against Bonaparte on 1 March and for refusing to allow a British naval contingent entrance 'in the name of the Allies' on the 8th (see chapter 1, note 47). In the autumn it would similarly stand up against invading Austrians. Anyone wishing to gauge the exact size of Bourbon gratitude for such staunchness can contemplate the miserable little pillar standing in the main square.

3. Which is what he'd in fact do – unavailingly – in 1830, when the Bourbons were finally thrown out.

4. Such as was left of it. In 1814 the entire French navy had been handed over to Britain under the terms of the peace treaty, except for one ship of the line, three frigates, and a number of smaller vessels.

5. Lainé, the rather unimaginative leader of the Liberal opposition, had led the protest against Napoleon's policies in 1814.

6. Juliette, taking refuge in numbers and having no intention of letting Constant into her bed, was simultaneously seeing M. Forbin. Forbin, an artist appointed by Louis to succeed Denon at the Louvre, was to go on a tour of Europe to collect articles for the King.

7. 'He,' Rilliet remarks with justifiable sarcasm, 'who a couple of months later would be commanding the Imperial Guard' – but would opt out because of an attack of gout on the eve of Waterloo.

8. Or anyway *ex post facto* will think he did. His famous *Mémoires de l'Outre-tombe*, which have to be studied for their style by every French schoolchild, are in reality a rhetorical hotch-potch written in the kind of inflated prose afterwards beloved by de Gaulle. These show Chateaubriand to be about the most unreliable historian one can imagine. Where he hasn't simply pinched his facts second-hand he indulges in unacknowledged hindsight.

9. *Charles Nodier*, in 1813, adds that this 'peculiar fixity had something redoubtable about it that sometimes still makes me shiver.'

10. In exile at Ghent Artois would 'invariably speak well of M. Fouché'.

11. In Paris, Napoleon, in a joking moment when Louis XVIII's ministers were discussed, would quip that Fouché was the King's 'Police Minister *in partibus*'.

12. All according to himself. Fouché's memoirs, written in exile at Trieste, were long held to be inauthentic. But experts, beginning with Frédéric Masson, have reversed that judgement, at least in part.

13. Actually he hadn't. As we've seen, he'd regarded Napoleon as *un personnage usé*, and foreseen anything except his making a comeback.

14. Mlle. Cochelet had been reader to Josephine and was now governess to Hortense's boys. She would leave vivid, if not wholly reliable, memoirs.

15. Bourrienne had appropriated 3.5 million francs from seized British goods, and greased his superior Talleyrand's palm with a third of the amount.

16. According to Frédéric Masson.

17. But Fouché's conclusion is probably true: 'This impromptu circumstance finally dissolved the mistrust that party had for me, and the very ones who until then had seen me as virtually a partisan of the Bourbons thereafter saw in me an enemy they'd proscribed.'

18. On 14 March. He'd just written to Clarke, Minister of War since Soult's resignation two days ago: 'I don't know what to think about the troops' morale. Tomorrow the Grenadiers will get going. I hope they'll be wise.' But next day: 'Not only won't the troops fight, they'll reinforce the enemy corps as soon as they meet it.' From Strasbourg Suchet wrote: 'I'm suspending the troops departure. Their morale can only make me think they'll defect.'

19. See *The Retreat*, pp.178, 179. Admittedly few of the men who'd marched through the clouds of Cossacks after Krasnoïe were still alive. But the grossly depleted ranks of the 1st and 2nd Grenadiers had, of course, been filled up with Line veterans for the 1813–14 campaigns. Digby Smith is of the opinion that it's impossible to know the number of Guard survivors from Russia still present in its ranks in 1815, but points out that of the 400–600 officers and other ranks who'd got back, many must have succumbed in Germany. The Grenadiers' and Chasseurs' composition in 1815 is perhaps relevant to the fiasco of the last fatal charge at Waterloo.

20. 'This scene will never efface itself from my memory,' the Duchess of Reggio goes on. 'It still makes me shiver, and yet under my pen I find it very far from the reality.'

21. 'It would be precisely these officers,' Sergeant Mauduit adds, 'whom we'd hear declaiming with the same fury against Napoleon on the morrow of the Waterloo disaster.'

22. British and American readers, sea-girt as they are, can hardly grasp the importance of France's fortresses in those days. These brilliant achievements of the great Vauban (1633–1707) guaranteed Europe's richest country against invasion; and the crucial political goal of France having 'natural' frontiers – the Alps, the Pyrenees and the Rhine – must also be understood in the same terms. Since most of Napoleon's campaigns had until 1814 been fought out on enemy territory, the fortresses' upkeep had been somewhat neglected. Lieutenant Beulay, returning from Russia, had been shocked to note how those at Lille were crumbling away. But Metz was an exception, and its elaborate fortifications – as Eugénie Oudinot had noticed in 1812 – were quite extraordinarily strong.

23. On St Helena Napoleon would observe, rightly, that Oudinot let himself be carried away by his wife's royalist sentiments.

Chapter 11: An Icy Reception

1. Or so it would be claimed at Ney's trial.

2. A popularity, Carnot will observe, he owed mainly to the Bourbons' catastrophic errors and to the pretensions of returned émigrés. Jean Tulard shrewdly points out that most of the peasants who were following him for any distance must have been day-labourers, since they seem to have had no difficulty leaving the farms.

3. Not quite obedient to his dead master's will, which stipulated that he marry 'the daughter or widow of an officer of my Guard', Louis Marchand, back from St Helena, would marry Brayer's daughter. If Napoleon didn't make his acquaintance until Lyons it was probably because Brayer had not been a general of the Guard.

4. Napoleon to Gourgaud at St Helena.

5. He who as a captain in the 7th Light Infantry had fought so intrepidly under the walls of Smolensk. See *The March*, p.193.

6. He adds: 'The 14th.' But though extremely vivid, Coignet's memoirs aren't always to be relied on in matters of detail. Four days earlier it had passed through from Orléans,

but halted at Avallon, where its Colonel Bugeaud had notified Soult of his men's disaffection and refusal to go further.

7. See *The Retreat*, p.417 *et seq.*

8. According to Louis Marchand, who may or may not have been present, 'the Emperor reproached the curé of the cathedral who from his high pulpit had been preaching fidelity to the established government, organising resistance to the Emperor's army, for stirring up civil war in the name of a God of peace and mercy, and told him he shouldn't meddle in other than spiritual matters, quoting several passages of Holy Writ, to which the curé neither replied nor should have.'

9. In fact this would be Napoleon's policy throughout the Hundred Days, in striking contrast to the Bourbons' vengeful attitude toward him.

10. By chance the present writer did the same. A narrow passage and stair leads to the first floor.

11. All researchers, latterly Kauffmann in his remarkable *The Dark Room at Longwood* (1998), note Ali's extraordinary memory and photographic eye for detail. Himself, Ali would afterwards often regret he hadn't kept a diary. Instead he checked over all the others known to him, and left his own account to Marchand, who'd retire here at Auxerre, not far from his friend and former colleague Ali, who after his return from St Helena would settle down at Sens.

12. Probably one of Napoleon's fibs at St Helena.

13. How could Fleury have known this? Of course it's possible he'd afterwards hear it from Bertrand at the Tuileries where Fleury, according to Napoleon, was altogether too fond of chatting and gossiping instead of getting on with his work in the office.

14. Thus Ney himself, at his trial.

15. At Tours a public subscription had been opened to reward anyone who killed the Usurper.

16. See *The March*, p.102.

17. Probably this last is a touch of local colour, added by Coignet *ex post facto*. During the Revolution it had been said that there was only man in the royal family, and that was Marie-Antoinette. Napoleon would transfer the compliment to her daughter after she'd tried to raise resistance against him at Bordeaux.

18. Maubreuil was a Chouan who in 1814 had waylaid Hortense's coach and robbed it of its diamonds etc.

19. Once again, Napoleon would scribble denials in the margin of Fleury's book, saying Girard should certainly have fired back if fired on. But Fleury quotes his letter. Girard would be mortally wounded at Ligny.

20. The old seven-span bridge over the Yonne, which at this point describes a broad curve to the left, would be dynamited to hold up the German advance in 1940. Only half an arch remains overshadowing an idyllic little park on the town side, a silent witness to that old tragedy.

21. He writes '26 March'. But Larreguy's vivid memories of the Yonne disaster have telescoped with his no less vivid ones of the Tuileries parade of that date.

22. For this and a few other details I'm indebted to Claude Manceron's deeply researched *Napoleon Recaptures Paris* (1968). The vase, he hears, has become a keepsake of her descendants. What happened to its contents he doesn't enquire, or anyway doesn't say.

23. See *The Retreat*, p.177 *et seq.*

Chapter 12: Hasty Departures

1. After fleeing from the Tuileries when it was stormed by the mob on 10 August 1792, and only surviving by throwing him-

self into the Seine, Hüe had faithfully reported back for duty and for several ghastly weeks had been the royal family's sole servant in the Temple Prison. Replaced by Cléry, he'd witnessed at close quarters the September Massacres, escaped by a miracle, been thrice imprisoned, and when the sole survivor, the future Duchess of Angoulême (then only a girl) had been kept in solitary confinement except for being allowed to walk in the Temple garden, he, at his own not inconsiderable expense, had rented an apartment overlooking it, and, to console her, had hired singers to perform specially composed songs she could hear from his open window. When she'd been exchanged for several leading republicans, among them Maret, Hüe had obtained special permission to follow her to Vienna; thereafter to Mittau in Lithuania, where he'd entered Louis XVIII's service, and then to Warsaw and to Hartwell. Though today not so famous as his fellow-valet Cléry's account (recently reprinted), Hüe's published account of the royal family's sufferings had been widely read all over Europe.

2. Hüe has left us a list of them: 'Necklaces, earrings, belts, diadems, crowns, headdresses, clasps,' etc; 4,769 diamonds, many of them very large, among others The Regent; 1,770 precious stones and pearls, 54 sapphires, 211 turquoises, 236 rubies, 234 amethysts, and 'innumerable little diamonds uncounted in the ornaments, plus 105 diamond clusters arranged like ears of corn, 12 diamond palms and unmounted precious stones, gold plaques, crosses, decorations, etc, packets of unmounted diamonds and precious stones, the ones valued at 175,089 francs 21 centimes, and the others at 39,302 francs.'

3. Narbonne himself had died of typhus in 1813 besieged in Torgau, where he'd voluntarily taken command. An admiring Brun de Villeret gives a moving account of his last moments.

4. Clearly Villemain's rehearsal of Fontanes' long speech is composed with a lot of hindsight. How could he know at 7:00

am that Napoleon would arrive in a *calèche* at the Tuileries wicket that evening? Or that, in fact, Constant would be called to the Tuileries to draft an addition to the imperial constitution, and be delighted to do so? But no doubt the gist of his account is correct.

5. Alas, *la Visconti* would get no further than Saint-Denis before some unspecified affliction struck her down and obliged her to return to Paris – minus her jewellery.

6. It would be Rochechouart who, as governor of Paris, would have to make the arrangements for Ney's execution in December.

7. As yet the Champs-Elysées were not a street, but still half-park, half-countryside.

8. This aspect of the matter is stressed by Claude Manaron in his *Napoleon Recaptures Paris* (1968). It would not be until the reaction after 1830 that the Paris proletariat would again rebel, with the bloodiest results, as described by Georges Sand.

9. '…whose calm and impartial [*sic*] attitude,' Rieu adds, 'would save Paris from great disorders during the Hundred Days.'

10. As temporary Minister of the Interior the resourceful Beugnot had dealt with a knotty question of nomenclature by decreeing that all squares and streets should resume their pre-Revolutionary names. Place Louis XV had been renamed Place de la Concorde by the Directory in a pious hope of an end to civil discord.

11. Saint-Chamans swears he hasn't changed one word of 'this odd conversation'. He'd have all the difficulty in the world afterwards to convince the restored authorities he hadn't gone over to Bonaparte.

12. Allowing for many pockets of Bonapartist and anti-royalist sympathies, *eg* in the towns of Brittany and Normandy, one can get a rough picture of France's division in 1815 by drawing a diagonal line from the

Channel ports to Antibes. To the west of that line the majority was royalist.

13. Planat is certainly a most reliable witness. If a hero is someone who sticks to his principles through thick and thin, then the handsome Flahaut, who may have been an excellent officer in the field, is very definitely not one of 1815's heroes, except in a purely battlefield sense. Otherwise he seems to have inherited his father Talleyrand's total faithlessness. Grossly unfaithful to Hortense, who adored him, he would even (according to Planat) be in a hurry to quit Napoleon after Waterloo. Stricken off Fouché's proscription list thanks to Talleyrand's intervention, he'd afterwards go over to England, be lionised by Piccadilly drawing rooms, and finally, completely deserting Hortense, marry into the English aristocracy.

14. 'In this way,' Planat concludes, 'Évain was in fact retained in his position and didn't even leave it after the Second Restoration.'

15. Houssaye writes melodramatically: 'It seemed that the beheaded spectre of Louis XVI was coming down the steps of the Tuileries with his brother' – the brother who'd done absolutely nothing to save him.

16. It probably would have, if *Radet*, a native of Varennes who afterwards became head of Napoleon's military police, hadn't barricaded the bridge to prevent the huge berline from crossing it and thus reaching Bouillé's hussars and the Belgian border. He would also play a part in 1815.

17. The Arc de Triomphe had been temporarily finished off in wood for Napoleon to drive under it with Marie-Louise in 1810. But last year Allied troops bivouacked in the Champs Elysées had chopped up its façades' elaborate sculptures for firewood. By 1814 its four pylons had risen to a height of 19.54 m, the base of its Roman arches that were to support the uppermost section. It was flanked by two customs buildings, with classical columns, later demolished. For an interesting history of the Arc de Triomphe, see Georges Poisson's article in *Revue du Souvenir Napoléonien*, December 2000–January 2001.

Chapter 13: 'It Seemed he'd Just Come Back from a Journey'

1. Since Marchand says 'up' it was evidently not the private apartments, just behind the horseshoe-shaped staircases, which until 1810 he'd shared with Josephine. He had then sent an order from Vienna to wall up the door between them: a rather brutal way, one can't help thinking, of forewarning her of divorce.

2. '*Aussitôt son arrivée*' can hardly be taken literally, since he'd hardly go (*parcourir*) through the gardens in the small hours!

3. Always under pressure of business, he'd probably never noticed all this before – no more than he had ever noticed the extraordinary fittings of his carriage ('I never had time'), captured at Waterloo, of which on St Helena he would read a detailed description (in an English newspaper) after Blücher had given it to Wellington and it had been put on display in London.

4. And – though Fleury certainly doesn't know about it – attempted suicide.

5. They would bring him to within an inch of the guillotine, from which he'd only make a sensational escape thanks to the resourcefulness of his wife (see chapter 3, note 8). Though he'd been Bonaparte's ADC in 1796 and could claim the firing squad, the returning Ultras would insist, to Lavalette's horror, that he be guillotined in the Place de Grève as an example.

6. Ferrand would be a witness against him at his trial.

7. Summoned to the Tuileries to explain his part in the Maret affair, Napoleon, 'seeing me in the distance, came up to me with looks that went straight through my head.' And Cambacérès had got such a ticking off as he'd never forget, for ordering the conspirator Malet's* execution

without waiting for his orders: 'Have you forgotten that the brightest jewel in my crown is the right to pardon? I don't know why I'm not severely punishing you.'

8. The document would be adduced against Lavalette at his trial as proving he'd treasonably seized the Post Office. Ferrand would declare that in entering the Post Office Lavalette had announced: 'In the Emperor's name I take possession of the postal administration.' Lavalette's own account seems more in line with his character.

9. A constitutional monarchist at heart, Molé is still only thirty-four. Napoleon's attention had first been drawn to him by his book, written in his twenties, recommending a system of government based on his view of human nature. Refusing an immediate post, he'd afterwards been promoted to ministerial rank. Molé's health seems to have been shattered when hiding during the Terror. His father, an eminent civil servant of the Ancien Régime, had been guillotined despite his faithful servant's last-minute appeal to Fouquier-Tinville just as he'd been getting into the fatal tumbril. Molé himself was a constitutional monarchist, but opposed to 'English' ideas.

10. Fouché would use the same ploy again in July, to control Louis XVIII's return. Astute and adept as he was, he too is middle-aged; has only certain manoeuvres in his repertoire.

11. 'And since that moment I've never seen either of them again,' Saint-Chamans concludes. From the extreme circumstantiality of his account we understand that Saint-Chamans, even in 1831, was still defending himself against suggestions that he'd gone over to Napoleon during the Hundred Days.

12. Saint-Chamans would remember all this as happening long before dawn and that it had still been 'pitch dark', except for the 'candles gleaming out from every window'. But this is impossible. We know from all our other eyewitnesses that Napoleon

didn't leave Fontainebleau until midday. Such errors are cautionary.

13. This is the only reference to Montholon – today gravely indicted by the Swedish researcher Sten Forshuvud and his apostle Ben Wieder of being Napoleon's assassin – I've been able to find during the Hundred Days. Frédéric Masson too, in his scathing account of his character and career, says that though he makes a brief appearance here on the Fontainebleau road, neither can he find any account of what that slippery playboy was up to during the Hundred Days.

14. Last year a royalist crowd had, of course, pulled down Napoleon's statue from it.

15. 'Which,' Routier adds indignantly, 'we'd be shamefully accused (after the Hundred Days) of having pillaged!'

16. Next day they would present it all to Napoleon, who gave each of them that didn't already have it the cross of the Legion of Honour, and the cross of the Reunion to those who did.

17. 'We shall see anon,' writes Routier, 'what this list, found at the War Ministry, would be worth to me after our disasters!'

18. At the Tuileries Napoleon would at first not even receive him, causing Gourgaud to shut himself up in one of the attics, threatening to commit suicide if he didn't. After a few days he'd be taken back into favour. For Gourgaud's hyper-emotional nature, see also *The Retreat*, pp. 354–5. It's possible Planat, writing his memoirs, would bear some kind of a grudge against him for – at the last moment, once again by hysterical tantrums – ousting him from going to St Helena. Napoleon had first chosen Planat, as much the more intellectual companion. It's even possible he, if he'd been at Longwood House, might have seen through Montholon's murderous designs (as elucidated by Sten Forshuvud and Ben Wieder). But Gourgaud's wildly possessive and jealous behaviour ('After all,' Napoleon would say, 'I couldn't go to bed with

him!') would eventually become utterly unbearable, so that in the end he'd leave in a hurry, and betray the real state of affairs at Longwood to Hudson Lowe and to Lord Balfour, in London, causing Hudson Lowe to still further tighten up his restrictions. It would only be afterwards, in Belgium, he'd revert to the role of Napoleonic hero.

19. Where on the eve of the fall of Paris last year Serrurier* had burnt 1,600 captured enemy standards, to prevent them being retaken. And whence, that same summer, the retiring army would remove at least part of the great collection of models of France's fortresses' plans. Mercer would write of the Prussians packing them up. They have recently (1999) been reopened to the public.

20. Closely comparing various accounts of the same event, it's interesting to see a) their different tones and mnemonic interpretations, and b) the odd gaps that arise. Obviously Routier's otherwise very detailed memory of the events of that, for him, ever-memorable day, censors the equally truthful and detailed Saint-Chamans' cavalry escort, even though it consisted of a whole regiment, 500 men!

21. Saint-Chamans says at 10:00 pm.

22. Certainly a grossly subjective overestimate. Modern analysis shows that there can't have been anything like this many.

BIBLIOGRAPHY

Abrantès, Laure June duchesse d'. *Mémoires de la Duchesse d'Abrantès. Intro-duction et notes d'A. Ollivier*. Paris, 1958. See also Chantemesse.

Ali (see Saint-Denis).

Angoulême, Marie-Thérèse-Charlotte, duchesse d'. 'Souvenirs de 1815. Manuscrit inédit de la duchesse d'Angoulême publié par François Laur-entie' in *Le Correspondant*, August 1913, pp.650–82.

Bainvel, Pierre-Marie. *Épisode de 1815. Souvenirs d'un écolier en 1815, ou Vingt ans après*. Paris, 1846; also 1874.

Barras, Paul-Jean-François-Nicolas, vicomte de. *Mémoires de Barras, membre du Directoire*, 4 vols. Paris, 1895–6.

Bary, G.A.R. *Cahiers d'un rhétoricien de 1815*. Paris, 1890.

Belliard, Augustin-Daniel. *Mémoires du comte Belliard, lieutenant-général, pair de France, écrits par lui-même, receuillis et mis en ordre par M. Vinet, l'un de ses aides-de-camp*, 3 vols. Paris, 1842.

Bernardy, Françoise de. *Son of Talleyrand*. London, 1956.

Beugnot, Jacques-Claude. *Mémoires du comte Beugnot, ancien ministre (1783–1815), publiés par le comte Albert Beugnot, son petit-fils*, 2 vols. Paris, 1866; also 1959.

Beulay, Honoré de. *Mémoires d'un grenadier de la Grande Armée (18 avril 1808–18 octobre 1815). Préface du commandant Driant*. Paris, 1907.

Boigne, Mme. de. *Récits d'une Tante*. Paris, 1908.

Bonaparte, Napoléon. *Correspondance de Napoléon 1er, publiée par ordre de l'Empereur Napoléon III*, 24 vols. Paris, 1868.

Bourienne, Louis-Antoine Fauvelet de. *Bonaparte intime. Préface et notes de B. Melchior-Bonnet*. Paris, 1960; and three earlier editions, entitled *Mémoires de. . .*, 1829, 1899–1900 (5 vols) and nd (3 vols).

Bro, Louis. *Mémoires du général Bro 1796–1844, publiés par son petit-fils le Baron Henry Bro de Comères*. Paris, 1914.

Brun de Villeret, Louis. *Les cahiers du général Brun, baron de Villeret, pair de France, publiés et présentés par Louis de Saont-Pierre*. Paris, 1953.

Burney, Fanny. *Letters and Journals*. Oxford, 1972.

Carnot, Lazare. *Mémoires sur Carnot, par son fils*, 2 vols. Paris, 1861–3; also 1893 and 1907.

Castellane, Victor-Elisabeth Boniface, comte de. *Journal du maréchal de Cas-tellane 1804–1862*, 5 vols. Paris, 1895–7.

Castelot, André. *Napoléon et les Femmes*. Paris, 1998.

Chaboulon, Fleury de. *Mémoires, avec annotations manuscrites de Napoléon 1er, publiés par Lucien Cornet*. Paris, 1901.

Chantemesse M. *Le roman inconnu de la duchesse d'Abrantès.* Paris, 1927.

Chastenay-Lantry, L-M-V. *The Notebooks of Captain Coignet.* London, 1986.

Chevalier, Jean-Michel. *Souvenirs des guerres napoléoniennes, publiés d'après le manuscrit original par Jean Mistler et Hélène Michaud.* Paris, 1970.

Cochelet. *Mémoires sur la Reine Hortense et la famille impérialé.* Paris, 1837.

Coignet, Capitaine Jean-Roch. *Cahiers.* Paris, 1883.

Constant, Benjamin. *Journaux intimes, edition intégrale.* Paris, 1952.

— *Mémoires sue les Cent Jours.* Paris, 1961.

Cuneo d'Ornano. *Napoléon au Golfe Juan, par M. le chevalier Cunéo d'Ornano.* nd.

Davout, Maréchal Louis-Nicolas, Prince d'Eckmühl. *Correspondance du maréchal Davout, 1801–1815, avec introduction et notes par Ch. de Mazade,* 5 vols. Paris, 1885.

Denniée, P.P. *Itinéraire de l'Empereur Napoléon.* Paris, 1842.

Dhombres, Jean & Nicole. *Lazare Carnot.* Paris, 1997.

Drouet d'Erlon, Jean-Baptiste. *Vie militaire écrite par lui-même.* Paris, 1944.

Dupuy, Victor. *Souvenirs militaires de Victor Dupuy, chef d'escadron de Hussards (1794–1816), publés par le général Thoumas.* Paris, 1892.

Fabry. *Itinéraire de Bonaparte.* 1816.

Fezensac, M. le Duc de. *Souvenirs militaires de 1804 à 1814.* Paris, 1863.

Flahaut, Charles de (see Bernardy, Françoise de).

Fouché, Joseph. *Mémoires de Fouché. Introduction et notes de Louis Madelin.* Paris, 1945.

François, Charles. *Journal du capitaine François (dit le Dromadaire d'Egypte), 1793–1830,* 2 vols. Paris, 1903–4.

Frénilly, François-Auguste-Fauveau de. *Souvenirs du baron de Frénilly, pair de France, publiés avec introduction et notes par Arthur Chuquet.* Paris, 1909.

Gaillard, Maúrice-André. *Un ami de Fouché d'après les mémoires de Gaillard, par le baron Despatys. Préface de Louis Madelin.* Paris, 1911.

Gobineau, Louis. *Mémoires due comte Louis de Gobineau. Èdition critique par Jean Puraye.* Brussels, 1955.

Gourgaud, Gaspard. *Journal de Saint-Hélène, 1815–1818. Edition augmentée d'après le manuscrit original. Préface et notes d'Octave Aubry.* Paris, 1947.

Griois, Lubin. *Mémoires du général Griois, 1792–1822,* 2 vols. Paris, 1909.

Guiraud, Baron. 'Journal de ma vie, publié par G. Castel-Cagarriga', in *Revue des Deux Mondes,* September 1967, pp.62–86, and March 1968, pp.200–10.

Hayman, Peter. *Soult, Napoleon's Maligned Marshal.* London, 1990.

Henckens, Lieutenant J.L. *Mémoires se rapportant à son service militaire au 6ème Régiment de Chasseurs à cheval francais de février 1803 à août 1816. Publiés par son fils E.F.C. Henckens.* The Hague, 1910.

Hortense de Beauharnais. *Mémoires de la reine Hortense, publié par le prince Napoléon av des notes de Jean Hanoteau,* 3 vols. Paris, 1927.

Hourtolle, E.G. *Ney, le brave des braves*. Paris, nd.

Hüe, François. *Souvenirs du baron Hüe, publiés par le baron de Maricourt*. Paris, 1903.

Jubé, Charles. *Les Cent Jours. Passage de l'Empereur à Grenoble. Journal du colonel de gendarmerie Jubé*, in *Revue Retrospective*, 1895, pp.73–100.

Laborde. *Quarante-huit heures de garde aux Tuileries*. Paris, nd.

Lamartine, Alphonse de. *Mémoires*. Paris, nd.

Larreguy de Civrieux, Silvain. *Souvenirs d'un cadet*. Paris, 1912.

Las Cases, Emmanuel. *Mémorial de Sainte-Helène*, with a preface by Jean Tulard, presentation and notes by Joël Schmidt. Paris, 1968.

Lavalette, Antoine-Marie Chamans, Comte de. *Mémoires et souvenirs du comte de Lavalette, (1769–1830), édition présentée et annotée par Stéphanie Giocanti*. Paris, 1994.

Lefol, Lieutenant-Général Baron Étienne. *Souvenirs sur le Pryntané de Saint-Cyr, 1814–1815*. Versailles, 1854.

Levavasseur, Octave. *Souvenirs militaires d'Octave Levavasseur, officier d'artilleri, aide de camp du maréchal Ney, pubvliés par le commandant Beslay*. Paris, 1914.

Macdonald, Jacques-Etienne-Joseph-Alexandre. *Souvenirs du maréchal Macdonald duc de Tarente. Introduction par Camille Rousset*. Paris, 1892.

MacKenzie, Norman. *The Fall and Flight from Elba, 1814–1815*. London, 1982.

Madelin, Louis. *Histoire du Consulat et de l'Empire*. Paris, 1910.

Manceron, Claude. *Napoleon Recaptures Paris*. English translation, London, 1968.

Mancy, Gindre de. Narrative in *La Sentinelle du Jura*, April 1870.

Marbot, Antoine-Marcelline. *Mémoires du général baron de Marbot*, 3 vols. 26th edition, Paris, 1891.

Marchand, Louis. *Mémoires de Marchand, premier valet de chambre et eécuteur testamentaire de l'Empereur, publiés d'après le manuscrit original par Jean Bourguignon*, 2 vols. Paris, 1952–5.

Maret, Hugues Bernard, duc de Bassano. *Souvenirs intimes de la Révolution et de l'Empire, receuillis et publiés par Mme. Ch. de Sor*, 2 vols. Brussels, 1843.

Marmont, Marshal A.L.F. *Mémoires*, 9 vols. Paris, 1857.

Mauduit, Hippolyte de. *Histoire des derniers jours de la Grande Armée ou souvenirs, documents et correspondance inédite de Napoléon en 1814 et 1815*, 2 vols. Paris, 1847–8.

Molé, Mathieu. *Souvenirs d'un témoin de la Révolution et de l'Empire (1791)*. Geneva, 1943.

Montalivet, Marthe-Camille Bachasson de. *Fragments et souvenirs*. Paris, 1899.

Noailles, Marquis de. *Le Comte Molé (1781–1855). Sa vie, ses mémoires*. Paris, 1922.

Nodier, Charles. *Souvenirs, épisodes et portraits pour servir à l'histoire de la Revolution et de l'Empire, par Charles Nodier*, 2 vols. Paris, 1831.

Noël, Colonel Jean-Nicholas-Auguste. *Souvenirs militaires d'un officier du Premier Empire, 1795–1832.* Paris, 1895.

Norvins, Jacques Marquet de Montbreton de. *Souvenirs d'u historien de Napoléon,* 3 vols. Paris, 1896–7.

Orléans, Louis-Philippe duc d'. *Mon Journal. Evénements de 1815.* Paris, 1849.

Ouvrard, Gabriel-Julien. *Mémoires de G.-J. Ouvrard sur sa vie et ses diverses opérations financières.* Paris, 1826.

Pellizzone, Mme. Jeanne-Julie Moulinneuf. 'Les Cent Jours à Marseille. Journal de Mme. Pellizone, publiés par Félix Tavernier', in *La Provence historique,* 1959, pp.150–81.

Peyrusse, Guillaume-Joseph-Roux. *Mémorial et Archives de M. le baron Peyrusse, trésorier général de la Couronne pendant les Cent-Jours.* Carcassonne, Lajoux, 1869.

Pion des Loches, Antoine-Augustin. *Mes Campagnes (1792–1815). Notes et correspondance du colonel d'artillerie Pion des Loches, mises en ordre et publiées par Maurice Chipon et Léonce Pingaud.* Paris, 1889.

Planat de la Faye, Nicolas Louis. *Vie de Planat de la Faye, aide-de-camp des généraux Lariboisière et Drouot, officier d'ordonnance de Napoléon 1er. Souvenirs, Lettres et Dictés et annotés par sa veuve.* Paris, 1895.

Pons de l'Hérault, André. *Souvenirs et anecdotes de l'Ile de'Elbe, publiés d'arprès le manuscrit original par Léon G. Pelissier.* Paris, 1897.

Randon, Jacques-Louis-Alexandre. *Mémoires du maréchal Randon,* 2 vols. Paris, 1875–7.

Reggio, Duchess of (see Stiegler).

Rieu, Jean-Louis. 'Mémoires de Jean-Louis Rieu', in *Soldats suisses au service étranger.* Geneva, 1910.

Rilliet, Frédéric-Jacques-Louis. 'Journal d'un sous-lieutenant de cuirassiers', in *Soldats suisses au service étranger.* Geneva, 1910

Roch-Godart. *Mémoires du général-baron Roch Godart, 1792–1815, publiés par J.B. Antoine.* Paris, 1895; new edition Flammarion, nd.

Rochechouart, Louis-Victor-Léon, Général Comte de. *Souvenirs sur la Révolution, l'Empire et la Restauration, publiés par son fils.* Paris, 1889.

Roguet, François. *Mémoires militaires du lieutenant-général comte Roguet, colonel en second des grenadiers à pied de la Vieille Garde.* Paris, 1862–5.

Routier, Léon-Michel. *Récits d'un Soldat de la République et de l'Empire (1792–1830), publiés par son fils le colonel Routier.* Paris, 1899.

Rumigny, Marie-Théodore Guilly, comte de. *Souvenirs du général comte de Rumigny, aide de camp du roi Louis-Philippe (1789–1860).* Paris, 1921.

Saint-Chamans, Alfred-Armand-Robert. *Mémoires du général comte de Saint-Chamans, ancien aide-de-camp du maréchal Soult, 1802–1832.* Paris, 1896.

Saint-Denis, Louis-Etienne. *Mameluck Ali, Souvenirs sur l'Empereur Napoléon, présentés et annotés par Christophe Bourachot.* Paris, 2000.

Savary, Anne-Jean-Marie-René, duc de Rovigo. *Mémoires du duc de Rovigo. Edition nouvelle refondue et annotée par Désiré Lacroix.* Paris, 1900.

Schuerman, Albert. *Itinéraire Général de Napoléon 1er.* 2nd edition, Paris, 1911.

Smith, Digby. *Napoleon's Regiments.* London, 2000.

Soldats Suisses au service de la France. Geneva, nd.

Stiegler, Gaston. *Le maréchal Oudinot, Duc de Reggio, d'après les souvenirs inédits de la maréchale.* 2nd edition, Plon, Paris, 1894.

Talleyrand-Périgord, Charles-Maurice de, Prince de Bénévent. *Mémoires de Talleyrand. Introduction, notes et établissement du texte par P-L. et J-P. Couchoud,* 2 vols. Paris, 1957.

Thibaudeau, Antoine-Clair. *Mémoires de A.C. Thibaudeau.* Paris, 1913.

Thiébault, Dieudonné-Paul-Charles-Henri. *Mémoires du général baron Thiébault, publiés sous les auspices de sa fille, Mlle. Claire Thiébault, d'après le manuscrit original par F. Calmettes,* 5 vols. Paris, 1893–5. One-volume excerpts by Robert Lacour-Gayet. Paris, 1962.

Tulard, Jean. *La Vie Quotidienne des Français sous Napoléon.* Paris, 1978.

— *Napoléon: Le pouvoir, la nation, la légende.* Paris, 1997.

— *Les Vingt Jours. Louis XVIII ou Napoléon? 1er–20 mars 1815.* Paris, 2001.

Üxkull, Baron Boris von. *Arms and the Woman, the Diaries of Baron Boris von Üxkull, 1812–1829,* translated by Joel Carmichael. London, 1966.

Véron, Louis-Désiré. *Mémoires d'un bourgeois de Paris, par le docteur Louis Véron, comprenant la fin de l'Empire.* Paris, 1853–5.

Villemain, Abel François. *Souvenirs contemporains d'histoire et de littérature, Les Cent-Jours,* 2 vols. Paris, 1864.

Vitrolles, Eugène d'Arnauld, baron de. *Mémoires de Vitrolles. Texte intégral établi par Eugène Forgues, présenté et annoté par Pierre Farel,* 2 vols. Paris, 1950.

Weider, B. & Hapgood, D. *The Murder of Napoleon.* New York, 1982.

Young, Norwood. *Napoleon in Exile,* vol 1. London, 1915.

Index